MANAGEMENT ACCOUNTING IN
THE DIGITAL ECONOMY

MANAGEMENT ACCOUNTING IN THE DIGITAL ECONOMY

Edited by

ALNOOR BHIMANI

OXFORD
UNIVERSITY PRESS

OXFORD
UNIVERSITY PRESS

Great Clarendon Street, Oxford OX2 6DP

Oxford University Press is a department of the University of Oxford.
It furthers the University's objective of excellence in research, scholarship,
and education by publishing worldwide in

Oxford New York

Auckland Bangkok Buenos Aires Cape Town Chennai
Dar es Salaam Delhi Hong Kong Istanbul Karachi Kolkata
Kuala Lumpur Madrid Melbourne Mexico City Mumbai Nairobi
São Paulo Shanghai Taipei Tokyo Toronto

Oxford is a registered trade mark of Oxford University Press
in the UK and in certain other countries

Published in the United States
by Oxford University Press Inc., New York

British Library Cataloguing in Publication Data

Data available

Library of Congress Cataloging in Publication Data

Data available

ISBN 0-19-926038-9

1 3 5 7 9 10 8 6 4 2

Typeset by Newgen Imaging Systems (P) Ltd., Chennai, India
Printed in Great Britain
on acid-free paper by
T.J. International Ltd., Padstow, Cornwall

CONTENTS

LIST OF CONTRIBUTORS

AMIGONI, Franco, is Full Professor of Management Accounting and Control Systems at Bocconi University and Senior Lecturer at the Management Accounting and Control Department of SDA Bocconi School of Management. From 1991 to 1996, he was the Dean of SDA Bocconi School of Management. He has published several papers on the design of management control systems and the impact of information technologies on the evolution of accounting. His research interests are in the fields of integrated performance measurement systems, innovations in management accounting and corporate governance.

ANDERSON, Shannon, is an Associate Professor of Management at the Jesse H. Jones Graduate School of Management of Rice University. Prior to joining the faculty at the Jones School she taught for 9 years at the University of Michigan Business School. She earned a doctorate in Business Economics at Harvard University and a BSE in Operations Research at Princeton University. Her research focuses on designing and implementing performance measurement and cost control systems to support management decision-making and has been published in the *Accounting Review, Accounting, Organizations and Society, Accounting Horizons, Production and Operations Management*, the *International Journal of Flexible Manufacturing Systems*, and the *Journal of Management Accounting Research*. She is also co-author of the book *Implementing Management Innovations*. Before returning to school to pursue her doctorate, Professor Anderson worked as an engineer for General Motors Corporation. Professor Anderson is a member of the American Accounting Association and INFORMS and currently serves as an Associate Editor of the *Journal of Management Accounting Research* and *Management Science* and on the editorial boards of the *Accounting Review, Management Accounting Research, Accounting, Organizations and Societies*, and *Service Operations Management*.

ANDON, Paul, M.Com. (Hons.) CA is a Lecturer from the School of Accounting at the University of New South Wales, Sydney, Australia. Paul currently teaches undergraduate financial and management accounting. His main research interests are in the areas of customer reporting/profitability, knowledge management and 'new economy' performance measurement. Prior to joining UNSW, Paul was employed at PricewaterhouseCoopers within their Assurance and Business Advisory Services division, specializing in technology, communications, and entertainment clients. Paul is an Associate of the

Institute of Chartered Accountants in Australia. He has published in the *Australian Accounting Review* and *Pacific Accounting Review*.

BAXTER, Jane, Ph.D. FCPA is from the School of Accounting at the University of New South Wales, Sydney, Australia. Jane teaches and researches in the area of management accounting. Jane has designed and teaches courses on stakeholder value management, innovation and intangible resources. Her current research interests encompass innovation, knowledge management, and the structuring of the accounting and finance function. Jane has published in *Behavioral Research in Accounting, Journal of Management Accounting Research, Pacific Accounting Review, Australian Accounting Review* and *Accounting, Organizations and Society*.

BHIMANI, Alnoor (Al), is a Reader in Accounting and Finance at the London School of Economics where he has been teaching since 1988. He obtained an MBA from Cornell University (US) and a Ph.D. from the LSE and is also a Certified Management Accountant (Canada). Al has co-authored a number of books, including *Management Accounting: Evolution not Revolution* (CIMA 1989), *Management Accounting: Pathways to Progress* (CIMA 1994) and *Management and Cost Accounting* (Pearson 2003). He has also edited *Management Accounting: European Perspectives* (OUP 1996). Al has written numerous articles in scholarly journals and serves on the editorial board of several journals. He has undertaken management accounting related fieldwork in a variety of global enterprises and has presented his research to corporate executives and academic audiences in Europe, Asia, and North America.

CAGLIO, Ariela, Ph.D. in *Economia Aziendale e Management* at Bocconi University, is an Assistant Professor of Management Accounting and Control Systems at Bocconi University and Lecturer at the Management Accounting and Control Department of SDA Bocconi School of Management. She has published some contributions on the evolution of the accounting profession, integrated information systems, and internet-based companies. Her research interests relate to the impacts of information technologies on both the organization of accounting activities and accounting system and management control of networked firms.

Salvador Carmona is a Professor of Accounting and Management Control at Instituto de Empresa. Salvador's research interests are management acounting in high-tech environments and management accounting change from an historical perspective. His papers have been published in journals such as *Abacus*; *Accounting Historians Journal; Accounting, Organizations and Society*; the *European Accounting Review*; the *European Journal of Operational Research*; *The International Journal of Production Economics*; *Management Accounting Research*; *Management Learning*; and *The*

Scandinavian Journal of Management. He serves on the editorial board of several academic journals.

CHAPMAN, Chris, gained his doctorate from the London School of Economics and Political Science before moving to the University of Oxford as a University Lecturer in Management Studies and Fellow in Accounting at Linacre College. His research interests focus on the role of accounting and accountants in financial management and performance evaluation. Emphasizing the social and organizational aspects of these processes he has published in journals such as *Accounting, Organizations and Society*, *Management Accounting Research*, and *European Accounting Review*. Chris sits on the editorial board of *Accounting, Organizations and Society*.

CHUA, Wai Fong, took up the headship of the School of Accounting at the University of New South Wales in 2000 where she has been a Professor since 1994. Prior to joining UNSW in 1985, Wai Fong taught at the University of Sheffield (1981–1982) and Sydney University (1983–1985). She teaches and researches primarily in the area of management accounting. Her current research projects include an examination of the role of financial and non-financial controls in the professional service firms and the operation of 'digitized' accounting technologies. Her other research interests include the historical professionalization of accounting and accounting in the public sector. She has published widely in international journals including *The Accounting Review*, *Accounting, Organizations and Society*, *Contemporary Accounting Research*, *Critical Perspectives on Accounting*, and the *Journal of Management Accounting Research*. She is on the editorial boards of several journals and on the Academic Board of the Institute of Chartered Accountants in Australia.

DITILLO, Angelo, Ph.D. in *Economia Aziendale e Management* at Bocconi University, is an Assistant Professor of Management Accounting and Control Systems at Bocconi University and Lecturer at the Management Accounting and Control Department of SDA Bocconi School of Management. He has published papers on financial shared service centres, transfer pricing, and knowledge-based organizations. His main research interests are in the area of management accounting and control of knowledge-intensive firms, multinational corporations, and networks.

GORDON, Lawrence A., is the Ernst & Young Alumni Professor of Managerial Accounting and Information Assurance, and the Director of the Ph.D. Programme at The Robert H. Smith School of Business, University of Maryland, College Park. His Ph.D. is in Managerial Economics from Rensselaer Polytechnic Institute. He is the author of more than seventy-five articles, published in such journals as *The Accounting Review*, *Journal of Financial and Quantitative Analysis*, *Accounting, Organizations and Society*,

Journal of Accounting and Public Policy, *Decision Sciences*, *Journal of Business Finance and Accounting*, *Accounting and Business Research*, *Managerial and Decision Economics*, *ACM Transactions on Information and System Security*, *Communications of the ACM*, and *Management Accounting Research*. Dr Gordon's current research emphasizes the importance of utilizing concepts from managerial accounting and economics within an information-based economy. Dr Gordon also is the author of several books, including *Managerial Accounting: Concepts and Empirical Evidence*. In addition, he is the Editor-in-Chief of the *Journal of Accounting and Public Policy* and serves on the editorial boards of several other journals.

GOSSELIN, Maurice, is a Professor in the École de Comptabilité at Université Laval in Québec City, Canada. Professor Gosselin has worked several years in practice as a Chartered Accountant and a Certified Management Accountant before becoming a faculty member at Université Laval. He completed his doctoral degree at Boston University in 1995. He has published several papers in academic journals, including *Accounting, Organizations and Society*. His research and teaching interests are in the areas of cost management and performance measurement in organizations operating in the digital economy.

GRANLUND, Markus, holds a Ph.D. in Economics and Business Administration and is currently an Acting Professor of Information Systems Science at the Turku School of Economics and Business Administration, Finland. His research interests cover a wide range of technical and behavioural issues in management accounting. His current research concerns the effects of ERP-systems on management accounting practices, as well as management control and information systems in new economy firms. He teaches on several MSc courses and executive programmes. He is also collaborating on several joint projects with major Finnish companies. Dr Granlund has published numerous articles in peer-reviewed accounting and management journals.

HARTMANN, Frank, is a Professor of Management Accounting at the Universiteit van Amsterdam and director of the Amsterdam Graduate Business School. He holds an MSc in Business Economics from Erasmus University in Rotterdam, and a Ph.D. from Maastricht University. He researches and publishes nationally and internationally on management control, performance measurement, and the methodology of accounting research. He served and serves on the editorial boards of various national and international journals. He is board member of the Dutch professional institute of certified controllers that supervises graduate management accounting education in The Netherlands.

KREINER, Kristian, is a Professor of Organization at the Copenhagen Business School, Denmark. He studies how things get organized and coordinated—by design and plan, and by accident and spontaneous action. The empirical focus of his research is on exotic organizations—knowledge-intensive, temporary, virtual and/or community-based ones. His interests include project management, knowledge management, technology management, product design and innovation. Kristian Kreiner is the editor of the *Scandinavian Journal of Management*.

KÜPPER, Hans-Ulrich, is the director of the Institute of Production Management and Management Accounting at the Munich Business School (University of Munich). He also heads the Bavarian State Institute of Research and Planning for Higher Education. He received his doctorate and 'habilitation' at the University of Tübingen. Later he became a full professor at the universities of Essen, Darmstadt, and Frankfurt a/M. He is the author of several books on production theory, scheduling, cost accounting and codetermination. He has also published in several German and international journals—mainly in the areas of management accounting, controlling, university accounting, and business ethics. He is co-editor of the fifth edition of the *Handwörterbuch der Betriebswirtschaftslehre* (Lexicon of Business Economics) and of the *Handwörterbuch Unternehmungsrechnung und Controlling* (Lexicon of Accounting and Controlling).

LOEB, Martin P., Ph.D. (Northwestern University) is a Professor of Accounting and Information Assurance and a Deloitte & Touche Faculty Fellow at the Robert H. Smith School of Business, University of Maryland, College Park. His papers span several business disciplines and have been published in leading academic journals including *The Accounting Review*, *ACM Transactions on Information and System Security*, *American Economic Review*, *Contemporary Accounting Research*, *Journal of Accounting Research*, *Journal of Law and Economics*, *Journal of Public Economics*, *Management Accounting Research*, and *Management Science*. He served on numerous editorial boards and is currently an editor of the *Journal of Accounting and Public Policy*.

LUKKA, Kari, is a Professor of Accounting at the Turku School of Economics and Business Administration, Finland. Kari's research interests and his international publication record cover a wide range of management accounting as well as accounting theory and methodology topics. In addition to being the editor of *European Accounting Review*, he also acts as a reviewer for several international journals. Kari is also a Professor at the European Institute for Advanced Studies in Management (EIASM). He is a co-editor (with Professor Tom Groot) of the book *Cases in Management Accounting: Current Practices in European Companies* (Prentice Hall 2000). He also runs and chairs a series of biennial research conferences, jointly with Professor Michael Shields, entitled 'New Directions in Management Accounting: Innovations in practice and research'.

Jan Mouritsen is professor of management control Copenhagen Business School, Denmark. His research is oriented towards understanding the role of management technologies and management control in various organisational and social contexts. He focuses on empirical research and attempts to develop new ways of understanding the role and effects of numbers in organisations and society. He is intrested in translations and interpretations made of numbers throughout the contexts they help to illuminate. His intrests include intellectual capital and knowledge management, technology management, management control and operations management, new accounting and management control. Jan Mouritsen is on the editorial boards of about 10 academic journals in the area of accounting, operations management, IT and knowledge management, and he has published in journals including *Accounting, Organizations and Society*, *Management Accounting Research*, *Scandinavian Journal of Management*, *Accounting, Auditing and Accountability Journal* and *Critical Perspectives on Accounting*.

QUATTRONE, Paolo, is an Assistant Professor at the University Carlos III of Madrid, after having been *Marie Curie Research Fellow* at the Manchester School of Accounting and Finance from 1998 to 2000. He has taught accounting and business economics at the University of Catania (1997) and Palermo (1992–1996), where he earned his Ph.D. He has been an academic visitor at the Graduate School of Economics at the University of Kyoto (2001) and at the Säid Business School at the University of Oxford (2002). His current research interests are: management control systems in large organizations, accounting history, evolution of theories of knowledge, and the reform processes of universities.

ROBERTS, Hanno, is a Full Professor in Management Accounting and Control at the Norwegian School of Management. He has an MBA from the Rotterdam School of Management and a Ph.D. from the University of Maastricht. His main research interests are in the areas of Intellectual Capital, Management Accounting and Control of the Knowledge-intensive Firm, and in Knowledge-based Value Creation. He teaches MBA candidates in Norway, Germany, and Spain as well as holding visiting positions in Denmark, Finland, France, and Spain.

SEDATOLE, Karen, L., is an Assistant Professor of Accounting at the McCombs School of Business, The University of Texas at Austin. Karen earned her BSE in computer engineering from Baylor University, her MBA from The University of Texas at Austin, and her Ph.D. from The University of Michigan. Prior to her doctoral work, she was a systems consultant, designing and implementing customized client information systems used in forecasting, planning, and decision-making. Dr Sedatole's research interests are in management control systems, including issues related to performance measurement and rewards. Her current research examines the use of non-financial performance measures as leading indicators of financial performance, and the use of financial and non-financial performance measures in managerial incentive contracts and inter-organizational settings.

SJÖBLOM, Leif, is a Professor of Accounting and Control at IMD in Switzerland. His areas of academic interest are the restructuring of the telecommunications industry, performance measurement, cost management, and shareholder value creation. He is co-director of IMD's flagship Programme for Executive Development (PED) for high potential upper and mid-level managers from all over the world. Leif has previously worked in marketing and production in the telecommunications industry. He received his Ph.D. from Stanford Business School. He is also a Certified Management Accountant (CMA) and a Chartered Financial Analyst (CFA).

VAASSEN, Eddy H. J., is a Professor of Accounting Information Systems at Universiteit Maastricht. He is the director of the Postgraduate Programme Registered Controller, the Executive Master of Finance and Control Program, and the Maastricht Accounting Auditing and Information Management Research Center (MARC). Further, he is a technical advisor of Deloitte & Touche and co-chair of the annual European Conference on Accounting Information Systems. He has Dutch and international publications—including two textbooks—within the fields of AIS, Accounting, Auditing, and Control. Eddy is a member of the editorial boards of the *Journal of Digital Accounting Research*, the *Journal of Emerging Technologies in Accounting*, *Global Perspectives on Accounting Education and the Journal of Information Systems*. He is also an *ad hoc* reviewer for *The European Accounting Review* and AAA monograph and the *International Journal of Accounting Information Systems*.

LIST OF FIGURES

LIST OF TABLES

1

Digitization and Accounting Change

Alnoor Bhimani

There is mounting evidence that the deployment of digital technologies by organizations not only affects the economics of operational and managerial processes but also mobilizes extensive social and organizational effects. Digitization impacts the form, substance, and provenance of internal accounting information with attendant consequences on the behaviour and actions of organizational participants and on the functioning of enterprises more widely. Knowledge about the influence of the deployment of digital technologies on management accounting thinking, processes, and practices is starting to take shape. This book explores some of the issues that are coming to light.

Developing an understanding of what is signified by the notion of a 'digital economy' holds possibilities for explicating the rationale for action pursued in its name. Even refutation of the concept has consequences tied to what is negated. The term 'digital economy' has been used to capture different significances and has been applied interchangeably with other terms which themselves vary in meaning depending on context. Where it has been written about, the term digital economy is associated with economic changes entailing computer-based information exchanges. The term 'new economy' has also been used to suggest this and sometimes, to include an array of other changes in the nature and functioning of the economy and related social structures and processes. Industrial transformation is regarded as profound in writings about the new economy though there is still 'no consensus as to whether the new economy exists, what it implies and how it differs from the old economy' (Holmberg *et al.* 2002: 12). Similarly, economic conceptions of the transformation from the physical assets and products associated with agriculture, mining, and manufacturing to the realization of intangible products are central to writings about the 'information economy', the 'knowledge economy', the 'experience economy', and the 'network economy' (Bernstein 1998; Cooper 1983; Gilmore and Pine 1999; Jussawalla and Lamberton 1988; Katz 1986; Kling 1990; Kupier 2002; Liebowitz 2002; Robinson 1986; Schement 1990; Stalder 2002; Teece 2002). This is so even though widely varying arguments often underpin explanations of this transformation (Castells 1997, 2000, 2001; Christensen 1997).

Comments on an earlier draft of this chapter by Thomas Ahrens, Christopher Chapman, Ashraf Jaffer, and Shyam Sunder are gratefully acknowledged.

Commentators addressing specific features of the digital economy have tended to be partial in their use of the term. For instance, in his popularization of the term, Tapscott (1996) focuses on the role of information technology in organizations and proprietary commercial networks to highlight the promise of the internet in fostering electronic commerce. A more developed characterization is provided by Margherio *et al.* (1998) in *The Emerging Digital Economy* report published by the US Department of Commerce. In this and in an updated report by Henry (1999), the emphasis is on systems and services which utilize the internet. Brynjolfsson and Kahin (2002: 2) see the digital economy as 'the largely unrealised transformation of all sectors of the economy by the computer-enabled digitization of information'. This view accords with Kling and Lamb's (2002: 297) assertion that 'we should not conceptualise a digital economy in ways that make the Internet central by definition'. As such, they see the digital economy as 'including goods or services whose development, sale, or provision is critically dependent upon digital technologies'. Other writings use the term digital economy to connote exchange between physical structures and conceptual planes of reference via digital coding (OECD 1998; Schmid 2001).

In the context of addressing management accounting issues, the view that is taken of the digital economy needs to be specific enough as to enable concerns germane to the discipline to be addressed whilst also remaining sufficiently general as not to preclude possibilities which remain nascent still. For the purposes of this and chapters that follow, it is proposed that the digital economy be regarded as signifying digital interrelationships and dependencies between emerging communication and information technologies, data transfers along predefined channels and emerging platforms, and related contingencies within and across institutional and organizational entities. Such a conceptualization permits social, political, and economic preconditions, effects, and consequences to be explored. It also posits sufficient ground for taking account of contemporary management accounting concerns without delimiting boundaries of possible change. With this view of the digital economy, it is now possible to turn to some substantive issues of concern in the field of management accounting.

A Matter of Trust

History may or may not repeat itself, but the basis for change is often repetitive. Within management accounting writings, exhortations for change have been prevalent for some time. Two decades ago, Kaplan (1983) called for a 'new' management accounting predicated on an understanding of business processes as a departure from the mere reporting of enterprise activities based on often erroneous assumptions about their nature. The debate evolved into exhortations for accountants to enhance their understanding of the processes involved in the manufacture of goods and the delivery of services, and to explore the physical flow of resources *vis-a-vis* economic accounts of enterprise activities. Ultimately, the argument was for providing accountings that could be seen as more closely representing organizational realities so as to abet managerial endeavours (Cooper and Kaplan 1987; Kaplan, 1984, 1985; Kaplan and Norton 2001. Accounting thinkers subsequently documented novel internal accounting techniques such as backflush accounting, activity-based costing, target cost management, quality costing, and renewed approaches to measuring performance (see Ansari 1997; Brinker 1996; Bromwich and Bhimani 1994; Yoshikawa *et al.* 1993).

The extent to which reliance can be placed upon accounting information by managers is resurfacing as an issue in debates concerning the relevance of management accounting as digitization within organizations becomes more significant (Boiney 2000; Chandra 2001; Sutton 2000). As enterprises become increasingly concerned with the generation and the processing of digitized information relating to the production and delivery of physical and digital products and services, the challenge will be to sustain sufficient credence in the monitoring, measurement, and assessment of these altering organizational activities (Bhimani, 2003). Trust is core in this regard. If it can be claimed that 'trust is becoming the most important asset in the digital economy' (Colvin 2002: 25) then what comprises trust in internal accountings will likely see transformations. Novel accounting concerns centring around faith in numbers (Kaplan 1986) will once again emerge and contemporary control systems will no doubt continue to face calls for reforms. Accounting measures will seek to engender trust in contexts where what is bought, sold, or produced never assumes physical form. Although service products have always evidenced such characterization, the means by which they are delivered have not ordinarily defied desired transparency nor the potential for observation in the same way as digital processes. Counting based on observation or observations enabling evaluations to be made are not always amenable to operationalization in contexts where digital rather than physical transactions underpin enterprise activities. Digital processes often evade physical verification, and established modes of enumeration and evaluation will therefore likely come under question.

How far accounting information can be trusted is not subject merely to the development of more rational forms of capturing the economic consequences of organizational activities resting on digital processes. Human interpretations of the significance of deploying digital technologies and their representation in economic terms is also a relevant issue. Alterations in the capture and reporting of information as well as the changing nature of the product that is to be reported upon within digitized organizational contexts will likely have behavioural implications worthy of study. Behavioural accounting research which has traditionally documented similarities and variations in the uses and impacts of accounting information on individuals will raise new concerns, questions, and issues. At the individual level, digitization will affect the type of accounting information being reported as well as the manner in which it is used and the resulting consequences.

The accounting literature on the behaviour of groups of individuals indicates the existence of differences and variety which distinguishes some groups from others in dealing with accounting information. This research suggests that we cannot predict the behaviour of groups, organizations, or markets by considering average behaviour or even the range of behaviours of the ensemble of members (Carley 2002; Epstein and Axtell 1997; Wellman *et al* 1996). Enterprise activities are influenced by structure, culture, and the experiences of groups of organizational members (Kauffman 1993). How the nature of trust evolves in contexts where modes of information generation and exchange alter will be affected both by technical and social factors. The permeation of new digital technologies across different industrial contexts will mobilize different meanings and allegiances and bring about a diversity of reactions and consequences across different organizations. Management accounting will thereby undoubtedly continue to be shaped by forces of change which include technical, behavioural, and organizational dimensions.

Rethinking the Management Accountant

Emerging organizational systems of managing knowledge and, in particular, financially oriented information systems are viewed as loosening their structural rigidities to allow alternative conceptions of resource flows and transactions to be reported (Kaplan and Norton 2000; Mouritsen *et al.* 2001). In digitized information reporting contexts, hypertext based accounting reports can enhance this trend by, for instance, further allowing linkages and connections relating to different segments of the organization and constructions of networked views of organizational affairs to be represented (Liebowitz 2002). This renders possible the creation of more individualized styles of managing, which rest on the customizability of information that is both financial and non-economic. Accounting information systems may thus increasingly forgo standardization and instead stress high particularity in configurations of economic and related data (Granlund and Mouritsen 2003; Hedberg and Jönsson 1978; Scapens and Jazayeri 2003). The role of the management accountant may come to be predicated upon customizable information generation potential as well as the ready production of information profiles to trigger more creative managerial responses (Boiney 2000; Sutton 2000). Management accounting systems may, in some instances, become enablers of novel information production and providers of newly synthesized information reports to prod non-standard managerial reactions. In such contexts, comparative monitoring issues will surface.

Where the management accountant acts as a provider of the means for creating information profiles of organizational affairs, the manager's knowledge of the technology through which this is undertaken will not be paramount. Relying on the knowledge of other people can have effects which are considered as contributing purposefully to one's deployment of that knowledge. In this regard, one might suggest that to a level, 'ignorance is efficient' (Leadbeater 2000: 87) as far as accounting information users are concerned. But this will likely not be so for accounting information providers. What will matter will be the credibility of the management accountant in enabling information reconfigurations. This will require both an appreciation of technical information issues as well as adherence and commitment to reporting that which is deemed to faithfully represent organizational reality.

The rise of digitization which may in part occlude the transparency of organizational affairs, will impact on pressures to portray management accounting work as being technically and internally legitimate. This will prove particularly pertinent in the near future given that, in the recent past, the accountant's credibility in public accounting functions has been tarnished. Just as consumers rely on brands to guide their choices as product diversity and complexity grow, and as barriers to entry in many markets drop, so the linkage between the managerial task and the know-how of internal accountants will be shaped by the credibility which management accounting can engender within enterprises. The management accountant will need to project not simply traditional professionalism but the constitution of a digitally cognizant person. One which appeals to digital spaces in representations of managerial tasks and which combines simulation with traditional reality as well as corporate legitimacy (Jones 1997; Turkle 1997).

New Contingencies

Commentators on long term economic changes suggest that bureaucratic hierarchies are, in many contexts, being replaced by networks (Kauffman and Walden 2001; Stalder 2002). Moreover, organizations which invest in the digitization of product development, production and delivery, and in networks enabling resource allocation, coordination, and monitoring tend also to become more knowledge intensive (Nonaka and Takeuchi 1995; Stewart, 2001). In such contexts, knowledge becomes increasingly embedded and embodied in practices and experiences. But virtuality begets physicality. Structures of physical assets and the level of social interaction which emerge as a matter of course in traditional production contexts have to be created in knowledge intensive and digitally coordinated organizational platforms. This may in part be to signal the magnitude of the enterprise's economic significance as well as to create a work environment supportive of network continuity (Holmberg *et al.* 2002). The role of accounting alters in such contexts. Accounting for space utilization takes different connotations where production activities and operational processes assume alternative significances. Notions of cost management and financial control approaches will likely be affected by emerging meanings of economic effectiveness.

As the use of digital technologies and particularly of broadband access connections become more evident, work and play, the professional and the personal, office and home become desegmented. Physical boundaries are reshaped when digital connectivities are created and virtual spaces formed. Such alterations will affect prescriptive and actual management accounting systems designs in terms of cost management pursuits, and planning and control structures, and will generate both intended and unanticipated roles and contingencies relating to accounting information.

Scholars in management accounting have in the past shown much interest in the structural contingencies between management accounting systems characteristics and contextual level variables such as strategy, technology, size, form, and market uncertainty (Chapman 1997; Dent 1990; Gordon and Miller 1976; Hopwood 1989; Langfield-Smith 1997; Otley 1980). The digitization of organizational endeavours including the deployment of electronic technologies in the development, production and delivery of digital and physical products is inherently associated with many such organizational and environmental variables. Information technology permits new organizational forms and practices to emerge (Grover and Segars 1999). Organizational spaces which are deindividualized in bureaucratic industrial organizations can undergo 'reterritorialization' within new organizational structures (Salzer-Mörling 2002: 121). Structure may cease to lag strategy (Earl 2000; Lucking-Reiley and Spulber 2001) and technology may become both the basis and the product of accounting information content and form (Clark 1998). Size is often no longer physically measurable let alone a measure of information intensity or structure (Means and Schneider 2000) whilst market uncertainty and risk can become generic to systems design rather than elements of differentiation (Kauffman and Walden 2001). Possibly, such changes arise because the emergence of digital networks 'imply a lesser need for formal structure than the mechanical age with its factory paradigm and characteristic corporate hierarchies' (Rowland 1999: 341).

What is becoming clear is that in contexts where the contingencies between cost objects, structures of information capture, and the attributes of economic engagements submerge, decouple, or become reformulated, the basis for information systems design reflect changed notions of balance. Ultimately, certain features of management accounting systems may come to transcend past conceptualizations of rational linkages and appropriate novel contingencies in predicating formulations of organizational reality.

Virtual Possibilities

The ubiquity of digital technologies across an increasing array of organizational functions is in growing evidence. If the impact of advances in information technology are so significant that it can be proclaimed that 'the first ten years of the twenty-first century will be the digital decade' (Bill Gates at the February 2002 World Economic Forum) then with little doubt, organizational and managerial effects will follow. Management accounting processes and thinking will undoubtedly come under considerable influence also. The chapters that follow are intended to liven the debate surrounding the many possible consequences.

The chapters in the book are divided into three parts. Part 1 brings together chapters which discuss accounting and management control systems and wider structural shifts connected with the advent of digital technologies. Chapter 2 by Amigoni, Caglio, and Ditillo argue that many large firms have increasingly downsized and have become 'vertically disaggregated' leading to the emergence of flat and horizontal corporations, networks, and virtual organizations. Concurrently, information flow structures have been redesigned which provide some stability to novel combinations of market versus hierarchical organizational features. They suggest that where accounting information complexity is low, organizational integration is achieved by accounting information networks which exhibit a high degree of centrality. Conversely, high complexity results in integration achieved via a distributed accounting information network. Their research posits a framework through which to understand the manner in which emerging organizational structures combine with new accounting forms which may otherwise be deemed to be isolated phenomena.

In Chapter 3, Anderson and Sedatole argue that technological advances, deregulation, and changing competitive forces have altered what has traditionally been regarded as firm boundaries. Different collaborative forms between firms have implications for defining the contours of entities for performance measurement and management control purposes. They posit that different modes of management accounting accompany the emergence of hybrid organizational forms. Concerned also with the transformation of control systems, Chapman and Chua suggest in Chapter 4 that contemporary technologies disturb existing ways of organizing and affect the nature of relationships between managers. Traditional forms of management controls may become more intense but technologies which intensify processes of organizational virtualization will likewise raise questions concerning the easy applicability of traditional ideas of control.

Chapter 5 by Gordon and Loeb develops a game theoretic model of a market shared by two rivals to shed light on how expenditures on competitor analysis affect and are influenced by expenditures on information security. They posit wider term implications of security based information economy issues for the future of management accounting and warn that for management accounting to survive in the twenty-first century, the field will have to stake its claim in the present information-wired economy.

Chapter 6 concludes Part 1 with a discussion by Hartmann and Vaassen who argue that the digital economy has enabled new types of organizations to emerge, which have different control needs. Characteristic of the new demands being made on control are increased flexibility and the growing significance of knowledge as a production factor. They suggest ways in which new organizational forms can adapt their management accounting systems to enable more 'integrated' organizational control. Key to this adaptation is the recognition that due regard must be placed on knowledge, communication, and altered information needs.

Part 2 of the book brings together commentaries on more organizationally focused shifts in the face of digitization trends in the economy. Andon, Baxter, and Chua in Chapter 7 examine altered accounting controls in a post-industrial organizational context. They argue that accounting control has become a more digitized process leading to disembedded and intensified forms of control. They discuss a field study which illustrates this transformation. In Chapter 8, Carmona and Quattrone draw upon a 'new institutional sociology' frame of reference to study organizational changes and shifts in the management control system of an internet company. Their investigation reveals the role of a control system in shaping efforts to move the company toward e-business operations. Their study reflects on the comingling of technical, enterprise-specific and wider institutional factors in alterations in the internal functioning of an organization and its efforts to engage in e-business. Similarly, Mouritsen and Kreiner explore changes within an internet company in Chapter 9. They focus on the mobilization of management controls in the development of the company's growth and consider how this and other forms of institutionalization are not driven purely by a logic of operational efficiency or the search for profits. They depict how controls can be regarded as communicating the sellable proposition that organizational competencies can be linked and integrated into a rational and transferable whole.

Chapter 10 by Sjöblom documents case studies which suggest that a wide level 'new economy' mindset influenced organizational notions of the virtues of control. He suggests that over optimistic market size estimates for products that could be sold on the internet, the perception that companies had to compete in a market 'race' for the number one position, and inflated valuations driven by ambitious future revenue expectations—were factors that worked against prudent financial management in the companies investigated.

Part 3 of the book is a collection of chapters which consider forms of accounting transformations which may be pursued in specific contexts both in terms of practice and as concepts. In Chapter 11, Gosselin makes the argument that e-logistics will significantly impact management control systems and that this will mobilize further important adaptations. Gosselin identifies potential contingencies between altered logistical variables and control characteristics. In Chapter 12, Küpper argues that not-for-profit organizations have specific information systems structure requirements which can be met by information and internet technologies. He identifies technical requisites seen as appropriate in bringing about the effective design and use of information systems in not-for-profit organizations.

Lukka and Granlund in Chapter 13 suggest that within 'new economy firms', a tension exists between the tendency to stress creativity, flexibility, and ultimate freedom of operation and the 'normal' control demands of business organizations. They posit that management and financial controls need to be designed as loosely coupled systems such that they are solid but still light and simple so as not to dampen the creative and indeterminate processual aspects of such organizations. In Chapter 14, Roberts argues that knowledge is a source of competitive advantage and economic growth and that it can be fused to an extent with accounting interpretations centred around its registration, accumulation, allocation, and utilization. By interpreting knowledge as a form of intellectual capital and identifying separate elements of this capital, Roberts discusses ways in which accountability can be enhanced. His discussion focuses in particular on the interfaces between accounting and knowledge using a production process perspective.

The chapters in the book bring together a variety of views and observations on management accounting and control issues associated with the rise of the digital economy. The frames of reference are diverse. They draw upon different themes and issues being articulated from across a number of disciplines. Differing degrees of empiricism and theoretical argumentation underpin the many contentions made by the chapter authors. It is hoped that their observations will incite further thought and reflection on the management accounting and control implications of the growing ubiquity of digital technologies across organizational spaces.

References

Ansari, S. L. (1997), *Management Accounting: A Strategic Focus* (New York: McGraw Hill).

Bernstein, P. L. (1998), 'Are Networks Driving the New Economy?', *Harvard Business Review* (November–December): 159–66.

Bhimani, A. (2003), *Strategic Finance and Cost Management* (London: Management Press)

Boiney, L. G. (2000), 'New Roles for Information Technology: Managing Internal Knowledge and External Relationships', *Review of Accounting Information Systems*, 4/3: 1–10.

Brinker, B. J. (1996), *Handbook of Cost Management* (New York: Warren, Gorham and Lamont).

Bromwich, M. and Bhimani, A. (1994), *Management Accounting: Pathways to Progress* (London: CIMA).

Brynjolfsson, E. and Kahin, B. *Understanding the Digital Economy: Data, Tools and Research* (MA: MIT press).

Castells, M. (1997), *The Power of Identity (The Information Age: Economy, Society and Culture)* (Oxford: Blackwell Publishers).

Castells, M. (2000), *The Rise of the Network Society (The Information Age)* (Oxford: Blackwell Publishers).
—— (2001), *The Internet Galaxy: Reflections on the Internet, Business, and Society* (Oxford: Oxford University Press).
Carley, K. (2002), 'Organizational Change and the Digital Economy', in E. Brynjolfsson and B. Kahin (eds), *Understanding the Digital Economy* (MA: MIT Press), 325–51.
Chandra, A. (2001), 'Systems Issues in E-Commerce', *The Review of Business Information Systems*, 6/1: 41–50.
Chapman, C. S. (1997), 'Reflections on a Contingency View of Accounting', *Accounting, Organizations and Society*, 22/2: 189–205.
Christensen, C. M. (1997), *The Innovator's Dilemma* (Boston, MA: HBSP).
Clark, T. H. (1998), 'Information Technology and the Virtual Organization', *International Journal of Electronic Commerce*, 3/1: 4–7.
Colvin, G. (2002), "E-trust" *Fortune*, 29/4: 25.
Cooper, M. D. (1983), 'The Structure of the Information Economy', *Information Processing and Management*, 19: 9–26.
Cooper, R. and Kaplan, R. (1987), 'How Cost Accounting Systematically Distorts Product Costs', in W. Bruns and R. Kaplan (eds), *Accounting and Management: Field Study Perspectives* (Boston, MA: HBSP).
Dent, J. F. (1990), 'Strategy, Organization and Control: Some Possibilities for Accounting Research', *Accounting, Organizations and Society*, 15: 3–25.
Earl, M. (2000), 'IT Strategy in the New Economy', *Mastering Management* (London: FT Prentice Hall).
Epstein, J. and Axtell, R. (1997), *Growing Artificial Societies* (Cambridge, MA: MIT Press).
Gilmore, J. H. and Pine, B. J. (1999), *The Experience Economy* (Boston, MA: HBSL).
Gordon, L. A. and Miller, D. (1976), 'A Contingency Framework for the Design of Accounting Information Systems', *Accounting, Organizations and Society*, 1: 59–69.
Granlund, M. and Mouritsen, J. (2003), 'Introduction: Problematizing the Relationship Between Management Control and Information Technology' *European Accounting Review* 12:77–84.
Grover, V. and Segars, A. H. (1999), 'Electronic Commerce and Market Transformation', *International Journal of Electronic Commerce*, 3/4: 3–9.
Hedberg, B. and Jönsson S. (1978), 'Designing Semi-Confusing Information Systems for Organizations in Changing Environments', *Accounting, Organizations and Society*, 3/1: 47–67.
Henry, D. (June 1999), *The Emerging Digital Economy II* (Washington, DC: US Department of Commerce).
Holmberg, I., Salzer-Möling and Strannegärd, L. (2002), *Stuck in the Future: Tracing the 'New Economy'* (London: Bookhouse Publishing).
Hopwood, A. G. (1989), 'Organizational Contingencies and Accounting Configurations', in B. Fridman and L. Ostman (eds), *Accounting Development—Some Perspectives: A Book in Honour of Sven-Erik Johansson* (Stockholm: Economic Research Institute), 23–44.
Jones, S. (1997), *Virtual Cultures* (London: Sage).
Jussawalla, M. and Lamberton, D. M. (eds) (1988), *The Cost of Thinking: Information Economies of Ten Pacific Countries* (Norwood, NJ: Ablex Publishing).

Kaplan, R. (1983), 'The Evolution of Management Accounting', *Accounting Review*, 58: 390–417.

Kaplan, R. S. (1984), 'Yesterday's Accounting Undermines Production', *Harvard Business Review* (July–August).

——(1985), 'Accounting Lag: The Obsolescence of Cost Accounting Systems', in K. Clark and C. Lorenze (eds), *Technology and Productivity: The Uneasy Alliance* (Boston: Harvard Business School Press).

——(1986), 'Must CIM Be Justified by Faith Alone?', *Harvard Business Review* (March–April).

——and Atkinson, A. A. (1989), *Advanced Management Accounting* (Englewood Cliffs, NJ: Prentice Hall).

——and Norton, D. P. (2001), *The Strategy-Focused Organization* (Boston, MA: HBSP).

Katz, R. L. (1986), 'Measurement and Cross-National Comparisons of the Information Work Force', *The Information Society*, 4/4: 231–77.

Kauffman, R. and Walden, E. (2001), 'Economics and E-Commerce: Survey and Directions for Research', *International Journal of Electronic Commerce*, 5/1: 5–116.

Kauffman, S. A. (1993), *The Origins of Order: Self-Organization and Selection in Evolution* (New York: Oxford University Press).

Kling, R. (1990), 'More Information, Better Jobs? Occupational Stratification and Labor Market Segmentation in the United States Information Labor Force', *The Information Society*, 7/2: 77–107.

——and Lamb, R. (2002), 'IT and Organizational Change in Digital Economies', in E. Brynjolfsson and B. Kahin (eds), *Understanding the Digital Economy* (MA: MIT Press), 295–324.

Kupier, E. (2002), 'The Intangible World of Business: In Search of a Name for our Times', *CMA Management* (November): 12–14.

Langfield-Smith, K. (1997), 'Management Control Systems and Strategy: A Critical Review', *Accounting, Organizations and Society*, 22: 207–32.

Leadbeater, C. (2000), 'In Defense of Ignorance', *The Industry Standard Europe*, 2: 86–9.

Liebowitz, S. (2002), *Re-thinking the Network Economy: The True Forces that drive the Digital Marketplace* (New York: Amacon).

Lucking-Reiley, D. and Spulber, D. (2001), 'Business-to-Business E-Commerce', *Journal of Economic Perspectives*, 15/1: 55–68.

Margherio, Lynn, Henry, Dave, Cooke, Sandra, and Montes, Sabrina, (1998), *The Emerging Digital Economy* (Washington, DC: US Department of Commerce).

Means, G. and Schneider, D. (2000), *Meta-Capitalism* (New York: John Wiley).

Mouritsen, J., Larsen, H. T., and Bukh, P. N. D. (2001), 'Intellectual Capital and the "Capable Firm": Narrating, Visualising and Numbering for Managing Knowledge', *Accounting, Organizations and Society*, 26: 735–62.

Nonaka, I. and Takeuchi, H. (1995), *The Knowledge-Creating Company* (New York: Oxford University Press).

OECD (1998), *The Social and Economic Implications of Electronic Commerce*. (London: OECD)

Otley, D. T. (1980), 'The Contingency Theory of Management Accounting: Achievement and Prognosis', *Accounting, Organizations and Society*, 5: 413–28.

Robinson, S. (1986), 'Analyzing Information Technology: Tools and Techniques', *Information Processing and Management*, 22: 183–202.

Rowland, W. (1999), *Spirit of the Web: The Age of Information from Telegraph to Internet* (Toronto: Key Porter Books).

Salzer-Mörling, M. (2002), 'Changing Corporate Landscapes', in I. Holmberg *et al.* (eds), *Stuck in the Future: Tracing the "New Economy"* (London: Bookhouse Publishing), 107–34.

Scapens, R. W. and Jazayeri, M. (2003) 'ERP Systems and Management Accounting Change: Opportunities or Impacts?' *European Accounting Review* (12): 201–234.

Schement, J. R. (1990), 'Porat, Bell, and the Information Society Reconsidered: The Growth of Information Work in the Early Twentieth Century', *Information Processing and Management*, 26/4: 449–65.

Schmid, B. (2001), 'What is New about the Digital Economy?', *Electronic Markets*, 11/1: 44–51.

Stalder, F. (2002), 'The Network Paradigm: Social Formations in the Age of Information', *The Information Society: An International Journal*, 4: 2–14.

Stewart, T. A. (2001), *The Wealth of Knowledge: Intellectual Capital and the 21st Century Organization* (New York: Doubleday).

Sutton, S. G. (2000), 'The Changing Face of Accounting in an Information Technology Dominated World', *International Journal of Accounting Information Systems*, 1: 1–8.

Tapscott, Don (1996), *The Digital Economy: Promise and Peril in the Age of Networked Intelligence* (New York: McGraw-Hill).

Teece, D. J. (2002), *Managing Intellectual Capital* (Oxford: Oxford University Press).

Turkle, S. (1997), *Life on the Screen: Identity in the Age of the Internet* (New York: Touchstone).

Wellman, B., Salaff, J., Divitrova, D., Garton, L., Gulia, M., and Haythornthwaite, C. (1996), 'Computer Networks as Social Networks: Virtual Community, Computer Supported Cooperative Work and Telework', *Annual Review of Sociology*, 22: 213–38.

Yoshikawa, T., Innes, J., Mitchell, F., and Tanaka, M. (1993), *Contemporary Cost Management* (London: Chapman and Hall).

Part 1
The Transformation of Accounting and Management Controls

2

Dis-Integration through Integration: The Emergence of Accounting Information Networks

Franco Amigoni, Ariela Caglio, and Angelo Ditillo

Introduction

Whether depicted as strategic alliances, joint ventures, trading networks or seen as the product of firm strategy, industry structure, or local conditions (Ebers 1997), network forms of organizing have attracted the attention of management theorists, so that a rich literature on networking has developed over a long time (Aldrich and Whetten 1981; Jarillo 1988; Moss Kanter 1988; Nohria and Eccles 1992). Yet, in becoming fashionable and sometimes very widely used, the notion of 'network' has lost its meaning (Nohria and Eccles 1992). In the field of economic studies as a whole, the major theoretical strands of research on networking include concepts and methods borrowed by industrial economics, organizational economics, resource dependence theory, neo-institutional theory, industrial marketing, negotiation analysis, organizational behaviour, historical and evolutionary approaches, population ecology, radical and Marxian studies, and social network theory. All these perspectives have helped management theorists to develop a more comprehensive overview, as each of them have contributed to unveiling a multiplicity of aspects relating to networks.[1]

This research has been supported with government funds allocated to the *'Young Researchers' Project 2000*. We would like to acknowledge the valuable contributions by Al Bhimani, Chris Chapman, and Jan Mouritsen.

Though this contribution is the result of the integrated effort and collaboration of the three researchers, Ariela Caglio has written parts 1 and 2, and Angelo Ditillo part 4. These two latter authors have also jointly developed part 3 and the conclusions. Franco Amigoni is the author of part 5, providing evidence taken from some research projects carried out at CESAD (the Research Centre in Business Administration of Bocconi University, chaired by the Author himself) in 2000–2001.

[1] *Industrial economics*, being concerned with incomplete or mixed forms of 'quasi-integration' (Blois 1972), studies different classes of production costs as explanatory variables of network efficiency. By contrast, *resource dependence theory* distinguishes among types of dependence as possible predictors of networks, indicative of a broad range of networking phenomena, as in the contribution by Pfeffer and Salancik (1978). Dependence is a central notion as well within the *neo-institutional approach*: inter-organizational forms of cooperation are created and sustained in order to avoid isolation and to gain legitimization (Baum and Oliver 1991;

Organizational economics has been one of the most widely used approaches: based on transaction cost economics, it considers that networks can be other than second-best arrangements with respect to market and hierarchy (Grandori and Soda 1995). More specifically, such an approach emphasizes governance costs as an explanatory variable of the nature and configuration of networks, which, balancing the properties of markets and those of hierarchies, are considered as optimal hybrid forms for regulating economic activities (Bradach and Eccles 1989; Powell 1990; Thorelli 1986; Williamson 1985). This theoretical point of view is often combined with the one proposed by *strategy*, which stresses the importance of firms' deliberate choices in the evolution of inter-firm relationships and structures. In particular, according to this perspective networks are the product of managerial choices—aimed at obtaining the best organizational arrangements to compete in their chosen markets (Lorenzoni 1992)—which allow firms to specialize in those activities of the value chain that are essential to their competitive advantage (Jarillo 1988: 35). In this sense, although economic forces drive the changes in organizational structures, such variables are moderated by individual firm strategies and preferences.

According to such approaches, market and hierarchy are seen as polar types of economic organization and are conceptualized as archetypes, or pure forms. Markets are seen to allow free and open competition: prices are determined by

Di Maggio 1986). In accord with organizational sociology, networks are said to be sensitive to pre-existing social relationships, which constrain the underlying economic relations: in fact, actors participating in a network reveal internalized values and norms whose nature is an important explanatory variable of inter-firm cooperative behaviour (Boisot 1986; Hamilton *et al.* 1990; Ring 1993). Likewise, from an *organizational behaviour* viewpoint, the importance of long-term inter-organizational relationships resides in the generation of cooperation and trust (Harrigan and Newmann 1990). According to this perspective, organizations choose to work together and closely for mutual benefit, as cooperation leads to a better overall performance. Also industrial marketing, whose research focus is on trade between organizations, has contributed to an understanding of interdependencies potentially existing between separate firms. Turnbull (1986), in particular, points out that, in industrial markets, the norm is represented by the existence of long-term and stable relationships characterized by mutual adaptation and change.

According to *negotiation analysis*, any network arrangement and any coordination problem can be expressed as a game (Axelrod 1984; Jarrillo 1988; Scharpf 1993), which can be used as a predictor of both network foundations and shape, while within *historical and evolutionary models*, both based on the work by Alfred Chandler (1990), the formation of networks is linked to the role of technology and learning (Nelson 1993).

Differing from all the approaches previously mentioned, the *population ecology perspective* studies specifically the causes of the endurance of inter-firm agreements, independently from the reasons of their emergence. Adopting a natural-selection perspective, legitimization has been pointed out to be one of the most important variables driving the selection processes regarding networks, whose survival is also influenced by public support and legislation.

Radical and Marxian studies give an original insight on networks: in fact, casting aside the question of networks effectiveness and efficiency, they examine those inter-firm agreements, which are based on power mechanisms and on class dominance (Moore 1979; Perucci and Potter 1989).

A final perspective on networks worth mentioning is the one of *social network theory*, which, originally belonging to the field of social psychology, has been successfully applied to economic research for analysing the emergence and evolution of informal structures of networks and the dynamics of network boundaries (Burt 1990; Laumann *et al.* 1980; Lomi 1991).

the actions of individuals. Information is available to everyone and it is possible to switch suppliers very easily. By contrast, in a hierarchy, different stages of the supply chain are owned and controlled by one single organization, which can adopt a wide range of vertical integration strategies and can enjoy different degrees of control on the allocation of resources (Zenger and Hesterly 1997).

As an alternative to these pure forms, hybrid structures may emerge when large firms evidence more flexible modes of organization to react quickly and effectively to market changes or when small firms decide to cooperate in order to achieve better business conditions, to pursue complex development efforts and to exploit synergies without vertically integrating. Such intermediate forms are a mixed mode operation in which elements of both market and hierarchy coexist.

Yet, there still seems to be a theoretical void in the aforementioned literature because these approaches have neglected issues concerning the stability of these intermediate forms over time.[2] The design of information flows as a way to safeguard such stability has been underestimated. This theoretical gap is in need of being addressed since, consequent to the widespread use of Internet technologies, it is the design and organization of information that has become a core explanatory variable of governance choices.[3] This provides our motivation for focusing on the information flows existing among stable networks of small, autonomous production or service units, and on information technology as a catalyst for the underlying changes. In this sense, within our framework of analysis, modern information technologies will be interpreted as an important enabler of the integration of more complex and varied information flows among networked firms.[4] These issues are, indeed, central when we speak about Accounting Information Networks (AINs) as a means of conferring stability to networking agreements.

---

[2] On this point see also Aldrich and Whetten, who explicitly point out the fact that 'studies of networks often overlook the question of network stability, whereas (...) the stability of networks must be treated as an empirical question' (1981: 385).

[3] The role of information has been described, analysed, and sometimes glorified, in several works on the topic (Schultze and Orlikowski 2001). Information is presented as being particularly enabling and assigned many central roles in organizations such as: a way of better seeing the physical organization (e.g. in the mirror world imagery of Rayport and Sviokla (1995)); an opportunity for partners to learn about each other (e.g. in the relationships described by Upton and McAfee (1996)); a means of constant self-renewal (Faucheux 1997); as the glue that binds the members of a virtual organization together (Davenport and Pearlson 1998); as a mechanism that absorbs increasing uncertainty (Feltham 1968; Feltham and Demski 1969). Yet, the constraining aspects of information deriving from its ambiguity, incompleteness, incorrectness, misrepresentation, as a result of its inappropriate structuring, have been completely neglected. Only recently in the last decade a more critical and convincing analysis of the role of information in relationships, alliances, and networks has been undertaken (Chapman 1998).

[4] More precisely, our interest in IT developments is motivated by the fact that they make the relationships that combine market and hierarchy features simultaneously possible. Mixed mode relationships existed even before the use of IT systems: nevertheless, the use of modern net technologies allows more articulated and more complex mixed mode structures to be managed (Holland and Lockett 1997).

In order to clarify the potential stabilization effects of information flows in networked structures, we begin with a brief review of organizational innovations, underlying an existing trend towards disaggregation, as a premise for providing a theoretical explanation for the existence of AINs. After exploring the functions and characteristics of an AIN, we thus present our argument that the diffusion of hybrid governance modes is always accompanied by a parallel phenomenon of information flows redesign. This latter depends on the level of informational complexity, which influences the features of the AIN. To support our theoretical considerations, we present some evidence of the various patterns AINs may assume.

Combining Dis-integration and Integration through Accounting Information Networks

As suggested in the preceding section, more and more firms have been joining the 'networking wave'. More specifically, evidence of network structures (Nohria and Eccles 1992) or of hybrid organizations (Williamson 1991) can be found whenever we speak about virtual corporations, cluster organizations, horizontal firms. Increasingly, large firms, in particular, have refocused and vertically disaggregated and conduct their businesses without relying on formal hierarchy. All these organizational experiments share the fact that they rely on small units, the basic building blocks of economic exchange, which can involve both internal (within firm) and external (between firms) networks. As a consequence, economic exchanges are more and more a mix of both market-like and hierarchical features (Holland and Lockett 1997; Zenger and Hesterly 1997).

However, Williamson (1985) was quite critical about the endurance of hybrid structures, due to the fact that such organizational forms usually have to face intense coordination difficulties, caused by lack of trust, rivalry, and costly decision-making processes. As a consequence, Williamson (1991) classified this governance structure as a temporal and unstable mode of transactions, disfavoured, in the long run, by both the market and the hierarchy. Also within strategy studies, the network is mainly viewed as a temporary form: for example, Miles and Snow (1992) conceived networks as temporary arrangements of disaggregated functions, which are more vulnerable than pure organizational forms and, consequently, deemed to decline. Some authors (D'Aunno and Zuckerman 1987; Van de Ven and Walker 1984) have also pointed to the fact that there is a life cycle in network management, eventually leading to the failure of networks. Consequently, the development of such intermediate forms, though long-surviving, contains the seeds of disintegration.

In contrast, more recent contributions (Holland and Lockett 1997; Zenger and Hesterly 1997) emphasize that pure forms rarely exist in reality: there is growing evidence that small units and firms have become the molecular building blocks of mixed mode structures, as not only more market-like exchanges are taking place within firms, but also hierarchical mechanisms increasingly support market transactions. Such evidence certainly discards the traditional assumption that markets and hierarchies represent discrete governance choices (Masten 1988; Milgrom and Roberts 1990; Powell 1990, Williamson 1991) confirming some earlier work on the viability of hybrid, intermediate forms (Bradach and Eccles 1989; Eccles 1981, 1985; Eccles and White 1988; Hennart 1993; Stinchcombe 1985).

In line with such view, we propose that disaggregation does not inevitably lead to disintegration. On the contrary, we believe that economic activity is converging within structures representing an optimal mix of market and hierarchical characteristics. The aforementioned contributions (Holland and Lockett 1997; Zenger and Hesterly 1997) maintain that this convergence is facilitated by some innovations in the field of information technology, organizational design, and performance measurement, which allow the implementation of relationships combining market-like and hierarchy-like features simultaneously. In this sense, they fill the theoretical gap between traditional notions of governance forms and emerging reality, while recognizing the importance of embedded assets and principles, which can effectively protect networks from stability problems and, consequently, from disintegration.

Yet, as anticipated in the introduction, one fundamental area is underestimated and partially left unexplored by these recent contributions: this concerns the design of information flows as a way to safeguard the permanence of mixed mode structures. Essentially, the relations characterizing hybrid forms can be explained by analysing the contents of micro-level linkages among organizations, that is: exchange content—the goods and services flowing between organizations; normative content—the expectations organizations have of one another given certain social characteristics or attributes; communication content—the passing of information from one organization to another (Mitchell 1973; Soda 1998). All these elements may be present in particular configurations, and investigators must specify which aspects represent their points of interest (Aldrich and Whetten 1981: 385).

Accounting Information Networks: A Definition

Starting from the aforementioned considerations, our contribution aims to focus not on inter-organizational structures themselves, but on the role of information in sustaining the stability of the linkages characterizing such structures.[5] In fact, as a consequence of the potentially powerful uses of information technology, it is information flows that have become a core explanatory variable and which

[5] Network stability can be thought of as a situation in which linkages between organizations within a bounded population remain the same over time (Aldrich and Whetten 1981: 391).

have bettered our understanding of the processes leading to the stability of mixed mode organizations.[6]

With such aim, we thus concentrate on the means to sustain these linkages, that is, on the AIN, whose existence is related to the need of managing a set of dis-integrated activities in an integrated manner. The term 'integrated' is intended here as referring to the need to guarantee compatibility, complementarity, and coherence of organizational behaviours, which derive from the sharing of all the pieces of information dispersed within the organization. In this respect, the functions of the AIN are related to its capacity of linking the sequential activities of processes (sequential integration) while activating all the dispersed resources and competencies, which are needed to manage such processes (cross-unit integration) and, finally, homogenizing different interpretive schemes used within decision-making processes (cognitive integration) (Galbraith 1973; Lawrence and Lorsch 1967; Weick 1979). In other words, if resources and activity flows are to be steadily carried on in a market-like mode within complex webs of autonomous units, it is necessary that the underlying information flows be regulated through shared rules, procedures, and a common information system. In this sense, an AIN is the information system, comprising cross-firm accounting rules and procedures, designed to overcome organizational boundaries and to be shared at the level of the network as a whole.

More specifically, *AIN(s)* can be defined as

multilevel information systems aiming at organizing, processing and sharing accounting information in order to: (1) Check the state of the relationships among the organizational units of mixed mode organizational structures (by verifying that the actions of the other party are in accordance with expectations.); (2) Master events by that relationship as an entity in itself (through planning a collaborative future by setting down what each party wishes to achieve from the collaboration, how feasible the goals and relative roles are and what actions need to be taken); (3) Support layered decision making processes.[7]

Within the AIN, accounting information is therefore used when trying both to check on the state of the relationships, and for mastery of events across more than one organization. For example, when autonomous firms decide to manufacture products or to provide services collaboratively, problems in understanding cross-organizational overhead allocations might arise in the absence of a common accounting information system and shared procedures for the calculation of product costs.[8] Similarly, given the fact that capacity limits in one

---

[6] From a review of the literature on network structures (Fulk and DeSanctis 1995; Grandori and Soda 1995; Holland and Lockett 1997), it is evident that information technology is explicitly recognised as a fundamental tool for the design of new organisational solutions.

[7] In providing the definition of AINs we are consistent with Tomkins (2001), according to whom the need for information in mixed mode structures can be understood only by distinguishing between two different types of information: to support trust and for mastery of events.

[8] On this purpose Nicolini *et al.* (2000) describe the problems which may arise in the construction industry, while Barber *et al.* (2000) refer to similar difficulties in understanding cost of quality exercises cross-organizationally.

firm could affect the whole network, inter-organizational responsibilities and budgets are necessary to construct a budget running across organizational boundaries. Investment appraisal also takes an inter-organizational dimension: in fact, the risk of one single firm could influence the financial risk of the whole network as perceived by the market. Starting from these considerations, suggesting the need, for mixed mode structures, to develop cross-organization cost management, budgeting, and financial analysis, we maintain that complexities related to information organizing, processing, and sharing across organizational units can be solved not by developing new accounting techniques (Tomkins 2000) but by re-examining the notion of accounting information systems, thus the need of introducing the concept of AIN.

The multiplicity of decision levels of an AIN resides in the fact that it acknowledges both the organizational and inter-organizational effects; views decisions as a function of both the cross-organizational shared context and the single units' cognitive processing; allows a dynamic balance for both routinized information collection and problem solving as specified by collective context and *ad hoc* information gathering done by single units for decision-making; permits alternatives to be evaluated at the level of both the whole networked organization and the single molecular units.[9] The consistency between these various levels is guaranteed by the use of a common language of communication, that is to say the accounting language, which functions as a frame, an integrative structure, providing shared interpretations of events thereby serving two roles: meaning assignment and linking mechanism (Boland 1993; Boland and Tenkasi 1995).

In this sense, the design of an AIN draws attention to the organization of accounting information in order to guarantee the existence, functioning, and permanence of mixed mode organizations. In fact, it is the way in which the various pieces of accounting information are located and transferred, leading to multiplex relations of communication, that makes certain accounting information flows as a suitable channel to support organizational stability, transforming disintegration into dis-integration.

The Impact of Informational Complexity on the Configuration of Accounting Information Networks

While recognizing that information flows may be considered as a core explanatory variable of organizational forms, this section of the chapter examines fundamental concepts related to the needs for, and organization of

---

[9] On this purpose see the *Multilevel Parallel Process Model Approach* proposed by Corner *et al.* (1994).

accounting information of mixed mode structures that blend components of markets and hierarchies.

In fact, the integration and stabilizing potentialities of accounting information cannot be taken for granted and our analysis needs to be taken further to describe the way in which the information is organized to produce these potentialities.[10] According to the organizational literature, one of the most important characteristics of an organizational network is represented by the difference in the relevance of its various actors and/or nodes (Freeman 1979). Usually the key or critical actors are located in a strategic position with reference to the resources and processes (Soda 1998). In the same way, it is possible to argue that one of the critical features for the functioning of an information network is represented by the location of information. The information network is designed to guarantee the positioning of information, where it is necessary and where it is cheaper to manage it (Arrow 1974).

According to the same literature, the *locus* of information (in other words where it is processed and managed within an organization, be it either a single firm or a network) seems to be related to its level of complexity (Bavelas 1951). The complexity variable has been studied by many authors, in different disciplines, assigning different meanings to this term. For example, in the decision theory, it was related to the uncertainty of decisions and depended on the possibility to assign a probability to a specific event (Knight 1986). Yet, this variable has assumed, over time, new and more articulated meanings in the organizational literature that can be applied to the concept of accounting information and that help distinguish between different types of accounting information configurations.

According to Grandori (1999) informational complexity is made up of two different dimensions: computational complexity and epistemic complexity. Both can help shed some light on the organization of accounting information. Computational complexity is related to variability, number of elements, and knowledge of events probability. What follows is a description of these various aspects and of their application to accounting information.

Variability derives from the context in which an activity takes place and which can affect its results (Williamson 1975); from the nature of the transformation objects and the transformation process (Perrow 1967); from the change rate and volatility of customers' needs (Hannan and Freeman 1977). For the purposes and the content of our analysis, variability depends on the context in which accounting information is produced and used, the nature of both accounting information and accounting information processing, the change rate and volatility of accounting information users' needs. More specifically, the level of variability of the contexts in which accounting information is used can be expressed in this way: the higher the number of uses, the higher the number of exceptions in accounting information treatment and

---

[10] On this point, see footnote 3.

interpretation, and the higher the level of change rate and volatility, the higher the level of variability. The problem is that it is not possible to classify, within the same organization, situations as possessing either a high level or a low level of variability in absolute terms, but within the same organization, these opposite situations may coexist, and the underlying accounting information flows need to be managed differently. The *number of elements* refers to the number of objects (actors, actions, contextual factors, etc.) and possible combinations of them involved in a specific activity (Simon 1955). In our terms, the higher the number of units that need to be represented by accounting, the number of decision levels and events affecting accounting information, and the need to drill down and combine synthesis and analysis at the same time, the higher the number of elements involved in accounting information. This is especially true when the focal tasks of a specific unit are affected by those performed in related units (Hirst 1981) as happens in a mixed mode organization. By following these lines of reasoning within the same organization it is possible to have both some accounting information with a high level of articulation and for which the combination of synthesis and analysis is essential, and more disarticulated accounting information related to single events. The two pieces of accounting information coexist and require a different treatment.

The last aspect of informational complexity refers to the possibility to assign *probability* to *events* (Knight 1986). The lower the possibility to assign probability to the events represented by accounting information, the higher the level of complexity.

Informational complexity is also characterized by the epistemic dimension, which refers to the level of knowledge completeness about the states of the world, preferences, relationships between causes and effects, behaviours and/or results. In our framework, the incompleteness of knowledge on *the states of the world* refers to the impossibility to forecast exactly which events may affect accounting information, providing therefore only a partial meaning to the accounting information available (Hirshleifer and Riley 1979).

The uncertainty about *preferences* is related to the uncertainty over the objective for actions. In terms of our analysis, this means that when the uncertainty over the objective for actions is low, accounting information, by providing a way of comparing the achievable and the desirable, introduces a powerful element to structure the decision-making process. In addition, it can facilitate coordination and integration of organizational activities by computational means. When the uncertainty over the objectives of organizational action is high, accounting information promotes particular positions and values. It does not reflect agreed objectives, but seeks to articulate and further particular ends. It may reflect what has already been decided upon and executed (Hopwood 1980).

The knowledge about *causes and effects relationships* can vary from complete knowledge, which exists when individuals are certain of the outcome associated with a given action, to incomplete knowledge, which exists where individuals are uncertain of the consequences of their actions (Hirst 1981; Ouchi 1977; Ouchi and Maguire 1975; Thompson 1967).

Finally, epistemic complexity refers to *observability of events and measurability of outputs*. Measurability depends on the completeness and sophistication of output measures (Abernethy and Brownell 1997; Kirsch 1996; Ouchi 1977, Rockness and Shields 1984). This affects the capability to evaluate ex post economic actions and their consequences. This means that some accounting information is more difficult to be read, interpreted, and understood because it refers to events that are more difficult to observe and measure. In this case the level of complexity is high.

Starting from this brief review of the literature, informational complexity can be interpreted as a multidimensional concept. Yet, in the analysis that follows we will consider only the combinatory effect of all the aforementioned elements leading to either a high degree or a low degree of informational complexity. This latter can affect the network's characteristics in terms of its centrality (Bavelas, 1951; Freeman *et al.* 1980).[11] This is coherent with Galbraith's view (1973) according to which organizations respond to uncertainty (informational complexity in our terminology) by increasing their capacity to process information (Feltham 1968; Feltham and Demski 1969). This can be achieved by means of two different strategies: the first involves investments in centred information systems that allow economies to be made on the transmission and treatment of information, thus increasing the capacity to deal with computational complexity. However, when computational complexity overcomes a certain limit and is accompanied by epistemic complexity, it is necessary to adopt a different strategy, that is to say the distribution of information processing where decision-making is located. This leads to a further advantage of guaranteeing that all relevant information is taken into consideration in the decision processes.[12]

Following these lines of reasoning, when informational complexity is low, integration between the various units of mixed mode structures is achieved by means of accounting information networks with a high degree of centrality. Conversely, when informational complexity is high, integration requires that accounting information is embedded in a densely connected web of interactions between the different nodes of an AIN, coincident with a low degree of centrality. The possibility to manage accounting information with different degrees of centrality derives from the peculiar nature of the AIN's intelligence. This latter can be defined as the gathering, storing, elaborating, and

---

[11] The term centrality has been taken from the social network literature, which has operationalized this concept in many different ways: for example, degree centrality, betweenness centrality, closeness centrality, and eigenvector centrality. For a review of these measures see Wasserman and Faust (1994), Soda (1998), Chapman (1998). In the context of this chapter, centrality refers to whether accounting information is mainly processed at the centre or at the periphery of a given network.   [12] On this point see: Grant (2001).

distributing of information (Pennings 1981; Sawney and Parikh 2001).[13] The location of this intelligence can be decoupled into back-end and front-end. The first type—the back-end intelligence—is usually embedded in a shared infrastructure at the network's core. Such form of intelligence is, therefore, centralized, robust, scalable, and standardized. The second type of intelligence, the front-end type, can be fragmented at the network periphery, and is characterized by decentralization, flexibility, personalization, and conceptualization (Sawney and Parikh 2001).

The nature of the front-end intelligence is very different from the nature of the back-end intelligence: the former is needed for interaction, while the latter is suitable for processing and storing information. They are complementary but, if decoupled, they empower each other, since back-end intelligence can be efficiently consolidated in a shared infrastructure so that front-end intelligence, freed from basic processing and storing functions, can be customized according to the needs of any final user (Sawhney and Parikh 2001). Complete decoupling is effective only when the level of informational complexity is low. In other cases, the two types of intelligence cannot be completely separated because the back-end intelligence is shaped according to the specific needs of the front-end intelligence. In this framework accounting represents a *lingua franca*, that is, a shared code for information exchange,[14] which enables individual pieces of intelligence to flow and be recombined anywhere along the network.

Evidence from the Field: Financial Shared Service Centres and e-Reporting

From an empirical point of view, AINs with a high degree of centrality can be observed in practice in the emergence of shared service centres, which may be defined as *'autonomous operating units aggregating resources, activities and competencies that provide services to different businesses and geographical entities within an organization'* (Beretta *et al.* 2000). Evidence of the diffusion of these organizational solutions applied to accounting activities shows that thirty-five companies, operating in various industries (electronic, chemical, distribution, service, and others), have already implemented one or more financial shared service centres across Europe. The number of such firms is high given that the financial shared service centre solution has been applied mainly by American corporations since the early 1990s and has started to proliferate in Europe during the early twenty-first century. In addition, it is an organizational solution that is adopted primarily by big

---

[13] Note that Pennings (1981) introduces the concept of organizational intelligence as a tool to forecast and absorb uncertainty. This is consistent with our argument that accounting information flows can be considered as a means to manage complexity.

[14] This is consistent with Shannon and Weaver's model of communication (1949).

multinational companies (Ditillo and Pistoni 2000). The growing number of companies adopting financial shared service centres is driven mainly by the pursuit of cost reduction and quality improvement.[15]

Financial shared service centres can be considered as evidence of AINs with a high degree of centrality because they consolidate specific operations in one location while, at the same time, developing a strong customer orientation that may potentially provide higher quality services at a lower cost (Jarman 1998). They try to match the level of efficiency achievable with the processing of accounting information in one single location with the customer focus of distributed operations of analysis and interpretation (Amigoni and Beretta 2000; Krempel 1998). They are based on an underlying *relational model* that fosters a *partnership* between suppliers of accounting services and their corresponding internal customers. Suppliers and internal customers are considered as separate units but combine their interests thanks to the information flows that foster the consistency between the activities carried out by the financial shared service centre and the functionalities demanded by the internal users (Bray 1996; Jarman 1998; Macrì and Nigro 1995; Ulrich 1995).

Shared service centres are structurally configured to produce and exchange definable accounting activities, tend to be measured as separate units and, finally, are normally rewarded directly for their performance. The evidence coming from the analysis of some firms (Accenture, IBM, Pirelli, 3M, Fiat, Whirlpool, Alcoa, Exel) supports these considerations and suggests that companies are attempting to both introduce output indicators to measure the centres' services (such as the number of invoices issued, the number of transactions recorded, and so on) and use incentive mechanisms that are strictly related to specific results of the financial shared service centre (Beretta *et al.* 2000).

On the other hand, the relationship between the financial shared service centre and its internal customers is regulated by the use of service level agreements and operating level agreements. Evidence shows that while service level agreements normally include the description of the services provided, the volume indicators and the prices/rates applied for them, the operating level agreements contain the duties of the financial shared service centre's customers in terms of, for example, the activities the customers carry out, the qualitative standards of the information the customers provide and, finally, the penalties for breaking the rules (Ditillo and Pistoni 2000). The characteristics of both kinds of agreement seem to be related to two different variables: the specificity of the contributions supplied by the financial shared

---

[15] Other evidence of the diffusion of the phenomenon can be found in Sandell R. C. *'The Shared Service Center: Catalyzing World-Class Performance'*, Price Waterhouse LLP, 1997, and *the Global Shared Services Benchmark Survey* undertaken by the Research International sponsored by Ernst&Young between October 1997 and January 1998. This last survey provides some data relating to the information management activities supported by shared services, like data warehouse management, data architecture management, information provision, end-user support, analysis and reporting, and technology architecture.

service centre and the level of informational complexity embedded in the services provided (Grandori 1995; Williamson 1981).

In terms of specificity, the analysis of the aforementioned firms shows that the activities performed by financial shared service centres are usually trans-action-based and routinized, with a low level of specificity. On the other hand, in terms of informational complexity, the same evidence shows that this is high, because it is not possible to specify in advance the quantity and time of service provision. For this reason long-term exchange contracts that include quality, responsiveness, and reliability are normally used.

In brief, it is possible to argue that the relationship between the financial shared service centre and its customers is a mixed mode relationship that combines at the same time market elements (exchange of definable outputs, measurement, and reward of specific performance) and hierarchical elements (the use of long-term exchange agreements that go beyond service and price to include responsiveness and reliability to deal with unexpected contingencies and events) (Beretta *et al.* 2000; Zenger and Hesterly 1997).

The question is whether financial shared service centres can be considered as organizational solutions with the necessary level of flexibility and respon-siveness for the accounting information processes of mixed mode structures. The analysis of some cases (Amigoni and Beretta 2000) shows that the activities per-formed by financial shared service centres are characterized by a high level of standardization. This is due to the specific characteristics of these activities, which are, as argued before, transaction-based and routinized. Yet, this stan-dardization does not necessarily prevent a proper level of flexibility. In fact, if correctly interpreted, standardization is the process of simply eliminating non-value added activities and at the same time maintaining the necessary level of adaptation to local needs. This combination of standardization, on the one hand, and flexibility and responsiveness, on the other, is the result of a continuous process of information sharing driven by information and com-munication technologies, which leads to a cross-fertilization between finan-cial shared service centres and their customers (Beretta 2000).

To conclude, financial shared service centres can add value to the accounting information processing and provision by means of procedures and systems' stan-dardization, deriving from the use of generally accepted practices and common accounting standards and leads to the necessary level of information integration to stabilize and prevent the disintegration forces of mixed mode structures.

On the other hand, the emergence of distributed AINs, that is, with a low degree of centrality, can be observed in the adoption of internet technologies supporting reporting processes. In fact, in the field of accounting, the lever-age on internet technology has translated into the emergence of a new electronic-reporting (e-reporting) architecture to manage the reporting process wholly electronically.

A fundamental principle of e-reporting is storing report content in an elec-tronic file format within digital libraries, which can be accessed by different users, not only in order to view specific reports, but also to customize some basic formats according to their information needs. Report versioning refers to the ability to create and store multiple versions of the same report information. Report mining means that report files can be interrogated by rules engines that allow, for example, to look for exceptions in the report data or to subdivide reports in smaller portions in order to analyse only the information that users really need. Finally, report searching, like common web searches, enables users to enter a keyword, get back a list of reports that match the search criteria and review the information online. The main benefits of such functionalities, as shown by anecdotal evidence,[16] include reducing the cost of transaction processing, delivering real-time accounting information, as well as improving the quality of accounting information itself. Therefore, e-reporting assumes a much wider range of accounting information output formats, so that through report versioning, mining, and searching, accounting data can be processed locally in order to customize analysis and interpretation.

Apart from specific functionalities, e-reporting is novel in that accounting information can be communicated electronically using universal, open standards. This means, ultimately, that by leveraging the internet, it is possible to solve the trade-off between richness and reach, which was typical of the traditional reporting process. By 'reach', we mean connectivity, i.e. the number of people who can share accounting data. 'Richness' refers to three important aspects of information, i.e. bandwidth,[17] customization and interactivity (Evans and Wurster 1997: 73).

Generally speaking, in the past, the communication of rich reports required either proximity or dedicated information channels, whose costs limited the audience that could benefit from reporting data. Conversely, the communication of reporting information to a large number of people, dispersed at the peripheries of firms, was detrimental for the bandwidth, the customization as well as the interactivity of the reporting process. In fact, the traditional concepts of span of control and hierarchical reporting were predicated on the conviction that communication of accounting information could not be rich and broad simultaneously (Evans and Wurster 1997: 74).

On the contrary, many of the recent organizational experiments—be they called virtual corporations, e-companies or extended enterprises—are indeed based on the solution of the aforementioned trade-off, enabled by internet technologies, which enhance single firms' capabilities to operate within broad coalitions of allies and to outsource all but critical activities.[18] As the use of e-reporting expands, business collaborations become more feasible, easier to establish, operate, and revise. Accounting information capabilities, in many

---

[16] On this point see: Caglio (2002).

[17] Bandwidth refers to the amount of information that can be moved from sender to receiver in a given time (Evans and Wurster 1997: 73).

[18] Some well-known examples of networked companies using e-reporting are Cisco Systems, CHL and Pirelli (case studies presented at the CESAD workshop on E-Administration (2001)).

instances, are replacing the need for well-defined structural boundaries and organizational hierarchies as well as for formal processes and layers of staff.[19] In fact, e-reporting may be fundamental to mixed mode organizations in that it supports decision-making processes, while enabling each nodes of the network both to check the relationships with all the other nodes in real time, and to act collaboratively, before strategic opportunities disappear, in order to develop business possibilities.

In this sense, e-reporting represents an AIN with a low degree of centrality, within which the same piece of accounting information can be used and re-used, interactively and creatively, in any locus of the network, in order to deal with contexts and events characterized by a high degree of informational complexity. Through the use of web-based applications, reporting becomes an on-going process. Accounting information role is no longer related to policing adherence to pre-determined courses of action, but rather focuses on enabling the management of the business forward in terms of future possibilities and outcomes.[20] Accounting information within e-reporting is undergoing a process of refinement such that complex and ambiguous events can be captured and fitted into an informational representation that provides an integrative frame of reference going beyond the boundaries of each single firm. In this way, each node in the AIN is mobilized as a locus for accounting information management and its contribution to the overall process is highlighted.

Moving reporting onto more accessible relational databases is 'opening up' accounting information, and the use of the internet as a means to support reporting processes is expanding their scope so that within mixed mode structures, it is possible to speak about 'reportals' instead of simple reporting systems. Such reportals provide a web-based gateway for employees, managers, and trusted business partners to share accounting information with varying degrees of access.[21] This is an example of an AIN with an extremely low degree of centrality, providing an integrative framework for all the relationships among the 'molecular' units of a mixed mode structure, which exist as they are made visible through accounting information flows.

Conclusions

Previous contributions on organizational forms posited the existence of two extreme governance structures of market and hierarchy. Only recently, the attention has been devoted to intermediate forms of hybrid networks or

---

[19] On this subject see: Amigoni (2001).

[20] On this 'double' role of accounting see: Chapman 1998.

[21] Users of a reportal can perform a wide range of functions regarding the accounting information provided: for example, they can navigate the reports, they can chart or tabulate report data, they can export information in a range of formats for further analysis and they can attach a specific report to an e-mail message. See: Caglio 2002.

virtual organizations. The argument made here is that these mixed mode forms would be difficult or infeasible to implement without the existence of AINs.

Our analysis, by leveraging on the concept of AIN, is new to accounting research, and provides a framework for developing our comprehension of accounting information flows within emerging organizational contexts. More specifically, it is suggested that stability to potentially unstable mixed mode structures is contingent on the design of either AINs with a high degree of centrality or distributed AINs. The evidence provided represents an attempt to draw out and understand some instances behind the patterned variations of AINs. While the framework presented here is not intended to be confined only to the phenomena under discussion, some *caveats* are necessary when trying to extend our interpretation to other accounting related trends.

In recognizing that AINs are the main stabilizing mechanisms of mixed mode structures, we do not want to neglect the role of other variables that influence the relationships between the molecular units of networked forms, that is, trust and control. Some authors argue that these variables are important prerequisites for the existence of inter-firms relations. However, without departing from the arguments of these commentators,[22] we suggest that trust and control may often be a result rather than a cause. More specifically, with reference to AINs, we argue that trust and control may emerge as a consequence of the integrative capabilities of accounting information flows, leading to closer relationships and collaborative actions.

To conclude, there are some further research issues that are raised by the arguments presented here: first, the use of social network analysis, applied to the field of accounting, in order to test the specific characteristics of AINs in practice; second, the use of this body of techniques for describing and understanding complex multi-level accounting information flows embedded in organizational communication; and finally, the organization processes involved in the formation and functioning of AINs. In this sense, the proposed interpretive scheme is not intended as a comprehensive treatment of newly raised accounting issues, but rather as a suggested starting point for empirical work on the proposed model. Initial exploratory studies should provide new avenues of research as well as contribute to our knowledge of accounting information management.

References

Abernethy, M. A. and, Brownell, P. (1997), 'Management Control Systems in Research and Development Organizations: The Role of Accounting, Behavior and Personnel Controls', *Accounting, Organizations and Society*, 22/3–4: 233–48.

---

[22] See, for example: Koza and Lewin 1998; Tomkins 2000.

Aldrich, H. E. and Whetten, D. A. (1981), 'Organization-sets, Action-sets, and Networks: Making the Most of Simplicity', in P. C. Nystrom and W. H. Starbuck (eds), *Handbook of Organizational Design* (Oxford: Oxford University Press), 385–408.

Amigoni, F. (2001), 'Tecnologie e attese degli stakeholders: il loro ruolo nelle misurazioni per il controllo di gestione', Paper presented at the conference *I sistemi di controllo di gestione tra old e new economy*, Bressanone.

——and Beretta, S. (2000), *Financial Shared Services* (Milano: Egea).

Arrow, K. J. (1974), *The Limits of Organization* (New York, London: W.W. Norton).

Axelrod (1984), *The Evolution of Cooperation* (New York: Basic Books).

Barber, P., Graves, A., Hall, M., Sheath, D., Tomkins, C. (2000), 'Quality failure costs in civil engineering projects', *International Journal of Quality and Reliability Management*, 17(4/5): 479–92.

Baum, J. A. C. and Oliver, C. (1991), 'Institutional linkages and organizational mortality', *Administrative Science Quarterly*, 36: 187–218.

Bavelas, A. (1951), 'Communication Patterns in Task-Oriented Groups', in D. Lerner and H. K. Lasswell (eds), *The Policy Sciences* (Stanford: Stanford University Press).

Beretta, S. (2000), 'I Centri Servizi Amministrativi: Logiche di costituzione e modalità di gestione', in F. Amigoni and S. Beretta, *Financial Shared Services* vol.14 (Milano: Egea).

——Ditillo, A., Pistoni, A. (2000), 'Financial Shared Service Centres: Hype and Reality', *European Business Forum*, Issue 3, Autumn.

Blois, K. J. (1972), 'Vertical Quasi-Integration', *Journal of Industrial Economics*, July: 253–72.

Boisot, M. H. (1986), 'Markets and hierarchies in a cultural perspective', *Organization Studies*, 7/2: 135–58.

Boland, R. J. Jr. (1993), 'Accounting and the Interpretive Act', *Accounting, Organizations and Society*, February/April: 1–24.

——and Tenkasi, R. B. (1995), 'Perspective Making and Perspective Taking in Communities of Knowing', *Organization Science*, 6/4, (July–August): 350–72.

Bradach, J. L. and Eccles, R. G. (1989), 'Price, Authority, and Trust: From Ideal Types to Plural Forms', *Annual Review of Sociology*, 15: 97–118.

Bray, P. (1996), 'Shared Services', *Management Accounting*, April: 42–3.

Burt, R. (1990), 'A study of structural holes as social capital and entrepreneurial opportunity', Working paper for *N.I.A.S. Symposium on 'Interdisciplinary Perspective on Organization Studies'*.

Caglio, A. (2002), 'E-Finance: The impact of net technologies on management control systems', Working paper.

Chandler, A. D. (1990), *Scale and Scope: The Dynamics of Industrial Capitalism*, (Cambridge: The Belknap Press of Harvard University Press).

Chapman, C. S. (1998), 'Accountants in Organizational Networks', *Accounting, Organization and Society*, 23/8, 737–66.

Corner, D. C., Kinicki, A. J., and Keats, B. W. (1994), 'Integrating Organizational and Individual Information Processing Perspectives on Choices', *Organization Science*, 5/3: 294–308.

D'Aunno, T. A. and Zuckerman, H. S. (1987), 'A Life-cycle Model of Organizational Federations: The Case of Hospitals', *Academy of Management Journal*, 12: 534–45.

Davenport, T. and Pearlson, K. (1998), 'Two Cheers for the Virtual Office', *Sloan Management Review*, 3: 51–65.

Di Maggio, P. J. (1986), 'Structural Analysis of Organizational Fields: A Blockmodel Approach', in B. M. Staw and L. L. Cummings (eds), *Research in Organizational Behavior* (Greenwich: JAI Press) Vol. 8, 335–70.

Ditillo, A. and Pistoni, A. (2000), '*Le modalità e i meccanismi di implementazione e di governo dei Centri Servizi Amministrativi: Risultati dell'analisi empirica*', in F. Amigoni and S. Beretta, *Financial Shared Services* (Milano: Egea).

Ebers, M. (1993), 'IT networks as organizational forms', paper presented at the 11th E.G.O.S. Colloquium The Production and Diffusion of Managerial Knowledge, Paris.

Eccles, R. G. (1981), 'The Quasifirm in the Construction Industry', *Journal of Economic Behavior and Organization*, 2: 335–7.

——(1985), *The Transfer Pricing Problem: A Theory for Practice* (Lexington: Lexington Books).

—— and White, H. C. (1988), 'Price and Authority in Interprofit Center Transactions', *American Journal of Sociology*, 94, S17–S51.

Evans, P. B., Wurster, T. S. (1998), 'Strategy and the New Economics of Information', *Harvard Business Review*, September–October: 71–82.

Faucheux, C. (1997), 'How Virtual Organizing is Transforming Management Science', *Communications of the ACM*, 40/9: 50–5.

Feltham, G. (1968), 'The Value of Information', *The Accounting Review*, October: 684–96.

—— and Demski, J. (1969), 'The Use of Models in Information Evaluation', *The Accounting Review*, July: 457–66.

Freeman, L. C. (1979), 'Centrality in Social Networks, I, Conceptual Clarification', *Social Networks*, 1: 215–39.

—— Roeder, D. and Mulholland, R. R. (1980), 'Centrality in Social Networks, II, Experimental Results', *Social Networks*, 2: 119–41.

Fulk, J. and DeSanctis, G. (1995), 'Electronic Communication and Changing Organizational Forms', *Organization Science, Focus Issue*, 6/4: 337–49.

Galbraith, J. (1973), *Designing Complex Organizations* (Reading, MA: Addison-Wesley).

Grandori, A. (1989), 'Reti Interorganizzative: Progettazione e Negoziazione', *Economia & Management*, 7: 28–40.

——(1995), *L'organizzazione delle Attività Economiche* (Bologna: il Mulino).

——(1999), *Organizzazione e Comportamento Economico*, (Bologna: il Mulino).

—— Soda, G. (1995), 'Inter-firm Networks: Antecedents, Mechanisms and Forms', *Organization Studies*, 16/2: 183–214.

Grant, R. M. (2001), 'The Knowledge-Based Approach to Organization Design', Paper presented at the conference on Information Flows in Knowledge Intensive Firms, Università Commerciale L. Bocconi.

Hamilton, G., Zeile, W. and Kim, W. J. (1990), '*The Network Structure of East Asian Economies*', in S. R. Clegg and G. Redding (eds), *Capitalism in Contrasting Cultures*, (Berlin: de Gruyter) 105–29.

Hannan, M. H., Freeman, J. (1977), 'The Population Ecology of Organizations', *American Journal of Sociology*, 82: 929–64.

Harrigan, K. R. and Newmann, W. H. (1990), 'Bases of Inter-Organization Co-Operation', *Journal of Management Studies*, 27: 417–34.

Hennart, J. (1993), 'Explaining the Swollen Middle: Why Most Transactions Are a Mix of "Market" and Hierarchy', *Organization Science*, 4: 529–47.

Hirshleifer, J. C. and Riley, J. G. (1979), 'The Analytics of Uncertainty and Information—An expository survey', *Journal of Economic Literature*, XVII: 1375–421.

Hirst, M. K. (1981), 'Accounting Information and the Evaluation of Subordinate Performance: A Situational Approach', *The Accounting Review*, LVI4 (October): 771–84.

Holland, C. P. and Lockett, A. G. (1997), 'Mixed Mode Network Structures: The Strategic Use of Electronic Communication by Organizations', *Organization Science*, 8/5: 475–88.

Hopwood, A. G. (1980), 'The Organizational and Behavioural Aspects of Budgeting and Control', in J. Arnold, B. Carsberg and R. Scapens (eds), *Topics in Management Accounting* (Southampton: Philip Allan).

Jarillo, J. C. (1988), 'On Strategic Networks', *Strategic Management Journal*, 9/1: 31–41.

Jarman, N. (1998), 'Shared Service Centres—Building for Europe', *Management Accounting*, June.

Kirsch, L. J. (1996), 'The Management of Complex Task in Organizations: Controlling the Systems Development Process', *Organization Science*, 7/1 (January–February): 1–21.

Knight, F. (1986) 'Risk, Uncertainty and Profit', in L. Putterman (ed.) *The Economic Nature of the Firm: A Reader* (Cambridge University Press).

Koza, M. P. and Lewin, A. Y. (1998), 'The Co-evolution of Strategic Alliances', *Organization Science*, 9/3: 255–64.

Krempel, M. (1998), *Shared Services* (London: The Economist Intelligence Unit).

Laumann, E., Marsden, P. and Prensky, D. (1980), 'The Boundary Specification Problem in Network Analysis', in R. Burt and M. Minor (eds), *Applied Network Analysis* (Beverly Hills: Sage) 18–34.

Lawrence, P. R. and Lorsch, J. W. (1967), *Organization and Environment. Managing Differentiation and Integration* (Harvard University: Division of Research, Graduate School of Business Administration).

Lomi, A. (1991), *Reti Organizzative* (Bologna, Il Mulino).

Lorenzoni, G. (a cura di) (1992), *Accordi, reti e vantaggio competitivo* (Milano, Etas Libri).

Macrì, D. and Nigro, G. (1995), 'Il Controllo Internal-Market Driven', *Sviluppo e Organizzazione*, Novembre–Dicembre.

Masten, S. (1988), 'A Legal Basis for the Firm', *Journal of Law, Economics, and Organizations*, 4: 181–98.

Miles, R. E. and Snow, C. C. (1992), 'Causes of Failure in Network Organizations', *California Management Review*, 34: 53–72.

Milgrom, P. and Roberts, J. (1990), 'The Economics of Modern Manufacturing: Technology, Strategy and Organization', *American Economic Review*, 80: 511–28.

Mitchell, J. C. (1973), 'Networks, Norms and Institutions', in J. Boissevain and J. C. Mitchell (eds), *Network Analysis* (Mouton: The Hague) 15–35.

Moore, G. (1979), 'The Structure of a National Elite Network', *American Sociological Review*, 44: 673–92.

Moss Kanter, R. (1988), *When Giants Learn to Dance* (London: Unwin Hyman).

Nelson, R. (1993), *National Innovation Systems. A Comparative Analysis* (Oxford: Oxford University Press).

Nicolini, D., Tomkins, C., Holti, R., Oldman, A., and Smalley M. (2000), 'Can Target Costing and Whole Life Costing be Applied in the Construction Industry?— Evidence From Two Case Studies', *British Journal of Management*: 303–24.

Nohria, N. and Eccles, R. G. (eds) (1992), *Networks and Organizations* (Boston: Harvard Business School Press).

Ouchi, W. G. (1977), 'The Relationships Between Organizational Structure and Organizational Control', *Administrative Science Quarterly*, 22 (March).

——Maguire, M. A. (1975), 'Organizational Control: Two Functions', *Administrative Science Quarterly*, 20 (December): 559–69.

Pennings, J. M. (1981), Strategically Interdependent Organizations, in P. C. Nystrom and W. H. Starbuck (eds), *Handbook of Organizational Design* (Oxford: Oxford University Press) 433–55.

Perrow, C. (1967), 'A Framework for the Comparative Analysis of Organization', *American Sociological Review*, 32 (April).

Perucci, R. and Potter, H. R. (1989), *Networks of power* (Berlin: de Gruyter).

Pfeffer, J. and Salancik, G. R. (1978), *The External Control of Organizations: A Resource Dependence Perspective* (New York: Harper and Row).

Powell, W. W. (1990), 'Neither Market nor Hierarchy: Network Forms of Organization', in B. M. Straw and L. L. Cummings (eds), *Research in Organizational Behavior* (Greenwich: JAI Press) 12, 295–336.

Rayport, J. F. and Sviokla, J. J. (1995), 'Exploiting the Virtual Value Chain', *Harvard Business Review*, 73: 75–85.

Ring, P. S. (1993), 'Processes facilitating reliance on trust in inter-organizational networks', Paper presented at the European Science Foundation conference 'Forms of Interorganizational Networks: Structures and Processes', Berlin.

Rockness, H. O. and Shields, M. D. (1984), 'Organizational Control Systems in Research and Development', *Accounting, Organizations and Society*, 9/2: 165–77.

Sawhney, M., Parikh, D. (2001), 'Where Value Lives in a Networked World', *Harvard Business Review*, January: 79–86.

Soda, G. (1998), *Reti tra imprese* (Roma: Carocci Editore).

Scharpf, F. W. (ed.) (1993), *Games in Hierarchies and Networks* (Frankfurt, Campus).

Schultze, U. and Orlikowski, W. J. (2001), 'Metaphors of Virtuality: Shaping an Emergent Reality', *Information and Organization*, 11: 45–77.

Shannon, C. and Weaver, W. (1949), *The Mathematical Theory of Communication*, (Chicago, IL: University of Illinois).

Simon, H. A. (1955), 'A Behavioral Model of Rational Choice', *Quarterly Journal of Economics*, 69.

Stinchcombe, A. L. (1985), 'Contracts as Hierarchical Documents', in A. L. Stinchcombe and C. A. Heimer (eds), *Organizational Theory and Project Management: Administering Uncertainty in Norweigian Offshore Oil* (Bergen: Norwegian University Press).

Thompson, J. D. (1967), *Organizations in Action* (New York: McGraw-Hill).

Thorelli, H. B. (1986), 'Networks. Between markets and hierarchies', *Strategic Management Journal*, 7: 37–51.

Tomkins, C. (2001), 'Interdependencies, Trust and Information in Relationships, Alliances and Networks', *Accounting, Organizations and Society*, 26: 161–91.

Turnbull, P. (1986), 'The "Japanization" of Production and Industrial Relations at Lucas Electrical', *Industrial Relations Journal*, vol.17 no.3.

Ulrich, D. (1995), 'Shared Services: Reengineering the HR Function', *Human Resources Planning Journal*, 18: 3, 12–24.

Upton, M. D. and Mcafee, A. (1996), 'The Real Virtual Factory', *Harvard Business Review*, 74: 123–33.

Van de Ven, A. H. and Walker, G. (1984), 'The Dynamics of Interorganizational Coordination, *Administrative Science Quarterly*, 29/4: 598–621.

Wasserman, S. and Faust, K. (1994), *Social Network Analysis: Methods and Applications* (Cambridge: Cambridge University Press).

Weick, K. E. (1979), *The Social Psychology of Organizing* (Reading: Addison-Wesley).

Williamson, O. E. (1975), *Markets and Hierarchies: Analysis and Antitrust Implications* (New York: Free Press).

——(1981), 'The Economics of Organization: The Transaction Cost Approach', *American Journal of Sociology*, 87: 548–77.

——(1985), *The Economic Institutions of Capitalism* (New York: The Free Press).

——(1991), 'Comparative Economic Organization: The Analysis of Discrete Structural Alternatives', *Administrative Science Quarterly*, 36/1: 269–96.

Zenger, T. R. and Hesterly, W. S. (1997), 'The Disaggregation of Corporations: Selective Intervention, High-powered Incentives, and Molecular Units', *Organization Science*, 8/3: 209–22.

3
Management Accounting for the Extended Enterprise
Performance Management for Strategic Alliances and Networked Partners

Shannon W. Anderson and Karen L. Sedatole

Introduction

Firm boundaries no longer define the relevant entity for performance management for many firms. Competitive forces, deregulated economies and technological advances have reduced the costs of transacting with external parties[1] and diminished the value of vertical integration. At the same time, the potential returns to collaboration have increased, as firms with unique capabilities join forces to more rapidly develop and deliver innovative products and services. Collaboration may take the form of franchises, licensing arrangements, joint ventures, or minority equity shares—arrangements that align the interests of participating parties through a shared profit opportunity and formal profit-sharing rules (Hansmann 1996; Hansmann and Kraakman 2000; Orts 1998). Alternatively, they may take a more amorphous form, using few mechanisms from contract law to structure their interactions or allocate the gains from trade. Terms that have been used to describe these relationships include: strategic alliances, strategic partnerships, consortia, strategic networks, cooperative interorganizational relationships, embedded relationships, extended enterprises, JIT II, and strategic supply chains (Das and Teng 1998, 1999; Dyer 2000; Dyer and Nobeoka 2000; Granovetter 1973; Granovetter 1985; Gulati 1995a, 1998; Gulati and Singh 1998; Gulati *et al.* 2000; Ring and Van de Ven 1994).

These organizational forms populate the vast middle ground of hybrids that lies between markets and hierarchies (Harbison and Pekar 1998; Williamson 1985, 1991). If evidence from US firms is representative, they account for a large and growing (more than 10,400 announced in the year 2000 as

We are grateful to Henri Dekker for comments on an early draft of the manuscript and to Steven Currall and Cyril Tomkins for helpful discussions about the material.

[1] In some countries the costs of using courts of law to settle disputes has also increased, making alternative dispute resolution mechanisms relatively more attractive.

compared to 3,730 in 1996) segment of the world economy (see Figure 3.1).
Accenture, a multinational consulting firm, estimates that the typical large US
company formed 177 alliances from 1997 to 2000 and that, for a quarter of
these companies, alliances will account for more than 40 per cent of their
market value by 2004 (www.accenture.com August 2001). In a survey of senior managers, 'more than 80 per cent of top executives consider strategic
alliances to be a prime vehicle for future growth' and they 'expect alliances
to account for 25 per cent of their company's market value within five years'
(Schifrin 2001*a*).

The new economy has not given birth to hybrid organizational forms. Rather,
the new economy has revealed them as instruments of competitive advantage.
The popular business press proclaims, 'the ability to attract partners and manage alliances...is the new core competency of the networked age' (Schifrin

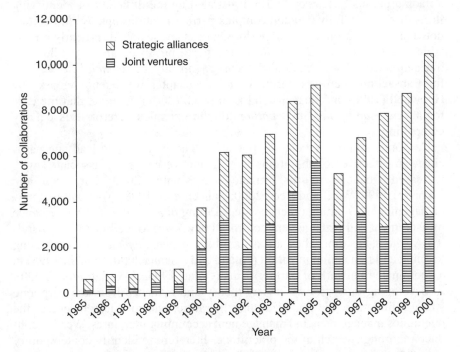

Fig. 3.1. The formation of collaborations through joint venture or strategic alliances,
1985–2000. A joint venture is defined as 'a cooperative business activity, formed by two
or more separate organizations for strategic purpose(s), which creates an independent
business entity, and allocates ownership, operational responsibilities, and financial risks
and rewards to each member, while preserving each member's separate identity/autonomy'.
A strategic alliance is defined as 'a cooperative business activity, formed by two or more
separate organizations for a strategic purpose(s), which does not create an independent
business entity, but allocates ownership, operational responsibilities, and financial risks
and rewards to each member, while preserving each member's separate identity/autonomy'.
(*Source*: Thomson Financial Services).

2001*a*) and major consulting firms are trumpeting partnering skills as the next competitive battleground (e.g., Harbison and Pekar 1998). Researchers are also finding that the ability to interact with suppliers in a partnership arrangement, termed 'relational capital', is a distinctive organizational capability that firms cultivate deliberately (Lorenzoni and Lipparini 1999). Although the research and teaching in some management disciplines reflect the trend toward collaboration as a mode of organizing economic activity, the field of accounting has generally been unresponsive to these changes.[2] In his Presidential Lecture at the 2000 American Accounting Association meeting on the future of accounting research, distinguished accounting scholar, Bill Kinney observed: 'We need to consider updating the accounting model to...measure and report on entities with "cloudy boundaries."...how should we account for an entity whose "inventory" is owned by another party and whose "fixed assets" are owned by a trading partner?' (Kinney 2001). Frustrated by the difficulty of identifying firms that successfully manage complex partner relationships, *Forbes* editors noted that 'measuring financial performance from the outside is nearly impossible' (Anonymous 2001: 64) in part because analysts do not track alliances. These examples focus on opacity of *financial accounting* for transactions between partners. In this chapter we extend remarks by Hopwood (1996) and Scapens and Bromwich (2001), to argue that the case for a new *management accounting* for the extended enterprise is equally compelling.

Corporate strategy scholars hypothesize that the ability to lead and participate in effective collaborations is a distinctive capability associated with increased financial returns (Anand and Khanna 2000; Lorenzoni and Lipparini 1999; Wolff and Reed 2000; Zaheer *et al.* 1998). We posit that new management accounting practices are fulfilling *old demands* for performance measurement and management control in *new ways* to facilitate this capability. At the same time, they are also fulfilling *new demands* for promoting learning and rich communication (Anand and Khanna 2000; Bianchi 1995) in a coordinated network of partner firms (Gulati 1995*a,b*; Gulati *et al.* 2000). In developing our case, we review theory and evidence from the corporate strategy literature, the organizational literature, and to a lesser degree, the operations management and management accounting literatures. We also conduct a thorough search of the practitioner literature to identify contemporary accounts of partner relationships. Our intent in the latter is to see whether anecdotes support our intuition that different modes of management accounting accompany the emergence of hybrid organizational forms. Our objective is to suggest a new research agenda for the extended enterprise that is linked

---

[2] Noteworthy exceptions include: Anderson *et al.* (2000), Baiman *et al.* (2001), Cooper and Slagmulder (2003), Gietzman (1996), Groot and Merchant (2000), Ittner *et al.* (1999), Miller and O'Leary (2002), Otley (1994), Seal *et al.* (1999), Tomkins (2001), and Van der Meer-Kooistra and Vosselman (2000).

to what has traditionally been termed management accounting research, but which challenges these boundaries using literatures that have begun to explore the contours of the new organizational landscape.

The section entitled 'The New Economy and the Extended Enterprise' provides a brief statistical description of the phenomena of newly emergent forms of strategic alliances and joint ventures. The section on Markets, Hybrids, and Hierarchies reviews theoretical and empirical studies of contingencies that portend the form, substance, and performance outcomes of interfirm relationships. The section on 'Determinants of Alliance Survival and Stability' examines the dynamics of the contingency relationship. Virtually all contingency studies attempt to determine the magnitude of exogenous shocks that precipitate costly realignments of strategy and structure, and the speed with which strategy, structure, and performance respond to these shocks. However, strategic alliances are somewhat unique because, absent exogenous shocks, the contingencies that predict the formation and success of a relationship leave few explanations for the high rate of failure of these relationships.[3] Researchers who study alliance failures appeal to a different set of contingencies associated with relational dynamics that are endogenous to the partnership (e.g. Anand and Khanna 2000; Das and Teng 2000; Doz 1996; Doz *et al.* 2000; Hughes *et al.* 1997; Madhok 1995; Madhok and Tallman 1998). For example, an extensive literature on interfirm relations examines the role of individual and organizational trust in enabling economic transactions that appear to be subject to severe hazards of opportunistic behaviour (e.g. Granovetter 1973; Lewis 1999; Ring and Van de Ven 1992, 1994; Zaheer *et al.* 1998; Zaheer and Venkatraman 1995). Trust may be based initially on observable 'reputations' in transactions with other partners; however, with repeated transactions, it may also be 'experiential'—based on private interactions between partner firms and their employees (Doz 1996; Doz *et al.* 2000; Van der Meer-Kooistra and Vosselman 2000). To the degree that trust serves as a complement to (Das and Teng 1998, 2001) or a substitute for (Gulati 1995*a*; Gulati and Singh 1998) alterative mechanisms for structuring and governing interfirm relations, the continually evolving state of experiential trust introduces a time-varying covariate that moderates the strategy and structure relationship (Dekker 2001).

It is tempting to draw parallels between the alliance literature reviewed in the sections on 'Markets, Hybrids, and Hierarchies' and in the section entitled 'Determinants of the Alliance Survival Stability', and the literature on the alignment of *firm* strategy, structure, and performance. However, the alliance literature is distinguished by the degree to which the questions are examined at several levels of analysis: the level of the transaction, the level of the

---

[3] Popular accounts estimate that 30 per cent of all alliances are 'abject failures' and that another 17 per cent experience some success but eventually disintegrate when priorities change or with top management turnover (Hutheesing 2001).

relationship between two firms, and the level of the network of relationships that binds several firms to a common goal.[4] We posit that the multi-level nature of alliance management is one source of new demands for management accounting and performance management.

In the section on 'Performance Management and Management Control in Strategic Alliance Networks' we consider three key components of a management accounting framework for strategic alliances: the governance structure (including the management of risk and trust), the performance measurement and control structure, and the process for managing the alliance network over time. We also present evidence from the practitioner literature that new practices are emerging and old practices are adapting to address the unique demands of management accounting in the extended enterprise of the strategic alliance network. The Conclusion summarizes the key components of management accounting for strategic alliance networks and concludes with the proposition that the examples of innovative and adapted practices found are indicative of a new area for research on management accounting in the extended enterprise.

The New Economy and the Extended Enterprise: Evidence on Strategic Alliances and Joint Ventures, 1985–2000

We use data from Thomson Financial Service's SDC Platinum Joint Ventures and Strategic Alliances Database to vividly illustrate our claim that a central feature of the new economy is permeable firm boundaries and increased use of collaboration to achieve competitive advantage. Strategic alliances and joint ventures have increased dramatically in the last decade—a threefold increase between 1990 and 2000 (Figure 3.1). The formation of collaborative initiatives has also outpaced the benchmark growth in the establishment of new firms. The US Census reports that the number of new firms grew by 8.7 per cent between 1992 and 1997 (http://www.census.gov/csd/susb/susb2.htm, October 2001). In the same period, the number of strategic alliances and joint ventures increased by 12.2 per cent. However, this aggregate statistic masks another trend. Specifically, strategic alliances, which are not accompanied by the formation of a formal third entity, have become more popular as compared to joint ventures, which rely heavily on contract law to enforce the terms of collaboration. Between 1990 and 2000, strategic alliances grew from 48 to 68 per cent of all announced collaborations.

The swell in collaborative activity has not affected all industries equally (Figure 3.2). The share and the absolute number of alliances formed in more traditional manufacturing industries (SIC codes 20–39) has declined from a

---

[4] For example, on the multi-level nature of trust, see Currall and Inkpen (2000) and on the multi-level nature of transactions costs see Gulati (1995*a*) and Anderson *et al.* (2000).

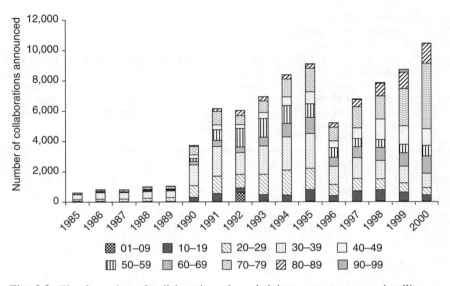

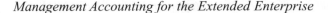

Fig. 3.2. The formation of collaborations through joint venture or strategic alliances, 1985–2000 for two digit SIC codes: SIC code definitions (http://www.census.gov/epcd/naics/nsic2ndx.htm): 01–09, Agriculture, forestry and fisheries; 10–19, Mineral industries and construction; 20–39, Manufacturing; 40–49, Transportation, communication and utilities; 50–59, Wholesale trade, retail trade; 60–69, Finance, insurance and real estate; 70–89, Service Industries; 90–99, Public Administration (*Source*: Thomson Financial Services)

combined share of 57.4 per cent, (2,139 announcements) in 1990 to a combined share of 13.6 per cent (1,413 announcements) in 2000. In contrast, service industries (SIC codes 70–89) showed a dramatic increase in the share and the number of collaborations formed during the period, 1990 to 2000—increasing from 16 per cent (609 announcements) to 54 per cent (5,627 announcements) of all collaborations. This extraordinary growth is not explained simply by growth in the service sector. (US Census data indicate that between 1992 and 1997 the number of manufacturing firms grew only 1.7 per cent, while the number of service firms grew by 13.3 per cent.) Rather, it reflects a significantly increased propensity among all service firms to employ collaboration strategies during the 1990s.

Data on the characteristics of collaborations reveal that the motivation for collaborations and the substance of collaborative activity has also changed (Table 3.1). In 1990, only 12 per cent of all collaborations were between partners of the same nationality. By 2000, the equivalent share was 47 per cent. What accounts for the increased use of collaborative arrangements within national borders? Deregulation and increased free trade play a major role in diminishing the use of international collaborations as a means of gaining access to world markets. However this is only part of the story. As the second column

Table 3.1 Characteristics of the activities of strategic alliance partners for collaborations that were first announced during the period, 1985–2000

Year	Per cent of partnerships involving partners of the same nationality	Per cent of partnerships with activities that cross national borders	Per cent of partnerships involving technology licensing	Per cent of partnerships involving shared research and development	Per cent of partnerships involving shared manufacturing	Per cent of partnerships involving shared marketing
1985	5.3	90.7	24.3	4.2	17.0	12.5
1986	13.1	81.7	16.9	4.2	15.6	12.1
1987	6.9	84.1	24.2	8.0	18.1	17.6
1988	14.0	75.6	18.8	8.4	15.5	14.1
1989	11.0	78.9	22.4	13.5	19.1	19.7
1990	12.0	67.6	15.5	17.7	18.7	29.9
1991	14.3	66.5	12.5	20.6	22.2	34.7
1992	37.3	58.0	13.1	25.3	21.4	42.6
1993	31.7	62.6	13.2	23.5	29.9	40.1
1994	33.6	63.9	14.8	22.4	30.2	33.8
1995	34.2	63.2	15.8	16.2	30.9	28.8
1996	33.3	61.7	17.2	13.5	26.6	25.1
1997	37.2	57.9	16.9	14.2	21.7	18.8
1998	40.2	56.0	16.3	6.9	21.1	15.7
1999	45.1	51.9	11.3	4.6	17.7	11.8
2000	46.9	51.7	3.3	5.7	10.3	10.7

Source: Thomson Financial Services.

of Table 3.1 indicates, even with the shift to local partners, in 2000, partnership activities remained heavily focused on those that crossed international borders for 51.7 per cent of collaborations (a decline from 67.6 per cent in 1990).

A more compelling explanation lies in the shift in the substance of collaborative activity. In the past, collaborations were often a mechanism for transferring technologies that were subject to impacted or tacit knowledge. Collaboration was necessary to permit a firm to earn profits on licensing proprietary technologies. During the 1990s it became more common for partners to *jointly* develop, produce, or market products and services. Indeed, in a survey of 2,000 alliances in 1994–5, the consulting firm, Booz-Allen & Hamilton, found that more than 55 per cent of alliances were between competitors (Harbison and Pekar 1998: 6, 19). The remaining columns of Table 3.1 chart the decline of technology licensing and the relative increase of joint activities. Related to the shift to collaborative activities is a subtle shift towards *networks* of collaborators. In 1985, 95 per cent of collaborations were between two partners; by 2000, only 86 per cent of collaborations were between two partners.

Reflecting on differences in early collaborative activity as compared to those of the new economy era, the early data are consistent with the strategy literature of the period (Porter 1980, 1985). This literature argued for joint ventures as a means of entering international markets, where local expertise and political influence could help bridge cultural divides and where government regulations might prohibit foreign entry without a local partner. Recent data are more consistent with contemporary resource-based views of the firm (e.g. Brandenburger and Nalebuff 1996; Hamel *et al.* 1989; Prahalad and Hamel 1989, 1990), in which strategic partnerships between capable specialists (including competitors) provide competitive advantage. The data suggest several important features of collaborations that have emerged in the new economy:

- The magnitude of collaborative activity has increased.
- The mechanisms of collaboration have changed.
- The participants in collaborations have changed.
- The motivation for collaboration has changed.
- The substance of collaborative activity has changed.

In the next section, we review key research findings from the strategy and organizational management literatures that explore these changes.

Markets, Hybrids, and Hierarchies: Theories of firm boundaries and alliance formation

Determinants of Firm Boundaries: Markets versus Hierarchies

Contemporary research on the determinants of firm boundaries takes as a starting point the 'New Institutional Economics' in which governance structure, rather than a production function, defines a firm (Williamson 1985). In this literature, researchers seek to explain why firms rely on markets (i.e. arm's-length transactions) to obtain some inputs but produce other inputs internally (i.e. vertical integration or hierarchies). In markets, price is the primary coordination mechanism and formal contracts reflect the mutually agreed-upon obligations of self-interested, transaction partners. Disputes that arise are often settled in a court of law. When firms opt for vertical integration, operations may be run in a centralized or decentralized fashion (e.g. using quasi-market mechanisms such as negotiated transfer prices); however, at the uppermost level of management, a common central authority oversees the interests of the firm and resolves disputes that arise at lower levels of the organization (Williamson 1991). Two theories have emerged to explain firms' choices between markets and hierarchies: the transaction cost minimizing view and the resource-based view.

   Transaction cost theory hypothesizes that firms choose an organizational form (i.e. markets or hierarchies) that minimizes the sum of production and transaction costs (Coase 1937). Transaction costs include the costs of negotiating and writing contracts, monitoring and enforcing compliance with contract terms, and resolution of contract disputes (Joskow 1987; Williamson 1985). The theory relies on two behavioural assumptions. The first is 'bounded rationality' of contract writers, which, along with uncertainty in the specification of the transaction itself or in the external environment, make complete contracts impossible or prohibitively expensive. Incomplete contracts and self-interested behaviour (the second behavioural assumption) of contracting parties, create the potential for opportunism and significant 'holdup costs' (Williamson 1985, 1991). Transaction cost economics theorizes that markets and hierarchies differ in their capacity to adapt to uncertainty and changing conditions and, thus, differ in the level of transaction costs. Firms integrate transactions with characteristics associated with high transaction costs, such as: uncertainty in defining the task or its completion, task complexity or interdependence, infrequency of transacting, and the necessity of investments in assets specific to the transaction (Milgrom and Roberts 1992; Williamson 1985). Empirical studies support the proposition that firms tend to subsume transactions that require investments in specific assets (Klein 1988; Masten *et al.* 1989; Monteverde and Teece 1982; Ulset 1996), that are fraught with uncertainty (Novak and Eppinger 2001; Ulset 1996), or are linked to other transactions (Anderson *et al.* 2000).[5]

Although transaction costs economics has become a fundamental theory of organizational design, recent research has identified two aspects of the theory that require further investigation. First, transaction cost economics does not encompass the effects of *other* costs such as those associated with the coordination of activities within and between firms (Lorenzoni and Lipparini 1999). Second, although the theory identifies interdependent transactions as a source of transaction cost, the nature and source of interdependencies has been insufficiently explored. Empirical studies typically use the individual transaction as the unit of analysis, ignoring interdependencies altogether. Interdependencies that merit investigation include technical interdependencies among inputs, such as those considered in Anderson *et al.* (2000), as well as interdependence among the firm and its network of suppliers that reflect 'relational capabilities' (Doz *et al.* 2000; Gulati 1995a; Gulati *et al.* 2000; Lorenzoni and Lipparini 1999; Ring and Van de Ven 1992).

The second school of thought on organizational design derives from Penrose's (1959) seminal work, and takes a resource-based view of the firm.[6]

---

[5] Shelanski and Klein (1995) provide a comprehensive review of empirical research on transaction costs.

[6] Related to the resource-based view of the firm are the organizational capabilities view (Lorenzoni and Lipparini 1999) and the property rights view (Grossman and Hart 1986) of the firm. In the organizational capabilities view firm competencies are the primary, albeit intangible, firm asset; in the property rights view, rare proprietary physical assets are the critical resource. In this chapter, we do not distinguish between tangible and intangible assets as sources of strategic capabilities.

According to this view, firm boundaries reflect strategic choices about the use of scarce, inimitable resources to achieve a sustainable competitive advantage (Prahalad and Hamel 1989, 1990). Scarce physical and human resources present firms with a range of opportunities. Penrose (1959: 25) distinguishes resource deployment decisions as the 'source of uniqueness' of individual firms. Theorists who hold the resource-based view tend to focus on the dynamics of firm strategy; for example, on how and why firms with seemingly identical initial resources deploy them differently. For example, Madhok (1996) and Bianchi (1995) focus on human capital and characterize the firm as a bundle of knowledge. They posit that resource deployment choices reflect efforts to use market interactions to stimulate learning and the creation of new human capital. Others consider the primary resource to be the firm's inimitable organizational capabilities and routines, for example, the ability to network with suppliers (e.g. Lorenzoni and Lipparini 1999).

In sum, both transaction cost economics and the resource-based view of the firm provide explanations for firm boundaries. The transaction cost view presents a more static view of firms setting boundaries to optimize costs that are known or anticipated, given a set of assumptions about human behaviour. The resource-based view presents firms engaged in a dynamic search for opportunities to deploy scarce resources in a manner that yields abnormal returns to entrepreneurial efforts. Although the theories differ, it is more accurate to view them as complements to one another rather than as competing theories of organizational form (Kogut 1988). The underlying motivation for boundary choices for a given firm depends on organizational context, and whether the transactions cost (e.g., cost reduction) approach to profit maximization is more likely to outperform the resource-based (e.g., market growth) approach (Kogut 1988: 330). In the next section we consider how both theories explain hybrid organizational forms.

Hybrid Organizational Forms

Between markets and hierarchies lies an array of hybrid organizational forms. Some, like joint ventures, franchises or other licensing arrangements, are backed by formal, legally enforceable contracts. Others, like strategic alliances and industry consortia, may operate without recourse to legal enforcement mechanisms (although, they may employ formal processes for managing the alliance). The first issue in considering hybrids in relation to theories of the firm is determining whether they represent stable organizational forms. Perhaps hybrid organizational forms are simply a 'way station' in the transition from markets to hierarchies, or vice versa. Indeed, in his seminal book on strategy, Michael Porter (1990: 613) claims that alliances are 'transitional devices rather than stable entities'. Given the high failure rate of alliances, this proposition seems reasonable. However, the sheer volume of collaborative activity in the last decade and the longevity of many relationships have caused many researchers to conclude otherwise (Menard 1995, 1996; Williamson 1985, 1991). Williamson (1991) promotes hybrids to the same level of prominence as markets and hierarchies and describes the adaptation characteristics of this governance mode and the types of transactions for which it is particularly well suited. Lorenzoni and Baden-Fuller (1995) observe, 'Most organizations oscillate between having ample creativity and little discipline, or too much discipline and not enough creativity.' They argue that a network of firms with a strong strategic centre yields an ideal middle ground. Thus, recent thinking in the academic literature suggests that hybrids are, in fact, stable organizational forms. The challenge for researchers is to reconcile these new organizational forms with existing theory, or to develop new theories that are consistent with the new organizational realities.

In transaction cost economics, the intensity of the profit incentive is a key advantage of markets; the superior coordination that is attained within the firm is the key advantage of hierarchies. Hybrids are characterized as having intermediate levels of incentive intensity and coordination ability (Ulset 1996; Williamson 1991).The theory predicts that hybrid governance forms emerge when transaction costs are sufficiently high to make market transactions too costly, but not high enough to justify vertical integration (Gulati *et al.* 2000; Menard 1995; Milgrom and Roberts 1992; Williamson 1985).[7] Thus, organizational forms align with a *continuum* of transaction costs, rather than assuming one of two extreme forms (e.g. markets or hierarchies).

Hybrid organizations employ one of three governance forms: equity joint ventures, in which two or more firms contribute equity to form an independent, jointly-owned entity; equity exchange, in which one or more firms take a minority equity stake in one another; and non-equity arrangements, where no equity is exchanged and a third organizational unit is not created. The first two approaches, which use equity to align partner interests, are generally considered to possess similar control characteristics, including the loss of high-powered incentives, of hierarchies. Non-equity alliances, on the other hand, possess control characteristics similar to arm's-length transactions (Gulati 1995*a*; Williamson 1991). Transaction cost economics predicts that transaction characteristics that prompted vertical integration will also favour equity over non-equity alliances. For example, firms are more likely to form equity alliances when appropriation hazards are high (Oxley 1997, 1999), or when uncertainty and asset specificity are high, such as in R&D activities (Buvik and Reve 2001; Gulati 1995*a*; Gulati and Singh 1998; Osborn and Baughn 1990; Pisano 1989, 1990; Pisano *et al.* 1988).

---

[7] Many researchers reject the characterization of hybrids or networks as lying on a 'continuum' between markets and hierarchies, arguing that they are distinct organizational forms (e.g. Osborn and Hagedoorn 1997; Powel 1990). Kogut (1988) notes that there is no conceptual reason to expect institutional choice to be linearly ordered, and that at a minimum, it is unlikely that interaction effects among asset specificity, uncertainty, and transaction frequency yield such an ordering.

Institutional factors that affect whether an alliance is likely to be sustainable compared to markets and hierarchies include appropriation risks, reputation effects, and uncertainty (Williamson 1991). When transactions require specific assets, the likelihood of sustaining a hybrid organization form declines as the risks of asset appropriation or devaluation increase. Over time, firms develop reputations as trustworthy (or untrustworthy) trading partners. In some circumstances, reputation can serve as a 'bond' against opportunistic behaviour that allows independent firms to engage in transactions that would normally be integrated within a firm. Moreover, as networks of firms become more 'embedded', or mutually dependent, reputations become intertwined and associated with an entity that represents the group of firms.[8] Loss of individual firm identity can serve to bind alliance partners together for a common mission and to reduce the risk of opportunistic behaviour among alliance partners. In general, hierarchies provide the greatest opportunity to orchestrate coordinated activities at low cost. Committed alliance partners may be able to nearly replicate coordination routines. However, when exogenous shocks are likely to affect trading partners differently, hierarchies are better able to mount a coordinated response because decision rights are concentrated with a single, like-minded management team. As a result, firms choose vertical integration over alliances when exogenous shocks are likely (Williamson 1991).

In sum, the transactions cost view of the firm incorporates hybrid organizational forms as a middle ground between markets and hierarchies. Like markets and hierarchies, the selection of a hybrid organizational form is influenced by the level of transactions and production costs, which in turn are influenced by the characteristics of the contemplated transaction and the relative production efficiency of the trading partners.

The resource-based view of the firm offers a different explanation for the formation of hybrid organizational forms; namely, as a source of sustainable competitive advantage (e.g. Doz and Hamel 1998). Transaction cost theory portrays the firm optimizing its profits over a range of alternative organizational structures for a transaction whose outputs are relatively well-understood. The resource-based view considers the possibility that firms enter alliances without well-specified goals or without a well-specified plan for attaining their goals, but with reason to believe that collaboration among uniquely qualified partners will create an opportunity for both parties to 'enlarge the pie' of their productive endeavours (Brandenburger and Nalebuff 1996; Doz 1996; Hamel *et al.* 1989). Studies that document the strategic role of alliances include: Gulati (1995*a,b*), Gulati and Singh (1998), Kale *et al.*, Kaufman *et al.* (2000), Lorenzoni and Lipparini (1999), Menard (1995), Ring and Van de Ven (1994), Tomkins (2001) and Williamson (1991). Evidence of positive

---

[8] Moore (1996) uses the metaphor of the business 'ecosystem' to describe the codependency of alliance partners.

financial returns to effective collaboration is found in: Anand and Khanna (2000), Lorenzoni and Lipparini (1999), Wolff and Reed (2000), Zaheer *et al.* (1998), Baum *et al.* (2000) and Stuart (2000). In a large sample study, Anand and Khanna (2000) find an association between alliance experience and abnormal market returns. Using survey results, Harbison and Pekar (1998: 1) report that strategic alliances 'produced a return on investment of nearly 17 per cent among the top two thousand companies in the world for nearly 10 years...50 per cent more than the average return that the companies produced overall'.

If we compare evidence on why firms profess to engage in strategic alliances (Kale *et al.* 2000; Tsang 2000) with the motivations suggested by transaction cost theory and the resource-based view of the firm, we find that both theories are consistent with the data on the growth of strategic alliances.[9] Consistent with the resource-based view, firms form alliances in order to leverage their existing capabilities in combination with those of strategic partners (Laseter and Ramdas 2001) and to develop inimitable relational capital (Adler 2001; Gulati *et al.* 2000; Lorenzoni and Lipparini 1999). Consistent with transaction cost theory, firms form alliances to achieve economic returns through greater production scale, more efficient risk sharing, and improved coordination and knowledge sharing[10] (Adler 2001; Dyer 2000; Dyer and Nobeoka 2000; Jensen and Meckling 1991). Dekker (2002) observes that the selection of a particular partner firm and the choice of alliance governance form are *simultaneously* made, and both are influenced by the nature and magnitude of transaction costs. This observation provides another potential link between the transaction cost and the resource-based views of the firm.

We also see evidence of conflict between the two theories. For example, while transaction cost economics posits that uncertainty induces firms to become more vertically integrated, Lorenzoni and Lipparini (1999) find that firms interact *more* with external supplier partners when uncertainty increases. Rather than absorbing the uncertainty within firm borders, they share the uncertainty with trusted partners. This is consistent with patterns of alliance formation in industries characterized by capital-intensive, uncertain product development activities such as film production in the entertainment industry, drug development in the pharmaceutical industry,[11] and oil and gas

[9] Kogut (1988) reviews evidence on the formation and stability of joint ventures in an effort to discriminate between transaction cost and resource-based theories of the firm. He finds evidence for both theories and concludes that 'the theories and their derived hypotheses will fare differently depending on contextual factors and the type of research questions being pursued' (p. 330).

[10] Theoretical models from the operations management literature also support the notion that innovative and close supplier relationships improve production efficiency through shared information (Cachon and Fisher 2000) and consequent inventory reductions (Cachon and Zipkin 1999).

[11] For Baxter International, a major pharmaceutical firm, motivations for entering alliances include filling gaps in its product pipeline and defending against competing new product technologies (Anonymous 2001: 94).

exploration in the energy industry. In the Japanese automotive industry, Okamuro (2001) finds the magnitude of risk sharing between supplier and buyer to increase with the 'intensity of the relation'. Similarly, Anand and Khanna (2000) find that in alliances, learning effects are more important when there is *greater* contractual ambiguity (i.e. the effects are stronger for R&D joint ventures as compared to marketing joint ventures). These papers suggest that strategic alliances are formed, not solely to reduce transaction costs, but also for the competitive advantages afforded by strategic collaborations.

In light of the benefits afforded by effective strategic alliances, the question arises, 'Why don't all firms develop strategic supplier alliances?' Although the benefits provide significant *inducements* for alliance formation, the ability of a firm to form supplier alliances is also a function of the *opportunities* to do so. Ahuja (2000) finds that alliance formation in the global chemicals industry is directly related to firms' alliance formation opportunities. Opportunities increase with the attractiveness of a firm to potential partners. Technological competence and past innovativeness (i.e. technical capital) and the ability to convert that competence into profitable products and services (i.e. commercial capital) attract alliance partners and increase the opportunities for alliance formation. Opportunities also accrue to firms that have established a positive reputation from prior alliance participation (i.e. embeddedness or social capital). In a study of the selection of alliance partners, Gulati (1995b) shows that the likelihood of two firms forming an alliance is higher when the firms have a prior alliance relation, when that prior relation is relatively recent, and when they share common ties to a third party. This social network perspective on alliance formation underscores the potential competitive advantage of relational capabilities.

Determinants of Alliance Survival and Stability

While the number of alliances has dramatically increased, over 60 per cent fail (Anonymous 2000);[12] that is, the hybrid organizational form dissolves without achieving the originally stated goals. Some end with recriminations and ill-will among partners. Others end as 'amicable divorces'. In this section we consider the prevalence of alliance failures from the perspectives of transaction cost economics and the resource-based view of the firm. We first consider failures of the hybrid organizational form alone. We then turn to failures of the organizational form that are associated with failures of the business premise for collaboration.

---

[12] See also tables 1 and 2 in Das and Teng (2000) for a more complete review of theoretical and empirical studies on the instabilities of strategic alliances and joint ventures and on the theories explaining strategic alliance instability, respectively.

As Porter (1990) suggests, alliances often transition to either a traditional market transaction or a hierarchy (e.g. acquisition or merger). Das and Teng (2000) propose that the 'stability' of an alliance rests on the ability of alliance partners to balance three pairs of competing tensions: cooperation/competition, rigidity/flexibility and short-term/long-term orientations. The first conflict, between cooperation (i.e. the pursuit of common benefits) and competition (i.e. the pursuit of self interest), recalls transaction cost economics concerns of opportunism (Das and Teng 1998; Parkhe 1993). The second conflict pits the need for flexibility in the alliance against the demands for stability that originate with the parent organizations. Thus, for example, the flexible relationships that are the hallmark of some hybrid organizational forms create different demands for performance management and interorganizational control than the more rigid modes of governance and control that are enacted within the firm (e.g. Harbison and Pekar 1998). Groot and Merchant find empirical evidence of this conflict in their study of international joint ventures. Finally, tensions build in an alliance when participants have different time horizons for alliance participation. Lorenzoni and Baden-Fuller (1995) also emphasize the importance of balancing these competing forces by suggesting that the successful, innovative network reconciles the flexibility of market relationships with the long-term commitment of hierarchical, centralized firms.

Das and Teng (2000) propose that the dynamics of an alliance are a function of shifts among the above-described tensions. A shift towards cooperation, rigidity and/or a long-term focus precipitates a migration from an alliance to *vertical integration*. In contrast, a shift towards competition, flexibility, and a short-term focus brings a migration towards a *market* transaction. Consistent with this view, Kogut (1989) finds that joint ventures are less likely to dissolve when the focus of activity is on research and development—a focus arguably requiring long-term cooperation—and when there are multiple ties among partner firms. Multiple ties reduce the probability of opportunistic behaviour because such behaviour is punishable by reciprocation in other transactions. Conversely, joint ventures are more likely to dissolve and revert to market transactions when there is more competitive rivalry among partners.

Transaction cost economics tends to focus on exogenous shocks that alter costs, or expectations thereof, for production or transactions. Williamson (1991) argues that the efficiency of a particular governance form is determined by its relative ability to support two types of adaptation to exogenous shocks: autonomous adaptation and cooperative adaptation. Autonomous adaptation is automatic, unconscious, and is the type of adaptation for which markets, using price as the mechanism, are best suited. Cooperative adaptation, however, is conscious, purposeful, and used when cooperation among the parties is necessary to adapt to the shock. Hierarchies are especially adept at this type of adaptation. Williamson (1991) suggests that alliances possess intermediate levels of both types of adaptation capability, offering a lower cost alternative to hierarchies in the presence of exogenous shocks requiring cooperative adaptation. Thus, according to transaction cost economics, a primary determinant of alliance performance and survival is the efficiency with which the alliance adapts to various types of exogenous shocks. In practice, however, we see alliance evolution and a high rate of alliance failure even in the absence of exogenous shocks. A different set of contingencies associated with relational dynamics is, therefore, needed to describe the evolution and high failure rates of alliances.

Alliances are vulnerable to failure because alliance partners are exposed to both 'performance risk' and 'relational risk' (Das and Teng 1996, 2001). Performance risk is the probability that alliance objectives will not be achieved, despite the full cooperation of the partners. This type of risk comes primarily from market forces such as competition, demand fluctuations, and changing government regulations—the exogenous shocks contemplated by transaction cost economics. While performance risk undoubtedly accounts for some alliance failures, it is mitigating this type of risk that motivates many firms to form alliances. Relational risk is the probability that partners will not cooperate, a risk that is unique to, and created by the formation of alliances among firms with potentially divergent interests (Das and Teng 2001). Das and Teng (2000) relate their three pairs of countervailing forces (described above) to the level of relational risk and the overall instability of alliances.

Since alliances are prone to failures that stem from relational risks, it is not surprising that two recurring themes in the strategy and management literature are that alliance success and performance are positively influenced by (i) *interpersonal, inter-group and interfirm 'trust'* (Adler 2001; Das and Teng 2000; Gulati 1995a; Hagen and Choe 1998; Jeffries and Reed 2000; Kale *et al.* 2000; Parkhe 1998; Tomkins 2001; Wicks *et al.* 1999; Zaheer and Venkatraman 1995) and by (ii) *network characteristics* (Granovetter 1985; Gulati *et al.* 2000; Rowley *et al.* 2000). In the sections below, we consider each of these factors as time-varying covariates of alliance performance and stability.

Trust in Alliance Relationships

The term 'trust' is used in a variety of ways in the management literature. Some studies refer to a game-theoretic type of 'calculative trust' in which participants behave in a manner promoting the common good only because it is in their best interest to do so (e.g., for reputation reasons) (Williamson 1993). In the transaction cost literature, transaction frequency promotes this type of trust. Common mechanisms for attaining this state of trust include substantial upfront investments in alliance-specific assets (e.g., physical or human capital) or significant exchange of equity that aligns firm interests. In effect, participants post a 'bond' that is forfeited (or substantially impaired) if the alliance is not productive. Madhok (1995) calls this type of 'mutual hostage exchange' the *structural* component of trust.[13] Others allow for a slightly more social interpretation and define trust as the objective expectation, based on experience and repeated interactions, that a partner will not behave in an opportunistic manner (Das and Teng 1998; Gambetta 1998; Gulati 1995*a*; Ring and Van de Ven 1992, 1994; Spekman *et al.* 2001; Tomkins 2001).[14] This definition is related to the notion of commitment (Spekman *et al.* 2001). Authors in this research stream are careful to point out that this definition relies on an *objective* assessment of probabilities and is, therefore, different from a purely psychological 'blind trust' (Adler 2001). Madhok (1995) argues that both the social (i.e. expectation) and the structural (i.e. calculative) components of trust are necessary but not sufficient conditions to sustain an interfirm relationship.

Das and Teng (2001) distinguish two components of social (or expectation) trust. 'Competence' trust is the assessment of the partner's *ability* to perform according to the agreement. 'Goodwill' trust is the assessment of his *intentions* to do so. Both assessments contribute to the overall level of expectation trust. Adler further expands the definition of trust. He defines a modern form of 'reflective trust' as encompassing (i) the familiarity of repeated transactions, (ii) the objective assessment of the other party's gains of opportunistic behaviour, and (iii) the confidence induced by prevailing values and norms. He argues that this type of trust is the primary coordinating mechanism of a third distinct governance form of 'community' (i.e. in addition to markets and hierarchies).

Irrespective of the calculative or expectational variety, trust reduces relational risk by replacing the fear of opportunistic partner behaviour with mutual confidence (Adler 2001; Das and Teng 1998; Das and Teng 2001). Inkpen and Currall (1998) identify the following consequences of trust: forbearance (e.g. refraining from opportunistic behaviour), reduced costs of governance (e.g. coordination and monitoring costs), increased relationship investments (e.g. specific assets), increased scope of activity, and increased performance of the partners.[15] Dyer (2000) discusses the role of trust in overcoming reluctance to invest in specific assets in the Japanese automobile industry. Others discuss

---

[13] Another structural component of calculative trust is the 'institution-based trust' described by Rousseau *et al.* (1998), in which firms consider the legal structures, social networks, or societal norms that surround and contribute to the context of the particular partnership. Thus, for example, a partnership that may be sustainable in a country with strong property rights law, may be rejected in a country that lacks similar support mechanisms.

[14] There are many categorizations of trust in the literature. Calculative trust is similar to 'deterrence-based' trust (Gulati 1995*a*) and the 'structural' component of trust (Madhok 1995). The confidence type of trust is similar to the 'behavioral' or 'social' component of trust (Madhok 1995), 'knowledge-based' trust (Gulati 1995*a*), 'process-based' trust (Dyer 2000) and 'cognitive-based' trust (Jeffries and Reed 2000). Distinctions are also made between interpersonal and interorganizational trust (Jeffries and Reed 2000; Kale *et al.* 2000; Zaheer and Venkatraman 1995). These are deemed to be distinct but related concepts and are both considered important to the success of interfirm relationships.

[15] Inkpen and Currall (1998) acknowledge the feedback mechanism between these consequences and antecedences such as 'assessment of competence' and 'individual attachment' of future trust levels.

the reduction in transaction costs—costs of search, contracting, monitoring, enforcement, and dispute resolution—when trust is high (e.g. Adler 2001; Dyer 2000; Gulati 1995*a*; Ring and Van de Ven 1994).

Empirical studies generally confirm trust as an important determinant of strategic alliance success. For example, in a survey of purchasing managers, Zaheer and Zaheer *et al.* (1998) find that conflicts and negotiation costs are lower and supplier performance higher when partners trust each other. Spekman *et al.* (2001) likewise document a positive relation between supply chain performance and trust between partners. In sum, trust allows transactions that would ordinarily be integrated because of specific asset investments and high transaction costs to be completed in the community of alliance partners (Hart 2001). Advantages of the market transaction, such as high-powered incentives, are preserved, while benefits of hierarchy such as knowledge-sharing and reduced need for other control mechanisms are retained (e.g. formal controls) (Adler 2001; Dyer 2000).

Network Relationships

The second determinant of alliance performance that has gained widespread attention among researchers is the strength and embeddedness of the network of alliance partners. A weakness of transaction cost economics research has been a focus on individual transactions in isolation of other, possibly related ones. Social network theorists argue that characteristics of the entire network of transacting parties within a value chain are an important determinant of performance (Gulati *et al.* 2000). The performance of a *specific* interfirm relationship is affected by the structure of the *network* and the degree to which firms are firmly embedded in that social network. Social networks promote trust and reduce transaction costs by enabling information sharing, strengthening reputation effects, improving coordination between firms, and facilitating the identification of potential partners (Gulati 1995*b*; Gulati *et al.* 2000). Rowley *et al.* (2000) provide empirical evidence that while the 'density' of a set of network ties is *positively* related to firm performance in environments demanding high investments in exploitation (e.g. steel industry), it is *negatively* related to firm performance in environments demanding high investments in exploration (e.g. semiconductor industry). Moreover, the positive relation between the 'relational embeddedness' (Gulati *et al.* 2000) of a firm (i.e. the strength of a partner relationship) and performance is weaker in dense networks.

It is important to note that the popular concept of supply chain management is distinct from the collaboration of firms in a value chain network (Lorenzoni and Baden-Fuller 1995). Supply chain management typically focuses on improving the logistics of placing and fulfilling orders and on better matching supply and demand to reduce inventory throughout the value chain. In contrast, participants in a strategic value chain network tend to focus on innovation opportunities and on developing and sharing new competencies.

Participants take a holistic view of the network and its collective ability to achieve competitive advantage. Lorenzoni and Baden-Fuller (1995) find that the most successful of these collaborations involve at least one very strong 'hub' firm that is the 'strategic centre' of the network. This strategic centre is much more than a contract broker and is not appropriately characterized as 'hollow', as are many firms that outsource core competencies. The strategic centre firm manages the agenda of the group by creating a vision that directs the energies of all participants. It also protects key brand images of the group and insures that core competencies are retained and developed and that innovative capacity is constantly renewed. Finally, the hub firm creates an environment of trust and reciprocity that motivates participants to perform in the interests of the group.

This brings us to the central concern of this paper. Specifically, what are the performance management, evaluation, and control needs of hybrid organization forms and how are they being met in the more successful examples that have emerged in the 1990s? In the section that follows we explore these questions using anecdotal evidence to illustrate the emergence of organizational practices aimed at facilitating alliance relationships.

Performance Management and Management Control in Strategic Alliance Networks

In crafting an alliance, partners make decisions about governance structure, and policies and procedures with the objective of enacting strategic goals while minimizing relational and performance risk. The previous sections reviewed the motivations and goals of alliance formation, the governance structures that are compatible with these motives, and evidence on the performance of these organizational forms. Much less has been written in the research literature about the policies and procedures that support alliance performance, including management accounting practices that help alliance partners manage performance of the extended enterprise. Yet business surveys and descriptions of successful alliances suggest that these are critical to the success of the alliance (e.g., Clement 1997; Harbison and Pekar 1998). A 1996 study by the Gas Research Institute (Clement 1997) of alliance practices in the oil and gas industry identified seven critical success factors, four of which have direct bearing on management accounting in strategic alliances:

- goals that are tied to profits for all parties;
- the use of quantitative measures of performance to mutually established goals;
- incentives for all parties to participate, and;
- the presence of an agreed upon process for regular evaluation of performance.

When *Forbes* (21 May 2001) compiled its ranking of firms that have been most successful in employing hybrid organizational forms to attain competitive advantage, it found the greatest variation in the area of 'partnering skills', the set of established practices for managing alliance relations.[16]

In this section, we consider three key aspects of performance management and management control in a strategic alliance network: alliance control (including the management of risk and trust), managing alliance performance (evaluation and performance measurement) and managing the evolution of the alliance (including partner selection and termination, managing learning and incentives). In these sections we cover topics typically considered within management accounting; however, we also consider unique demands that alliances place on management accounting. In each case we offer evidence from the practitioner literature that strategic alliances meet demands for management accounting information in both traditional and novel ways.

Alliance Control Practices

Confidence in an alliance partner comes from trust and control, both of which mitigate risk (Das and Teng 1998). Trust and control can be substitutes or complements. In some circumstances, trust is a substitute for formal control. For example, Gulati (1995a) finds that alliances are less likely to be equity-based when trust, as measured by the number of prior interactions between the participants, is high. Gulati and Singh (1998) show that fewer hierarchical type controls, such as formalized operating and dispute resolution procedures, are used when trust between alliance partners is high. Rowley *et al.* (2000) argues that a dense social network can also serve as a trust-based governance mechanism and an alternative to formalized controls. Trust is also a complement to formalized controls. Control mechanisms are more effective (Das and Teng 1998) and risk is reduced (Chiles and McMackin 1996) when trust is high.

In this section we hypothesize that successful strategic alliance networks will emphasize management control practices that support risk assessment and management and that foster the emergence of trust among relevant employees and firms within the alliance.

Managing Alliance Risk

As stated above, alliances are vulnerable to both performance and relational risk and different alliance governance structures are better suited to different sources of risk (e.g., equity alliances are better at mitigating relational risk,

---

[16] In contrast, *Forbes* (21 May 2001) found much more uniformity in the degree to which successful alliance partners had a strong reputation among its partners, had an extended alliance network, had distinctive assets, and used technology to further collaboration.

while non-equity alliances are better at mitigating performance risk) (Das and Teng 1996). Das and Teng (1999) posit further that management control techniques must be matched to both the type of risk present (i.e. performance or relational) and to the type of resources committed by alliance partners (i.e. property or knowledge). Property includes physical and financial assets with clear property rights that are protected by law. In contrast, knowledge is embedded in the organization and its employees, and is not legally protected.

Firms that commit property resources to an alliance and are primarily concerned with *relational* risk must focus on the protection of these assets. Das and Teng (1999) suggest a 'control' orientation in which the management of the alliance involves using contractual, equity, and managerial control mechanisms to protect assets from misuse. If the alliance partner perceives *performance* risk to be the primary risk, the alliance management objective changes. Partner firms have an incentive to maintain a 'flexible' management orientation to enhance the alliance's ability to adapt to changing environments and increase the likelihood of alliance success. Das and Teng (1999) suggest managing these types of alliances with short term, recurrent contracts that have clear exit provisions.

When the committed assets in an alliance are of the knowledge type, alliance partners cannot rely on legal means for protecting their resources and are, therefore, more vulnerable to partner opportunism. This is a particularly difficult situation given that the sharing of knowledge is frequently a primary reason for alliance formation. When firms are confident in the cooperation of their alliance partners (i.e. relational risk is perceived to be low), *performance* risk is the dominant risk. Management control in these alliances focuses on the production of knowledge and on the efficiency with which knowledge is transferred across firm boundaries. Das and Teng (1999) suggest that this 'productivity' orientation demands management controls that facilitate coordination of organizational routines and that maximize the efficiency of knowledge production and sharing. Rivera *et al.* (2001) argue that the characteristics of the people involved in the alliance and their compatibility are essential to learning in alliances. However, they caution that while increased operational control enhances coordination in knowledge sharing, it can also reduce the creative capacity of the alliance if it creates rigid, pre-approved paths for sharing knowledge.

If firms committing knowledge resources are primarily concerned with *relational* risk, the objective of the alliance management process is security of the firm's own knowledge and know-how. In this case Das and Teng (1999) suggest limiting the access of knowledge to the partner firm, and maintaining separate work locations. They stress the importance of clearly delineating knowledge-sharing intentions to avoid false expectations.

Dyer (2000) and Dyer and Nobeoka (2000) describe Toyota's management techniques for promoting information sharing with and among its suppliers, while assuring the confidentiality of proprietary knowledge. Kale *et al.* (2000)

likewise find that firms develop expertise and capabilities from alliance partners but are able to protect their own proprietary assets from supplier opportunism.

Managing the Emergence and Growth of Trust

A growing literature examines the role of individual and organizational trust in enabling economic transactions. Trust, as a static exogenous construct based on observable 'reputation' (and proxied by the number of previous partner ties), was argued above to be a determinant of alliance formation. One example of an external signal of quality reputation that has been widely adopted is the ISO 9000 certification programme (Anderson *et al.* 1999; Bergin 1996). However, trust may also be 'experiential'—based on private interactions between partner firms and their employees (e.g. Van der Meer-Kooistra and Vosselman 2000: 57). Inkpen and Currall (1998) note that structural components of trust, which may exist before the formation of an alliance, have different antecedents than the more dynamic, experiential types of trust, which are based upon human interaction.

The definitions of trust used in the literature are consistent with this dynamic view in that they allude to the process of *building trust* with repeated interactions (Das and Teng 1998; Gambetta 1998; Gulati 1995*a*; Ring and Van de Ven 1992, 1994; Spekman *et al.* 2001; Tomkins 2001). Trust grows (or deteriorates) over time as partners interact repeatedly. Alliance partners build trust by sharing information, preserving equity among partners, honouring (especially long-term) commitments, engaging in mutual risk-taking, demonstrating competence, and maintaining flexibility and a willingness to compromise in partner negotiations (Das and Teng 1998; Dyer 2000; Lewis 1999). Lewis (1999) identifies overt practices that firms often use to build trust within partnerships. For example, partner firms seeking to build trust engage in purposeful and extensive information sharing. They also achieve consensus on clear, *mutual* performance measures. Finally, to build trust, the governing body of the alliance must provide necessary resources and give clear direction to partner firms.

Evidence of overt activities to build and manage the emergence of trust is most prevalent among Japanese firms. Cooper and Slagmulder (2001) identify structural elements of the management system that promote trust in joint product development activities. Sheridan (1994, 1998) describes Sony Corporation's and Honda of America's programmes of sending consulting engineers to suppliers' locations to teach important technical skills and improve operating performance. Beecham (1999) describes a structured approach to performance management and goal setting used by Nissan to improve the 'codevelopment environment' between it and its suppliers. Dyer *et al.* (1998) describe Toyota Motor Company's partitioning of suppliers into three concentric circles. Each ring contains suppliers with different levels of embeddedness in and criticality to the 'Toyota family', as evidenced by governance relationships with

Toyota and the intensity of resource sharing between the firms. Dyer and Ouchi (1993) elaborate on how Toyota uses controlled competition among suppliers to generate a better product without consequently having a collapse of trust. A common thread in these stories is the use of accounting systems to facilitate the emergence of trust; for example, through shared accounting cost records (Frey and Schlosser 1993) and the creation of a ' "see through" value chain where both parties' costs and problems are visible' (Dyer 1996; Dyer and Ouchi 1993) and through complex mutual monitoring programmes (Dyer 1996; Richards 1995).

Distinctions are also made in the literature between *interpersonal* and *interorganizational* trust. The former is the trust between individuals and has both an emotional and cognitive component. The latter is purely cognitive and is the collective orientation towards another organization (Jeffries and Reed 2000). Practices that build interpersonal trust, such as stable employment of individuals involved and career paths that cross firm boundaries (Dyer 2000), also facilitate interorganizational trust (Zaheer and Venkatraman 1995; Zaheer *et al.* 1998). Inkpen and Currall (1998) argue that antecedents of inter-personal trust include the mutual attachment of individuals in both firms and the presence of boundary spanning managers. In a study of supplier partner-ships in the automotive and computer industries, Ittner *et al.* (1999) identify performance gains when trust-building practices such as frequent meetings (i.e. information exchange) are used. Frey and Schlosser (1993) note Ford and ABB explicitly engineered their partnership to create trust using a governance structure that brought about frequent encounters among employees and key managers. In 1999 United Airlines formed an alliance division to manage new partnerships and an executive 'keeps in *daily* contact with the partner's man-agement' (Anonymous 2001: 68).

Jeffries (2000) considers the dynamics of interpersonal and interorganiza-tional trust and problem-solving incentives among alliance partners. He sug-gests that when *either* interpersonal *or* interorganizational trust is high (but not both), partners have the strongest motivation to solve alliance problems. Kale *et al.* (2000) also link interpersonal trust to problem solving. In data collected from a survey of alliances formed by US-based companies, they find that trust affects 'the extent to which conflicts are managed in an inte-grative fashion'. Improved conflict resolution facilitates knowledge-transfer and deters opportunistic behaviour. As a result, alliance participants can gain capabilities from alliance partners while also protecting proprietary assets from opportunistic behaviour.

Finally, there is a dynamic relation between trust and information needs in interfirm relationships. Trust affects the sharing of different types of informa-tion differently. Trusting partners are more likely to share information related to know-how and capabilities (Adler 2001; Dyer 2000; Kale *et al.* 2000). On the other hand, trust may be an alternative to monitoring (Madhok 1995; Zaheer and Venkatraman 1995). That is, trusting partners need less information about partner activities and the fulfillment of partnership agreements. For example, Motoman, a supplier of industry robotic systems, and Stillwater Technologies, a contract tooling and machining company, describe their relationship as one 'based on trust and a handshake, not a written contract' (Sheridan 1997). This is consistent with the proposition by Ring and Van de Ven (1994) that increasing trust among partners leads to an increased reliance on informal negotiations relative to formal ones.

Tomkins (2001), however, suggests that the relation between trust and monitoring information is more complex than these authors suggest. Trust builds faster when information is more readily available in the early stages of the interfirm relationship. Top management played a crucial role in building trust in what was a previously poor relationship between Analog Devices and Teradyne. Trust grew out of their act of faith in 'opening books' to one another (Litsikas 1996). Moreover, partners' trust level and, therefore, their information needs may differ during the life of the partnership. Honda of America BP works with suppliers to improve their quality and cost, occasionally even sending Honda teams to suppliers' sites. Through these information-sharing experiences, suppliers can earn the right to move to higher levels of involvement in Honda's product planning and design efforts (Sheridan 1998). These examples illustrate how trust-building activities and the establishment of control and information systems are inextricably linked in interfirm relationships.

Managing Alliance Performance

In this section we argue that successful strategic alliance networks will manage alliance performance by providing effective leadership and direction, facilitating communication and learning, and by measuring and evaluating performance of the alliance network and of the network participants.

Providing leadership and direction

Lorenzoni and Baden-Fuller (1995) find that strategic networks have a strong firm at the centre of the network that takes primary responsibility for ensuring that the network creates value for all partners. The firm sets rules that govern partner responsibilities and building capabilities through simultaneous activities in structuring and strategizing. An executive at Honeywell, a defence industry and technology firm with over 100 alliances, echoes the importance of a central firm in the network, noting that 'whenever possible Honeywell avoids entering into 50–50 deals in which nobody is in control' (Anonymous 2001: 82).

Surveying the popular business literature, we find that for many firms, the first step in building a core competency in alliance management is the creation of a new, high-level management team dedicated to the task of developing alliance relationships. Ellram and Edis' (1996) study of one hundred matched pairs of buyer–supplier partners found that the most successful firms dedicated a team that had top management's support and involvement to managing the partnership. Examples from the business press include United Airlines' formation in 1999 of an alliance division to monitor and create new partnerships (p. 68), Johnson Controls' appointment of an executive to oversee each alliance (p. 70), and Coca-Cola's (p. 73) and IBM's (p. 77) appointment of a vice-president in charge of alliances and new ventures (Anonymous 2001). Alliance management groups are not an offshoot of corporate procurement, nor are they a simple variant on a merger and acquisition team, populated by financial, legal, and tax experts. Indeed, Accenture warns that too many firms assume that the issues of integration that arise in managing an alliance are similar to those of a merger or acquisition (www. accenture.com, August 2001). They argue that while integration and mutual adaptation are essential, they are achieved much more gradually and require continuous management by individuals skilled in diplomacy and with deep understanding of the core business objectives of the alliance network.

Facilitating communication and learning

If 'alliance capability' is to become a pervasive core competency of the firm, a key objective of these new corporate groups will be to capture and transfer alliance knowledge across the organization. Rivera *et al.* (2001) study alliance-specific mechanisms for learning, such as: the similarity of partners, the diversity of employees, and enabling processes and technologies that integrate the firms. As an example of the latter, Kodak developed and adopted a methodical approach for partnering with other firms in 1991 (Ellram and Edis 1996). The demand for standard practices and codified approaches to managing partner relations will increase with the number of alliance partners and the complexity of the portfolio of alliance governance structures used (www.accenture.com, August 2001).

In successful alliance networks, the central firm typically oversees and manages effective communications processes, including, but not limited to, electronically-based processes. Absent the bureaucratic processes of hierarchies, strategic alliances have the potential for making decisions faster. Indeed, in a survey of managers, executives report that in well-functioning alliances, decisions are reached 30–50 per cent faster than for comparable internal decisions in their firms. However, they note that multi-partner relationships, union settings, and communication styles that favour consensus-building can slow decisions even in alliances (www.accenture.com, August 2001). Lorenzoni and Baden-Fuller (1995) find that the central firm often sets the communications style for meetings among partners and actively monitors and documents information exchange.

The substance of communications is not limited to the perhaps narrow problem that the alliance seeks to address. It includes sharing ideas about customers, other suppliers, market trends, and general business practices. The density and breadth of information exchange suggests that substantial personal interactions are essential in strategic alliances. This is what we find in our review of popular business articles that describe effective partnerships (e.g., Anonymous 1996; Dixon 1999; Hendricks 1997; Sheridan 1997). In a description of Volkswagon's revolutionary factory in which suppliers work alongside VW employees on the auto assembly line, one executive says, 'A key challenge is the systematic integration of the activities of partners. This is accomplished through intense communication, which is made possible by their close proximity, as well as integrated information technology (Lima 1997)'.

Finally, effective communication and the exchange of information plays a key role in the *control* of interfirm relationships. Adler and others argue that alliances are particularly adept at transferring knowledge across organizational boundaries. Indeed, the sharing of information is a source of competitive advantage of alliances and a necessary condition for their success. Tomkins (2001) identifies the level of trust as a fundamental determinant of information needs within strategic alliances. Partnerships in which there is less trust require more information for monitoring and coordination. Tomkins asserts that the relation is more complex and dynamic than it appears, suggesting that trust, information needs and, consequently, control requirements likely change over the life of the partnership. Successful alliance networks must continually adapt to these changing information and communication needs, a task that requires effective personnel and technology management.

Clearly integrated information systems are an enabling technology for many alliances, even those that lack close proximity. For example, firms are using web-based intranets (among partners) to facilitate information exchange. At IBM, the top executive responsible for software alliances has a 'war room' with a wall covered with procedural charts for fifty-nine such alliances and monitors each from a Lotus Notes extranet on his laptop (Schifrin 2001*b*: 28). Cisco Systems uses the Internet to speed partner communications and to educate partners about its products (Schifrin 2001*b*: 79), Nuclear Management Company uses a Web-based intranet to post internal peer-group report cards (Schifrin 2001*b*: 82), and Hewlett-Packard invites prospective partners to submit proposals via its Web sites and provides a forum for tracking work in existing partnerships (Anonymous 2001: 78).

Measuring and evaluating performance

Whether it is facilitated by technology, as in the case of Nuclear Management Company's online peer report cards (Anonymous 2001: 82), or a component of personal communications, as in the case of the daily production meetings between Volkswagon supervisors and their on-site partners (Lima 1997), a key component of performance management of alliances is performance measurement and evaluation. Lewis (1999) likewise identifies accountability for results as a primary task of alliance control. Ellram and Edis' (1996) study of one hundred matched pairs of buyer–supplier partners found that the most successful relationships employed formal processes for mutual performance monitoring. However, even these firms acknowledged that this was one of the most difficult aspects of establishing the alliance relationship. Echoing this, Accenture concluded from a survey of executives involved in strategic alliances that 'measuring alliance performance is the newest, most imperfect branch of alliance management. Less than half of all alliances use formal measurements and only ten per cent find those they use sufficient' (www.accenture.com August 2001).

Although these systems may assist firms in mutually monitoring for the opportunistic behaviour that transaction cost economists fear, we found very little evidence of this in the descriptions of alliances in the popular press.[17] Rather, the focus appears to be on identifying opportunities for improved performance of the alliance and on facilitating the discovery of opportunities to innovate and expand the scope of alliance activities. Consider this description of performance measurement by Universal Card Services and TSYS:

> strategic intent [of the alliance] was reinforced when UCS created a set of measures to evaluate the quality of operations at both companies. TSYS has created 36–45 quality measures to monitor its operations' performance...Both UCS and TSYS post daily statistics on accuracy, speed, response time and customer satisfaction measures throughout the company...The goals for each measure were set through discussions between UCS and TSYS. The performance for each day is compared to the goal and a composite daily quality measure is computed and shared. Graphs comparing daily performance with targeted goals are available online to all the employees of TSYS and UCS as well as being prominently posted in both companies. These measures are used to chart the progress of the alliance (Sankar *et al.* 1995).

As is the case within firms, measures of performance are crucial to implementing control in interfirm alliances. Das and Teng (2001) identify three types of control mechanisms and suggest that the appropriate approach depends on the level and type of trust (goodwill or competence trust) that is present and on the type of risk (relational and performance risk) that the firms wish to mitigate. The first control mechanism, behaviour control, is a control of the *process* and is useful for reducing relational risk. Output controls, on the other hand, are better at reducing performance risk. Finally, social controls—informal controls designed to establish norms of behaviours—mitigate

---

[17] Perhaps this reflects the experience of a senior executive at a leading global insurance firm who remarked in an interview with us that

> ...most contracts and written agreements are put in a lawyer's drawer after they are written... People charged with enacting the alliance work together to achieve mutually desirable ends—trust builds over time and that becomes the basis for the business as it plays out. They don't tend to worry about the details of the initial agreement...If we have to pull out the agreement and bring in the lawyers it almost always means that something has gone terribly wrong and everyone loses.

This manager was a lawyer by training and his group's responsibilities included monitoring alliance relationships to ensure that partners upheld the firm's philosophies on corporate social responsibility.

both types of risk. Goodwill and competence trust enhance the effectiveness of all three types of control (Das and Teng 2001).

In addition to the control mechanism, firms choose the appropriate control *focus* and control *tightness*. These choices are continually re-evaluated in light of partner objectives and of existing trust levels and alliance performance (Groot and Merchant 2000). In a study of international joint ventures, Groot and Merchant find some evidence that control focus is broader—encompassing a broader set of performance indicators—when partner's objectives are more broadly defined and when past performance or trust levels are relatively low. Low past performance and low trust also will result in the use of tighter controls.

In sum, successful strategic alliance management involves leadership and direction, the facilitation of communication and learning, and performance measurement and evaluation. Partner relations, competitive forces, and economic conditions, however, are ever changing. This dynamic environment poses a significant challenge to management accounting, which must provide for information and control needs of the strategic alliance throughout its life. In the next section, we explore the management issues that arise with the evolution of strategic alliances.

Managing the evolution of alliances: formation and stability

Other than single-firm case studies, we are aware of only one research paper that examines the processes by which strategic alliances emerge using a large sample of firms. Doz *et al.* (2000) conduct a survey of 53 R&D consortia in an effort to understand how different formation processes affect alliance performance. In an exploratory analysis, they identify two paths of network formation. In the first path, the 'emergent process', changes in the environment, common interests, and similar views among potential members lead to alliance formation. The second formation path is an 'engineered process' by which a third party recognizes the opportunity for collaboration and triggers alliance formation. This path is more likely when interests are more dissimilar and interdependence is low. From the results of the exploratory analysis, Doz *et al.* (2000) make basic inferences and predictions about how the alliance formation process affects the manner in which consensus is reached by alliance participants, participant satisfaction with the alliance, and alliance longevity. Specifically, alliances formed by an emergent process tend to use formal boundaries to precipitate consensus building among partners. Engineered alliances develop consensus by establishing contractual terms that align partner incentives. Doz *et al.* (2000) propose that engineered alliances will face unmet expectations while members of emergent alliances experience both satisfaction and disappointment at various times throughout the alliance life. Moreover, the exploratory results suggest that although members of emergent alliances have stronger expectations of continuity of the alliance, they will terminate sooner than alliances formed by an engineered process.

Finally, Doz *et al.* (2000) find evidence that engineered alliances tend to lead to additional, emergent type alliances among the partners.

The competing forces framework for alliance success suggested by Das and Teng (2000) does not describe the evolutionary *process* by which the forces emerge or the *process* by which an imbalance in the forces is corrected or leads to a deterioration in the alliance form. There is little scholarly research that explores these processes, either conceptually or empirically. An exception is Ring and Van de Ven (1994). Taking as given the existence of an 'inter-organizational relationship' between two or more firms, they develop a theoretical framework for how relationships evolve over time. They describe 'the development and evolution of [an alliance] as consisting of a repetitive sequence of negotiation, commitment and execution stages (Ring and Van de Ven 1994)'. Negotiations and commitments can be formal or informal, and execution includes both role and personal interactions. The evolution of *role* relationships to *personal* interactions is proposed to increase with the alliance tenure of the firm agents involved. As reliance on trust among participants increases, *informal* contracts increasingly supplant *formal* ones. However, if expected duration of the alliances exceeds the expected tenure of the agents, then participants begin to *formalize* previously *informal* commitments. Finally, the probability that the parties will dissolve the alliance in response to a commitment breach decreases over the life of the alliance (Ring and Van de Ven 1994).

Focusing on the strategic network, rather than individual transactions, Lorenzoni and Baden-Fuller (1995) find that strategic networks that continually renew themselves by building new capabilities are most likely to survive as alliances. New capabilities may arise in a process of mutual adaptation as firms discover new ways to recombine their individual competencies (Rivera *et al.* 2001). Alternatively, they may arise with new partners joining the alliance. This points to another demand for management information in the appropriate selection of partners. 'A big difference between the successful and unsuccessful networks is that in the former, the central firm chooses partners based on careful consideration of strategic issues as well as the *"fit" or compatibility of management systems, decision processes, and perspectives'* (Lorenzoni and Baden-Fuller 1995, italics added).

Incentives and Rewards: Managing Partners' Share of Alliance Returns

Describing the control and governance structure that underpins successful strategic networks, Lorenzoni and Baden-Fuller (1995) remark:

Anglo-Saxon contracts are typically limited in the sense that partners are not expected to go beyond the contract. In contrast, in a network perspective, the behavior is prescribed for the unknown, each promising to work in a particular manner to resolve future challenges and difficulties as they arise ... Strategic centers also rely on trust, but utilize contracts and formal controls as a complement. Central firms develop rules for settling disputes... [and] ensure that rewards are distributed in a manner which encourages partners to reinforce the positive circle... None of the central firms we studied seeks to be the most profitable firm in the system... the task of the manager is one of designing a structure which provides an environment favorable for inter-actions to form and for new information to be generated. Such a structure is a network ... Information condensed through the network is 'thicker' than that condensed through the brokerage market, but is 'freer' than in the hierarchy.

Much more so than firms involved in a supply chain network, Lorenzoni and Baden-Fuller (1995) find that members of strategic networks seek to build partners' capabilities and are unusually aggressive in scanning the horizon for innovation opportunities, particularly those that involve partners sharing and modifying one another's technologies in a model of business growth that the authors describe as 'borrow-develop-lend'. They also find that it is quite com-mon for central firms to create 'races' among key partners for the discovery of new knowledge and capabilities with the expectation that the 'winner' will be rewarded, but that all partners will benefit from the discovery. Toyota's carefully controlled competitions among suppliers, where all parties survive to compete again, illustrate this concept of the central firm maintaining prof-itability of all players for the good of the network (Dyer and Ouchi 1993). This 'disciplined creativity' interjects competition that is often absent in hier-archies, while avoiding the 'winner take all' outcomes of competition that may limit the number of competitors who compete in subsequent stages of innovation. It is also a critical element that underpins the stability of the alliance by ensuring fair returns to all partners.

Conclusion

The past decade has seen a tremendous growth in strategic alliances and joint ventures across a variety of industries, providing evidence of the phenomena of newly emergent forms of collaborative interfirm relationships. The volume of this collaborative activity and the longevity of many of these relationships suggests that interfirm alliances do, in fact, represent a sustainable organiza-tional form. Despite this, strategic alliances have received little attention in the accounting academic literature.

Transaction cost economics suggests that hybrid organizational forms emerge in settings in which transaction costs are sufficiently high to make market transactions too costly, but not high enough to justify vertical integ-ration. The resource-based view of the firm offers a different explanation for the formation of hybrid organizational forms, namely, as a source of sustainable competitive advantage. Both theories suggest motivations and goals of alliances, the governance structures that correlate with these motives, and factors that affect the performance of these organizational forms. Empirical evidence supports many of these theoretical propositions. Yet we know very little about the policies and procedures that support performance attainment in the day to day life of the alliance, including management accounting practices aimed at helping firms manage performance of this extended enterprise.

The multi-faceted nature of alliance formation and alliance management and control creates new demands for management accounting. Performance measurement and control across organizational boundaries represent the adaptation of old management accounting techniques to this new setting of firm networks. New management practices of relationship management are evolving, facilitated by management accounting information to meet demands for interorganizational trust building, learning, and rich communication among partner firms. After reviewing the extant research related to strategic alliance formation and performance, we suggest a new agenda for management accounting research in the extended enterprise, an agenda linked to what has traditionally been termed management accounting research but that also challenges these boundaries. We consider three key challenges of managing a strategic network, taking as given a particular hybrid governance structure; specifically, managing alliance control (including risk and trust among partners), managing alliance performance evaluation, and managing the evolution of the alliance. In each case we offer evidence from the practitioner literature that strategic alliances are meeting demands for management accounting information in both traditional and novel ways, supporting our intuition that the new hybrid forms are sufficiently different from markets or hierarchies to demand different modes of management accounting.

Within a particular hybrid organizational form, the first significant challenge is *management control*. Management techniques and management accounting control mechanisms must be tailored to the type of assets (property or knowledge) committed to the alliance partnership and to the dominant type of risk (performance or relational) present. Moreover, trust among partners affects the perceived level of relational risk and, in some settings, substitutes for formal control mechanisms. Accounting information and trust levels are inextricably linked, in that trust levels among partners affect the extent to which information sharing is needed and the extent to which partner firms are willing to share information.

The second challenge for alliance partners is the *evaluation of alliance performance*. Observations of innovative and successful collaborative arrangements highlight the importance of a central firm responsible for overseeing network communications. Integrated information systems are important to alliance formation as is the consistent and objective measurement and evaluation of alliance performance. High-level management support, in the form of a distinct management team dedicated to alliance formation and management, is also frequently used in successful alliances. Emphasis on various types of control mechanisms (behaviour, output or social) is adapted to the type of risk present and the level of partner trust in the alliance.

Finally, the *management of alliance evolution* is the third challenge facing alliance partners. Management accounting information is increasingly important to the selection of alliance partners and the assessment of the compatibility of information systems and decision processes. Accounting information also plays an important role in the development of interfirm trust, which has implications for information needs and the use of formalized control mechanisms. Finally, accounting information is often the basis for learning within the partner network.

In sum, while the incorporation of strategic alliance networks into modern, extended enterprises places many traditional demands for control and evaluation on alliance partners, it also introduces new demands. Firms' innovative responses to these demands herald the advent of a new realm of research and teaching in management accounting.

References

Adler, P. S. (2001), 'Market, Hierarchy, and Trust: The Knowledge Economy and the Future of Capitalism', *Organization Science: A Journal of the Institute of Management Sciences*, 12/2: 215–34.

Ahuja, G. (2000), 'The Duality of Collaboration: Inducements and Opportunities in the Formation of Interfirm Linkages', *Strategic Management Journal*, 21/3: 317–343.

Anand, B. N. and Khanna, T. (2000), Do Firms Learn to Create Value? The Case of Alliances. *Strategic Management Journal* 21/3: 295–315.

Anderson, S. W., Daly, J. D., and Johnson, M. F. (1999), 'Why Firms Seek ISO 9000 Certification: Regulatory Compliance, or Competitive Advantage?' *Production and Operations Management*, 8/1: 28–43.

—— Glenn, D., and Sedatole, K. L. (2000), 'Sourcing Parts of Complex Products: Evidence on Transactions Costs, High-Powered Incentives and Ex-Post Opportunism', *Accounting, Organizations & Society*, 25/8: 723–50.

Anonymous (1996), 'The New Supplier Partnership: An Inside Story', *Nations Business*, 84/5: 21.

—— (2000), 'Alliance Management: Five Destructive Myths', *CMA Management*, 73/10: 14–15.

—— (2001), 'The Forbes Magnetic 40', *Forbes Best of the Web* (May 21): vol.167 no.2 61–107.

Baiman, S., Fischer, P. E., and Rajan, M. V. (2001), 'Performance Measurement and Design in Supply Chains', *Management Science*, 47/1: 173–89.

Baum, J. A. C., Calabrese, T., and Silverman, B. S. (2000), 'Don't Go It Alone: Alliance Network Composition and Startups Performance in Canadian Biotechnology', *Strategic Management Journal*, 21/3: 267–94.

Beecham, M. (1999), 'Cogent Theory', *Supply Management*, 4/1: 36–7.

Bergin, S. (1996), 'Monsanto's Mission: Total Customer Satisfaction', *Transportation and Distribution*, 37/7: 65–6.

Bianchi, M. (1995), 'Markets and Firms: Transaction Costs Versus Strategic Innovation, *Journal of Economic Behavior & Organization*, 28/2: 183–202.

Brandenburger, A. M. and Nalebuff, B. J. (1996), *Co-Opetition: 1. A Revolutional Mindset that Redefines Competition and Cooperations; 2. The Game Theory Strategy/That's Changing the Game of Business* (New York: Doubleday).

Buvik, A. and Reve, T. (2001), 'Asymmetrical Deployment of Specific Assets and Contractual Safeguarding in Industrial Purchasing Relationships', *Journal of Business Research*, 51/2: 101–13.

Cachon, G. P. and Zipkin, P. H. (1999), 'Competitive and Cooperative Inventory Policies in a Two-Stage Supply Chain', *Management Science*, 45/7: 936–53.

Cachon, G. R. P. and Fisher, M. (2000), 'Supply Chain Inventory Management and the Value of Shared Information', *Management Science*, 46/8: 1032–48.

Chiles, T. H. and McMackin, J. F. (1996), 'Integrating Variable Risk Preferences, Trust, and Transaction Cost Economics', *Academy of Management Review*, 21: 73–99.

Clement, J. P., III. (1997), 'Effective Collaboration Is the Key to Successful Operator/Supplier Relationships', *Oil and Gas Journal*, 95/41: 47–8.

Cooper, R. and Slagmulder (forthcoming), 'Interorganizational Cost Management and Relational Context', *Accounting Organizations and Society*.

Coase, R. H. (1937), 'The Nature of the Firm', *Economica*, 4/(13–16): 386–405.

Currall, S. C. and Inkpen, A. C. (2000), 'Joint Venture Trust: Interpersonal, Inter-Group and Inter-Firm Levels', in D. O. Faulkner and M. DeRond (eds), *Cooperative Strategy: Economics, Business, and Organizational Issues* (Oxford: Oxford University Press), 324–40.

Das, T. K. and Teng, B. (1996), 'Risk Types and Inter-Firm Alliance Structures', *Journal of Management Studies*, 33/6: 827–43.

——— (1998), 'Between Trust and Control: Developing Confidence in Partner Cooperation in Alliances', *Academy of Management Review*, 23/3: 491–512.

——— (1999), 'Managing Risks in Strategic Alliances', *Academy of Management Executive*, 13/4: 50–62.

—— (2000), 'Instabilities of Strategic Alliances: An Internal Tensions Perspective', *Organization Science: A Journal of the Institute of Management Sciences*, 11/1: 77–101.

—— (2001), 'Trust, Control, and Risk in Strategic Alliances: An Integrated Framework', *Organization Studies*, 22/2: 251–83.

Dekker, H. C. (2001), 'Control of Inter-Organizational Relationships: Theoretical Framework and an Empirical Investigation', Working paper, Vrije Universiteit Amsterdam, Amsterdam, The Netherlands.

—— (2002), 'Control of Information Technology Transactions: An Empirical Test of Appropriation Concerns, Coordinations Requirements and Social Embeddedness', Working paper, Vrije Universiteit Amsterdam, Amsterdam, The Netherlands.

Dixon, L. (1999), 'Jit Ii: Ultimate Customer-Supplier Partnership', *Hospital Material Management Quarterly*, 20/3: 14–20.

Doz, Y. L. (1996), 'The Evolution of Cooperation in Strategic Alliances: Initial Conditions or Learning Processes?' *Strategic Management Journal*, 17 (special issue): 55–84.

—— and Hamel, G. (1998), *Alliance Advantage: The Art of Creating Value through Partnering*. (Boston: Harvard Business School Press).

—— Olk, P. M., and Ring, P. S. (2000), 'Formation Processes of R&D Consortia: Which Path to Take? Where Does It Lead?' *Strategic Management Journal*, 21/3: 239–66.

—— and Ouchi, W. G. (1993), 'Japanese-Style Partnerships: Giving Companies a Competitive Edge', *Sloan Management Review*, 35/1: 51–63.

Dyer, J. H. (1996), 'How Chrysler Created an American Keiretsu', *Harvard Business Review* (July–August).

—— (2000), *Collaborative Advantage: Winning through Extended Enterprise Supplier Networks* (New York: Oxford University Press).

—— and Nobeoka, K. (2000), 'Creating and Managing a High-Performance Knowledge-Sharing Network: The Toyota Case', *Strategic Management Journal*, 21/3: 345–67.

—— Dong Sung, Cho and Wujin, Chu. (1998), 'Strategic Supplier Segmentation: The Next "Best Practice" in Supply Chain Management', *California Management Review*, 40/2: 57–77.

Ellram, L. M. and Edis, O. R. V. (1996), 'A Case Study of Successful Partnering Implementation', *International Journal of Purchasing and Materials Management*, 32/4: 20–8.

Frey, S. C., Jr. and Schlosser, M. M. (1993), 'ABB and Ford: Creating Value through Cooperation', *Sloan Management Review*, 35/1: 65–77.

Gambetta, D. (1998), 'Can We Trust Trust?' in D. Gambetta (ed.), *Trust: Making and Breaking Cooperative Relations* (Cambridge, MA: Basil Blackwell), 213–37.

Gietzmann, M. B. (1996), 'Incomplete Contracts and the Make or Buy Decision: Governance Design and Attainable Flexibility', *Accounting, Organizations and Society*, 21/6: 611–26.

Granovetter, M. (1985), 'Economic Action and Social Structure: The Problem of Embeddedness', *American Journal of Sociology*, 91/3: 481–510.

Granovetter, M. S. (1973), 'The Strength of Weak Ties', *American Journal of Sociology*, 78/6: 1360–80.

Groot, T. L. C. M. and Merchant, K. A. (2000), Control of International Joint Ventures', *Accounting, Organizations and Society*, 25/6: 579–607.

Grossman, S. and O. Hart (1986), 'The Costs and the Benefits of Ownership: A Theory of Vertical and Lateral Integration', *Journal of Political Economy*, 94: 691–719.

Gulati, R. (1995*a*), 'Does Familiarity Breed Trust? The Implications of Repeated Ties for Contractual Choice in Alliances', *Academy of Management Journal*, 38/1: 85–113.

—— (1995*b*), 'Social Structure and Alliance Formation Patterns: A Longitudinal Analysis', *Administrative Science Quarterly*, 40/4: 619–52.

—— (1998), 'Alliances and Networks', *Strategic Management Journal*, 19/4: 293–317.

Gulati, R. and Singh, H. (1998), 'The Architecture of Cooperation: Managing Coordination Costs and Appropriation Concerns in Strategic Alliances', *Administrative Science Quarterly*, 43 (4).

—— Nohria, N. and Zaheer, A. (2000), 'Strategic Networks', *Strategic Management Journal*, 21/3: 203–15.

Hagen, J. M. and Choe, S. (1998), 'Trust in Japanese Interfirm Relations: Institutional Sanctions Matter', *Academy of Management Review*, 23/3: 589–600.

Hamel, G., Doz, Y. L., and Prahalad, C. K. (1989), 'Collaborate with Your Competitors and Win', *Harvard Business Review*, 67/1: 133–140.

Hansmann, H. (1996), *The Ownership of Enterprise* (Cambridge, MA: Harvard University Press).

Hansmann, H. and Kraakman, R. (2000), 'Organizational Law as Asset Partitioning', *European Economic Review*, 44/(4–6): 807–17.

Harbison, J. R. and Pekar, P. (1998), *Smart Alliances: A Practical Guide to Repeatable Success* (Somerset, NJ: Jossey-Bass/John Wiley & Sons, Inc).

Hart, O. (2001), 'Norms and the Theory of the Firm', Working paper.

Hendricks, M. (1997), 'A New Twist on Just-in-Time Management Pays Off for Entrepreneurs and their Customers', *Entrepreneur* (May).

Hopwood, A. (1996), 'Looking across Rather Than up and Down: On the Need T. Explore the Lateral Processing of Information', *Accounting, Organizations and Society*, 21/6: 589–90.

Hughes, D., Griffiths, L., and Mchale, J. V. (1997), 'Do Quasi-Markets Evolve? Institutional Analysis and the Nhs', *Cambridge Journal of Economics*, 21/2: 259–76.

Hutheesing, N. (2001), 'Marital Blisters', *Forbes*, (May 21): 30–2.

Inkpen, A. C. and Currall, S. C. (1998), 'The Nature, Antecedents and Consequences of Joint Venture Trust', *Journal of International Management*, 4/1: 1–20.

Ittner, C. D., Larcker, D. F., Nagar, V., and Rajan, M. V. (1999), 'Supplier Selection, Monitoring Practices and Firm Performance', *Journal of Accounting and Public Policy*, 18(3): 253–81.

Jeffries, F. L. and Reed, R. (2000), 'Trust and Adaptation in Relational Contracting', *Academy of Management Review*, 25/4: 873–83.

Jensen, M. and Meckling, W. (1991), 'Specific and General Knowledge, and Organizational Structure', in L. Werin and H. Wijkander (eds), *Main Currents in Contract Economics* (Oxford: Blackwell), 251–74.

Joskow, M. (1987), 'Contract Duration and Relationship Specific Investments: Empirical Evidence from Coal Markets', *American Economic Review* 77, (March): 168–85.

Kale, P., Singh, M., and Perlmutter, H. (2000), 'Learning and Protection of Proprietary Assets in Strategic Alliances: Building Relational Capital', *Strategic Management Journal*, 21/3: 217–37.

Kaufman, A., Wood, C., and Theyel, G. (2000), 'Collaboration and Technology Linkages: A Strategic Supplier Topology', *Strategic Management Journal*, 21/6: 649–63.

Kinney, W. R. (2001), 'Accounting Scholarship: What Is Uniquely Ours?' *The Accounting Review*, 76/2: 275–84.

Klein, B. (1988), 'Vertical Integration as Organizational Ownership: The Fisher Body-General Motors Relationship Revisited', *Journal of Law, Economics and Organization*, 4: 199–213.

Kogut, B. (1988), 'Joint Ventures: Theoretical and Empirical Perspectives', *Strategic Management Journal*, 9/4: 319–32.

——(1989), 'The Stability of Joint Ventures: Reciprocity and Competitive Rivalry', *Journal of Industrial Economics*, 38/2: 183–98.

Laseter, T. and Ramdas, K. (2001), 'Product Types and Supplier Roles in Product Development: An Exploratory Analysis', Working paper.

Lewis, J. D. (1999), *Trusted Partners: How Companies Build Mutual Trust and Win Together*. (New York: The Free Press).

Lima, E. P. (1997), 'VW's Revolutionary Idea', *Industry Week*, 246/6: 62–7.

Litsikas, M. (1996), 'Cliches Aren't Just Quality Rhetoric', *Quality*, 35/4: 70–6.

Lorenzoni, G. and Baden-Fuller, C. (1995), 'Creating a Strategic Center to Manage a Web of Partners', *California Management Review*, 37/3: 146–63.

—— and Lipparini, A. (1999), 'The Leveraging of Interfirm Relationships as a Distinctive Organizational Capability: A Longitudinal Study', *Strategic Management Journal*, 20/4: 317–38.

Madhok, A. (1995), 'Revisiting Multinational Firms' Tolerance for Joint Ventures: A Trust-Based Approach', *Journal of International Business Studies*, 26/1: 117–38.

—— (1996), 'The Organization of Economic Activity: Transaction Costs, Firm Capabilities, and the Nature of Governance', *Organization Science: A Journal of the Institute of Management Sciences*, 7/5: 577–90.

—— and Tallman, S. B. (1998), 'Resources, Transactions and Rents: Managing Value through Interfirm Collaborative Relationships', *Organization Science: A Journal of the Institute of Management Sciences*, 9/3: 326–40.

Masten, S., Meehan, J., and Snyder, E. (1989), 'Vertical Integration in the US Auto Industry', *Journal of Economic Behavior & Organization*, 12: 265–73.

Menard, C. (1995), 'Markets as Institutions Versus Organizations as Markets? Disentangling Some Fundamental Concepts', *Journal of Economic Behavior & Organization*, 28/2: 161–82.

—— (1996), 'On Clusters, Hybrids, and Other Strange Forms: The Case of the French Poultry Industry', *Journal of Institutional and Theoretical Economics*, 152/1: 154–83.

Milgrom, P. and Roberts, J. (1992), *Economics, Organization and Management* (Upper Saddle River, NJ: Prentice-Hall).

Miller, P. and O'Leary, T. (2002), 'Appraising Investment in Systems of Complementary Assets: A Field Based Study of Inter-Firm Coordination Mechanisms', Working paper.

Monteverde, K. and Teece, D. (1982), 'Supplier Switching Costs and Vertical Integration in the Automobile Industry', *Bell Journal of Economics*, 13: 206–13.

Moore, J. F. (1996), *The Death of Competition: Leadership and Strategy in the Age of Business Ecosystems* (New York: Harper-Business).

Novak, S. and Eppinger, S. D. (2001), 'Sourcing by Design: Product Complexity and the Supply Chain', *Management Science*, 47/1: 189–204.

Okamuro, H. (2001), 'Risk Sharing in the Supplier Relationship: New Evidence from the Japanese Automotive Industry', *Journal of Economic Behavior & Organization*, 45/4: 361–81.

Orts, E. W. (1998), 'The Future of Enterprise Organization', *Michigan Law Review*, 96/6: 1947–74.

Osborn, R. N. and Baughn, C. C. (1990), 'Forms of Interorganizational Governance for Multinational Alliances', *Academy of Management Journal*, 33: 503–19.

—— and Hagedoorn, J. (1997), 'The Institutionalization and Evolutionary Dynamics of Interorganizational Alliances and Networks', *Academy of Management Journal*, 40: 261–79.

Otley, D. (1994), 'Management Control in Contemporary Organizations: Towards a Wider Framework', *Management Accounting Research*, 5: 289–99.

Oxley, J. E. (1997), 'Appropriability Hazards and Governance in Strategic Alliances: A Transaction Cost Approach', *Journal of Law, Economics and Organization*, 13/2: 387–409.

—— (1999), 'Institutional Environment and the Mechanism of Governance: The Impact of Intellectual Property Protection on the Structure of Inter-Firm Alliances', *Journal of Economic Behavior & Organization*, 38/3: 283–309.

Parkhe, A. (1993), 'Strategic Alliance Structuring: A Game Theoretic and Transaction Cost Examination of Interfirm Cooperation', *Academy of Management Journal*, 36/4: 794–829.

Parkhe, A. (1998), 'Building Trust in International Alliances', *Journal of World Business*, 33/4: 417–37.

Penrose, E. T. (1959), *The Theory of the Growth of the Firm* (London: Basil Blackwell Publishers).

Pisano, G. P. (1989), 'Using Equity Participation to Support Exchange: Evidence from the Biotechnology Industry', *Journal of Law, Economics, and Organization*, 5/1: 109–26.

——(1990), 'The R&D Boundaries of the Firm: An Empirical Analysis', *Administrative Science Quarterly*, 35/1: 153–76.

——Russo, M. V., and Teece, D. (1988), 'Joint Ventures and Collaborative Agreements in the Telecommunications Equipment Industry', in D. Mowery *International Collaborative Ventures in U.S. Manufacturing*, (Cambridge, MA: Ballanger) 23–70.

Porter, M. E. (1980), '*Competitive Strategy: Techniques for Analyzing Industry and Competitors*', New York: The Free Press.

——(1985), *Competitive Advantage: Creating and Sustaining Superior Performance* (New York: The Free Press).

——(1990), *The Competitive Advantage of Nations* (New York: The Free Press).

Powel, W. W. (1990), 'Neither Market nor Hierarchy: Network Forms of Organization', *Research in Organizational Behavior*, 12: 295–336.

Prahalad, C. K. and Hamel, G. (1989), 'Strategic Intent', *Harvard Business Review*, 67/3: 63–77.

——(1990), 'The Core Competence of the Corporation', *Harvard Business Review*, 68/3: 79–91.

Richards, L. (1995), 'Empowerment and Trust Key to Partnerships', *TQM Magazine*, 7/1: 38–41.

Ring, P. S. and Van de Ven, A. H. (1992), 'Structuring Cooperative Relationships between Organizations', *Strategic Management Journal*, 13/7: 483–98.

——(1994), 'Developmental Processes of Cooperative Interorganizational Relationships', *Academy of Management Journal*, 19/1: 90–118.

Rivera, M., Dussauge, P., and Mitchell, W. (2001), 'Coordination, Creation and Protection: Micro-Mechanisms for Learning from an Alliance', Working paper.

Rousseau, D. M., Sitkin, S. B., Burt, R. S., and Camerer, C. (1998), 'Not So Different after All: A Cross-Discipline View of Trust', *Academy of Management Review*, 3: 393–404.

Rowley, T., Behrens, D., and Krackhardt, D. (2000), 'Redundant Governance Structures: An Analysis of Structural and Relational Embeddedness in the Steel and Semiconductor Industries', *Strategic Management Journal*, 21/3: 369–86.

Sankar, C. S., Boulton, W. R., Davidson, N. W., Snyder, C. A., and Ussery, R. W. (1995), Building a Worked-Class Alliance: The Universal Card—Tsys Case', *Academy of Management Executive*, 9/2: 20–9.

Scapens, R. W. and Bromwich, M. (2001), 'Management Accounting Research: The First Decade', *Management Accounting Research*, 12/2: 245–54.

Schifrin, M. 2001a. 'Is Your Company Magnetic?' *Forbes Best of the Web*, (May 21): 16.

——2001b, 'Partner or Perish', *Forbes Best of the Web*, (May 21): 26–8.

Seal, W., Cullen, J., Dunlop, A., Berry, T., and Ahmed, M. (1999), 'Enacting a European Supply Chain: A Case Study on the Role of Management Accounting', *Management Accounting Research*, 10/3: 303–22.

Shelanski, H. A. and Klein, P. G. (1995), 'Empirical Research in Transaction Cost Economics: Review and Assessment', *Journal of Law, Economics and Organization*, 11/2: 363–9.

Sheridan, J. H. (1994), 'Leap of Faith' Pays Off', *Industry Week*, 234/14: 39–42.

—— (1997), 'An Alliance Built on Trust', *Industry Week*, 246/6: 67–70.

—— (1998), ' "Best" of Everything', *Industry Week*, 247/2: 13–24.

Spekman, R. E., Spear, J., and Kamauff, J. (2001), 'Supply Chain Competency: Learning as a Key Component', Working paper.

Stuart, T. E. (2000), 'Interorganizational Alliances and the Performance of Firms: A Study of Growth and Innovation Rates in High-Technology Industry', *Strategic Management Journal*, 21/8: 791–811.

Tomkins, C. (2001), 'Interdependencies, Trust and Information in Relationships, Alliances and Networks', *Accounting, Organizations and Society*, 26: 161–91.

Tsang, E. W. K. (2000), 'Transaction Cost and Resource-Based Explanations of Joint Ventures: A Comparison and Synthesis', *Organization Studies* 21/1: 215–242.

Ulset, S. (1996), 'R&D Outsourcing and Contractual Governance: An Empirical Study of Commercial R&D Projects', *Journal of Economic Behavior & Organization*, 30/1: 63–82.

Van der Meer-Kooistra, J. and Vosselman, E. G. J. (2000), 'Management Control of Interfirm Transactional Relationships: The Case of Industrial Renovation and Maintenance', *Accounting, Organizations and Society*, 25/1: 51–77.

Wicks, A. C., Berman, S. L., and Jones, T. M. (1999), 'The Structure of Optimal Trust: Moral and Strategic Implications', *Academy of Management Review*, 24/1: 199–16.

Williamson, O. E. (1985), *The Economic Institutions of Capitalism* (New York: The Free Press).

—— (1991), 'Comparative Economic Organization: The Analysis of Discrete Structural Alternatives', *Administrative Science Quarterly*, 36/2: 269–97.

—— (1993), 'Calculativeness, Trust, and Economic Organization Theory', *Journal of Law and Economics*, 36 (April).

Wolff, J. A. and Reed, R. (2000), 'Firm Resources and Joint Ventures: What Determines Zero-Sum Versus Positive-Sum Outcomes?' *Managerial and Decision Economics*, 21/7: 269–84.

Zaheer, A. and Venkatraman, N. (1995), 'Relational Governance as an Interorganizational Strategy: An Empirical Test of the Role of Trust in Economic Exchange', *Strategic Management Journal*, 16/5: 373–92.

Zaheer, A., McEvily, B., and Perrone, V. (1998), 'Does Trust Matter? Exploring the Effects of Interorganizational and Interpersonal Trust on Performance', *Organization Science: A Journal of the Institute of Management Sciences*, 9/2: 123–42.

4

Technology-Driven Integration, Automation, and Standardization of Business Processes
Implications for Accounting

Chris Chapman and Wai Fong Chua

> The computing revolution of the past two decades has so reduced information collection and processing costs that virtually all technical barriers to design and implementation of effective management accounting systems have been removed.
>
> (Kaplan and Johnson 1987: 6)

Since the above was written the scale and scope of developments in information technology have only increased. Today, companies are presented with an increasingly bewildering and expensive array of cutting edge, must have, technological developments to consider (e.g. ERP, EIP, SCM, CRM, SSC, B2C & B2B e-commerce, ASP[1]). Many of these developments represent the continuation of trends begun in previous generations of technologies. For example, today's analytical customer relationship management (CRM) software owes much to the data warehouse, which in turn owes much to the executive information system (EIS), and decision support system before that. Likewise today's business to business (B2B) e-commerce products can be seen as a direct descendant of yesterday's electronic data interchange (EDI) (Markus 2000). However, as will be discussed below, these technologies share new features that open up possibilities for new forms of organizing. Whilst at the time of writing the above quotation was almost certainly technologically optimistic, today the challenge lies in understanding what would constitute effective management accounting for the kinds of organizing and organizations that new technologies may help to bring about.

In considering these new technologies the academic information systems literature is acknowledging that they have brought about a major shift in the

---

We gratefully acknowledge the comments of Al Bhimani and Paolo Quattrone on earlier drafts of this chapter.

[1] Table 4.1 provides a brief glossary, but these technologies will be discussed in more detail below.

Table 4.1. A selected glossary of ERP-type technologies, adapted from Manchester (2000*b*)

ASP	Application service provider	A company that rents application services usually based on standard packages such as SAP, Oracle, etc.
B2B	Business to business	Communications between companies and their suppliers
B2C	Business to customer	Communications between companies and their customers
CRM	Customer relationship management	Software to manage and control relationships with customers
EAI	Enterprise application integration	A business initiative to link all IT systems together
EIP	Enterprise information portal	An initiative to bring all corporate information together under one 'seamless' regime and provide universal access using internet technology and other tools
ERP	Enterprise resource planning	Integrated software to control and manage the whole range of enterprise activity
SCM	Supply chain management	Software to automate the supply chain from procurement
SSC	Shared service centre	Software to centralize, manage, and control provision of administrative services
XML	Extensible mark-up language	A 'language' to define business documents so that they can be exchanged regardless of the computer platform

process of information systems implementation and development (Markus 2000). They turn on its head decades of received wisdom regarding bespoke software development, risk management, and the dangers of tight linkages between systems. As yet, however, there has been little published work looking at the implications of these technologies with regard to accounting. Where these technologies have been considered there has been a tendency for discussion to remain at a quite general level, with the implications for accounting often couched in terms of pre-existing accounting debates. Scapens (1997) and Fahy and Lynch (1998), for example, are both concerned about the implications of technology for the role of accountants along the lines of the more general debate on 'bean counters' and 'change agents' (exemplified by the survey on management accounting practice by the Institute of Management Accountants 1999). Another example would be Cooper and Kaplan (1998) who reiterate their concerns about lack of understanding of activity based costing (ABC) principles and warn that new technologies make this an even greater problem.

We do not disagree with the conclusions of these authors, but do feel that these new technologies (that we collectively label in this chapter as ERP-type) deserve more detailed study in their own right. Given the current scarcity of writings about these technologies in relation to accounting, in this chapter we present a brief review of the development of information processing technologies in organizations, noting specifically the trend towards the automation, integration and standardization of business process bound up with ERP-type technologies. The literature on information technology and organization clearly cautions against making simple cause and effect arguments; however, ERP-type technologies are suggestive of a number of specific developments that we will discuss below. We conclude the chapter with an analysis of the potential implications of such developments for accounting, the role of accountants and the role of accounting academics.

The Evolution of ERP-Type Technologies

A complete history of the introduction of information technology to organizations is beyond the scope of this chapter, however a brief history of the development of corporate information systems is useful. McNurlin and Sprague (1989) briefly outline the major trends that are of particular relevance in understanding the rationale for, and dramatic success of, ERP-type technologies. During the 1960s the introduction of computer technology to business processes took off in areas that involved large-scale routine transaction processing problems (e.g. payroll) using highly centralized mainframe technology. Over time, the range of activities managed through computer technology increased. For example, manufacturing resource planning (MRP) and related systems dealt with production scheduling and inventory management; later on databases tracked information in new areas such as sales and marketing.

During the 1970s discussions arose concerning how computer technologies could be employed not just in transaction or data processing, but about how such vast stores of records could be subsequently used as a source of information. Transaction data could be manipulated in new decision support systems to help managers make better decisions about their businesses. The advent of the personal computer in the 1980s and the development of local area networking technologies supported the development of increasingly sophisticated and localized decision support systems. Taking this decentralizing trend to its logical conclusion, a new form of computing, called 'end-user computing' was hailed as a paradigm shift (Panko 1988). However, such systems complemented rather than superseded previous forms of computing: managers used spreadsheets as well as using centralized systems.

By the early 1990s the business processes of large organizations were supported by many hundreds of separate information systems that had been developed in many different languages and that ran on many different hardware platforms. This fragmented pattern of development was largely the unplanned result of the interaction between a series of technological solutions and perceived business problems. An attempt to impose a façade of structure was brought to organizational information through the development of sophisticated decision support systems such as EIS. These systems were designed to provide senior executives with access to the sea of data that was held in the myriad corporate systems. Often these systems also provided some interpretation of information via tools such as traffic lighting (good numbers were shown in green, bad numbers in red). The advantage of these systems was that business information became available without the need to understand (or even know about) the individual systems in which it was stored.

As notions of corporate strategy took on a less top–down flavour, data warehousing subsequently emerged as a more general form of the EIS idea, aspiring to offer access to all information to potentially everyone in the organization. However, as with EIS before them, data warehouses represented yet another corporate information platform. To carry out their integrative role they performed the complex process of tapping into diverse corporate systems, taking information from them and presenting it in a common format (data scrubbing). Data warehouses were a step forward in terms of enhancing the benefits of corporate information systems but added further to costs. Even with a friendly and easy to access front-end to corporate information, and sophisticated analytical tools, the complexity, diversity, and incompatibility of information systems in most organizations was prohibitively costly to maintain. This fact became particularly apparent in industries such as retail banking. New entrants were unencumbered by (among other things such as a physical branch network) unwieldy 'legacy systems' that required specific and often non-transferable staff skills and training, supported by specific and often non-transferable technical support staff and vendor relationships (Gandy and Chapman 1997).

Enterprise resource planning (ERP) systems emerged as a solution to this problem of fragmentation and incompatibility. A common definition of ERP systems often cited in write-ups of ERP implementations (e.g. Hirt and Swanson 1999) is,

'ERP Software is designed to model and automate many of the basic processes of a company, from finance to the shop floor, with the goal of integrating information across the company and eliminating complex, expensive links between computer systems that were never meant to talk to each other'.

ERP packages such as SAP, took off in popularity with the introduction of a version that ran on client/server technology as opposed to mainframe computers (Scapens 1998). Traditional mainframe technology allowed the technology vendor to restrict customers to buying proprietary peripheral devices (storage units, terminals, printers, etc.) and to using software that was often leased not bought out right. Client/server technology broke this effective monopoly. Secondly with client/server it was much easier and cheaper to add capacity to corporate information system resources as the business grew. Finally the ubiquity of operating systems (such as Windows on PC) meant that the costs of training users were substantially reduced since applications that ran on their desktop PCs (clients) could act as interfaces to corporate information that was managed and stored on larger centralized machines (servers). The growing use of the web browser as the standard interface for data on the Internet and corporate intranets via enterprise information portals (EIP) has continued this trend.

The advantages of ERP systems went beyond the cost of information system provision however. The automation and integration of business processes involved in ERP systems also dramatically changed the way organizations could (must) operate. With an ERP system, a customer placing an order over the phone could receive instant confirmation as their credit limit and the availability of the products they were ordering was automatically checked. If the required product was not available it could be automatically scheduled for manufacture and an immediate estimated delivery date provided. Once the order was confirmed, the system could automatically update the relevant accounting systems and issue an invoice. One person could accomplish tasks that might previously have involved passing information between multiple managers for entry into, and retrieval from, multiple systems. The time taken to accomplish these tasks was also dramatically reduced. Davenport (1998) cites one case in which customer order fulfilment time dropped from 2 weeks to 24 h (cf. OECD 1999 for a comprehensive discussion of efficiency and cost gains supported by new technologies).

Increasingly the rationale behind the ERP system is being applied across the value chain. The ERP concepts of integration and automation can also be seen in electronic procurement systems and supply chain management (SCM) systems; in this case working beyond the boundaries of the firm in the processes of interaction between a company and its suppliers. Such systems allow for the automation of authorization of expenditure, billing, and payment and at the same time ensure the use of chosen suppliers. This has operational benefits in terms of speed and support for purchasing decisions, but on top of these benefits, purchasing information automatically feeds into internal control systems regarding spending limits, budgets, etc., and can also be used as the basis of negotiations regarding price, quality, and delivery terms.

At the other end of the value chain are CRM systems (CRM, also continuous relationship management). One advantage of CRM technology is increased convenience for customers since they can make enquiries and place orders via whatever channel they choose (e.g. phone, e-mail, web page, fax, letter, etc.). Operational-CRM systems feed such requests directly into corporate ERP systems allowing for faster and cheaper service delivery, and for automatic updates on order status, and the automatic processing of invoices and payment. Analytical-CRM systems capture information about customer interactions (such as when they last called for information, when and what they last ordered). The idea is that by presenting the organization with a rich source of information on customer habits and preferences, new products and services can be developed and tailored accordingly. This task is supported by the kind of analytical data mining tools developed for data warehousing.

Another area in which new technologies are introducing automation and integration to business processes is the shared service centre (SSC). Again the SSC approach is claimed to deliver substantial cost reductions for large corporations by replacing the local provision (either within separate divisions or within the company as a whole) of various administrative services such as accounts payable, payroll, technical support, etc. with one centralized service. Under the SSC approach, transaction information from the corporate ERP is automatically fed into the remote systems, allowing the remote management and delivery of necessary but routine services.

Finally, the use of the term e-commerce broadly maps onto the above technologies but implies the use of the Internet as the technological basis of many of the above forms of inter- and intra-firm communication. B2B e-commerce maps broadly onto SCM and SSC, B2C (business to customer) e-commerce onto CRM. Many companies that originally provided ERP systems have either through acquisition or internal development expanded their product range to offer the whole range of ERP-type technologies (e.g. extended-ERP, Plaut (1999*a,b*)).

In summary, the role of information technology in organizations might be seen in terms of three stages. Initially technology was applied to the automation of existing business processes, there followed a concern for the development of decision support capabilities, and contemporary discussions revolve around the ways in which ERP-type technologies might substantially increase the 'virtualization' of organizations and their interactions with others.

ERP-Type Technologies and Standardization

Whilst ERP systems themselves are increasingly considered 'old' (James and Wolf 2000), newer technologies such as CRM and SCM continue, and build on, the distinguishing characteristics of ERP systems. We would argue that the distinctive characteristics of ERP-type technologies are their drive towards the integration, automation, and standardization of business processes.

In the early days of ERP technology the idea of standardization of processes was not always well received, and attempts were made to tailor the package to the processes of the purchasing company. Recent write-ups of ERP implementations (e.g. Austin and Nolan 1998, 1999; Hirt and Swanson 1999) stress that this is now regarded as too expensive. Modifying ERP software is very costly. Modification is time consuming both in the first instance and when it comes to subsequent upgrading of software. Second, it is increasingly regarded as too risky since alterations to ERP packages often invalidate support agreements with the vendor, and given the complexity of ERP software, may well have unanticipated implications for the system once in operation. Vendors increasingly claim that contemporary ERP packages represent best-practice processes that should be adopted by all companies in an industry (e.g. Manchester 2000*a*; Markus 2000).

To say that ERP-type technologies require standardized business processes, however, is not to say that they are inflexible, but that they are flexible in a highly specific way. Over time the major ERP-type vendors have brought out a wide variety of industry specific versions of their products (e.g. SAP offers its product tailored for the specific needs of more than twenty industrial sectors ranging from education to telecommunications). A commonly cited example of the necessity of such industry specific versions would be the very different requirements of business that manufacture discrete products (e.g. industrial components), from those that are process based (e.g. cake mix). Within industry specific packages there are many (in the case of SAP, thousands) tables of options that can be set to adapt the operation of the package to the specifics of the business.

Despite this flexibility, however, the attempt to automate business processes necessitates some standardization. Unlike people, computers can only operate within a precisely structured framework of decision rules. Business processes must be precisely specified. Diversity and flexibility must be expressed formally in terms of parameters of a function, business processes become algorithms, or protocols.

'Before a transaction can be successfully completed, the mandatory SAP document must be created. This occurs only after strict validation of entries. Uniform data structures must be used, and the transaction must obey clear-cut rules about posting. The SAP document identifies the rules used for each line item' (Blain 1999: 25).

ERP-type technologies effectively bring the operating principles of computers and computer networks to organizations and their business processes. The Internet and most of contemporary e-commerce is fundamentally based on the TCP/IP protocol, however, the principle of protocols is long established, and, whilst the detail varies, the principle remains unchanged (e.g. Tanenbaum 1981). Figure 4.1 shows how TCP/IP maps directly onto the much older International Standards Organization (ISO) 7 layer model. This earlier model has established the idea of creating a global set of networking protocols as a means of enabling communication between computers, independently from the many

ISO seven layer model		TCP/IP
(7) Application		Application
(6) Presentation		
(5) Session		
(4) Transport		Transport
(3) Network		Internet
(2) Data Link		Subnet
(1) Physical		

Fig. 4.1. How TCP/IP relates to the earlier ISO seven Layer network model

technologies (both hardware and software) involved. The rationale of both models is to break up the complex task of information transmission into a series of structured tasks grouped together in layers. The purposes of each layer is to provide services to the higher layers, shielding those layers from the details of how the offered services are actually implemented. The layers communicate with each other using established protocols that govern the format and nature of possible interactions.

The result is that the whole range of processes or layers involved in the transmission of information across a computer network are integrated, yet at the same time the individual processes can be managed quite independently subject to compliance with agreed rules for the nature of inputs and outputs. Viewed as a part of the overall process of transmitting information, the specific details of machinery associated with given tasks need not be considered.

To elaborate this idea using less technical language, say for example, that you wish to send a colleague in another institution an email. The operation of layered network protocols means that you do not need to know which email application your colleague uses, nor what kind of local area network (LAN) they are connected to, nor whether the link between their and your LAN is based on twisted pair or fibre optic cabling. The task of sending the email is broken into a series of sequential tasks, which take place in the various layers. This means that your computer, the LAN to which it is connected, or indeed the technology relating to any stage of the process may be replaced, upgraded or changed to improve its performance independently, as long as the new technology supports the agreed protocols for interaction with its neighbouring processes.

This organizing principle of breaking the overall task up into discrete blocks with strictly defined rules for passing inputs and outputs between them allows for what might be considered as integrated-independence. ERP-type technology employs a similar organizing principle to the relationships between business processes. The clarity and accessibility of information regarding the interactions of different modules in an ERP package has opened the way for greater competition in the ERP market. James and Wolf (2000) describe the recent development of middleware products that make it easier to select specific modules from different ERP vendors allowing purchasers to select the individual modules from each vendor that best fit their needs and to make them work together as an integrated system. In the next section we will discuss how this rendering of business processes as protocols presents opportunities for such integrated-independence, supporting new arrangements of organizations, around both traditional and newly emerging value chains.

ERP-Type Technologies, Organizational Form, and Management Control

A major contemporary concern has been the emergence of new forms of organizing. Kraft and Truex (1994) provide an extensive list of possible new organizational forms: virtual enterprise; dissipative organization; imaginary organization; adaptive organization; learning organization; flex firm; agile enterprise; pulsating organization; network organization; and post modern organization. While these terms are not necessarily identical with each other, they all point to an argument that new technologies loosen the constraints on the structure and development of organizations (e.g. Castells 1996; Kaplan and Sawhney 2000).

Castells (1996), for example, discusses the ways in which technology releases organizations from the geographical constraints that frequently required the colocation of very different employees engaged in very different activities (e.g. research and development scientists and telephone clerks). In technology-supported network forms, appropriate physical environments could be selected for individual groups of workers independently of geography, with communication technologies providing the means for integration of their activities. At one extreme the nature of 'appropriate' might simply indicate cheaper (e.g. labour costs), however the concept of the milieu indicates the geographic concentration of various specialist facilities that might support a given type of activity. The classic example here is Silicon Valley.

Some authors have been sceptical about the emergence of such 'virtual' forms however. Winter and Taylor (1996) wonder why, since communications technology that can compress time and space have been around for a long time, should we expect virtualization now? We would argue that the presence of technology is a necessary but not sufficient condition for the emergence of more virtual forms of organizing. The drive towards standardized business processes of ERP-type technologies is a crucial factor in driving 'virtualization' by opening up possibilities for integrated-independence. The barriers to the formation and sustainability of network forms of organizing are lowered through this potential solution to the challenge of co-ordination that network forms create.

Chesbrough and Teece (1996) discuss the issue of coordination in virtual forms, critiquing the notion that fluid organizational forms with constantly forming and reforming relationships will become ubiquitous. They argue that such organizations might be more or less appropriate depending on the nature of innovation and change in an industry. Virtual organizations, they argue, are good at autonomous innovation within a given framework. In terms of the analogy between network protocols and business processes made above, autonomous innovation and process improvement within the operations of particular network members is highly plausible given the detailed protocols determining the characteristics, and patterns of flow, of resources (physical, financial, informational) to be passed between them.

Chesbrough and Teece (1996) go on to point out, however, that this form of organization might be less successful when some systemic change requires the members of the network to respond in a co-ordinated way. Following the analogy, such systemic change would require a rewriting of the protocols that govern interactions between network members. The problem is that we do not yet understand how such a network organization might go about determining what appropriate changes might look like, or making necessary trade-offs between the interests of the constituent parties to the network in effecting change.

Chesbrough and Teece suggest this type of systemic co-ordination might be possible if the network was centred around a strong leader (they cite Toyota as an example) which could impose direction, however as they point out, in such circumstances the networks 'function more like integrated companies than like market-based virtuals'. In making this comparison to integrated companies Chesbrough and Teece (1996) draw attention to the overtly hierarchical nature of such supplier networks. However unlike integrated companies engaged in such activities, the virtual form of operation acts to reduce costs and risks for the major company at the core of the network, pushing uncertainty into the smaller firms that make up the periphery.

The balance of power in the network form described by Castells (1996), and supported by technology driven integrated-independence might be more evenly distributed than in traditional supplier networks described above, however. Balance may be gained since service providers need not be restricted to providing services to only one customer. For example, Shell Services International started as the internal shared service provider to the five key businesses of the Royal Dutch/Shell Group. It is now a separate company that is expected to be profitable as a separate business entity with clients both inside and outside the Shell group of companies. It has offices world-wide and employs 4,700 people (Quinn *et al.* 2000).

The market of corporate function and service provision could potentially become more competitive before a shakeout consolidates the market into one dominated by giant, global service providers. The growth of such multi-organization activity and the development of ERP-type technologies specifically targeting the flow of information between firms has led to the development of organizations that own and manage the ERP-type software and hardware itself, thus adding another organization to the network, the application service provider (ASP).

Such new forms of organization present a major challenge to traditional models of management control based on the dichotomy between centralization and decentralization. Major questions are, how the members of the network enterprise will collectively negotiate a mutually satisfactory strategic direction in the absence of a dominant player to take the role of central co-ordinator, and what role traditional accounting inscriptions will play in the control and emergence of such networks?

In the absence of a dominant actor to provide direction, the solutions to the problem of control presented by many 'virtual enthusiasts' owe much to the work of Burns and Stalker (1961) and their concept of organic organizations. Characteristic features of 'virtual' organizations are the temporary and changing nature of relationships and a facility for flexibility (e.g. Byrne 1993; Creed and Miles 1996; Handy 1995; Miles and Snow 1992), but now between rather than within organizations. As technology advances so the pace of fluidity is argued to increase (Werbach 2000). In writing about the management control issues faced by such organizations authors tend to fall back on the concept of trust as vital.

'In the network form, efforts to apply traditional control mechanisms are generally ineffective. As noted earlier, there is broad agreement that trust requirements are high for networks to perform effectively', Kramer and Tyler (1996: 30).

The ways in which trust either emerges or functions is rarely discussed in detail, however. Yet there is much evidence to suggest that attention to such social aspects of organization is vital. Whilst authors have pointed out the potential for communications technology to allow co-ordinated activity regardless of geographical distance, this ability is constrained by the nature of the interaction between parties. There is a considerable body of work that suggests that the nature and effectiveness of interpretation of business information is heavily dependent on the social context in which it takes place (Boland and Tenkasi 1995; Brown and Duguid 1996, 2000; Chapman 1998; Hill 1991). A traditional problem for new technologies was the issue of how they might complement informal information flows that are often vital in keeping operations working (as highlighted by the effectiveness of 'working to rule' as a form of protest).

With previous forms of technology, individuals were less closely bound to the system, retaining some freedom to depart from standard procedures. Several studies of the introduction of technology to business processes document the desire by users to 'work around' the system (e.g. Austin and Nolan 1999; Orlikowski 1991). Orlikowski (1991) in her study of the introduction of productivity tools into the work of software consultants traces changing working patterns. She describes how consultants would some times engage in 'work arounds' when they wished to try out a speculative idea without being forced by the system to complete all the ancillary documentation until they were certain that it would work. The integration and scope of contemporary ERP-type systems means that operating outside of the embedded business decisions becomes increasingly difficult. Sotto (1997: 39) sums up this issue well,

'When it mediates organizational action in a given domain, information technology tends to dictate the range of strategic choices available rather than those which are humanly assessed'.

As ERP-type technology spreads into more and more aspects of business operation, the impact of their integration, automation, and standardization becomes exponentially more significant as they crowd out informal systems and actions. ERP-type technologies attempt to take 'local' business processes and embed them within themselves. Any idiosyncratic or personal knowledge that used to be bound up with the way in which individuals carried out their assigned roles are analysed and constrained such that they can be expressed through rigorous techniques such as event process mapping (Blain 1999).

ERP-type technologies, therefore shift the balance of significance away from the idiosyncratic local knowledge towards the delivery of standardized outputs based on standardized inputs. Schulze and Boland (2000) are an example of a recent case study that builds on Giddens' (1990) argument that new technologies might disembed social relations from local contexts rendering them independent of time and location.

The ramifications of such disembedding of process are likely to develop over a long period subsequent to the initial technology implementation. In thinking about this, a simple example from the experiences of a university ERP implementation is helpful. Prior to their ERP implementation, individual departments ran their courses and degrees independently. Discussions of student progress took place in the context of a relationship between a student and an expert individual, namely the faculty member allocated to them. With the introduction of the ERP system came a move to standardize course credits across all departments. Once this was achieved it became possible to take marks from different courses and calculate a weighted average mark (WAM). This opened up possibilities for a concise ranking of students that could be used for the distribution of honours to those at the top of the list, and support to those at the bottom. As a result a new post was created specifically to monitor and act on WAMs. Notions of objective evaluation came to transform what had been a local and personalized process, resulting in a reshaping and redistribution of the task of tracking student progress away from academics to administrative staff.

The complex interactions between the technical and the social mean that even in the face of a consistent trend towards standardized processes driven by ERP-type technology, the network form described by Castells is only a possibility, not an imperative. A recent study by Kraut *et al.* (1999) suggests that as yet organizations tend to exhibit network characteristics only in specific areas of operation rather than as an all-embracing organizing principle. Emerging evidence suggests that ERP-type technologies are purchased and subsequently deployed for a wide variety of reasons (e.g. Markus 2000). Commonly documented objectives are integration, automation, and control, but also flexibility, responsiveness, and enhanced decision support. This ambiguity is underscored by the substantial body of work demonstrating the danger of making simple causal argument in relation to technology and organization (Hill 1991; Markus 1997, 2000; Orlikowski 1991; Quattrone and Hopper 2001; Robey and Azviedo 1994; Sotto 1997; Winter and Taylor 1996; Zuboff 1988). Notwithstanding this complexity, in the next section we will consider some of the possible implications of ERP-type technologies for accountants, accounting, and accountability.

Implications for Accountants, Accounting, and Accountability

Zuboff (1988) documents two possible trajectories for occupational groups when information systems are introduced to their work. One possibility is that the information system seeks to directly replace their expertise by incorporating and automating decision-making, downgrading the occupational group away from managerial status. Zuboff refers to this process as automating. A happier (for the occupational group) possibility is what Zuboff refers to as informating, whereby unwanted (often repetitive) aspects of work are automated shifting the nature of remaining work upwards in managerial status as the information system supports enhanced levels of decision-making (both in terms of quantity and quality).

Accountants are used to associating advances in technology with enhancements in their managerial status. With the introduction of early transaction processing systems, accountants were made directly responsible for the management of information technology itself until continuing change and increasing complexity led to the creation of independent IS departments (McNurlin and Sprague 1989). Boland and O'Leary (1988) analyse the way in which advertisements for information technology aimed at accountants explicitly played on the image of technology raising the accountant (predominantly depicted as male) above detail work and gaining new clerical subordinates (predominantly depicted as female) to manage. The quotation that opens this chapter clearly presents technology as a developmental opportunity for accountants.

The way in which ERP-type technologies may change modes of operation in terms of the nature of business processes raises the question of whether or not the historical development of increasingly informated accountants will continue. The spread of ERP-type technologies is predicated on, and an indication of, an increase in the structured representation and operation of business activity. In such an environment we would expect the prevalence and significance of accounting as an organizational practice to increase. Various commentators such as Orlikowski (1991) and Sotto (1997) have discussed how these technologies have the potential to significantly increase control and accountability, creating a solid basis for the creation of virtual panopticons. However, whilst such moves would suggest that accounting as a form of control might well increase its organizational significance, from an institutional perspective there are some potentially very threatening implications for accountants themselves. ERP-type technology can create visibility and accountability automatically through technology, both within organizations, and between them and their stakeholders.

Internal Financial Reporting

Inside organizations the twin aspects of automation and integration that characterize ERP-type technology dramatically reduce the necessity for employing management accountants to collect information, prepare reports, and police adherence to agreed standards and operational procedures. The enhanced possibilities for control, both in terms of reduced scope for individual discretion, and automated monitoring of activity, of integrated information environments has been well documented (Orlikowski 1991; Sotto 1997;

Zuboff 1988). As ERP-type technologies extend their coverage, the metaphor of business as machine becomes increasingly appropriate. Bashein *et al.* (1997), in a series of case studies, carefully draw out the disciplinary effect of built in audit trails and the automatic generation and distribution of exception reports for unauthorized access attempts, etc.

Bashein *et al.* (1997) describe how new technology forces companies to address the question of who should have access to what information head on. Previously this issue could be approached piece-meal or not at all, however, contemporary technology means that without some action, all information might be available to all employees, and potentially all customers and suppliers. The technology does not remove traditional problems such as the separation of responsibility and oversight, but does provide a clear framework within which such issues can be dealt with. Once decided, information access policies are automatically implemented and enforced, with the system itself providing many tools that operate as a kind of self-audit of this process.

Exception reporting can really become just that with the technology automatically generating tailored reports that detail exceptions specified by operational managers. Email warnings can be generated based on the amount of over-spend in absolute or percentage terms, the number of repeat occurrences, and so on. All of these parameters can be set by the managers themselves, without recourse to accountants in collecting or interpreting the resulting information.

Recent studies of the impact of ERP systems on the work of management accountants (e.g. Quattrone and Hopper 2001; Westrup 2000) point to the problems caused by the shifting areas of responsibility brought about through the implementation of ERP systems. Both cases discuss how ERP systems can perversely create significant data integrity problems. Prior to the implementation of such systems operational managers may have thought of their role as purely operational, with others (such as accountants), having responsibility for the reporting of information regarding their activities. Once ERP-type technologies are in place however, operational managers must adapt to the fact that their interactions with the system are automatically captured and distributed. So if they mistakenly enter an invoice amount it may be fed directly and immediately into their budget, the materials ordering system, etc.

The process of adaption to ERP-type technologies is made more difficult by the frequent imposition of new vocabularies to describe existing and re-engineered processes. For example, one major ERP product will not allow the term 'department' which must be labelled instead 'cost centre'. The same package requires the use of the standard term 'materials' (as opposed to a more specific label such as books for a publisher, say). Even where such systems allow for the customization of terminology, the cost of making such changes means that it is often easier to 'just stick with what the system says'.

One of the promises of ERP-type technologies was the ability to access previously disparate sources of information to gain valuable insights into key business processes or customer buying habits through data mining. However, given the efforts required to learn new ways of interacting with both systems and colleagues, using new vocabularies, it seems likely that it may be some time before the initial promise of the technology can begin to be fulfilled. Another stumbling block here is the current unfriendliness of the interfaces of standard ERP systems. Current developments mean that increasingly users can use a spreadsheet type interface to access corporate data, but unfamiliarity with the means to query data is likely to provide a role for management accountants for some time.

The discussion above suggests that whilst much management accounting work might become automated, issues of managing data integrity and basic information retrieval may well increase to compensate. As such the outlook for management accountants may not seem threatening. ERP-type technologies may ultimately have a significant impact on existing management accounting career structures by creating a new set of relationships between management accountants and other managers, however.[2]

A significant area of such disturbance relates to the provision of accounting services via a single SSC. Richison *et al.* (1997) reported that management accounting was the largest area of growth in outsourcing activity, Cecil (2000) cites outsourcing and standardization of services as major objectives of the SSC approach. Fulk and DeSanctis (1995) argue that issues of cost management and control lie behind much outsourcing activity, since outsourcing turns fixed costs into variable ones presenting organizations with more flexibility, but further reinforces the drive towards standardization of process through the requirement to negotiate a service level agreement.

We can understand the relationship between this growth in outsourcing and ERP-type technologies better by looking at the findings of Widener and Selto (1999). These authors examined the reasons behind the decision to outsource (or not) the internal audit function. As predicted by the transaction cost economics literature, they found a strong negative correlation between asset specificity and outsourcing of internal audit. ERP-type technologies, by introducing standardization and disembedding local idiosyncrasies act to reduce the local specificity of such services.

Some aspects of management accounting will be more susceptible than others to provision via SSC, in particular the more mundane reporting aspects (e.g. such as managing data integrity, and basic system support discussed above). The trend described above towards the automation or outsourcing of routine aspects of management accounting will very likely appeal to contemporary management accountants who are dismissive of 'just reporting' and are constantly seeking to develop the more strategic, business advisory aspects of their work (Ahrens and Chapman 2000). However, whilst contemporary

---

[2] Although as documented in Quattrone and Hopper (2001) ERP systems may, with sufficient effort, attempt to reproduce a pre-existing set of relationships.

management accountants may well benefit from such a shift, the implications for management accountants as an occupational group are potentially worrying.

Current entry-level management accounting jobs in large organizations involve a considerable amount of 'just reporting'. Through carrying out such tasks management accountants develop an intimate knowledge of idiosyncratic local processes and how to accommodate them. Over time, and as higher levels of professional examinations are passed, management accountants work progresses onto systems dealing with new areas of a business and ultimately onto more analytical work that offers opportunities for greater interpretation of information as well as its provision. A clear aspect of contemporary career structures within large organizations is that trainee management accountants frequently move through a variety of placements. Contemporary British management accountants frame their career development in terms of the search for exposure to new and relevant experience (Ahrens and Chapman 2000).

Whilst ERP-type technology enables the global and instantaneous flow of information, this information will require considerable interpretative and analytical skills. Contemporary management accountants can claim to act as a strategic advisor based on their past experiences and relationships, but the basis of future generations' claims to expertise may be undermined by ERP-type developments such as the SSC. If increasing amounts of reporting work are automated and centralized in corporate SSCs, or worse still in out-sourced ones, this career development path may disappear. Entry-level management accounting jobs may no longer take place at all, or may take place in separate companies that cannot offer the same route to advancement through intimate exposure to operational issues. In as much as contemporary management accountants may currently provide valuable interpretations of corporate performance and positioning, such changes are not simply of concern to the accounting profession itself.

External Financial Reporting

ERP-type technologies also present the possibility of major changes in the sphere of financial reporting. A commonly reported reason for investment in ERP-type technologies is the opportunities they represent to introduce firm-wide (often global) corporate charts of accounts (Austin and Nolan 1998, 1999; Bashein *et al.* 1997). A common corporate chart of accounts allows for quicker, cheaper, and faster corporate consolidated accounting. An interesting step towards the development of a truly global chart of accounts is the extended business reporting language (XBRL) developed by the AICPA together with 30 other organizations including accounting regulatory bodies, public practice firms, and technology vendors (Wright 2000). The project is not yet complete, but their eight level taxonomy of business reporting categories is freely downloadable from their web site (www.xbrl.org) for study and comment.

The development of XBRL paves the way for ERP-type management of the financial reporting process. The project aims to standardize the categories of financial reporting, promising enormous leaps forward in the timeliness, accessibility, and cost of corporate reporting of financial information. The approach reduces cost not just in terms of automating much calculation, but also by supporting the easy distribution of resulting information through a variety of channels, from the traditional annual report to the corporate web page. If companies (or third parties) made available XBRL information via their web sites, then it would be a small step to develop applications that could instantly retrieve a company's financial information, apply US GAAP, IASC etc., accounting standards, and generate appropriate financial statements.

The widespread use of such technology would introduce a new dynamics into the accounting standards harmonization debate. A more radical possibility is that XBRL might potentially displace existing institutions responsible for the development of accounting standards altogether. At present bodies such as FASB, IASC, etc. present in their various standards a portfolio of accounting decisions relating to many different areas. Under the current technology of reporting users must opt for a set of accounts that complies with the entire portfolio, or engage in a laborious process of adjustments. Just as middleware has allowed users to mix and match between the modules of different ERP-vendors, a format such as XBRL could allow users to selectively choose the accounting conventions they wish to apply, or even to entirely make up their own. Clearly in the past such analysis was possible, but the widespread use of an XML format to provide corporate financial information would make such analysis virtually effortless.

Implications for Research

In this chapter we have argued that ERP-type technologies might encourage a change in the shape of firms and the flow of their business processes, facilitating new forms of inter-firm co-operation and embedding business processes within technology. In short, ERP-type network technology might help to promote network enterprises. ERP-type technology has brought about economies of speed, scope (through promotion of downstream, upstream, and sideways integration), size (through promotion of globalization). It has achieved some degree of spatial compression. However there is a limit to the efficiencies achieved. The efficiencies of ERP-type technology that require standardization also mean the potential loss of idiosyncratic flexibility re-emphasizing the importance of face-to-face contact. That would explain the evidence of technopoles (Castells and Hall 1994). These authors suggest that spatial proximity continues to matter; it is important to travel up to Tokyo or Silicon Valley to promote innovation. These new technologies threaten to disintermediate accountants' traditional roles. Understanding these new organizational dynamics of innovation and control will be vital for accountants if they are to sustain the organizational significance they currently enjoy.

Even where the technologies themselves might be considered mature, studies have shown that their organizational consequences vary, between organizations and across time (Markus 2000; Quattrone and Hopper 2001). For example, Markus (2000) reports that whilst sophisticated data mining was the rationale for many data warehousing projects it is not yet a widespread practice. Instead, many such systems fulfil the role of streamlining existing internal reporting processes. In the case of ERP, at the time of writing there is virtually no published material that studies accounting and this technology. This article has drawn together research from a number of fields and attempted to sketch out some of the issues that these new technologies raise for accounting and accountants. The need for research into these issues in accounting is great since ERP-type technologies (and others) are rapidly spreading and at the same time evolving.

Markus (1997) calls for the acceptance in the information systems literature of research that takes the form of scientific observation informed by understanding of technology. Whilst the developments and implications that we suggest are clearly susceptible to examination from a number of perspectives, we would suggest that all of the above points towards the need for direct and careful analysis of these issues in the field. The call for more field-studies in accounting is hardly new, however, the development and increasing spread of ERP-type technologies, with their potential to radically alter the field of accounting, does add a new urgency. In relation to this final point, it is worth considering that for those interested in the study of accounting, it is increasingly unclear that making accountants and their work the focus of research is appropriate. ERP-type technologies enhance and support the structured representation and management of activity, and so would seem to increase the organizational significance of accounting, however, at the same time these technologies raise serious questions as to whether or not such accounting activity will be carried out by accountants in the future.

References

Ahrens, T. and Chapman, C. (2000), 'Occupational Identity of Management Accountants in Britain and Germany', *European Accounting Review*, 9/4: 477–98.

Austin, D. and Nolan, R. (1998), *Cisco Systems, Inc.: Implementing ERP*, Harvard Business School Case 9-699-022.

————(1999), *Tektronix, Inc.: Global ERP Implementation*, Harvard Business School Case 9-699-043.

Bashein, B., Markus, L., and Finley, J. (1997), *Safety Nets: Secrets of Effective Information Technology Controls* (Financial Executives Research Foundation).

Blain, J. (1999) *Special Edition Using SAP R/3*, 3rd edn (Indianapolis, IN: QUE).

Boland and O'Leary (1988), 'Behind the accountant: Images of accounting and information machines in advertising 1910–1970', Working paper, Urbana Champagne.

Boland and Tenkasi (1995), 'Perspective Making and Perspective Taking in Communities of Knowing', *Organization Science*, 4/6: 350–72.

Brown, J. S. and Duguid, P. (1996), 'Organizational Learning and Communities-of-Practice: Toward a Unified View of Working, Learning, and Innovation', in M. Cohen and L. Sproull (eds), *Organizational Learning* (London: Sage), 58–82.

————(2000), *The Social Life of Information* (Cambridge, MA: Harvard Business School Press).

Burns, T. and Stalker, G. M. (1961), *The Management of Innovation* (Tavistock).

Byrne, J. (1993), 'The Virtual Corporation', *Business Week*, (February 8th): 37–41.

Castells, M. and Hall, P. (1994), *Tecnopoles of the World: The Makings of 21st Century Industrial Complexes*. London: Routledge.

Castells, M. (1996), *The Rise of the Network Society* (Oxford: Blackwell).

Cecil, R. (2000), 'At your Service', *Management Accounting*, 78/07: 32–3.

Chapman, C. S. (1998), 'Accountants in Organisational Networks', *Accounting, Organizations and Society*, 23/8: 737–66.

Chesbrough, H. and Teece, D. (1996), 'When is Virtual Virtuous?', *Harvard Business Review*, 74/1: 65–73.

Cooper, R. and Kaplan, R. (1998) The Promise—and Peril—of Integrated Cost Systems, *Harvard Business Review*, (July–August): 109–19.

Creed, W. and Miles, R. (1996), 'Trust in Organizations: A Conceptual Framework Linking Organizational Forms, Managerial Philosophies, and the Opportunity Costs of Controls', in R. Kramer and T. Tyler (eds), *Trust in Organizations: Frontiers of theory and research* (London: Sage), 16–38.

Davenport, T. (1998), 'Putting the Enterprise into the Enterprise System', *Harvard Business Review* (July–August): 121–31.

Fahy, M. and Lynch, R. (1998), '*Enterprise Resource Planning (ERP) Systems and Strategic Management Accounting*', paper presented at EAA conference, Bordeaux, France.

Fulk, J. and DeSanctis, G. (1995), 'Electronic Communication and Changing Organizational Forms', *Organization Science*, 6/4: 337–49.

Gandy, T. and Chapman, C. (1997), 'Data Warehousing—Unleashing the Power of Customer Information', *Chartered Banker*, 3/5: 10–42.

Giddens, A. (1990) *The Consequences of Modernity* (Stanford, CA: Stanford University Press).

Handy, C. (1995), 'Trust and the Virtual Organization', *Harvard Business Review* (May–June): 40–50.

Hill, S. (1991), 'Technological Change and the Systematisation of Organizational Culture', in S. Aungles (ed.), *Information Technology in Australia* (New South Wales University Press), 92–112.

Hirt, S. G. and Swanson, E. B. (1999), 'Adopting SAP at Siemens Power Corporation', *Journal of Information Technology*, 14: 234–51.

Institute of Management Accountants (1999), '*Counting More, Counting Less: Transformations in the Management Accounting Profession*.

James, D. and Wolf, M. (2000) 'New Life from an Old System', *McKinsey Quarterly* (May 5th): 88–91.

Kaplan, R. and Johnson, R. (1987), '*Relevance Lost: The Rise and Fall of Management Accounting* (Harvard Business School Press).

Kaplan, S. and Sawhney, M. (2000), 'E-Hubs: The New B2B Marketplaces', *Harvard Business Review* (May–June): 97–103.

Kraft, P. and Truex, D. (1994), 'Post-Modern Management and Information Technology in the Modern Industrial Corporation', *IFIP Transactions, Transforming Organizations with Information Technology*, A-49: 113–27.

Kraut, R., Steinfeld, C., Chan, A., Butler, B., and Hoag, A. (1999), 'Coordination and Virtualisation: The Role of Electronic Networks and Personal Relationships', *Organization Science*, 10/6: 722–40.

Manchester, P. (2000a), 'Rich Rewards Yet to be Unlocked', *Financial Times Survey: E-Business and Beyond* (July 19th): I.

——(2000b), 'The ABC of TLAs...', *Financial Times Survey: E-Business and Beyond* (July 19th): II.

Markus, L. (1997), 'The Qualitative Difference in Information Systems Research and Practice', in A. S. Lee, J. Liebenau, and J. I. DeGross (eds), *Information Systems and Qualitative Research* (Chapman Hall).

——(2000), 'Conceptual Challenges in Contemporary IS Research', *Communications of the Association of Information Systems*, 3 (February, Article 4): 1–15.

McNurlin, B. and Sprague, R. (1989), *Information Systems Management in Practice*, 2nd edn (Prentice Hall).

Miles, R. and Snow, C. (1992) 'Causes of Failure in Network Organisations', *California Management Review*, 34/4: 53–72.

OECD (1999), *The Economic and Social Impact of Electronic Commerce* (Organization for Economic Co-operation and Development).

Orlikowski, W. (1991), 'Integrated Information Environment or Matrix of Control? The Contradictory Implications of Information Technology', *Accounting, Management and Information Technology*, 1/1: 9–42.

Panko, R. (1988), *End User Computing: Management Applications and Technology* (John Wiley & Sons).

Plaut (1999a), *Increasing Business Performance Through ERP* (Plaut International Management Consulting White Paper).

Plaut (1999b) *eBusiness or No Business* (Plaut International Management Consulting White Paper).

Quattrone, P. and Hopper, T. (2001), 'What Does Organizational Change Mean? Speculations on a Taken for Granted Category', *Management Accounting Research*, 12: 403–35.

Quinn, B., Cooke, R., and Kris, A. (2000), *Shared Services. Mining for Corporate Gold* (Pearson Education Limited).

Richison, T., Duff, P. and O'Neill, M. (1997), 'Daring to Outsource the Financial Functions: A Call for Help', *Financial Executive*, 13/6: 16–21.

Robey, D. and Azvedo, A. (1994), 'Cultural Analysis of the Organizational Consequences of Information Technology', *Accounting, Management and Information Technology*, 4/1: 23–37.

Scapens, R. (1998), 'SAP: Integrated Information Systems and the Implications for Management Accountants', *Management Accounting*, 76/8: 46–8.

Schulze, U. and Boland, R. (2000), 'Place, Space and Knowledge Work: A Study of Outsourced Computer System Administrators', *Accounting, Management and Information Technologies*, 10/3: 187–219.

Sotto, R. (1997), 'The Virtual Organization', *Accounting, Management and Information Technology*, 7/1: 37–51.

Tanenbaum, A. S. (1981), *Computer Networks* (Prentice Hall).

Widener, S. and Selto, F. (1999), 'Management Control Systems and Boundaries of the Firm: Why do Firms Outsource Internal Auditing Activities?', *Journal of Management Accounting Research*, 11: 45–73.

Werbach, K. (2000), 'Syndication—The Emerging Model for Business in the Internet Era', *Harvard Business Review* (May–June): 85–93.

Westrup, C. (2000), 'Enterprise Resource Planning Systems and the role of Management Accountants: Aspiration and Evidence', paper presented at Management Accounting Research Group Conference, London School of Economics, 6th April.

Winter, S. and Taylor, J. (1996), 'The Role of IT in the Transformation of Work: A Comparison of Post-Industrial and Proto-Industrial Organization', *Information Systems Research*, 7/1: 5–21.

Wright, I. (2000), 'Parlez-Vous XML ou XBRL', *Accountancy*, 125: 72–3.

Zuboff, S. (1988) *In the Age of the Smart Machine: The Future of Work and Power* (New York: Basic Books).

5
Expenditures on Competitor Analysis and Information Security
A Managerial Accounting Perspective
Lawrence A. Gordon and Martin P. Loeb

Introduction

As economies around the world are becoming ever more information based, all aspects of business operations are facing significant challenges and opportunities. Management accounting is no exception in this regard. Indeed, management accounting is experiencing an identity transformation. This transformation is the result of the fact that the Internet, plus related developments like data mining techniques, have given 'information power' to everyone in an organization. Thus, management accounting researchers and practitioners no longer have a monopoly on designing and using information systems for organizational planning and control. If management accounting is going to survive the twenty-first century, it is essential for the field to stake out a claim in this information-wired economy.

Management accounting researchers have a keen interest in studying the interplay among information, strategy, and managerial decision-making. Two aspects of the information economy that have particular relevance to this area of interest for management accounting are competitor analysis (CA) and information security (IS). Accounting researchers and practitioners have already shown an interest in pursuing these areas. Nevertheless, with the exception of Gordon and Loeb (2001), little has been done to link CA and IS. The key purposes of this chapter are to build upon the Gordon and Loeb (2001) work, by modelling the strategic relation between expenditures on CA and IS, and to show that management accounting issues play a central role in effectively understanding the link between CA and IS. Hence, the strategic relation between CA and IS seems to be one more important area in the information economy in which management accounting researchers and practitioners (in their role as business advisors/consultants) should stake out a claim.

The authors wish to thank Duane Helleloid for comments on an earlier version of this chapter. Financial support for this research was provided in part by a grant form the National Security Agency's Laboratory for Telecommunications under the University of Maryland Institute for Advanced Computer Studies (UMIACS).

Competitor Analysis and Information Security

Competitor Analysis

Organizational strategy refers to the way a firm positions itself relative to the competition. Thus, organizational strategy involves analysing the competition and seeing where your firm can gain a competitive advantage. The process of collecting, analysing, and using information about market rivals (i.e. competitors) in order to enhance a firm's strategic position and, in turn, its profitability is referred to as CA. In the academic literature, research dealing with the strategic aspects of CA is usually traced to Porter (1980, 1985). The strategy oriented literature on CA is now quite extensive (e.g. Chen 1996; Chen and Miller 1994; Ghoshal and Westney, 1991; MacMillan *et al.* 1985; Miller and Chen 1994; Prescott and Smith 1987; Young, 1987; Zajac and Bazerman 1991). Data mining specialists, who focus on analysing large sets of data, have also become interested in CA activities (e.g. Hirji 2001). CA activities within organizations have led to the emergence of the Society of Competitive Intelligence Professionals (SCIP), an organization for professionals working in the field. The SCIP membership is both large and rapidly growing.

Accounting researchers, including management accounting researchers, have also become interested in CA (e.g. Bromwich 1990; Guilding 1999; Jones 1988; Shank and Govindarajan 1988,1992; Simmonds 1982, 1986). In essence, accounting researchers and practitioners have focused on analysing the accounting-related data of competitors. The more a firm knows about the operations of its competitors, as reflected in the accounting data, the better its chances of successfully competing with such competitors. Bromwich (1990: 44) makes this point when he writes, '... accountants should not restrict their attention to the cost structure of the firm for which they work. They, additionally, need to focus on the cost structures of all firms in the market and those likely to enter the market.' Indeed, CA of such management accounting issues as revenues, cost structure, asset composition, and margin of safety can be of immense help in gaining a competitive advantage.

The wealth of firm-specific data now available on the Internet has greatly enhanced what can be gleaned from CA activities related to management accounting issues. For example, by using the US Securities and Exchange Commission (SEC) EDGAR database (see www.SEC.gov), one can easily gather enough data to run simple regression models to derive a ball-park figure of a competitor's cost structure, breakeven point (in sales) and margin of safety. In addition to the firm-specific data gathered by such organizations as the SEC, there are millions of individual bits of information being transmitted about firms on a daily basis. These bits of information trickle out in articles in the newspapers, professional magazines, and public statements made by company executives. The analysis of these bits of information, via modern data mining techniques, can also facilitate the CA activities of a firm.

Guilding (1999) provides empirical evidence on the use and perceived helpfulness of management accounting related CA activities. In particular, based on a questionnaire survey of 230 New Zealand-based companies, he finds that the following five management accounting related CA activities are in greater use than suggested by the limited management accounting literature in the area: (i) competitor cost assessment, (ii) competitive position monitoring, (iii) competitor appraisal based on published financial statements, (iv) strategic positioning and (v) strategic costing. He also finds evidence that the demand for these management accounting related activities exceeds the supply of information on these activities.

Information Security

The term information security (IS), as used in this chapter, is broadly interpreted to include the following activities: (a) protecting information from unauthorized users, (b) making information available on a timely basis to authorized users, (c) protecting information from integrity flaws, and (d) detecting information security breaches, if, and when, they occur. Managers, engineers, computer scientists, and others who face the day to day responsibility for information security in organizations, naturally have a strong practical interest in IS issues. Most of the academic work on IS has been done by computer scientists and engineers. Their research is centred around the technical design issues (e.g. use of encryption, access controls, and firewalls) aimed at reducing the frequency of security breaches (e.g. see Denning and Branstad 1996; Sandhu *et al.* 1996; Simmons 1994). In addition to computer scientists and engineers, academicians specializing in management issues have done research in the IS field. This line of research focuses on the behavioural aspects of preventing IS breaches (e.g. Straub 1990; Straub and Welke 1998).

The importance of information security in an information-based economy cannot be overstated. Indeed, an entire field of research, education, and practice has emerged to meet the demands related to information security issues. There are now numerous academic and professional journals devoted exclusively to issues surrounding information security. Many universities are now offering graduate degrees in the area and various professional organizations have been created to bring together practitioners in the field. In this latter regard, the Computer Security Institute (CSI) is probably (or at least it claims to be) the 'leading international membership organization created specifically for information security professionals' (*Computer Security Journal*, 2003: i).

Accounting researchers and practitioners, including those in management accounting (a field centred around the design, use, and control of information systems), have also shown an interest in information security (e.g., Gordon and Loeb 2002). Much of this work falls under the heading of information assurance or assurance services (e.g. Elliott and Pallais 1997; King and Schwartz 1997). The information assurance perspective, which is closely aligned with the attestation function in auditing, tends to focus on providing guarantees of an information system's security, rather than on the activities associated with making the system secure. Of course, the distinction between information security and information assurance is blurred, at best, and so these terms are often used interchangeably. In fact, consulting activities (by both accounting and non-accounting firms) in the area are usually performing services of both an information security and information assurance (as defined above) nature. For the purposes of this chapter, we use the term information security to include all the activities related to securing, and guaranteeing such security, of an information system (i.e. we use information security as the generic term to include assurance services).

There can be little doubt that accounting (including management accounting) practitioners have recognized the opportunity afforded them in the area of information security by the transformation of the economy to one that is information based. In this regard, assurance services provided by practising accountants often adhere to the Control Objectives for Information and related Technology (COBIT) standards developed by the Information Systems Audit and Control Foundation (see http://www.isaca.org/cobit.htm). In terms of research opportunities, McCracken (2000: 83) states it well when she notes that, 'The market for information systems assurance is fairly young and therefore a prime area for research... A better understanding of this area is essential for both practitioners and academics as we determine the optimal strategy for proceeding in this area... It is also a market where CAs/CPAs are expected to have a competitive advantage (SysTrust).' Joel Demski, the current president of the American Accounting Association and one of the world's leading management accounting researchers, recommends that information assurance be an integral part of a university education in accounting (Demski 2002: 1, 3). Contemporary textbooks in auditing have already begun the process of integrating information assurance services into the educational process for accounting students (e.g. Kinney 2000; Messier 2003).

Combining CA and IS

From the above discussion, one can see that individually CA and IS activities provide exciting opportunities for the field of accounting in general, and management accounting in particular, in prevalent information-based economy. These opportunities have been recognized and some management accountants are starting to stake out a claim in these areas. Nevertheless, the fields of CA and IS essentially have developed as two distinct areas. One noted exception in this regard is the paper by Gordon and Loeb (2001) (hereafter referred to as GL). GL argue that, although the fields of CA and IS have developed as distinct fields, these fields are logically linked. They pursue this argument by noting that firms which engage in CA activities should also expect to be a target of the CA systems of their market rivals. Furthermore, they also point out that a natural response to CA is for firms to devote some of their resources to

IS in order to reduce likelihood that strategic information will reach the hands of competitors. In this regard, GL (2001: 41) argue that '...the more your competitors analyze your firm's activities, the more valuable it becomes for your firm to view information security as a competitive response'.

In essence, GL suggest that there is a game theoretic connection between the IS expenditure decisions of one firm and the CA expenditure decisions of rival firms. GL's argument is consistent with the view expressed by Zajac and Bazerman (1991: 39), when they note that, 'A major potential contribution of game theory to the strategic management area is the recognition that competitive actors need to fully consider the contingent decisions that other parties will make.' GL's view is also consistent with the 'attacker–attackee' view expressed in the computer security literature. For example, Jajodia and Millen (1993: 85) note that, 'Computer security is a kind of game between two parties, the designer of a secure system, and a potential attacker.' As of 2003, however, the game theoretic aspects of CA and IS have not been modelled. By providing such a model, with particular emphasis on the implications for expenditure decisions related to CA and IS, it becomes clear that management accounting concepts are essential elements of the game-theoretic framework proposed by GL. Thus, the information-wired economy offers yet another exciting opportunity for management accounting. To better understand this opportunity, we next present the model and then discuss its implications.

The Model

We examine a setting in which two rivals share a lucrative (i.e. profitable) market. Each of the two firms must decide on the amount to spend for CA and the amount to invest in IS. Each firm's expenditures on CA enables the firm to capture a portion of the market's profits currently earned by the firm's rival, less the cost of the firm's expenditures on CA. Expenditures on IS by a firm serve a number of functions, including reducing the threat that the firm's information system will be breached by the firm's rival or by others (e.g. malicious individuals who hack without any monetary incentive to do so). In the absence of CA activity by its rival, each firm would find it optimal to spend some positive amount on IS. By investing in IS beyond this benchmark level, a firm can diminish the effectiveness of their rival's expenditures on CA. In making the decision to invest in this incremental IS, the cost and effectiveness of IS need to be considered. In such a setting, expenditures on CA merely partition the market but do not expand it. Hence, the optimal joint (cooperative) solution would be for both rivals to make no expenditures on CA and to make no *incremental* expenditures on IS (i.e. no expenditures beyond the benchmark levels). However, in the absence of such cooperation, determination of the levels of expenditures on CA and IS may be analysed by viewing the situation as one of a non-cooperative zero-sum game.

Consider a market in which fixed profits of K are initially divided between two rival firms. Firm 1's initial profits are denoted as $\theta_1 K$, where $\theta_1 = \theta \in (0,1)$

and firm 2's initial profits are denoted as $\theta_2 K$, where $\theta_2 = (1 - \theta)$. Let $C_i \geq 0$ represent firm i's expenditures on CA and, for $i = 1, 2$, let $P_i \geq 0$ (for protection) represent firm i's (*incremental*) expenditures on IS (beyond the benchmark level). Each firm selects a level of CA in hopes of attaining some of the profits initially secured by its rival. Similarly, each firm selects a level of IS in order to reduce the effectiveness of the rival's expenditures on CA. Furthermore, we let $\alpha \in (0,1)$ be a constant representing the maximum portion of a firm's initial profits that could be lost to a rival that rationally selects its level of expenditures on CA. That is, each firm, knowing that its rival acts rationally, would be confident that $1 - \alpha$ of its initial share of profits would not be taken away by its rival through CA. One may think of α as a measure of the productivity of CA. For simplicity, we assume that α is the same for both firms.

The profit function of each of the two rivals is composed of five parts. The first part is $\theta_i K$, the firm's initial profits. The second part is the firm's gain from its expenditures on CA, gross of the firm's CA costs, denoted $R_i(C_i, P_j|$ $\alpha, \theta, K)$, where $i, j = 1, 2$ and $j \neq i$. We assume that each $R_i(\cdot)$ function is sufficiently smooth, that is, has continuous first and second partial derivatives; that as C_i increases, that is, as the firm increases it expenditures on CA, $R_i(\cdot)$ increases at decreasing rate; and as P_j increases, that is, as the rival firm increases its expenditures on IS, $R_i(\cdot)$ decreases at decreasing rate. Furthermore, $R_i(\cdot)$ increases with (*a*) increases of α, the maximum fraction of the rival firm's initial profits that the firm could take by rationally investing in CA activities, (*b*) increases in total market profits, K, and (*c*) increases in the firm's initial profit share, θ_i (hence, $R_1(\cdot)$ increases in θ and $R_2(\cdot)$ decreases in θ). The third part of firm i's profit function is the loss from firm j's CA activities, $-R_j(C_j, P_i| \alpha, \theta, K)$, where $i, j = 1, 2$ and $j \neq i$. The final two parts of the firm i's profit function are the reduction in profits due to expenditures for CA and IS, $-C_i$ and $-P_i$, respectively. Thus, firm 1's profits can be written as:

$$\Pi_1(C_1, P_1, C_2, P_2) = \theta K + R_1(C_1, P_2| \alpha, \theta, K)$$
$$- R_2(C_2, P_1| \alpha, \theta, K) - C_1 - P_1 \qquad (1)$$

and firm 2's profits can be written as:

$$\Pi_2(C_1, P_1, C_2, P_2) = (1 - \theta)K + R_2(C_2, P_1| \alpha, \theta, K)$$
$$- R_1(C_1, P_2| \alpha, \theta, K) - C_2 - P_2 \qquad (2)$$

Note that $\Pi_1(C_1, P_1, C_2, P_2) + \Pi_2(C_1, P_1, C_2, P_2) = K - C_1 - P_1 - C_2 - P_2$, so that from a social welfare viewpoint, expenditures on CA and IS represents a lump sum loss. Similarly, the two rivals acting cooperatively would set $C_1 = P_1 = C_2 = P_2 = 0$. However, the trouble with such a cooperative solution is that each rival would have an incentive to cheat on such an agreement and invest in CA (assuming that such an investment were unobservable by the rival firm).

We model the expenditure game being played by the two rivals as a noncooperative static game of complete information. Hence, each firm knows both profit functions (1) and (2), although each firm does not know its rival's choice of level of expenditures on CA and IS at the time it makes its own CA and IS decisions. The Nash equilibrium of this game gives predicted levels of each firm's expenditures on CA and IS such that each firm's expenditures are the optimal response to the predicted expenditures of their rival. As an intermediate step in the calculation of the Nash equilibrium, we examine firm i's reaction curves, $\hat{C}_i(P_j)$ and $\hat{P}_i(C_j)$. These curves specify how the firm would optimally react to the levels of expenditures on IS and CA of the rival firm j (if firm i were to know these levels at the time of its CA and IS decisions). Note from equations (1) and (2) that each firm's optimal reaction expenditure level of CA is independent of the rival's choice of expenditure level on CA and that the firm's optimal reaction expenditure level of IS is independent of the rival's choice of expenditure level on IS. Firm i's reaction curves $\hat{C}_i(P_j)$ and $\hat{P}_i(C_j)$ are determined by maximizing $\Pi_i(C_1, P_1, C_2, P_2)$ with respect to C_i and P_i, and are (for interior, that is, strictly positive, solutions) implicitly defined by the first-order conditions:

$$\frac{\partial R_i(\hat{C}_i(P_j), P_j \mid \alpha, \theta, K)}{\partial C_i} - 1 = 0 \tag{3}$$

and

$$\frac{\partial R_j(C_j, \hat{P}_i(C_j) \mid \alpha, \theta, K)}{\partial P_i} + 1 = 0 \tag{4}$$

for $i, j = 1, 2$, $i \neq j$. To ensure each firm would rationally select a level of expenditures on CA such that the fraction $1 - \alpha$ of each firm's initial profits will not be taken away by the rival's CA activities, we assume $R_i(\hat{C}_i(0), 0 \mid \alpha, \theta, K) \leq \alpha \theta_j K$ for $i, j = 1, 2$, $i \neq j$. That is, if firm j selects not to invest in CA or IS ($C_j = P_j = 0$), then firm $i \neq j$, is assumed to be able to increase its profits, gross of its cost of CA, by at most $\alpha \theta_j K$. Note that since $R_i(\hat{C}_i(P_j), P_j \mid \alpha, \theta, K) \leq R_i(\hat{C}_i(P_j), 0 \mid \alpha, \theta, K) \leq R_i(\hat{C}_i(0), 0 \mid \alpha, \theta, K)$, our assumption implies that $R_i(\hat{C}_i(P_j), P_j \mid \alpha, \theta, K) \leq \alpha \theta_j K$ for $i, j = 1, 2$, $i \neq j$. The reaction curves $\hat{C}_1(P_2)$ and $\hat{P}_2(C_1)$ will together determine the Nash equilibrium values C_1^* and P_2^*; similarly, the reaction curves $\hat{C}_2(P_1)$ and $\hat{P}_1(C_2)$ will together determine the Nash equilibrium values C_2^* and P_1^*.

In order to gain insights about the nature of the equilibrium, we examine a class of R_1 and R_2 functions with specific functional forms consistent with the general forms discussed above. In particular, we specify the profit functions for firm 1 and firm 2 as:

$$\Pi_1(C_1, P_1, C_2, P_2) = \theta K + 2\sqrt{C_1}\left[\sqrt{\frac{\alpha(1-\theta)K}{2}} - \sqrt{\beta P_2}\right] - C_1$$

$$-2\sqrt{C_2}\left[\sqrt{\frac{\alpha\theta K}{2}} - \sqrt{\beta P_1}\right] - P_1 \tag{5}$$

and

$$\Pi_2(C_1, P_1, C_2, P_2) = (1 - \theta)K + 2\sqrt{C_2}\left[\sqrt{\frac{\alpha\theta K}{2}} - \sqrt{\beta P_1}\right] - C_2$$

$$-2\sqrt{C_1}\left[\sqrt{\frac{\alpha(1 - \theta)K}{2}} - \sqrt{\beta P_2}\right] - P_2 \qquad (6)$$

where $\beta > 0$ is a parameter measuring the efficiency of the protection (IS) system. As β increases (decreases) the effectiveness of expenditures on information security increases (decreases). As with the parameter for the efficiency of the CA system, for simplicity, we use one parameter for the efficiency of each of the rivals IS system.

The reaction curves $\hat{C}_1(P_2)$ and $\hat{C}_2(P_1)$ (derived from the first-order conditions corresponding to equation (3) together with the second-order conditions $\partial^2\Pi_i/\partial C_i^2 < 0$ showing how each firm optimally sets their level of expenditures on CA as function of their rivals level of expenditures on IS are found to be:

$$\hat{C}_i(P_j) = \begin{cases} \left[\sqrt{\frac{(\alpha\theta_j K)}{2}} - \sqrt{\beta P_j}\right]^2 & \text{for } P_j \le \dfrac{\alpha\theta_j}{2\beta}K \\ 0 & \text{for } P_j > \dfrac{\alpha\theta_j}{2\beta}K \end{cases} \qquad (7)$$

for $i, j = 1, 2$ and $j \neq i$. Similarly, the reaction curves $\hat{P}_1(C_2) = \beta C_2$ and $\hat{P}_2(C_1) = \beta C_1$, showing how each firm optimally sets their level of IS expenditures as function of their rivals level of expenditures on CA, were found by maximizing (5) with respect to P_1 and (6) with respect to P_2.

The reaction curves $\hat{C}_1(P_2)$ and $\hat{P}_2(C_1)$ will together determine the Nash equilibrium values C_1^* and P_2^*; similarly, the reaction curves $\hat{C}_2(P_1)$ and $\hat{P}_1(C_2)$ will together determine the Nash equilibrium values C_2^* and P_1^*. The Nash equilibrium is illustrated in Fig. 5.1, and the algebraic representation of the equilibrium expenditure levels of CA and IS are given below:

$$C_i^* = \frac{\alpha\theta_j K}{2(\beta + 1)^2} \qquad (8)$$

and

$$P_i^* = \frac{\alpha\beta\theta_i K}{2(\beta + 1)^2} \qquad (9)$$

for $i, j = 1, 2, j \neq i$.

From equations (8) and (9), it follows immediately that the firm with the smaller initial share of total profits spends more on CA and less on IS than does the rival with the larger initial share of total profits. It also follows immediately from equation (8) that the amount spent on CA increases with (a) increases in α, the measure of productivity of CA, (b) increases in θ_j, the rival's share of initial profits, (c) increases in K, the size of the total market (as measured by total profits prior to the expenditures on CA and IS by both firms), and (d) decreases in β, the productivity of IS. Similarly, from

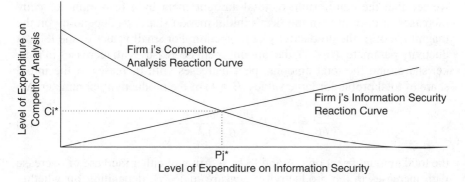

Fig 5.1. Nash equilibrium for firm i's competitor analysis level of expenditures and firm j's information security level of expenditures.

equation (9), it follows immediately the amount spent on IS increases with (*a*) increases in α, the measure of productivity of CA, (*b*) increases in θ_i, the firm's initial share of total profits, (*c*) increases in K, the size of the total market. Note, however, that since:

$$\frac{\partial P_i(\beta)}{\partial \beta} = \frac{1}{2} \alpha \theta_i K \frac{1 - \beta}{(1 + \beta)^3},$$ (10)

sign $\partial P_i(\beta)/\partial \beta$ depends on whether β, the productivity of IS, is greater or smaller than one. If the productivity of IS is small ($\beta < 1$), the amount invested in IS increases with increases in the productivity of IS; if the β is large (i.e. $\beta > 1$), then the amount invested in IS decreases with increases in the IS productivity parameter. When the productivity of IS is small, a small increase in the productivity of IS makes an increase in the expenditures on security justified by the added protection from the rival's attacks. However, when the productivity of IS is large, a small increase in the productivity of IS reduces the rival's attacks by a large amount, even when IS expenditure is somewhat reduced.

Let T_i denote the total amount spent in equilibrium by firm i on both CA and IS. Therefore, since $\theta_j = 1 - \theta_i$, we have:

$$T_i = C_i^* + P_i^* = \frac{1}{2} \alpha K \frac{(1 - \theta_i) + \beta \theta_i}{(\beta + 1)^2}.$$ (11)

From (11), we see that the total amount spent by a firm for CA and IS will increase with K, the total size of the market, and with α, the measure of productivity of CA. As:

$$\frac{\partial T_i}{\partial \theta_i} = \frac{1}{2} \alpha K \frac{\beta - 1}{(\beta + 1)^2},$$ (12)

we see that the equilibrium of total amount spent by a firm monotonically increases or decreases in the firm's initial market share, θ_i, depending on the magnitude of β, the productivity of protection. For small values of the IS productivity parameter ($\beta < 1$), the amount spent decreases with increases in market share, and the total amount spent increases with increases in the initial share of total profits for large values ($\beta > 1$) of the productivity parameter. As:

$$\frac{\partial T_i}{\partial \beta} = -\frac{1}{2}\alpha K \frac{\beta\theta_i - 3\theta_i + 2}{(\beta + 1)^3},$$ (13)

the total amount spent on CA and IS by a firm will either increase or decrease with increases in the productivity measure of IS, β, depending on whether $\beta < 3 - \frac{2}{\theta}$ or $\beta > 3 - \frac{2}{\theta}$. Therefore, since β is positive, a sufficient condition for the sum of the firm's equilibrium expenditures on CA and IS to be decreasing in β is that $\theta_i < \frac{2}{3}$. Also, since $3 - \frac{2}{\theta} < 1$, another sufficient condition for the firm's total expenditures to be decreasing in β is that $\beta > 1$. Therefore, if one firm does not dominate the market (in the sense that its initial profit share is greater than or equal to $\frac{2}{3}$) or if the measure of productivity of IS is greater than one, an increase in the productivity of IS results in firms' reducing their total expenditures for the sum of CA and IS.

Next, we compare the total amount spent for CA and IS by firm 1 with the amount spent by firm 2. From (11), we find that a necessary and sufficient condition for $T_1 > T_2$ is:

$$2\theta(\beta - 1) > +\beta - 1.$$ (14)

Therefore, $T_1(\theta) > T_2(\theta)$ if and only if $\theta > \frac{1}{2}$ when $\beta > 1$ and $T_1(\theta) < T_2(\theta)$ if and only if $\theta > \frac{1}{2}$ when $\beta < 1$. That is, the firm with highest initial share of total profits spends more (less) than the other firm when the productivity of IS is high (low).

Now let $T = T_1 + T_2$ denote the total amount spent in equilibrium by both firms on both CA and IS. Hence:

$$T = C_1^* + P_1^* + C_2^* + P_2^* = \frac{\alpha K}{2(\beta + 1)}.$$ (15)

From (15), we see that in equilibrium total expenditures on CA and IS increase with increases in the size of the total market and the productivity of CA, and decrease with increases in the productivity of IS. Since from a social welfare viewpoint, the expenditures are a deadweight loss, social welfare would increase with improvements in the productivity of IS and decrease with improvements in the productivity of CA. Finally, note that T is independent of θ. That is, the combined amount spent on CA and IS by the two firms is independent of how initial profits were distributed between the two rival firms. Note from (11) that each firm's total expenditures on CA plus

IS does depend on θ. Hence, the reason that the combined expenditures for both rivals does not change must be due to changes by each firm that exactly offset the changes made by the other firm.

Finally, we examine the effect of the equilibrium CA and IS activities on the profits of each firm both gross and net of the costs of these activities. Since expenditures on CA and IS do not increase the size of the market in our model, at least one, and possibly both, of the firms must be worse off than with their respective initial profit positions. The effect of expenditures on CA and IS on a firm's profits, gross of the costs of CA and IS, can be calculated by substituting the equilibrium levels of these activities as given in equations (8) and (9) into equations (5) and (6), and rearranging terms to yield:

$$\Pi_i(C_1^*,P_1^*,C_2^*,P_2^*) + C_i^* + P_i^* - \theta_i K = \alpha K \frac{1 - 2\theta_i}{(\beta + 1)^2}, \tag{16}$$

for $i = 1, 2$. The sign of the right hand side of (16) is positive when $\theta_i < 0.5$ and negative when $\theta_i < 0.5$. This leads immediately to the following:

Proposition 1. *The firm with the smaller share of initial profit will gain profit share gross of its costs of CA and IS, while the firm with the larger initial share of profits will lose profit share (both gross and net of its cost of CA and IS) from the CA/IS expenditure game.*

Note that if the firm has a large initial profit share, the firm cannot refuse to play the CA/IS expenditure game in order to avoid losing part of its profits. Since the equilibrium levels (C_i^*, P_i^*) reflect the best strategy available to the firm, selecting zero levels of CA and IS will only put the firm in a still more unfavourable position.

Adding $\theta_i K - C_i^* - P_i^*$ to both sides of (16) and again using (8) and (9), results in the expression for the profits of each firm net of the costs of CA and IS:

$$\Pi_i(C_1^*, P_1^*, C_2^*, P_2^*) = \theta_i K + \frac{1}{2}\alpha K \frac{1 - 3\theta_i - \theta_i \beta}{(\beta + 1)^2}. \tag{17}$$

A firm is a net gainer from CA and IS if and only if the last expression in equation (17) is positive. Hence, the following proposition follows directly from equation (17).

Proposition 2. *A necessary and sufficient condition for a firm's net profits in equilibrium to increase from expenditures on CA and IS is that $\theta_i < 1/(3 + \beta)$.*

Thus, for a given value of the productivity measure of IS, β, there exists a level of initial profit share such that if the firm has an initial profit share less than that value, the firm will have net profits increase under the Analysis/IS game. Moreover, the greater the productivity of the IS system, the smaller the firm's initial profit share must be for the firm to have profits increase by playing the CA/IS expenditure game. Since $\frac{1}{3} > 1/(3 + \beta)$ as $\beta > 0$, the following follows directly from Proposition 2:

Corollary. *A necessary condition for a firm's net profits to increase as a result of the CA/IS expenditure game is that the firm's initial profit share is less than $33\frac{1}{3}\%$. A sufficient condition for a firm's net profits to decrease as a result of the CA/IS expenditure game is that the firm's initial profit share is greater than or equal to $33\frac{1}{3}\%$.*

Proposition 2 and its corollary show that firms with a small portion of initial profits will gain from playing the CA/IS expenditure game, and firms with a large portion will lose from the game. For initial profit shares less than $33\frac{1}{3}$ per cent, the firm may either be a net gainer or loser depending on the relative size of the productivity parameter for IS and the size of the initial profit share. Note also that the productivity parameter for CA, α, and the total initial profits, K, affect the magnitude of the gain or loss, but not the sign. Although the specific cutoffs given in Proposition 2 and its corollary are dependent on the functional form of the profit function, one would expect the result that firms with a small initial share are likely to be winners and those with large initial shares are likely to be independent of the specification of functional form.

Implications

The above model can be summarized in terms of five generic equilibrium results. These results are:

1. The amount spent on CA increases with the rival's initial share of total profits (i.e. decreases with its own initial share), increases with the size of the total market, increases with productivity of CA, and decreases with increases in the productivity of IS.

2. The amount spent on IS increases with increases in the size of the firm's initial share of total profits, increases with the total size of the market, and increases with increases in the productivity of CA. The amount spent on IS increases (decreases) with increases in the productivity parameter of expenditures on IS for low (high) values of the IS productivity parameter.

3. The firm with the higher initial profit share spends more on IS and less on CA than does the firm with the smaller initial profit share. The total amount spent by a firm on both CA and IS increases (decreases) in the firm's initial share of total profits for high (low) levels of productivity of IS. In environments in which the productivity of IS is high (low), the

firm with the higher initial profit share spends more (less) in total on IS and CA than does the firm with the smaller initial profit share.

4. The total amount spent by both firms for both CA and IS is independent of the initial distribution of total profits, but increases with increases in the size of the total market, increases with increases in the productivity of CA and decreases with increases in the productivity of IS.

5. Gross of the costs of expenditures on CA and IS, the firm with the larger initial profit share sees profits at equilibrium decline from the firm's initial profit level. The firm with the smaller initial profit, sees profits gross of CA and IS expenditures increase. Net of expenditures on CA and IS, a firm's initial share of market profits must be considerably less than half, in order for the firm to have equilibrium net profits greater than initial profits. Furthermore, the maximum initial share of market profits that leads to a firm benefiting from the CA and IS decreases as the productivity of IS increases. Hence, it is likely that both firms will see their net profits decline from the CA and IS activities. (Recall, that a firm cannot unilaterally set both CA and IS to zero and expect not to lose even more.)

Measuring and using economic phenomena such as revenues, expenditures, and productivity measures are fundamental activities of accounting, in general, and management accounting, in particular. The empirical literature in management accounting, as reviewed by Itner and Larcker (2001), provides strong evidence attesting to this claim. Our analysis, as summarized above, provides important implications for real-world markets in the modern information economy. Management accounting researchers and practitioners are well poised to use and empirically test these implications. Three of these implications, and suggestions on how they may be used and tested, are discussed further.

The first, and most general implication that can be drawn from our model is that decisions by firms regarding their expenditures on CA and IS are logically dependent on the total market size, a firm's share of the market's profits, and the productivity of CA and IS. In addition, there is a fundamental interaction between the CA expenditures of one firm and the IS expenditures of another firm. This latter point is particularly important and means that, in deciding on how much to spend on CA and IS, each firm also should consider the expenditure decisions on CA and IS by its competitor. In their role as business advisors/consultants, management accountants would want to make sure that their firms are considering CA and IS expenditures in a joint decision-making framework. Indeed, given their expertise on issues related to cost behaviour and allocations, we believe that management accountants are uniquely qualified to advise firms in this area.

The above implication could be empirically tested by management accounting researchers via a study of various firms competing within a given industry. If such a study were restricted to publicly traded firms, market-related data and profit-related data would be available for analysis. However, data on the expenditures and productivity of CA and IS would have to be gathered by other means (e.g. from a survey or case studies). Assuming that the requisite cross-sectional data could be obtained, a set of simultaneous equations could be developed to test the above arguments (along the lines used in the studies by Keating 1997 and Holthausen *et al.* 1995). The empirical model specification would regress CA and IS on the following independent variables: size of the total market for a given industry, market shares of each participating firm in the industry, and each firm's share of the industry's total profits. In addition, the CA equation would have IS as an independent variable and the IS equation would have CA as an independent variable. Finally, each equation would have to have another independent variable for model identification purposes (e.g. the CA equation might include a variable related to the firm's growth strategy, and the IS equation might include a variable related to a firm's security break-in history). The empirical model described above to test the first implication of our model would lend itself to testing several specific hypotheses regarding each one of the independent variables in the model, as well as the simultaneity of CA and IS expenditures.

A second implication of our model, which is clearly related to the first implication, is the argument (hypothesis) that a firm with a small share of the market's (industry's) profits (i.e. less than $33\frac{1}{3}$ per cent) would experience net gains in its profit share (while other firms in the same market will experience losses in their profit shares) by increasing expenditures on CA. Indeed, as a firm strategy, it may make sense for firms with a small percentage of an industry's profits to ramp up its expenditures on CA. In their role as business advisors, management accountants would want to encourage their firms to act in accordance with such a strategy. Once again, given their expertise on issues related to profit analysis, we believe management accountants are uniquely qualified to advise firms in this area.

This second implication also suggests that CA expenditures and a firm's share of profits are logically dependent on one another, suggesting the need for identifying the empirical model specified above. However, to empirically test this second implication, management accounting researchers would want to consider longitudinal data. More to the point, it would be interesting to study this issue by constructing a 'before' and 'after' event study, where the event in question is increased expenditures on CA (along the lines adopted in the study by Haka *et al.* 1985). The variable of interest would then be the level of industry profit share before and after the event. A matched pair design would make such a study all the more powerful. A compliment to such a study could be to assess the stock market effect of any publicly announced expenditures on CA.

For the third implication from our model, which is also related to the first two implications, consider a firm that produces many goods (or services) and faces different rivals for the different products it produces. Our analysis suggests that such a firm would have an incentive, whenever possible, to allocate indirect corporate expenses to the most profitable business segments (both in terms of the absolute size of the firm's profits and the firm's relative share of the total market's profits). By allocating indirect expenses in this manner, it will make these business segments look less profitable than may actually be the case. Hence, competitors in the most profitable lines of business would likely underestimate total market profitability and the potential gains from CA activities, thereby leading to a reduction in CA expenditures for that market. Since this implication is inexorably intertwined with indirect cost allocation, and since indirect cost allocation is central to management accounting, practitioners and researchers in the field would have a comparative advantage in using and conducting research on issues related to this hypothesis. Specifically, practitioners could provide advice on selecting a cost system that incorporates a cost allocation system that is most favourable for the firm, and researchers could design an empirical test of the cost shifting hypothesis (i.e. the hypothesis that firms respond to rivals by shifting indirect costs to the most profitable product line).

Concluding Comments

Management accounting, which has always been centered around the use, value, and implications of information for internal decision-making, is a discipline poised to be at the centre of business in the information economy. Research developments in the areas of CA and IS opened up several opportunities in this regard. The study of the interaction between CA and IS promises to be another fruitful area for management accounting in the prevalent information-based economy. In this chapter, we have used a game theoretic model to analyse how expenditure decisions on CA and IS affect one another. The model of two rivals sharing a market fixed in size gave rise to several equilibrium results. In addition, the model suggests some important implications for management accounting.

As an abstract representation of reality our model, as are all models, is subject to limitations. Among the limitations are the following four concerns. First, we have modelled the CA/IS game as a static game. Second, the only asymmetry in our model is the share of initial profits of each rival. Third, our analysis only considers two rivals and we have specified a particular functional form of the profit functions in order to get closed-form solutions. Fourth, as with most game theory models of firm behaviour, we have assumed that decision makers within the rival firms behave in a completely rational manner.

Of course, the validity of the implications presented in this chapter is an empirical issue. Hence our discussion also suggested ways management accounting researchers can empirically test the implications. Given the importance of CA and IS decisions to firms operating in an information-based economy, we hope management accounting researchers will pursue such empirical tests.

References

Bromwich, M. (1990), 'The Case for Strategic Management Accounting : The Role of Accounting Information for Strategy in Competitive Markets', *Accounting, Organizations and Society*, 15/1, 2: 27–46.

Chen, M.-J. (1996), 'Competitor Analysis and Interfirm Rivalry: Toward a Theoretical Integration', *Academy of Management Review*, 21/1: 100–134.

——and Miller, D. (1994), 'Competitive Attack, Retaliation and Performance: An Expectancy-Valence Framework', *Strategic Management Journal*, 15/2: 85–102.

Computer Security Journal (2003), 'What is the Computer Security Institute', 19/1: i.

Demski, J. S. (2002), 'President's Message', 'Accounting Education News', *American Accounting Association*, Winter: 1, 3.

Denning, D. E. and Branstad, D. K. (1996), 'A Taxonomy of Key Escrow Encryption Systems', *Communications of the ACM*, 39/3: March: 34–40.

Elliott, R. K. and Pallais, D. M. (1997), 'Are You Ready for New Assurance Services', *Journal of Accountancy*, 183/6: June: 47–51.

Financial Account Standards Board (1997), *Statement of Financial Accounting Standards No. 131*, 'Disclosures about Segments of an Enterprise and Related Information'.

Ghoshal, S. and Westney, D. E. (1991), 'Organizing Competitor Analysis Systems', *Strategic Management Journal*, 12/1: 17–31.

Gibbons, R. (1992), *Game Theory for Applied Economists* (Princeton, NJ: Princeton University Press).

Gordon, L. A. and Loeb, M. P. (2001), 'The Economics of Investment in Information Security', Working paper.

—— (2001), 'A Framework for Using Information Security as a Repsponse to Competitor Analysis Systems', *Communications of the ACM*, September: 70–5.

—— (2002), 'The Economics of Information Security Investment', *ACM Transactions on Information and System Security*, November: 438–457.

Guilding, C. (1999), 'Competitor-Focused Accounting: An Exploratory Note', *Accounting, Organizations and Society*, 24/7: 583–95.

Haka, S. F., Gordon, L. A., and Pinches, G. E. (1985), 'Sophisticated Capital Budgeting Selection Techniques and Firm Performance', *The Accounting Review*, 60/4: October: 651–669.

Holthausen, R. W., Larcker, D. F., and Sloan, R. G. (1995), 'Business Unit Innovation and the Structure of Executive Compensation', *Journal of Accounting and Economics*, 19/2,3: 279–313.

Hirji, K. K. (2001), 'Exploring Data Mining Implementation', *Communications of the ACM*, 44/7: July: 87–93.

Itner, C. D. and Larcker, D. F. December (2001), 'Assessing Empirical Research in Managerial Accounting: A Value-Based Management Perspective', *Journal of Accounting and Economics*, 32/(1–3): December: 349–410.

Jajodia, S. and Millen, J. (1993), 'Editors' Preface', *Journal of Computer Security*, 2/2,3: 85.

Jones, L. (1988), 'Competitor Cost Analysis at Caterpillar', *Management Accounting* (US), October: 32–38.

Keating, A. S. (1997), 'Determinants of Divisional Performance Evaluation Practices', *Journal of Accounting and Economics*, 24/3: 243–273.

King, R., and Schwartz, R. (1998), 'Planning Assurance Services', *Auditing: A Journal of Practice & Theory*, 17/Supplement: 9–36

Kinney, W. R. (2000), *Information Quality Assurance and Internal Control for Management Decision Making* (New York: McGraw-Hill).

McCracken, S. A. (2000), 'Discussion of An Analysis of the Market for Systems Reliability Assurance Services', *Journal of Information Systems*, 14/Supplement: 83–5.

MacMillan, I. C., McCaffery, M. L., and van Wijk, G. (1985), 'Competitor's Response to Easily Imitated New Products: Exploring Commercial Banking Product Intro-ductions', *Strategic Management Journal*, 6: 75–86.

Messier, W. F. (2003), *Auditing Assurance Services: A Systematic Approach*, 3rd edn (New York: McGraw-Hill/Irwin).

Miller, D. and Chen, M.-J. (1994), 'Sources and Consequences of Competitive Inertia: A Study of the U.S. Airline Industry', *Administrative Science Quarterly*, 39/1: 1–23.

Porter, M. E. (1980), *Competitive Strategy: Techniques for Analyzing Industries and Competitors* (New York: Free Press).

—— (1985), *Competitive Advantage: Creating and Sustaining Superior Performance* (New York: Free Press).

Prescott, J. E. and Smith, D. C. (1987), 'A Project-Based Approach to Competitive Analysis', *Strategic Management Journal*, 8: 411–423.

Sandhu, R. S., Coyne, E. J., Feinstein, H. L., and Youman, C. E. (February 1996), 'Role-Based Access Control Models', *IEEE Computer*, 29/2: February: 38–47.

Shank, J. K. and Govindarajan, V. (1988), 'Making Strategy Explicit in Cost Analysis: A Case Study', *Sloan Management Review*, Spring: 19–29.

———— (1992), Strategic Cost Management: The Value Chain Perspective', *Journal of Management Accounting Research*, Fall: 179–198.

Simmons, G. J. (1994), 'Cryptanalysis and Protocol Failures', *Communications of the ACM*, 37/11: November: 56–64.

Simmonds, K. (1982), 'Strategic Management Accounting for Pricing: A Case Example', *Accounting and Business Research*, 12: 206–14.

—— (1986), 'The Accounting Assessment of Competitive Position', *European Journal of Marketing*, 20/1: 16–31.

Straub, D. W. (1990), 'Effective IS Security: An Empirical Study', *Information Systems Research*, 1/3: 255–76.

—— and Welke, R. J. (1998), 'Coping with Systems Risk: Security Planning Models for Management Decision Making', *MIS Quarterly*, 22/4: December: 441–69.

Young, M. A. (1987), 'Sources of Competitive Data for the Management Strategist', *Strategic Management Journal*, 10: 285–293.

Zajac, E. J. and Bazerman, M. H. (1991), 'Blind Spots in Industry and Competitor Analysis: Implications of Interfirm (MIS)Perceptions for Strategic Decisions', *Academy of Management Review*, 16/1: 37–56.

6

The Changing Role of Management Accounting and Control Systems

Accounting for Knowledge Across Control Domains

Frank G. H. Hartmann and Eddy H. J. Vaassen

Introduction

Commentaries on major economic cycles in human civilization have identified three ages of economic evolution: the agrarian age, the industrial age, and the information age (e.g. Hope and Hope 1997; Toffler 1990). These ages are determined by the dominant factors of power and production, and their implications extend to the wider business disciplines. The ages partially overlap and therefore cannot be exactly positioned on a time scale. Differences also exist between different countries' paces of development. The agrarian age lasted roughly until the second half of the eighteenth century in the Western world, and was followed by the industrial age. The industrial age saw an overlap with the information age over several decades, so that we presently find ourselves in a transitional stage between the industrial and the information age. This is reflected in the way in which our thinking about management and accounting is changing.

The agrarian age can be characterized by the power of the guilds that were governed on the basis of unambiguous agreements between the members. As a result, competition was virtually non-existent, and control was centralized. The industrial era may be characterized by the severe concentration of power in increasingly bigger, centrally controlled corporations that are mainly involved in production activities, with moderate competition. Our traditional conceptions of control and management accounting, focusing on the optimization of internal processes by achieving predetermined plans, have developed in this context.

The information era is characterized by the emergence of new organizational forms that go beyond industry boundaries, national borders, and markets, and that seem to defy central control. This 'third wave' economy is dominated by service organizations including those in the trade sector and the financial sector (Hope and Hope 1997). Here information is the key competitive factor.

Slogan wise, communication is not a part of the economy; it *is* the economy (Kelly 1998). Physical production activities—the traditional core competencies of many organizations, are frequently outsourced to countries with lower wage levels, leaving the role of product development to the developed economies. Moreover, the service sector rather than the production sector increasingly dictates the conditions under which contracts are settled between product developers and manufacturers. Over the last decade, in particular, the acknowledgement of 'knowledge', 'communication', and 'information' as the main production factor have brought further refinement to the business and management implications of the information age. Globalization has become the label of this trend toward world spanning activity, and worldwide competition.

From a managerial accounting perspective, the changes in the economy, in industries and individual firms alike, must be supported by the firm's accounting and control infrastructure (cf. Bromwich and Bhimani 1994). In order for knowledge employment to be effective and efficient, coordination within and between firms is essential, focusing on people's collaboration with each other and learning from each other. However, there is no reason to suspect that the more traditional roles of accounting and control will disappear, thus posing a tension between demands for flexibility and control. The thrust of this chapter is that the accounting information and control systems in contemporary organizations must be able to support this dual role. The remainder of the chapter is organized as follows. The section on The 'New Economy' as a Concept, discusses selected elements of the 'new economy'. These are subsequently linked with characteristics of the 'new organization' that emerge in response. From these developments follows an exploration of the strengths and weaknesses of traditional management accounting and control systems. The section on The 'New Organization' as a Response then illustrates how management accounting and control systems could adopt insights from knowledge management, if they are to meet the needs of organizations which simultaneously demand control and flexibility. This section is conceptual in nature and illustrates how traditional conceptual control frameworks might include the control of the accounting information system and the communication process. This chapter ends with some concluding remarks.

The 'New Economy' as a Concept

Belief in the existence and importance of the 'new economy' moves up and down with the fortunes of organizations taking part in it. It is without doubt, however, that electronic activities—or e-activities—play an increasingly important role in the current economic environment and provide the most visible and fundamental departure from the industrial age thus far. Trade via the World Wide Web is growing, and e-entrepreneurship seems to outsmart—if not outperform—its traditional counterpart. These developments serve not only as indicators of the true start of any 'new economy', but have initially also been perceived as signals of the immediate obsolescence of the old rules of the 'organization game'. However, their effects on traditional accounting and control systems in organizations remain to be explored. First, although the 'new economy' has been introduced as the overall label for a set of developments innovating on traditional ways of doing business, it is a label whose meaning and importance have yet to be determined. Second, the brief hype in the e-industry in the late 1990s was followed by a severe economic downturn, suggesting that the new rules are not a perfect safeguard against economic risks. With hindsight, estimations of the value of these companies, based on 'new' valuation principles, appeared to have been overly optimistic. This not only resulted in the impossibility of offsetting negative cash flows by positive future expectations, but above all suggests the continued importance of more traditional accounting and control systems. Despite the fact that the current economics are indicative of the continued importance of the traditional laws of economic viability, and moreover, the traditional need for control, there should be little doubt that the nature of business is drastically changing. For this reason, the concept of the new economy is used below as a unifying label of more fundamental and structural changes in the economy currently observable.

The changes of the new economy reflect in the ways of doing business, in the role of information and in the application of information and communication technology (ICT) (Vaassen 2002). In the new economy the number of potential competitors is increasing. Following Porter's (1980) terminology, information exchange causes both buyers and suppliers to be better informed and consequently to have more bargaining power in relation to the company. Producers recognize the opportunities of substitute products more quickly, resulting in their faster and larger availability. Increasing competitive forces require companies to be able to react much more attentively to changing market conditions. The need for specialist knowledge of products, local markets, and the necessity to employ a wide variety of production technologies, and information and communication technologies, is leading organizations to form cost effective alliances, partnerships, and joint ventures. In this setting, outsourcing and the so-called economical networks are the new and dominant forms of cooperation. Economical networks require high-quality information provision between the affiliated partners, and between the economical network and third parties. Economical networks may even exist as so-called virtual organizations in which the activity range is dominated by electronic transactions (Vaassen 2002). The success of this type of organization is highly dependent on the quality of information provision. The flow of physical goods and money is less important than the accurate and timely information about the location and the state of the physical goods and money. Companies may not have own inventories, but know about the vendors that can supply the goods their clients have ordered, or the warehouses which store these goods.

The 'New Organization' as a Response

The characteristics of the new economy, as those mentioned above, may have become household words, but their consequences for the organization have not. Indeed, it is equally difficult to talk about the 'new economy' as it is to talk about the 'new organization' since both concepts are generalizing labels rather than analytic descriptions. However, practitioners and theoreticians in the field of management and information management alike point to the development of new organizational forms that abandon traditional design prescriptions in which top–down command and control, fixed structures, rationality, and hierarchy are portrayed as guarantees for corporate success (Peters 1987; Senge 1990). In the industrial age, organizational thinking has been dominated by normative theories about the design of tasks, the design of the organization, the fixed drivers of profit maximization, and the benefits of hierarchy-based authority (cf. Fayol 1949; Taylor 1911; Weber 1946).

The contingency theory of organizations (e.g. Lawrence and Lorsch 1967), positing that organizations should fit their environment, attempted to portray a dynamic relationship between the organization and its environment, but never challenged the industrial view of organizations as mechanisms with a single goal, dedicated to transforming well-defined inputs into well-defined outputs. In such organizations, the central managerial challenge is 'control', since these organizations cannot attain a different set of goals, nor perform a different set of tasks until after consciously made adjustments by and to the organization have been made. In such organizations, organizational control comes in three flavours—strategic, tactical and operational—corresponding with the levels of the organizational hierarchy (e.g. Anthony 1981).

These normative theories of 'management by control' continue to be applied today. Many 'old economy' firms still rely on classical management philosophy, with the associated controls such as detailed work procedures, standardized products, rules and directives, performance evaluation, compliance-based rewards, and selection and placement. Also some modernistic contributions to management theory still bear the related birthmarks of top–down management (Kaplan and Norton 1996). For our purpose, it is important to understand how these classical ideas relate to the modern concepts of information exchange and knowledge. In the classical organization, employees are valued because of their ability to contribute to the efficient functioning of a fixed structure. Importantly, in this type of organization knowledge resides in the organization and not in the individuals working in the organization. This type of organization therefore encourages employees to obey operational orders that are embedded in the organization's strategy and tactics. They should be aware of their functions and roles in the complete organization instead of being interested in the intrinsic characteristics of their duties, and question these. This type of organization may suffice for stable tasks under stable circumstances, as well as for changing tasks under predictable circumstances. Simply stated however, when the circumstances become subject to change or get less predictable, employees should be able to question the rightness of their task assignments and adjust their actions in accordance with new situations.

The classical organization is therefore juxtaposed by the 'new organization' in which the assumptions about the conditions of stability, the exchange of information, and the location of knowledge are radically different (Drucker 1988). In new economy firms, knowledge resides in the heads of the people within the organization. These firms are knowledge-intensive and their core employees are knowledge workers such as technicians who monitor computer-controlled machines instead of machine operators (Drucker 1993; Nonaka and Takeuchi 1995; Quinn 1992). The new organization gives its knowledge workers discretion over their own actions, instead of demanding obedience to external norms (cf. Clegg 1990). Ideally, the new organization is self-organizing, reflective, and has an inherent ability to meaningfully revitalize itself and adjust to changing circumstances. Volberda (1996, 1998) refers to this type of organization as the 'flexible firm'. Some important characteristics of the traditional organization and the new organization are depicted in Table 6.1.

Although the new organization can be described from a multitude of perspectives and levels of analysis, some generalizations are important for our purpose. The new organization is not primarily aimed at mass production from a blunt cost minimization perspective. Rather, it tries—driven by market expectations—to customize its products as much as is economically efficient. For reasons of efficiency, synergy is sought in deliberately limiting the choice

Table 6.1. Characteristics of traditional and 'new' organizations

Characteristic	Traditional organization	New organization
Production routine	Mass production	Mass customization
Technology imperative	Technological determinism	Technological discretion
Information systems	Legacy information systems	Multi-purpose information systems
Task demarcation	Well-defined tasks	Ambiguous tasks
Task complexity	Simple tasks	Complex tasks
Core labour force	Core of production workers	Core of knowledge workers, and periphery of part-time and temporary workers
Tightness of labour relations	Life-time employment	Employability
Degree of specialization	Integration	Outsourcing
Decision-making	Centralized	Decentralized, workers being empowered
Managerial challenge	Control	Flexibility
Dominant control mode	Cybernetic	Interactive
Perfect control	Achieving ex ante plans	Realizing ex post potential

options customers have in components and processes to choose among. Thus, customization may be reduced to a limited number of different types of goods and services. Similarities with serial piece production exist, but the time-to-market of each series is significantly shorter than in traditional serial piece production (Vaassen 2002). Technology, including ICT, is considered as given in the traditional organization whereas in the new organization it is considered discretionary, and an active management tool. An important consequence of this technological discretion is that the accounting information systems of the new organization may take many forms, but have in common that they serve multiple purposes and are able to capture all data relevant for decision-making, internal as well as external (Fan *et al.* 2000). The new organization, because of its needed flexibility has less well-defined tasks than the traditional organization because tasks may be non-routine, ambiguous, and complex (Peters 1987; Volberda 1996). As a result, employees must have greater abilities to work and think independently.

Knowledge workers constitute the core workforce in the new organization, in contrast with production workers that need well-defined command and control lines. The labour market adapts to the need of organizations. As a consequence of their higher potential, workers become more mobile and will easily make the changeover from one employer to another. This is not considered to be a flaw but a prerequisite for constant rejuvenation of the organization and yielding genetic diversity (Prahalad and Bettis 1986). Also, as a result of its knowledge intensity and the need for more skilled and educated workers, the new organization is necessarily more specialized than the traditional organization. The trade-off is that the workers in the new organization must be empowered to make key decisions themselves. Hence, decentralization is an important theme in the new organization (Simons 1995; Volberda 1998).

Finally, in the new organization a departure of the traditional cybernetic control model can be observed in favour of a more interactive model in which continuous alignment of central functions is the key tenet. Perfect control in this type of organization is *not* to achieve a predetermined plan, but to realize its potential. As we will argue below, this requires extending control outside its traditional boundaries, to acknowledge the information and communication processes required.

The Need for 'New' Accounting and Control Systems

Traditional Notions of Control

It is questionable, at this stage, whether our current understanding and models of management accounting and control in organizations suffices to describe the impact of such a wide variety of developments to organizational design. To start understanding the impact of the mentioned changes in organizations on the role of accounting and control systems, they will be confronted with the classical—and presently still dominant—model of cybernetic control in this first section, and the associated use of cybernetic management accounting techniques in practice. The discussion below elaborates on this confrontation, by considering the extensions in three established control frameworks from the extant literature. We subsequently evaluate these frameworks from the perspective of the need for control in the new organization.

The managerial accounting and control literature offers a variety of definitions of the classical concepts of control and management control that fit the three stage management cycle of strategy, tactics, and operations (e.g. see Merchant 1998; Otley and Berry 1980; Simons 1995, 2000). As Otley and Berry (1980) note however, connotations of the term 'control' essentially boil down to only two ideas, *dominance* and *coordination*. Combined with its *goal orientation* and its *intentional nature* (e.g. Ouchi 1979), these definitions present management control as a set of rational and formal activities aimed at organizational goal attainment. Lowe (1971) extensively defines a management control *system* as:

a system of organizational information seeking and gathering, accountability and feedback designed to ensure that the enterprise adapts to changes in its substantive environment and that the work behaviour of its employees is measured by reference to a set of operational sub-goals (which conform with overall objectives) so that the two can be reconciled and corrected for.

The rationality and formality of control are best illustrated by the general control model that presents management control as an essentially cybernetic process, consisting of four steps following a systematic order (e.g. Anthony 1981: 8):

First, a standard of desired performance is specified. Second, there is a means of sensing what is happening in the organization and communicating this information to a control unit. Third, the control unit compares this information with the standard. Fourth, if what is actually happening does not conform to the standard, the control unit directs that corrective action be taken, and the directive is conveyed as information back to the entity.

The best-known example of a cybernetic control process is the functioning of a thermostat that controls room temperature. As Anthony (1981: 8) explains, 'The thermostat has a preset standard of the desired temperature in a room. It receives information about the actual temperature. If the actual temperature differs from the standard temperature, the thermostat directs the heating unit or the cooling unit to turn itself on.'

The cybernetic model finds a direct example in the practice of budgeting as a traditional management accounting technique (Hartmann 2000). Until the late twentieth century, budgeting has been broadly portrayed as the administrative process of setting targets and evaluation of their subsequent achievement. The budgeting model focuses on this essential cycle, and would regard the bureaucracy surrounding budgeting as 'noise'. It is recognized, however, that it is more fruitful to think of budgeting including its wider, sometimes dysfunctional, impact on organizational and individual behaviours (Hope and Hope 1997). Those who portray budgeting as an ideal practical representation of the cybernetic model therefore forget that the control model is indeed a *cybernetic model* of control and not a model of *cybernetic control*. In this sense, Fisher (1995: 26) noted, 'The cybernetic definition does not explicitly define the mechanisms and performance measures that constitute a control system, but rather defines the formal control process.' This means that the simplicity of the thermostat analogy helps to understand the essential meaning of 'control', but may hinder the understanding of the required characteristics of control systems in the reality of the new organizations. Conversely, deviations from cybernetic control, such as those described below, do not automatically mean discarding the underlying cybernetic notion of control. These deviations, which occupy the remainder of this section, show that the cybernetic model can be extended in different ways. One such way involves the extension of the thermostat analogy toward a more complex and adaptive 'climate control device'. Such a device has sensors for temperature, humidity, and air pressure, not only in the room where the temperature must be controlled, but also outside that room, and even outside the building.

In general, numerous meteorological measures are used to arrive at accurate weather forecasts, to have leading indicators of future temperatures and to 'pro-actively' adjust heating or cooling. The number of people in the room may be determined as well as their activities, moods, and physical conditions to optimize room temperature. Clearly, this form of control is still essentially cybernetic, but regards the *macro-goal* of creating a desirable room atmosphere, rather than the *micro-goal* of constant temperatures regardless of changing needs for certain temperatures. The earlier mentioned *Balanced Scorecard* philosophy may be seen as the most prominent and practical example of such *macro-systems* (Kaplan and Norton 1996), since it proposes a causal chain of operational and financial indicators to control organizations. It is clear however, that, in a cybernetic sense, the multi-dimensional performance indicators in the scorecard are not fundamentally different from the one-dimensional performance targets in the traditional accounting budget. In a similar way, developments in *Value Based Management and Strategic Cost Accounting* extend beyond the micro control level (Ittner and Larcker 2001). Table 6.2 depicts differences between these alternative cybernetic accounting and control models, along the four steps in the control process outlined above (Anthony 1981).

Extending the Cybernetic Control Model

A more fundamental extension of the traditional control model is found by elaborating on the notion of the *object* of control. In our view, the new organization denotes the trend to fundamentally move beyond the cybernetic idea

Table 6.2. The cybernetic control model and its extension

Step in control process	'Micro' cybernetic control model	'Macro' cybernetic control model
1. Standard setting	Few, clear, stable, and operational goals	Many, ambiguous, changing, and abstract goals
2. Performance measurement	Outputs clearly measurable	Difficult to measure individual contributions to macro-outputs
3. Performance evaluation	Outputs clearly interpretable	Difficult to interpret results in view of multiple goals
4. Feedback for corrective actions	Ex ante set definition of possible actions and single loop learning	Ex post action choice based on experience and double loop learning

of fixed standards of performance—whether few or many, accounting or non-financial—and from cyclical information exchange along the organizational hierarchy. More generally, it recognizes that control does not deal with a single mechanical process—whether simple or complex—but with the behaviour of deliberately empowered humans. Since the cybernetic control model is a closed model, it does not account for the dynamic and unpredictable environment of the new organization—with its ambiguous, multiple, and constantly changing goals (e.g. Volberda 1996). Workers within such an organization should be self-organizing and independent, rather than obedient in their task execution. They may consequently be more motivated by incentives that reflect their perceived contribution to organizational goals, than by incentives based on some 'subjective' short-term performance target. Examples of firms that, in the recent history, got caught in their competences and related investments in fixed assets are numerous, including such giants as IBM, GM, and DEC (Vaassen 2002). Here, short-term targets focused employees' attention on achieving budgeted sales of existing products, rather than reward behaviour to search for 'unpaved' paths, experiment, and hence have a more long-term, organization-wide focus.

This questioning of the cybernetic model of control is to some extent visible in earlier attempts to describe organizational learning as a multiple loop cybernetic process (e.g. Argyris and Schön 1978). The accounting and budgetary literature has never really caught up with such. Other attempts to describe control in action have introduced a multitude of controls to a world more complex than that of pure cybernetics (e.g. Otley and Berry 1980). The *conceptual control framework* by Ouchi (1979) distinguishes between market control, clan control, and bureaucratic control, answering the question how organizations succeed in organizing and regulating their affairs, consciously or not. Merchant's (1982) *control objects framework* originally was a clear exponent of the cybernetic model, answering the question how managerial behaviour can be 'kept on track'. It was loosely based on the contingency framework from Thompson (1967), absorbing the behavioural and social aspects of Ouchi (1979), yet viewed management control systems as supporting the organization's top–down hierarchy. Its recent inclusion of *cultural controls* means a clear extension of the underlying cybernetic model (Merchant 1998). This requires management working toward a culture that stimulates experimentation and adapting the organizational structure (including its accounting information systems) to deal with changing environmental conditions. Sharp is an example of this policy (Vaassen 2002). The framework on *strategy implementation* by Simons (1995, 2000) provides a third extension of strict cybernetics, explicitly accounting for the typical environmental circumstances of contemporary organizations and extending the notion of control from top–down diagnosis to cross organizational interaction. The demands for the organization's information and communication infrastructure remain unclear, however.

Control Typologies and the New Organization

To evaluate the relevance of these frameworks for the new organization, Table 6.3 summarizes the frameworks for management control from Ouchi (1979), Merchant (1982, 1998), and Simons (1995, 2000) from the perspective of the new organization. The remainder of this section discusses to what extent these typologies cover important characteristics of the new organization, such as flexibility and the importance of information and knowledge transfer.

Ouchi's *conceptual framework* enriched the traditional cybernetic control model in various ways. His classification relies on the control of *people*, and attempts to balance the hiring of qualified people with the managerial system

Table 6.3. Three frameworks for control

Framework	Ouchi (1979) 'Concepts of control'	Merchant (1982) 'Objects of control'	Simons (1995) 'Levers of control'
Focus	Positive, conceptual, and explanatory	Normative and managerial	Conceptual, managerial
Organizations need control systems to ...	... organize and regulate their affairs	... keep behaviours of managers 'on track'	... implement the strategy of the organization
Control in action is ...	... the combination of prototypical, formal, and informal control mechanisms	... formally designed instruments and procedures	... the ways in which various organizational uncertainties can be managed
Control typology	Clan control, bureaucratic control, market control	Personnel and cultural controls, action controls, result controls	Beliefs systems, boundary systems, diagnostic systems, interactive systems

to instruct, monitor, and evaluate—initially—non-qualified people. In this sense, this framework incorporates the creation and sharing of knowledge, specifically in *clans*. Although conceptually usable, the framework lacks specific design parameters that may serve as a checklist for developing a mature control system. Hence, it is indeed a *conceptual* framework, underlying more applicable frameworks, such as the Merchant (1982, 1998) framework. Merchant's classification attempts to derive a classification of controls that organizations 'may work with'. Additional control tools enrich the repertoire of the typical cybernetic type of control. Although abstract, the three types of controls reflect alternative, and observable, options to control the *behaviour* of managers. Merchant's framework may be used as an overall checklist for the design of control systems at the operational level. Hence, this framework is intended to support control systems aimed at the effective and efficient execution of specific tasks with certain goals, thus still relying on cybernetics.

Simons' (1995, 2000) framework distinguishes between four, so-called, levers of control, which relate to interactive control systems—that deal with strategic uncertainties, boundary systems—that put limits to organizational actions, diagnostic control systems—that provide performance data, and beliefs systems—that shape organizational culture and vision. These classes of controls do not directly point to a specific set of operational controls, but rather seem to redefine control in terms of implementing strategy in an uncertain world, thus at least recognizing that control systems should support constant flexibility and change.

To what extent do the three frameworks of control thus support the needs of the new organization? The three frameworks may all contain elements useful to the new control environment, but are also incomplete. Since innovation, knowledge, and flexibility go hand in hand, the levers of control may provide a suitable framework in the new environment, although its instruments may still show considerable fit with the *objects of control framework* (cf. Roberts 1998). Ouchi's *conceptual control framework* contains a unique notion of control—market control—that may prove to be superior to any other control mechanism within the new organization. The overall framework, however, lacks specificity to support strategy implementation. Bureaucratic control comprises both results controls and action controls, which are primarily *diagnostic*. These controls, which are essentially cybernetic, may well be applicable at the organizational level, for measuring the accomplishment of organizational goals in more traditional ways. *Clan control* corresponds with *personnel controls* and *cultural controls*, which in turn have much in common with *beliefs systems* and *boundary systems*. They all address the importance of the individual employee's role in control, hinting at self-control, empowerment, team spirit, and flexibility. The *interactive controls* that bridge the gap between strategy formulation and implementation cannot be found in any of the other frameworks. They are the clearest deviation from top–down controls and address the way in which other controls are used, rather than forming a separate form of controls. Therefore, the few empirical studies available to date show that interactive control seems to go hand in hand with more traditional and cybernetic accounting and control systems, such as systems in which the accounting budget is central (e.g. Abernethy and Brownell 1999). Simons' case study on Codman and Shurtleff (e.g. Simons 1999) provides a clear illustration of the same.

As a conclusion, the above frameworks in combination may serve some of the needs of the new economy and its organizations. *Market control* systems may create self-selection mechanisms. In the flexible labour market, workers that do not fit into the specific culture of an organization will have the incentive to adapt or leave. Action controls and results controls are predominantly aimed at organizational goals, safeguarding performance in traditional financial terms. Organizations may define goals at a strategic level, and diagnostically control them, but without assuming the possibility of their direct translation to lower levels in the organization. The frameworks suggest that other controls may be more effective at these lower levels. Cultural and personnel controls aim at creating a desirable work attitude among empowered knowledge workers. Overall, interactive control systems aim at managing strategic uncertainties between different levels of the organizational hierarchy. Overall, several parallels between extant control frameworks and the new organization can be found. Yet, the models still focus on the control of operational business and management processes. What is missing, in our view, is the explicit recognition of the information and communication infrastructure that underlies these processes, and that is paramount to their ultimate effectiveness in the new organization. The next section therefore proposes an extension of traditional control models that may fill this void.

Management Control and Knowledge Management

A New Perspective for Management Control

Over the past decade, a growing literature addresses the significance of *knowledge* for firm success (e.g. Drucker 1993; Edvinsson and Malone 1997; Nonaka and Takeuchi 1995; Stewart 1997; Sveiby 1997). Demarest (1997) defines knowledge in this context as, 'the actionable information embodied in the set of work practices, theories-in-action, skills, equipment, processes and heuristics of the firm's employees'. In this conception, knowledge is regarded as the single most important production factor of the contemporary organization, and *knowledge management* as its most important challenge. However, the emphasis on knowledge has not yet affected current management control thinking that still revolves around the traditional factors, labour and capital. This may be due to the fact that knowledge management is considered to belong to the domain of top management and their responsibility in strategy formulation (cf. Hope and Hope 1997; Nonaka and Takeuchi 1995), but its implications go further indeed. As we illustrated above, control frameworks have moved beyond micro cybernetics to include more realistic assumptions about the new organization, but while focusing on people they do not explicitly address their knowledge, or the ways in which they develop and use knowledge within the organization. We think that this may be the logical step further, and that our current understanding of control systems can be enriched from a knowledge management perspective, positioning knowledge as the central object of control and extending control to the accounting information system and the communication process.

Knowledge management as the normative field of applied management originates in a positive knowledge-based theory of the firm, as proposed, amongst others, by Grant (1996, 1997). The chosen label—knowledge-based theory of the firm—hints at the classical micro-economic theory of the firm that aims to explain the existence of firms and their behaviour on markets. The knowledge-based theory of the firm opens up the firm's black box, to explain how the management of knowledge determines the firm's structure, its existence, its boundaries, its external behaviour, and ultimately its competitive position. Because a significant part of an organization's knowledge is created and resides in the heads of its members, the knowledge-based theory of the firm explicitly recognizes the importance of people in organizations, but it goes beyond their behaviour to include the information and communication systems in organizations that store and transfer knowledge (Demarest 1997).

Grant (1996) explains the existence of firms from two interpersonal, knowledge-related factors—*cooperation* and *cross-learning*—which are paramount in the management of organizations. Cross-learning involves the transfer of tacit, personal, and specialized knowledge from one organizational member to other members. In complex organizations, however, knowledge transfer is not always desirable or possible since it is time-consuming and costly, and will ultimately exceed workers' cognitive abilities. As a result, specialization occurs among employees. The essence of firms is that they allow employees to specialize, while establishing mechanisms to guarantee that individuals work together, integrating their functional specializations and knowledge bases. The knowledge management perspective thus predicts that firms will integrate specialist knowledge in such a way that the costs of communication and coordination are minimized. It also proposes that management processes are essentially about supporting *knowledge creation* and about organizing cooperation between different knowledge specializations, which is called *knowledge integration*. In an extreme case, cooperation between knowledge specializations may even exceed organizations' boundaries. Many companies, such as Nike, Intel, and Microsoft (Vaassen 2002), have long-term alliances with the apparel industry by forming tight network organizations in which they specialize in performing a few unique functions along the value chain and outsource the remaining functions to their partners. In these networks, any form of information and communication will be applicable contingent upon the degree of routine in task fulfilment.

Knowledge Creation and Integration and the Need for Management Control

To minimize communication and coordination, Grant (1996) proposes four mechanisms to integrate knowledge in organizations: *rules and directives, sequencing, routines*, and *group problem solving and decision-making*, which mirror the control elements in Merchant's (1982, 1998) objects of control framework. Rules and directives are vehicles for communicating personal knowledge to the organization, or in other words, for transforming tacit into explicit knowledge by creating a set of operating procedures about how to perform certain tasks. Rules and directives are typical instances of action controls. Sequencing refers to time-patterned sequences of activities so that each specialist's input occurs independently through being assigned a separate time slot: a subsequent activity cannot take place before the preceding activity is finished to a certain pre-defined degree. Just like rules and directives, sequencing is a manifestation of action controls. Merchant (1998) uses the terms 'fool-proofs' or 'poka-yokes' to refer to sequencing, indicating that no discretion exists with respect to the sequence of activities to be performed. Computer applications often use a similar concept in that they force users to follow a fixed sequence of steps through a programme, supported by screen layouts. Routines are relatively complex multi-person behaviours that are triggered by a relatively small number of signals or choices. As such, they constitute automated stimulus–response patterns. Teams that are used to working in a specific team-setting, typically make use of routines, thereby minimizing communication during the job, like the surgeon and his team operating on a patient. However, routines still require some controls to be built into the organization. Examples of such controls are pre-action reviews, which are action controls, and the hiring of qualified personnel, which are cultural and personnel controls. Group problem solving and decision-making is, other than the former three who are basically of a logistic nature, a communication-intensive control mechanism.

Galbraith (1973) has asserted that impersonal coordination mechanisms should always be supplemented by personal and group coordination mechanisms. In terms of the objects of control framework, cultural and personnel controls should always perform the role of disciplines over action and results controls. Since efficiency in organizations increases with the use of impersonal coordination mechanisms that economize on communication, group problem solving and decision-making is restricted to non-routine, unusual, complex, and important tasks. As we asserted before, in existing economy and organizations, more and more tasks fit this description. So, here group problem solving and decision-making will be the dominant control mechanisms, and information provision and communication form the core processes. Logistic companies, such as the Dutch railways (NS), have rules and directives, routines, and sequences for routine situations, which are replaced by group problem solving when exceptions occur, like accidents or engine failures. Built-in flexibility allows the NS to handle accidents and engine failures in an almost routine manner which, because of the frequency of their occurrence, are commonplace as a result. In case of incidental, high exposure variations, such as strikes, hooliganism, terrorist attacks, and acts of nature, group problem solving will become dominant.

Managing knowledge integration—which essentially is knowledge sharing and employment—is but one element of knowledge management. AT&T used its marketing and distribution knowledge to enter the credit card market, 3M combined the expertise of the adhesives, abrasives, coatings, and non-woven technologies divisions to create 'never rust' plastic soap pads as a response to customer complaints about rusting steel wool pads (Leonard-Barton 1995). The creation of knowledge in the heads of an organization's workers—which essentially is knowledge development—logically precedes the integration of knowledge in organizations (Grant 1996, 1997). Knowledge creation is a *creative* process, which is less predictable and controllable than knowledge integration, but the above mentioned controls do have a role here as well. The management control literature already recognizes that important triggers of creativity are group processes—such as group problem solving and decision-making (e.g. Scott and Tiessen 1999). Rules, directives, sequencing, and routines ascertain that the organization allocates scarce managerial resources to innovation instead of control. However, the most important control objects that enhance creativity and innovation relate to organizational culture and personnel (Merchant 1982, 1998) and beliefs systems (Simons 2000).

Control in the New Organization

Although the discussion above may suggest the relative simplicity of integrating knowledge management into control frameworks, it does not suffice to merely point out the existing parallels, nor is indeed such integration simple. This section outlines the direction for extending control frameworks from a knowledge management perspective, to include the information system and the communication process, supporting knowledge creation and integration. In this wider perspective, three domains exist which are central to the control of organizations. These domains are depicted in Figure 6.1.

The control framework comprises the 'business domain', the 'communication domain', and the 'information domain', which are causally linked. In the business domain the organization's essential business processes take place. Essential business processes are those processes that make up an organization's logistic core—or value chain—and constitute its presence in the external (market) environment. Examples of such processes include purchasing, selling, production, decision-making, and human resource management. It is our conjecture that traditional control frameworks have thus far only addressed this business domain of control. The second domain houses

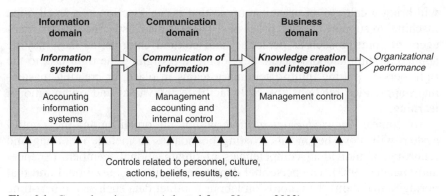

Fig. 6.1. Control environment (adapted from Vaassen 2002)

the processes through which information and is communicated for and about the business processes. The central objects of interest are the internal reporting processes and procedures. This is typically the domain of traditional management accounting, which is severely challenged today (e.g. Ittner and Larcker 2001; Kaplan and Norton 1996) and of internal control (Vaassen 2002). The *information domain* contains the technology employed to communicate information. The information domain is not about the content of information and communication but about its *form*. Its central objects are the organization's information systems and ICT applications. This domain is generally regarded to belong to the separate field of *accounting information systems* (Romney and Steinbart 2000). This model, however, proposes to link the domains, recognizing that they form a causal chain in which 'good' business controls require 'good' controls in the preceding information and communication domains. Furthermore, the model suggests that the control elements, that were previously restricted to the business domain, may also be effective in these earlier domains, thus extending traditional control frameworks.

The dependence of control in the business domain on controls in the other domains is easily illustrated. Control of knowledge in the business domain refers to knowledge creation and integration. Information and communication exchange between organizational members leads to the sharing of ideas, thoughts, facts, and the like. When doing so, the control system should support making an 'inventory' of available knowledge and required knowledge. Knowledge creation bridges the gap between available and required knowledge, and although not predictable, the role of internal control is paramount. While it cannot directly support the creative processes of knowledge development, it should facilitate the information and communication processes that lead to knowledge development by assuring that reliable and relevant information is provided (Romney and Steinbart 2000). This process is greatly enhanced by employing company-wide information systems that also capture external information. In addition, a sound internal control system will bring a calm to an organization so that it can function as a 'well-oiled machine' to support creative processes. There is also a specific role for management controls such as personnel and cultural controls, as they may be applied to stimulate knowledge development. Assigning the right task to the right person, putting multi-disciplinary teams in place, or creating master–mate–apprentice relationships, will facilitate individual and organizational learning.

To control *knowledge integration* within an organization, the control system will move beyond its existing boundaries to include recording and reporting of individual competencies of organizational members (Spencer and Spencer 1993). The personnel department is the organizational unit that normally maintains the records on labour contract data such as the part-time factor, and gross salary of the worker, but may also maintain data on individuals' specific competencies—such as education, experience, personality type, skills, preferences for specific tasks, performance, encountered problems, conflicts with others. Any HRM-module within a company-wide information system can be employed to meet this information need. Another type of knowledge sharing deals with the content of the knowledge as present within an organization. This knowledge is not necessarily concentrated at the personnel department, but rather dispersed within the organization. Knowledge sharing is not just the effective and efficient use of an organization's information systems. Often a much more important element of knowledge sharing is the creation of such an organizational culture that everybody automatically makes his knowledge available to anyone else within the organization. Especially beliefs systems and cultural controls provide the tools to move organizational culture into this desired direction.

The *integration* of knowledge is often not more than combining knowledge workers' proprietary information, skills, experiences, and attitudes with task characteristics. Personnel controls will play an important part here since they facilitate an optimal person–task alignment with respect to education, experience, personality characteristics, cognitive style, knowledge, skills, and the like. In the new organization, by definition, personnel controls are of prime importance, but the current descriptions of the role of personnel in organizations, provided by available framework, do not link well with knowledge. In the new organization, workers will feel an intrinsic responsibility for their task fulfillment. As soon as they enter an organization at conditions both the employer and the employee agree upon, they implicitly state that they will do their utmost to do whatever is in the organization's interest and refrain from anything that may bring harm to the organization. After initial selection and placement—which process is strongly guided by the worker himself—the worker goes through an assimilation process that educates him about the core organizational values. If these values do not match with his personal values he will exit the organization. This market mechanism continues to work for every newly hired employee. However, this very same mechanism also works for every existing employee because the organization is likely to change over

Table 6.4. Knowledge-based framework for control

Characteristics	Business domain	Communication domain	Information domain
Control is...	...the effective way in which knowledge is created and integrated	...the effective processes of communicating reliable and relevant information	...the efficient design and working of information systems
Object of control	*Business processes* Purchasing, selling, production, servicing, HRM, etc.	*Communication* Reporting on financial and operational, internal and external situation	*Information system* ICT applications
Perfect control is...	...enabling the quick adaptations to environmental changes	...providing relevant and reliable information on time to users	...dynamic and constant optimization of ICT employment
Examples of controls	*Business Controls* Personnel, cultural, action, results, beliefs (= routines, sequencing, rules and directives, group problem solving, and decision-making)	*Communication Controls* Action and results controls (system controls), directed at information quality, personnel and cultural controls to ensure knowledge and motivation	*Information controls* Personnel and cultural controls to ensure knowledge and motivation for ICT employment

time, potentially creating an atmosphere that is not in agreement with the atmosphere this employee desires. In this seemingly tinkering approach to organizational control, knowledge is exploited to a maximum, enabling workers to learn and adapt swiftly to changing circumstances, thereby never losing the organizational well-being out of sight.

The above discussion provides a first overview of the many links between the controls in the three domains. The types of controls required for the three domains are further illustrated in Table 6.4. In line with the earlier overviews of control systems, this table outlines the objects of control in the three domains, and provides examples of control types for the information and communication domain.

Concluding Remarks

Although some may question the true emergence of a 'new economy', it cannot be doubted that new organizations emerge bearing similar structural characteristics, even across various different industries. This chapter has argued that our understanding of the structure of these organizations might be increased by focusing on the management of knowledge, communication, and information, rather than on the traditional management of labour and capital through top–down hierarchical relationships. This implies that traditional management control typologies, whose focus has already shifted from pure cybernetics to employee behaviour, should be extended to capture elements of knowledge management. In the analysis of these new organizations, the traditional three-fold planning and control cycles—strategic, tactical, and operational—are replaced by an alternative three-fold classification of control domains; the business domain, the communication domain, and the information domain. Although these domains do not mean a complete departure from the control elements and instruments in the traditional typologies, they do mean a fundamental refocus on the control questions brought about by the central roles of knowledge, information, and communication in contemporary organizations.

References

Abernethy, M. A. and Brownell, P. (1999), 'The Role of Budgets in Organizations Facing Strategic Change: an Exploratory Study', *Accounting, Organizations and Society*, 24: 189–205.

Anthony, R. N. (1981), *Planning and Control Systems. A Framework for Analysis* (Boston: Harvard Graduate School of Business).

Argyris, Ch. and Schön, D. (1978), *Organizational Learning* (Reading, MA: Addison-Wesley).

Bromwich, M. and Bhimani, A. (1994), *Management Accounting: Pathways to Progress* (CIMA). London.

Clegg, S. R. (1990), *Modern Organizations—Organization Studies in the Postmodern World* (London: Sage Publications).

Demarest, M. (1997), 'Understanding Knowledge Management', *Long Range Planning*, 30/3: 374–84.

Drucker, P. F. (1988), 'The Coming of the New Organization', *Harvard Business Review* (January–February): 45–53.

——(1993), *Post-Capitalist Society* (Oxford: Butterworth Heinemann).

Edvinsson, L. and Malone, M. S. (1997), *Intellectual Capital. Realizing your Company's True Value by Finding its Hidden Brainpower* (New York: Harper Business).

Fan, M., Stallaert, J., and Whinston, A. B. (2000), 'The Adoption and Design Methodologies of Component-Based Enterprise Systems', *European Journal of Information Systems*, 9: 25–35

Fayol, H. (1949), *General and Industrial Management* (London: Pitman).

Fisher, J. (1995), 'Contingency-Based Research on Management Control Systems: Categorization by Levels of Complexity', *Journal of Accounting Literature*, 14: 24–53.

Galbraith, J. (1973), *Designing Complex Organizations* (Addison-Wesley).

Grant, R. M. (1996), 'Toward a Knowledge-Based Theory of the Firm', *Strategic Management Journal*, 17 (Winter Special Issue). 109–122.

—— (1997), 'The Knowledge-based View of the Firm: Implications for Management Practice', *Long Range Planning*, 3 (June): 450–54.

Hartmann, F. G. H. (2000), 'The Appropriateness of RAPM: Toward the Further Development of Theory', *Accounting, Organizations and Society*, 25/4–5: 423–57.

Hope, J. and T. Hope. (1997), *Competing in the Third Wave. The Ten Key Management Issues of the Information Age* (Boston, MA: Harvard Business School Press).

Ittner, Ch. and Larcker, D. F. (2001), 'Assessing Empirical Research in Managerial Accounting: A Value-Based Management Perspective', *Journal of Accounting and Economics*, 32/1–3: 349–69.

Kaplan, R. S. and D. P. Norton. (1996), *The Balanced Scorecard, Translating Strategy into Action* (Boston, MA: Harvard Business School Press).

Kelly, K. (1998), *New Rules for the New Economy. Ten Ways the Network Economy is Changing Everything* (London: Fourth Estate).

Lawrence, P. R. and Lorsch, J.W. (1967), *Organization and Environment, Managing Differentiation and Integration* (Boston: Harvard).

Leonard-Barton, D. (1995), *Wellsprings of Knowledge: Building and Sustaining the Sources of Innovations* (Boston, MA: Harvard Business School Press).

Lowe, E. A. (1971), 'On the Idea of a Management Control System: Integrating Accounting and Management Control', *The Journal of Management Studies*, 8: 1–12.

Merchant, K. A. (1982), 'The Control Function of Management', *Sloan Management Review* (Summer): 43–55.

—— (1998), *Modern Management Control Systems* (Upper Saddle River: Prentice Hall).

Nonaka, I. and Takeuchi, H. (1995), *The Knowledge-Creating Company. How Japanese Companies Create the Dynamics of Innovation* (New York: Oxford University Press).

Otley, D. T. and Berry, A. J. (1980), 'Control, Organization and Accounting', *Accounting, Organizations and Society*, 5: 231–44.

Ouchi, W. G. (1979), 'A Conceptual Framework for the Design of Organizational Control Mechanisms', *Management Science* (September). 833–48

Peters, T. J. (1987), *Thriving on Chaos* (New York, NY: Knopf).

Porter, M. E. (1980), *Competitive Strategy: Techniques for Analyzing Industries and Competitors* (New York: Free Press).

Prahalad, C. K. and Bettis, R. A. (1986), 'The Dominant Logic: A New Linkage Between Diversity and Performance', *Strategic Management Journal*, 7/6: 485.

Quinn, J. B (1992), *Intelligent Enterprise: A Knowledge and Service Based Paradigm for Industry* (New York: The Free Press).

Roberts, H. J. E. (1998), 'Management Accounting and Control Systems in the Knowledge-Intensive Firm', paper presented at the 21st Annual Congress of the European Accounting Association, Antwerp, Belgium.

Romney, M. B. and Steinbart, P. J. (2000), *Accounting Information Systems*, 8th edn (Upper Saddle River, NJ: Prentice Hall).

Scott, T. W. and Tiessen, P. (1999), 'Performance Measurement and Managerial Teams', *Accounting, Organizations and Society*, 24/3: 263–78.

Senge, P. (1990), 'The Leader's New Work: Building Learning Organizations', *Sloan Management Review* (Fall): 7–23.

Simons, R. (1995), *Levers of Control. How Managers Use Innovative Control Systems to Drive Strategic Renewal* (Boston: Harvard Business School Press).

—— (2000), *Performance Measurement & Control Systems for Implementing Strategy* (Upper Saddle River: Prentice Hall).

Spencer, L. M. and Spencer, S. M. (1993), *Competence at Work: Models for Superior Performance* (New York, NY: John Wiley & Sons).

Stewart, T. A. (1997), *Intellectual Capital. The New Wealth of Organizations* (London: Nicholas Brealey).

Sveiby, K. E. (1997), *The New Organizational Wealth. Managing and Measuring Knowledge-Based Assets* (San Francisco: Berrett-Koehler Publishers).

Taylor, F. W. (1911), *The Principles of Scientific Management* (New York: Harper & Row).

Thompson, J. D. (1967), *Organizations in Action* (New York, NY: McGraw-Hill).

Toffler, A. (1990), *Powershift: Knowledge, Wealth, and Violence at the Edge of the 21st Century* (New York: Bantam Books).

Vaassen, E. H. J. (2002), *Accounting Information Systems: A Managerial Approach* (Chichester: John Wiley & Sons).

Volberda, H. W. (1996), 'Toward the Flexible Form: How to Remain Vital in Hypercompetitive Environments', *Organization Science*, 7/4: 359–74.

——(1998), *Building The Flexible Firm: How to Remain Competitive* (Oxford: Oxford University Press).

Weber, M. (1946), in H. H. Gerth and C. Wright Mills (eds), *From Max Weber: Essays in Sociology* (New York: Oxford University Press).

Part 2
Reflections on Organizational Shifts

7

Management Accounting Inscriptions and the Post-Industrial Experience of Organizational Control

Paul Andon, Jane Baxter, and Wai Fong Chua

Introduction

The idea that management accounting information may be used to control organizational functioning is not new—indeed, this has constituted one of the cornerstones of our disciplinary discourse (Emmanuel *et al.* 1990; Horngren *et al.* 2000). However, given that the so-called post-industrial economy is sustaining 'new' modes of inter- and intra-organizational functioning (Castells 1996; Harvey 1989; Rifkin 2000), the process of organizational control, and accounting's role in it, becomes a topic of renewed interest. Will accounting continue to be connected to organizational functioning in familiar ways or will accounting control emerge in new and different forms? This chapter explores such issues.

In this chapter we argue that organizational control, and accounting's role in it, has become an increasingly digitized and technologically enabled process. New 'centres of calculation' (Latour 1987: 216) have arisen within post-industrial organizations which, in turn, are facilitating more disembedded and intensified forms of accounting control. We examine and illustrate this post-industrial phenomenon of organizational control within a call centre context. Data have been drawn from a case study of an Australian call centre operation, which processes in excess of 12 million customer enquiries each year.

The remainder of the chapter is structured in the following way. We commence with an overview of accounting and control in industrial organizations. This is followed by an outline of the emerging nature of accounting and control in post-industrial organizations. This is then illustrated in the context of the changing practices of the case organization. We conclude by considering the disciplinary implications of this account.

Accounting and Control in the Industrial Organization

There have been many different constructions of organizational functioning and accounting's connection to it within the literature. Burchell *et al.* (1980), for example, outline a variety of organizational roles for accounting: first, accounting may assume a decision-support role within organizations; second, accounting may promote dialogue within organizations; third, organizational learning may be facilitated by accounting; and, finally, accounting information may provide the impetus for novel forms of organizational functioning. However, the most enduring characterization of accounting's role in the industrial organization has been as an enabler of 'efficiency' and 'effectiveness' (Emmanuel *et al.* 1990: 29). The dual mantras of 'efficiency' and 'effectiveness' have endowed accounting with a central role in maintaining organizational control—in ensuring that organizational objectives are pursued and that resources are used wisely in moving towards such ends. And whilst subsequent and sporadic debate may have emerged to question this means–end relationship between accounting and organizational functioning (Cooper *et al.* 1981), such debate has been conducted at the disciplinary periphery and in counterpoint to this entrenched and prevailing viewpoint.

Indeed, the ways in which the rhetoric of efficiency and effectiveness connects accounting to the industrial organization has become a central part of the contemporary research agenda. Whilst a number of different research approaches have been adopted to investigate this issue (e.g. see Covaleski and Dirsmith 1983, 1988; Hopper and Armstrong 1991), we will confine our attention to that research, which draws upon the writings of the late French social scientist, Michel Foucault. This is the literary corpus which articulates most closely with the ideas that we will draw upon in our investigation of accounting in post-industrial organizations.

Foucault's work on 'discipline' (1977) has provided a platform for many interesting renderings of accounting control in industrial organizations. More particularly, Foucault's description of Bentham's panoptican (a type of building that enables an overseer in a central tower to watch the activities of all the occupants—such as the incarcerated, the insane, or the industriously employed) provides a metaphor that has recast accounting control and its quest for efficiency and effectiveness into a more dismal and constraining language. Foucault writes:

the major effect of the Panoptican: to induce . . . a state of consciousness and permanent visibility that assures the automatic functioning of power. So to arrange things that the surveillance is permanent in its effects, even if it is discontinuous in its action; that the perfection of power should tend to render its actual exercise unnecessary; that this architectural apparatus should be a machine for creating and sustaining a power relation independent of the person who exercises it. (1977: 201)

Drawing on this, systems of accounting control have been examined for the ways in which they create and perpetuate an unrelenting form of organizational surveillance from a distance. As a consequence, accounting inscriptions have become associated with the regulation or 'governance' of organizational functioning, as well as the unequal power/knowledge relationships between the controller and the controlled.

The seminal work by Miller and O'Leary (1987) illustrates the application of this perspective in a study of the emergence of standard costing and budgeting systems in the early 1900s. Miller and O'Leary argue that standard costing and budgeting have embedded a detailed knowledge of individual organizational participant's behaviour in accounting systems. Accounting systems became the panoptican of the industrial organization, highlighting the economic contribution of organizational participants and the extent of their wastefulness and inefficiency. Behavioural deviations from prescribed norms, such as standard costs or budgetary targets, are made visible by accounting systems. This enables subsequent management intervention in 'out-of-control' work processes. In brief, accounting systems are characterized by Miller and O'Leary as being instrumental in the production of 'docile' and compliant organizational participants in the industrial age.

As a further illustration, Knights and Collinson (1987) adopt a Foucauldian lens in their study of the impact of accounting systems on male manual workers in a heavy manufacturing context. Faced with the possibility of their own redundancy, these workers accepted unquestioningly financial data that demonstrated the need for greater stringency and cost control, particularly with respect to the level of total labour costs. The workers were unable to rally against the 'concreteness' of the accounting figures, as Knights and Collinson describe it (1987: 472). They had implicitly accepted the classification of labour as an 'expense' to be minimized at the discretion of management. Knights and Collinson correspondingly argue that accounting had become a way of 'disciplining the shopfloor' (1987: 457). In effect, these workers were participants in their continued subordination to the extant managerialist power/knowledge regime that characterized their organization in particular, and industrial society more generally.

As such, it may be argued that accounting prospered in industrial organizations, such as those considered by Knights and Collinson (1987) and Miller and O'Leary (1987), because accounting inscriptions sustained the networks of interests and power/knowledge relationships that were embedded in their design—strong vertical hierarchies, authoritarian management roles, and Taylorized production functions (Harvey: 1989). Accounting was an efficient and effective form of discipline: it ensured the bodily engagement of workers in the production function in parsimonious ways, but it also ensured that management remained ever watchful and vigilant with respect to prevailing interests of capital.

Accounting in the Post-Industrial Organization

However, the argued transition to a post-industrial economy is transforming organizational functioning in radical ways (Castells 1996; Harvey 1989). Organizational boundaries have become less distinct as various forms of outsourcing and strategic partnering grow to be more commonplace (Doz and Hamel 1998). Organic designs reflect the emergence of knowledge-based forms of organizational leadership (Drucker 1998). The product/service offerings of the post-industrial organization are subject to continued pressures for change and innovation (Christensen 1997). Overall, post-industrial organizations confront more time-intensive and globalized forms of competition (Harvey 1989). And quantum leaps in information processing technology have contributed to this revolution in organizational functioning (Castells 1996). These changes in organizational functioning, in turn, have generated debate about the emerging nature of control in post-industrial organizations. In particular, we will outline an argument that organizational control is becoming an increasingly disembedded and intensified process.

The increasing disembeddedness of organizational control is attributed to the 'lifting out' (Giddens 1991: 18)—or replication across time and space— of local systems of surveillance. A quest for competitive advantage, through the diffusion of 'best practice,' has resulted in many post-industrial organizations adopting systems of organizational control from leading-edge business units or external consulting firms and business solution providers, such as SAP. The relatively recent digitization of accounting inscriptions has accelerated the translation of systems of surveillance from one time and place to another, contributing to a sense of intensification that accompanies the disembedding of post-industrial organizational controls.

It is of significance to note, moreover, that the digital translation of accounting inscriptions is a feature of contemporary organizational functioning that was absent from the pre-industrial and industrial contexts analysed by Foucault, and his influential followers within the accounting literature. Vast amounts of information about customers, employees, production processes, and so-on are now stored in the digitized databases of post-industrial organizations. And it is a reliance upon this particular media to accumulate, process, and disseminate information that is changing the constitution of organizational control. As Poster has stated, digitized repositories constitute a form of 'Superpanoptican, a system of surveillance without walls, windows, towers or guards' (1990: 93). In short, digitization has enabled organizational control to be exercised in almost any place and at almost any time.

As such, virtual representations of organizational functioning have changed the post-industrial experience of the spacing and timing of organizational control (Giddens 1991; Lyon 2001; Poster 1990). The post-industrial experience of organizational control is no longer as local or as partial as it was once perceived. Lyon argues that this has been brought about, in part, by the integrative capabilities of organizational databases or their 'leaky' quality (2000:8). Huge amounts of digitized information can be passed with ease from one application to another, and from one site to another. Also the ability to retrieve, process, and analyse this information at any time or place means that surveillance does not need to occur in real-time or in its real-life context. Rather surveillance may now take place within the boundaries of the computer screen or the perimeters of a paper report (Ihde 1998). As a result, organizational control becomes a more disembodied or 'over-there' process (Ihde 1998: 351) as technologically mediated interactions enable the physical separation of the controller and the controlled (Wiley 1999). But it is the 'invisibility' (Lyon 2001: 25) of digitization that most acutely reinforces the post-industrial experience of the timing and spacing/disembedding and intensification of organizational control. Indeed, some of the organizational participants interviewed in our case study will comment on their uncomfortable sense of an omniscient and omnipresent form of 'Big Brother' embedded in the technology that enables their work.

However, before moving to a consideration of the case study and the ways in which it exemplifies this post-industrial experience of organizational control, we consider briefly the continued connection between accounting and organizational control. How may we account for accounting's resilience? Arguably, it is the nature of accounting inscriptions which provides part of the clue. Accounting generates *numerical* inscriptions of organizational functioning, for example, production output, sales revenue, cost expenditure, and so-on. And these inscriptions are particularly useful in the process of surveillance because of their mobility, stability, and combinability (Latour 1987: 223). Accounting inscriptions are mobile in that they can be moved quite readily to the sites where surveillance takes place, such as a particular manager's office or personal computer. Accounting inscriptions are also stable—numbers travel well, they do not deteriorate or change as they are moved around organizations. And accounting inscriptions are combinable, such numbers may be added, subtracted, divided, and multiplied to provide relevant and additional insights into organizational functioning (for instance, the level of profitability, sales growth, return on investment, gearing, and so-on). Additionally, the numerical nature of accounting inscriptions has allowed their digital translation to occur with relative ease, and this has served to intensify the mobility, stability, and combinability of accounting inscriptions and their role in virtual forms of organizational control.

Accounting and Control in a Post-Industrial Organization

An Outline of the 'Old'

We were monitored fairly closely in those days—for our supervisors used to walk, and do the walk around, and make sure that you were doing . . . your work and didn't have a break. You only had a break every three hours and that was just a ten minute break and then you had your meal break. . . . They just stood at a, like a podium and overlooked the floor.

This is an excerpt from an interview with a 'call girl' who has worked in the call centre operation of our Australian case organization for over 30 years.[1] Her descriptions of the working conditions that she encountered early in her career are typical of the ways in which we have come to think of control in the industrial organization. Control was a very physical process. It involved the copresence of the controller and the controlled; the call girls were clearly visible to their supervisor and the supervisor's continued watchfulness was conveyed to the call girls through his pacing and strategic placement in their work environment. This resulted in the production of 'docile bodies' (Foucault 1977: part 3). The call girls submitted to a work regime that involved sitting in a defined place for a relatively long period of time. Any breaks were monitored closely and timed. Managing time, and managing the ways in which the call girls used their time, became the key to control in this organization.[2] In many respects, surveillance, and its goals of efficiency and effectiveness, involved ensuring that the call girls were busy and answered all incoming calls quickly.[3] As this call girl stated, it was important that 'you were on the boards, doing your work all the time'.

An Elaboration of the 'New'

Thirty years later, the basic construction of organizational control in this call centre operation remains unaltered. The management of labour and time continues to dominate the discourse. As the Financial Controller explained, 95 per cent of the call centre budget is comprised of labour costs. And a recent activity-based analysis of the call centre cost structure confirmed that time was the 'ultimate driver' of the consumption of call centre resources. Yet things were different, the process of surveillance within the call centre operation had changed and these changes may be attributed, in the main, to advances in technology.

Advances in technology have enabled telephony to become a digitized process, rather than one dominated by 'plugs and cords' or 'desktops' and 'pushbuttons'. Highly accurate and invisible surveillance of a 'consultant's'[4] calls is now undertaken, providing a rich repository of data for analysis and management intervention. The daily activities of each consultant are monitored by 'the system' at 5 min intervals. The next day, a team leader is

---

[1] Refer to Appendix for information on the research site and method.

[2] There was a very brutish aspect to organizational control in this case organization. Another interviewee indicated that the supervisor would often walk around with a ruler in his hands. There were also reports of supervisors who would pinch the legs of the call girls to ensure that they were wearing stockings and appropriately attired for work.

[3] The manager of the call centre operation indicated that 'speed of answer' had remained a dominating priority for the last 20 years.

[4] The call centres were now staffed by 'consultants' (both male and female).

presented with a computerised simulation of each consultant's performance.[5] A variety of time-based performance measures—'the stats'—are compiled. Measures of the call centre performance include: average calls per hour; the percentage of call time that a customer spends on hold; 'wrap time' or the amount of time that a consultant spends doing any paper work after a customer hangs up; 'adherence to schedule' or the extent to which a consultant is logged on to the system in conformance with their schedule (that specifies starting times, breaks, and lunch times); and 'average handling time' or the average time spent both on a call and its subsequent 'wrap up').

The most closely monitored measure of performance, however, is the average handling time (AHT). Very clear performance benchmarks have been established for this. Consultants are expected to conform to an AHT of approximately 235 seconds per call. Unacceptable deviations from this standard become the subject of management investigation. One team leader outlines her rules for managing time: 'we only need to focus on people outside the bell curve. So yeah, I mean you have, if you go through the stats it's easy to pick out—I look at anyone over 300 [seconds] and that's being generous...Anyone who's particularly low, maybe 170 [seconds], again that's being really generous'.

Despite the availability of such detailed 'stats' about a consultant's daily activities, team leaders rely on other forms of surveillance as well. Team leaders conduct regular 'ride ons' with a consultant: a team leader will sit next to a consultant for about 45 min each month and monitor the verbal interaction between the customer and a consultant,[6] in addition to assessing the consultant's procedures.[7] Team leaders also continue to invoke and preserve the more visceral tradition of control within the call centre. Direct observation remains an important part of the team leader's management repertoire.[8] As one team leader put it:

it is easy for a person to do it right [during a ride on], you might be sitting with him and he might be spot on but the minute you turn your back—that is why the team manager's role is so crucial because it is not just on the time that he spends monitoring him, how he talks to a customer. It's every minute of every day, observing how people react to situations and to people around them. So that's where observation, call it observation, but by observation means, I mean, watching your people and getting to know your people. That's going to tell you who has got the attitude I think and who doesn't. So that is something that can't be measured or can't be taken away from the role of team manager. Part of the job has to be that.

---

[5] A team leader is responsible for the performance of 16–20 consultants within the call centre operation.

[6] The team leader would wear headphones to monitor calls.

[7] Remote monitoring of calls, whilst technologically possible, was not undertaken because of extensive trade union resistance to the process.

[8] Direct observation was facilitated by the fixed seating plan and the cell-like layout of the call centre.

Experiencing the 'New'

Participants in the case organization experienced the transition to a more technologically enabled system of surveillance in a variety of ways. For those
organizational participants who worked in a support capacity within the call
centre operation, the detailed performance information was perceived as
being particularly beneficial. By normalizing consultant behaviour around the
AHT, much of the 'variability' in organizational functioning has been
removed, facilitating the planning process. Scheduling has become easier and
there is now less risk associated with the management of labour costs. Greater
casualization of the labour force is possible as a consequence, and excess
capacity has been shed through a series of redundancies.

But there are more reservations than approbations expressed about 'the
system' by call centre consultants—those organizational participants whose
behaviour is digitized and monitored. Consultants are particularly concerned
by the way in which 'the system' is changing the nature of customer relationships. One interviewee perceived them as less 'friendly'. Predominantly, however, consultants were concerned that they could not offer a 'quality' service
within the 235 seconds time frame. A consultant stated:

I don't like the time schedule, that's all. You know, like monitoring your own time
because sometimes it is not always possible because of the calls that you have, so it is
very hard to keep to that deadline, you know; they really want you to. I think that it is
going away from the customer service to time and I don't think that you can give both.
I'm from the old school...I think the focus is going off customers...Always in the
back of our mind is time, time, time.

And whilst one team leader indicated that some flexibility accompanies the
evaluation process, she was adamant that service could be accomplished 'in
the time frames'.

Consultants, on the other hand, are generally united in their perception that
such time-based measures of performance are 'too rigid'. Assessing consultants on their ability to manage time only, in their opinion, gives an inaccurate
and incomplete representation of their role in customer relationships.
Measures, such as AHT, do not take into account a consultant's ability to: 'win
back' customers; solve difficult problems on the spot (and thereby save more
expensive forms of follow-up); build rapport; follow procedures; or cross-sell
other products and/or services. One consultant was particularly outspoken in
this regard: 'But the best service hasn't got a measure. The best service is relative, if you like, to the customer's perception.' As a consequence, consultants
attributed a decline in 'morale' to the performance measurement regime.
Nonetheless, the consultants responded to their situation in a relatively understanding way: 'the statistical data is important to the business. We really need

to have statistical data because it enables us to identify our effectiveness. It is necessary for business to be profitable.'[9]

The measures were perceived as being 'effective for the company' but not 'for the actual workers'.

Our research also uncovered more personal accounts of the experience of post-industrial surveillance too. One consultant, for example, described the exhaustion, which she felt at the end of a working day, propelled by the AHT metric:

I find it mentally really, really gruelling because you will finish afterwards and, on average, take eleven calls an hour. That can be 77 to 100 calls a day. You will find that you brain is swinging in information because you've just gone at 100 miles an hour and as soon as you finish one call, you are back in to take another one. So you constantly have a stream of calls. I mean, in a sense, it's really hard.

However, it is the way that consultants feel during the working day that is more telling. There is a sense of the loss of personal freedom.[10] The public and the private have become blurred as a consequence of the surveillance process. The following consultant's story is noteworthy:

I think the scariest thing for people is the fact it feels as though they are monitored in everything now whereas before it was just your adherence. Now it feels as though every little part of what you do is [part of the organization]. Well, I had it explained to me by [my team leader] one day and he said, 'I went to look for you because you were off the phones and Sydney [head office] had called to find out why there was one person off line. And then I went looking for you and I found out that you were on the toilet. So I had to go back and let them know in Sydney that, yeah, you're on a toilet break.' That's how much it is monitored, just as an example. You can't even go to the loo without them knowing. ... But I thought that was interesting that they know exactly when you are going to the toilet. You feel like leaving a little note or putting a thing around your neck!

Consultants described the operation of the control system in terms of 'Big Brother'. One consultant felt as if there were 'eyes and ears on you everywhere'. Another experienced a feeling of someone 'looking over your shoulder'. Even one team leader (who exhibited a remarkable and spontaneous 'Latourian turn') admitted that the mode of operation of the control system contributed to this sense of individual discomfort and disquiet:[11] 'A lot of the

[9] This quotation has been cited from an interview with a Team Manager who worked previously in customer service positions.

[10] There was also a feeling of regret that the spatial demands of the surveillance system had disrupted established friendships. Consultants were required to sit in a designated seat; there was no choice. This created a sense amongst consultants that it was 'just work and not much else'.

[11] There was one demurring comment, however. One long serving call girl/consultant remarked that, whilst she did not like the statistics, she felt that this unobtrusive approach had created a relatively more relaxed work atmosphere, in comparison to the 'ruler brandishing' supervisors that she encountered on first entering the call centre environment.

staff don't like the calcs, you know, the statistics. ...too much like Big Brother, you know, too much supervision, not direct supervision, but supervision from, you know, *from a distance emphasis added* [emphasis added]'.

This system of call centre surveillance has created a powerful form of post-industrial panoptican in the case organization. Its invisible and virtual nature has constituted a qualitative experience of the consciousness of control. The time-based measures implemented to monitor the consultants' activities are experienced as continuing, systematic, and probing in their application.

Accomplishing the 'New'

The consultants from this call centre operation responded to such a context of post-industrial organizational control in two countervailing ways—on the one hand, they submitted to 'the system' and, on the other, they subverted 'the system'. The consultants were implicated in both the continuing operation of the system of surveillance *and* ongoing attempts to undermine the veracity of 'the stats'.

First, with respect to the accomplishment of submission, as has been indicated previously, the consultants have developed a fairly simple mental map that enables them to resolve the dilemma of their personal experiences at the 'front line,' with a need to achieve organizational goals. They are able to rationalize their situation through a demonstrated empathy with the objectives of the call centre operation. A consultant made the following illustrative remark:

It's like most jobs, you get put in the front and you just learn and most of the time it is not unreasonable. But you can usually empathise with the company and empathise with the customer. So you can see both sides of it, so you work on both ends of it, you know what I mean. I can understand your problem but I can also understand the company's problem with getting there.

Sympathy and submission are mutually reinforcing values within the call centre.

More fundamental, however, is the connection between 'the stats' and the consultants' sense of worth, facilitating their submission to such detailed monitoring and measurement of work-based behaviours. 'The stats' create normalized evaluations of the self. Consultants are able to appreciate their 'averageness', 'above averageness' or 'below averageness' as a result of the process of organizational control. And such performance-based measures are linked to 'job satisfaction' by the consultants. One consultant stated, for example:

I think the measures are, basically, fairly significant in terms of people knowing exactly where they are at. And they will have a goal to aim at, particularly if there is something set there for them, or they themselves can set some sort of targets for themselves if there is no targets from the company. I think from the point of view it creates a bit of job satisfaction, the fact that someone's got something to aim for, rather than just doing the same thing over and over again.

The strength of this link between the constitution of the self and 'the stats' is further illustrated by the ways in which particular consultants signal potential problems in performance to their team leaders in a proactive fashion. One long-serving consultant stated:

I myself know that when I had a really, really lousy day, where you have been held up on calls, either due to the customers or time processes with the testers and things like that, I might say, 'Look, I'm a little over the time that has been allowed. I've had a really busy morning. And, you know, it will probably affect my stats.'

A sense of individual achievement was one of the consequences of the consultants' submission to 'the stats'.

Second, there were aspects of resistance to the system of surveillance within this call centre operation too. The consultants responded to the performance measurements system by 'working the stats' (i.e. engaging in 'dysfunctional' forms of behaviour). And the team leaders acknowledged, for example, that the consultants 'play silly buggers with the phone'. There were a number of 'tricks' that particular consultants would perform to increase their adherence and average handling time, for instance:

people started sharing techniques up here, the way you get nice and high [performance ratings] and that's logging out in five minute blocks because the management systems that manages adherence works in five minute blocks—and scales things up and down anywhere in the middle. So someone might miss their break by a minute and then sit in traffic for another four minutes to go out of traffic on the five minute dot and they could achieve near perfect adherence.... When we have bad weather we've got lots of irate customers blah, blah, blah. Generally, your AHT can increase. Consultants were actually wrapping the calls up quicker and I suppose not logging complaints so they could stay within that range. So, you know, there's a lot of negative consequences from those sorts of things.

And whilst some consultants have a well-earned reputation ('icons') because of an ability to 'work the stats', other consultants, in comparison, were far more naïve and uninterested in engaging in this process of subversion. One such ingenuous consultant stated: 'you have to be very good to work them . . . I could never do it. There, I've given it away . . . I don't know many of them [the tricks], but I know it can be done. You hear enough in the lunch room and that sort of thing.'

Managing the 'New'

This ongoing dualism of submission/subversion provided management with a platform to introduce a generally well-received programme of change into the call centre operation. The deficiencies and dysfunctions of the extant performance measurement system were recognized (and capitalized on) by a keen new manager. He envisioned a future in which the coercion of time-based measures would be matched by a concern for the quality of service. The

Balanced Scorecard (BSC) was seen as the way forward—a very powerful way of ensuring compliance with an even more comprehensive listing of performance measures (see Kaplan and Norton 1996). The newly designed BSC monitors measures relating to 'operations' (cost-based measures), 'customer service' (customer satisfaction measures), and 'people' (employee satisfaction and performance measures).[12] And as this change agent and new player stated sagely: 'it's a good piece of rhetoric saying "balance". Who can argue against something that you say is "balanced"?'. Indeed.

The management hopes residing in this attempt to reconfigure the postindustrial experience of control in the call centre operation turn on the desired effects of the BSC. Management believes that the introduction of the BSC will make the consultants' jobs 'more interesting'. The consultants will be required to understand a range of business drivers and their interplay. The manager of the call centre operation stated:

The beauty is that [the BSC] gives us more confidence and understanding of our business and being able to sell our business, both internal and external, in a way of saying . . . we understand our business, we understand the cost drivers of our business. We understand the impacts, you know, the cause and effect impacts. That, in itself, is powerful and that will help me manage. . . . It won't be managing by perceptions and it will help me, perhaps, have the knowledge to move the business forward.

The architect and advocate of the BSC, however, had more far-reaching aspirations for the project. He was championing the BSC in an attempt to control the range of interpretations that abounded regarding organizational functioning. He stated:

I don't hold out hopes that we will be perfect in that way [vis-à-vis the performance metrics]. . . . What we wanted to achieve . . . when you can go to the consultants, testers, team managers, centre managers, anywhere in Australia and say, 'What are our business drivers? How do you get measured?' And they all say the same thing.

Nonetheless, despite this manager's desire for certainty and consensus, there was still a range of possibilities surrounding the fate of the BSC initiative. There were factors that augured well for this project's success. The consultants were generally quite positive about the formal connection that was being forged between costs and customers. As an illustration, it was stated: 'Well, again, we are going through a transition with the [BSC project], changing the measures to quality and customer focus compared to costs—which has been a big bee in my bonnet over the last couple of years, so that's a big improvement'. As such, the BSC more closely paralleled the consultants' philosophy of customer relationship management than the extant performance measurement system. And herein lies the irony of this case: the consultants were prepared to submit to a more extensive performance measurement

[12] Two versions of the BSC had been proposed during the period of the field work.

regime because they perceived that the BSC had shifted the focus from those time-based measures that formed the basis of their resistance.

The consultants also reacted favourably to the change process *per se*: very optimistic about it [BSC]. . . . 'I've liked the fact that they have got consultants involved in the process'. But this process also elicited some substantial reservations from management. One manager from the call centre operation stated that the focus on consultant involvement may prove to be the death knell of the BSC: 'we had champions [usually team leaders/consultants] in the centres that were rolling things out, bypassing the centre managers—and yet they [the centre managers] were the ones who were going to be driving behaviours'. Another manager expressed some doubt about the level of organizational participants' understanding of the 'balanced approach' itself, despite its rhetorical persuasiveness. He indicated that the rebuilding of individuals' causal maps, reconnecting control to a new series of performance measures and drivers, 'is not happening at the moment'.

As to whether the BSC creates a network of calculations that more strongly links the interests of managers, consultants and customers—only time will tell!

Disciplinary Resonances

Management accounting inscriptions and the technological have become increasingly intertwined in the post-industrial organization. The digitization of management accounting inscriptions has served to intensify the experience of post-industrial organizational control. Organizational participants are increasingly conscious of the operation of technologically enabled systems of control, despite the invisibility of their operation. And, as this case illustrates, such an experience of the intensification of control may be attributed to the changed timing and spacing of technologically enabled systems of surveillance. These systems have a capability to operate in real-time, simulating organizational functioning with greater immediacy and a richness of data-points than was possible in the industrial organization. For instance, in the call centre operation that we studied, behaviour was monitored at 5 min intervals, providing a very detailed account of consultants' performance. Also deviant behaviour, such as unscheduled or lengthy breaks, could result in the almost immediate intervention of call centre management into the activities of consultants in remote locations. As such, these digitized systems of surveillance have intensified the scope of post-industrial organizational control, enabling them to operate across far greater geographic spaces by disembedding accounting inscriptions from their local origins. Digitization has enabled the translation of local actions into inscriptions that reside in global knowledge repositories. The organizational (and inter-organizational) trajectory of accounting inscriptions is both unknown and unknowable in the post-industrial organization—particularly when coupled to the dissemination of financial information over the internet.

Nonetheless, as our case also illustrates, digitized forms of organizational control have emerged as an adjunct to, rather than as a replacement for inter-personal forms of organizational surveillance. Physical observation *continues* to be undertaken by the team leaders and the call centre management, despite the availability of comprehensive daily statistics on the performance of every consultant under their control. As such, there are important forms of implicit managerial knowledge, used in the control of organizational functioning, that cannot be made explicit in numerical accounting inscriptions and the media of digitized repositories. Local and unarticulated knowledge remains an important component of the control process in post-industrial organizations.

Similarly, local knowledge also constitutes an important part of the reper-toire of the 'controlled'. It is local knowledge that enables the 'controlled' to engage in the subversion of, and resistance to digitized forms of organiza-tional surveillance. For example, the consultants whom we studied were able to invoke their particular knowledge of customers' circumstances in order to challenge management's view of organizational functioning and to character-ize it as uncaring, unconcerned with quality, and fiscally-driven. It was local knowledge that enabled the consultants to treat 'the system' as a bit of game, manipulating 'the stats' and undermining the integrity of the accounting inscriptions. In many ways, these local forms of knowledge and modes of operating constitute an antidote to post-industrial forms of pessimism. Yet subversion and resistance appear to be matched by equal measures of sub-mission to, and rationalization of post-industrial forms of organizational con-trol. The intensification of surveillance outlined in this case, as well as the proliferation of performance measures, occurred only as a result of the chronic compliance of the consultants in the call centre.

It is these enigmas and tensions present in digitized forms of surveillance which constitute an interesting and challenging set of problems for future accounting research in a post-industrial context. The tensions between the vis-ibilities of digitized performance measures and the invisibility of their operation, as well as those between local accomplishments and global configurations of organizational functioning, sustain a research agenda which arguably promises both great empirical insight and theoretical interest.

APPENDIX

Research Note

The data used in this chapter were generated as part of a larger research project. This project investigated an Australian call centre operation over an 11 month period, commencing in August 2000. The call centre operated in 22 locations and employed approximately 1,900 full time equivalent staff at the time of the study. A summary of the data collection process is outlined below.

Table 1. Schedule of interviews

Interview number	Date	Interviewee	Approximate duration (min)
1	6 November 2000	Financial Controller	60
2	6 November 2000	Business Operations Manager	90
3	4 December 2000	Strategic Project Leader	30
4	20 December 2000	Strategic Project Leader II & III	60
5	15 January 2001	Business Analysts	60
6	19 January 2001	Centre Manager	90
7	29 January 2001	Team Leader	135
8	6 February 2001	Centre Manager II	135
9	7 February 2001	Service Technician	30
10	7 February 2001	Team Leader II	30
11	7 February 2001	Consultant	45
12	7 February 2001	Consultant II	30
13	7 February 2001	Team Leader III	45
14	7 February 2001	Team Leader III	30
15	17 March 2001	Team Leader IV	60
16	17 March 2001	Consultant III	45
17	17 March 2001	Consultant IV	45
18	18 March 2001	Commercial Operations Manager	90
19	21 May 2001	Business Operations Manager	30
20	25 May 2001	General Manager	60
21	12 June 2001	Executive General Manager	60

Table 2. Meetings observed

Meeting/event	Approximate duration	Number attended	Approximate total hours
Weekly national management meeting	1 hour for each meeting	25	25
Teleconference hookups and meetings on performance measures	Varied between 30 min and 3 hours in length	15	30
Performance measurement workshop	2 days	1	16
Strategy and project seminars	2 days each	3	64
Management conferences	2 days each	2	32
Other	Variable	5	21

References

Burchell, S., Clubb, C., Hopwood, A., Hughes, J., and Nahapiet, J. (1980), 'The roles of accounting in organizations and society', *Accounting, Organizations and Society*, 5: 5–27.

Castells, M. (1996), *The Rise of the Network Society* (Oxford: Blackwell).

Christensen, C. M. (1997), *The Innovator's Dilemma* (Boston, MA: Harvard Business School Press).

Cooper, D. J., Hayes, D., and Wolf, F. (1981), 'Accounting in Organized Anarchies: Understanding and Designing Accounting Systems in Ambiguous Situations', *Accounting, Organizations and Society*, 6: 175–91.

Covaleski, M. A. and Dirsmith, M. W. (1983), 'Budgeting as a Means for Control and Loose Coupling', *Accounting, Organizations and Society*, 8, 323–40.

——————(1988). 'The Use of Budgetary Symbols in the Political Arena: An Historically Informed Field Study', *Accounting, Organizations and Society*, 13: 1–24.

Doz, Y. L. and Hamel, G. (1998), *Alliance Advantage* (Boston, MA: Harvard Business School Press).

Drucker, P. (1998), 'The Coming of the New Organization', in *Harvard Business Review on Knowledge Management* (Boston, MA: Harvard Business School Press).

Emmanuel, C., Otley, D., and Merchant, K. (1990), *Accounting for Management Control,* 2nd edn. (London: Chapman & Hall).

Foucault, M. (1977), *Discipline and Punish: The Birth of the Prison* (Middlesex: Peregrine Books).

Giddens, A. (1991), *Modernity and Self-Identity: Self and Society in the Late Modern Age* (Cambridge: Polity Press).

Harvey, D. (1989), *The Condition of Postmodernity* (Cambridge: Basil Blackwell).

Hopper, T. and Armstrong, P. (1991), 'Cost accounting, controlling labour and the rise of conglomerates', *Accounting, Organizations and Society*, 16, 405–38.

Horngren, C. T., Foster, G., and Datar. S. M. (2000), *Cost Accounting: A Managerial Emphasis,* 10th edn, (Princeton, NJ: Prentice Hall International, Inc).

Ihde, D. (1998), 'Bodies, Virtual Bodies and Technology' in D. Welton (ed.) *Body and Flesh* (Malden, MA: Blackwell), 349–57.

Kaplan, R. S. and Norton, D. P. (1996), *The Balanced Scorecard* (Boston, MA: Harvard Business School Press).

Knights, D. and Collinson, D. (1987), 'Disciplining the Shopfloor: A Comparison of the Disciplinary Effects of Managerial Psychology and Financial Accounting', *Accounting, Organizations and Society*, 12: 457–77.

Latour, B. (1987), *Science in Action* (Cambridge, MA: Harvard University Press).

Lyon, D. (2001), *Surveillance Society* (Buckingham: Open University Press).

Miller, P. and O'Leary, T. (1987), 'Accounting and the construction of the governable person', *Accounting, Organizations and Society*, 12, 235–65.

Poster, M. (1990), *The Mode of Information* (Cambridge: Polity Press).

Rifkin, J. (2000), *The Age of Access* (London: Penguin).

Wiley, J. (1999), 'No Body is "Doing It": Cybersexuality' in J. Price and M. Schildrick (eds), *Feminist Theory and the Body* (Edinburgh: Edinburgh University Press), 134–9.

8

Operations, Purchase, and Sales in Hyperreality

Implications for Management Control from the Perspective of Institutional Sociology

Salvador Carmona and Paolo Quattrone

Introduction

Extant knowledge about the functioning of management control systems in the e-business environment has overwhelmingly focused on the technical side of systems (i.e. Chorafas 2001; Glover *et al*. 2001; Greenstein and Feinman 2000). In contrast, little is known about the extent to which management control systems interplay with the new structures and organizational forms that emerge from Internet commerce. At the same time, new institutional sociologists suggest that organizational survival is not only tied to conformity to institutional pressures as to acceptable behaviour, but also to effectiveness in the development of instrumental work (Dirsmith *et al*. 2000: 516; Meyer and Rowan 1977; Scott and Meyer 1983). A study that investigated how management control systems forge organizational understandings to enable firms' e-business practices, would enhance our knowledge about Internet commerce as well as contribute to the sociology of management control systems.

Empirical evidence to support the present chapter investigation has been gathered from Peony Ltd,[1] a family-owned firm that launched an Internet commerce division (ICD) in spring 1999 to sell online gifts and souvenirs to the millions of tourists and temporary residents that visited the region where the firm is established. Our data gathering spanned from September to November 2001 and consisted of twenty-seven open interviews with top, middle managers, and

We would like to express our gratitude to the personnel of Peony Ltd. for providing us with a rewarding research setting and to Al Bhimani for his helpful comments on an earlier draft of this chapter. This project is funded by the CICYT (Spain) grants # SEC 98-0282 and 01-657. Salvador Carmona is grateful to the School of Accountancy and Information Systems of Arizona State University and to the project PR 2001-0093 for support during 2001–2.

[1] The names and some of the events reported in this study are slightly disguised for confidentiality reasons.

employees. Aside from interview notes taken, Peony also provided free access to the minutes of its board of directors, internal memoranda, and external reports used in their decision-making process.

This chapter connects to the prior concerns of researchers in several ways. First, as noted by DiMaggio (1991), the establishment of a new formal structure usually faces internal opposition in so far as resources are diverted from pre-existing structures and, thus, those vested with interests in the old structures will protest. Removal of organizational opposition, we contend, might explain why some ideas or techniques achieve remarkable visibility and success (i.e. privatization, outsourcing) while others fail to do so (Hasselbladh and Kallinikos 2000: 700). Therefore, investigating the role of management control systems in enabling Internet commerce might shed some light over the qualitative and quantitative techniques that served purposes of support to such new forms of business.

Second, organizational survival depends on both a firm's compliance with institutional demands and the attainment of a performance threshold (Deephouse 1999; Dirsmith *et al.* 2000). As noted by Dirsmith *et al.* (2000: 516), investigating this relationship constitutes more than a promising research area as long as 'it concerns the practical human affairs of everyday work in contemporary organizations'. In spite of the importance of the relationship between institutional demands and organizational performance for research and practice, Dirsmith *et al.* (2000: 515) have echoed the early claim of Scott and Meyer (1983: 141), and contend that we know too little about the intertwinement between instrumental work processes and the symbolic display of rational organizational practice in response to institutional pressures. Our study attempts to contribute to the sparse, though growing, accounting literature that addresses the interplay between economic and institutional arguments (Granlund and Lukka 1998*a*; Granlund *et al.* 1998), in the development of organizational forms. In particular, we attempt to address the extent to which the rhetoric of management control systems mediates institutional and economic rationalities.

Third, our study addresses a family-owned firm that installed a new corporate division to develop commerce on the Internet. As shown below, the enactment of such a division involved the deployment of a management control system that blended purpose-built traits with logics imported from the brick and mortar division. As noted by Amat *et al.* (1994), family-owned firms of small and medium size enact forms of control that depart from those overwhelmingly reported in top-tier, premier outlets. Further, our focal organization used different systems of management control in each of its divisions. Therefore, the examination of the functioning of two management control systems in the same firm, albeit in different divisions, might also enhance our present understanding about their role in shaping different organizational visibilities.

The remainder of this chapter is structured as follows. The theoretical background of our investigation is described first. It is followed by an outline of the setting. The last section discusses our conclusions and poses some suggestions for future research in this area.

Institutional Theories and Management Accounting: The Framework of Institutional Sociology

Since calls have been made to study accounting in its organizational and social context (e.g. Burchell *et al.* 1980, 1985), the contribution of institutional theories to the debate in accounting and, specifically, in management accounting has been gradually increasing. The literature has witnessed, during the 1990s, the proliferation of works using the vocabularies and categories of institutional approaches (e.g. Carmona *et al.* 1998; Carruthers 1995; Carruthers and Espeland 1991; Meyer 1986) and various perspectives have so far entered the scene of the debate in management accounting. Such interest may be attributed to the relevance of institutional arguments in explaining change and stability in contemporary economies and society and, ultimately, to its research potentials in enhancing our understanding about processes of management accounting change. We do not attempt to provide an exhaustive and complete review of the contributions adopting such a perspective but will briefly discuss previous arguments and themes and their ties to the theoretical part of this chapter.

The contributions in this field are multifaceted. In some cases the institutional arguments are left hidden in the theoretical approach informing the study. The works by Malmi (1997) on the difficulty of drawing clear-cut distinctions between success and failure in the implementation of an ABC system, and by Granlund and Lukka (1998*b*) on the evolution of management accounting practices in Finland may be considered examples of this typology. In other instances, the use of an institutional theoretical framework is made explicit and constitutes the core of the entire contribution. This is the case, for example, of those increasing numbers of works which use Gidden's structuration theory to interpret the dialectic between management accounting change and stability (e.g. Scapens and Roberts 1993) and combine it with the *Old Institutional Economics* of Veblen and North (e.g. Burns and Scapens 2000) or with the *New Institutional Sociology* of DiMaggio and Powell (e.g. Granlund 2001). Concepts such as isomorphism (see below) and legitimation are nowadays common tools used in management accounting theorization (i.e. Covaleski *et al.* 1996 and Malmi 1999, as examples of use of these two categories in accounting studies, respectively).

The use of institutional theories has not been exempt from criticism (see the concluding section of this chapter). However, it is undisputed that institutional theories can contribute to enlightening the role that management accounting systems have in enacting, internalizing and/or resisting to external environmental pressures (see Ahrens and Chapman 2002; Bjørnenak 1997; Vaivio 1999). The present chapter is inserted in this emerging stream of studies and seeks to contribute along this direction.

Institutional theory attributes the diffusion of new organizational forms to compliance with institutional pressures (Meyer and Rowan 1977; Strang and Meyer 1993). A central tenet of institutional sociology is that organizational contexts are 'characterized by the elaboration of rules and requirements to which individual organizations must conform if they are to receive support and legitimacy' (Scott and Meyer 1983: 149). Such rules and requirements are known as institutions, which in turn are defined as 'cognitive, normative, and regulative structures and activities that provide stability and meaning to social behaviour' (Scott 1995: 33). Organizational conformity to institutional pressures help avoid external claims of irrationality and inappropriate behaviour and confer legitimacy and resources and enhance their viability. As noted by institutional sociologists, 'being technically efficient is not the only path to organizational survival. Achieving legitimacy in the eyes of the world, state, powerful professions, or society at large, is another effective survival strategy' (Carruthers 1995: 317).

Compliance with environmental pressures arguably makes organizations resemble each other or, as termed by institutional sociologists, become isomorphic (DiMaggio and Powell 1983). There are three forms of institutional isomorphism: coercive, mimetic, and normative. Coercive isomorphism mainly stems from the action of the state (i.e. by enacting environmental regulations that instil substantial changes in production and managerial processes of firms). Normative isomorphism arises from the action of the professions (i.e. the audit profession sets rules and norms that exert a significant impact on the administrative procedures of firms). Lastly, mimetic isomorphism is the outcome of organizational imitation, that is, firms mimic practices of counterparts regarded as successful (i.e. imitation of total quality management practices). Accordingly, isomorphism invests firms with legitimacy, which in turn is defined as 'the generalized perception or assumption that the actions of an entity are desirable, proper, or appropriate within some socially constructed system of norms, values, beliefs, and definitions' (Suchman 1995: 574).

Isomorphism, thus, enables the diffusion of organizational forms that will ultimately become institutionalized. Tolbert and Zucker (1996) proposed a general model of the institutionalization process that involved three stages. Pre-institutionalization, which implies generation of a new structural arrangement in response to specific organizational problems. At this stage, the new structure is created for technical reasons. Semi-institutionalization, which occurs when a social consensus develops regarding the value of the structure. Lastly, full-institutionalization develops when the structure perpetuates over time and becomes taken for granted by social participants. As Berger and Luckman (1967: 58) would put it, this occurs when a structure is seen to exist 'over and beyond' the individuals that supported it.

The mere adoption of institutionalized practices by firms, and the concomitant enhancement of their legitimacy, does not guarantee organizational survival in the long term. As Dirsmith *et al.* (2000: 516) point out, firms' survival

requires the blend of conformity to institutional pressures and the development of instrumental work processes in an effective manner. Nevertheless,
both dimensions are interrelated: 'there is ... an important interplay between
technical "as is" arguments and institutional "as should be" arguments,
implying that both factual and judgmental propositions are always present in
an argument' (Granlund *et al.* 1998: 435). In short, 'legitimation cannot be
systematically separated from "reality" ' (Granlund *et al.* 1998: 435; see also
Giddens 1984). Though it is argued that 'firms with persistent net resource
outflows will eventually fail' (Deephouse 1999: 148), it is debatable of the
level of organizational performance that guarantees the long-term survival of
an individual firm, as this is contingent on industries, geographical areas, and
ownership structure (Gimeno *et al.* 1997).

The Setting

Antecedents

Peony, Ltd was founded in 1982 to operate in the business of corporate gifts
and souvenirs. By the time of its inception, the firm was a family-owned concern that gathered a considerable part of the fortune of Mr Perez. In the mid-
1960s, Mr Perez started operations in the bridal and gift retail business and,
by the mid-1970s, ran and owned four profitable shops that attracted a client-
ele of wealthy people and firms. By the late 1970s, Mr Perez realized that
firms were increasingly demanding customized gifts (i.e. merchandise with a
firm's logo stamped on it). This perception was reflective of discussions in the
local chamber of commerce and attendance at business workshops and semi-
nars. In short, Mr Perez realized that firms gave increasing strategic importance to issues of corporate image that might provide him with significant
business expansion opportunities. Drawing in part on his lifetime savings, the
sale of one of the shops and two bank loans, Mr Perez launched Peony to
operate in this emerging market.

Peony was located in a county that experienced considerable industrial,
tourist, and demographic expansion (i.e. its population increased by 40 per cent
during the period 1925–99). Further, the area benefited from active govern-
mental policy to attract high-tech and clean industries as well as tourist-
related firms, which Mr Perez deemed receptive to issues of corporate image.
In this environment, Peony became a successful early entrant into the corporate
gift and souvenir market.

Starting Commerce on the Internet

By the second half of the 1990s, Peony became a dominant vendor in the segment of large firms that operated in its region. It attained 34 per cent of the
corporate gift market. Further, Peony counted leading high-tech firms and

hotel networks among its regular customers. As most of Peony's high-tech customers were in the process of installing Enterprise Resource Planning (ERP) systems, increasing demands from influential customers for Peony to implement a similar system were reported in the minutes of the board of directors' meetings. Intensification of these demands led Mr Perez to follow the Peony's procedures and request an investment assessment from the finance department. The report made clear that such investment would not comply with the 2-year payback requirement that Peony had established as a rule of thumb to assess capital budgeting projects. Further, the report raised concerns as the cost estimates supplied by the provider, especially an over-estimation of the technological savvy of Peony's employees that would require costly training. However, the report confirmed that it would be a crucial move for the firm to set up a system permitting electronic interfacing with critical customers. Lastly, the report attached a memo from the marketing depart-ment, which regarded Peony's social network with customers as a main asset of the firm and pointed out that such a network might deteriorate if imper-sonal forms of business were enforced. Lastly, Mr Perez summarized his posi-tion in a memo forwarded to the board of directors:

The report on the financial assessment of the ERP implementation has merit and is technically correct. It aptly acknowledges measurement problems of a crucial aspect: the benefits that Peony could gain by interfacing sales with our customers. It is clear to me that maintenance of our market niche advises implementation of such systems, as consistently noted in conversations held with our most important customers... The marketing department makes a point about the importance of our social network with customers and I will lead a team to design a plan that should enable Peony to enrich its social network with customers in spite of the deployment of ERP systems in our firm.

By early autumn 1998, the implementation of an ERP system along with exten-sive purchasing of computers and up-to-date software to curb the eventual Y2K effects resulted in Peony's over-capacity for information systems processing. This was shown in a compelling report made by Mr Perez's elder son, Ed, who joined the firm after earning a masters degree in information systems manage-ment. The report was circulated within Peony and led Mr Perez to conceive of new business opportunities from the sunk costs. In particular, Mr Perez thought of the potential online market arising from the millions of tourists that visited the region each year and that made extensive shopping of souvenirs and gifts.

From the marketing department, Mr Perez learnt that Peony could target three different segments through Internet commerce: (i) some 5 million tourists a year, who visited a region's world-class attraction; (ii) visitors who spent some 12 million hotel-nights in the metropolitan area, as reported by the chamber of commerce. In particular, the report of the marketing department indicated that Peony could focus on some one million, upper class visitors to the recreational facilities of the county (i.e. golf resorts); and (iii) a high, though non-quantified, number of elders who spent 6 months a year in the metropolitan area, escaping from the cold season of their Northern home-towns. Interestingly, housing for the elderly concentrated on three locations, whose share of elder neighbours ranged from 70 to 75 per cent of total population. This was deemed a potentially easy target for the sales force. Finally, the report echoed surveys of consultancy firms about the motivation of online shoppers, which consistently stressed that shopping on the Internet was chosen for convenience (73 per cent), to avoid crowds (69 per cent), and to save time (63 per cent).

The finance department prepared an assessment report on the prospects of e-business for Peony. The report stated that most long-term investments had already been made and actually constituted sunk costs for the firm. Additional investment requirements were regarded as 'minimal' and, thus, there was little doubt about the financial prospects of such business:

[to start operations on the Internet], we will need just some minor investments in fixed assets and software packages, and hiring as many as three people in the information management area. Marketing costs may be important during the start-up stage but will turn into operational levels pretty soon. Commerce on the Internet is a significant challenge for Peony that will enable us to profit from present sunk costs in our systems of electronic data processing as well as in personnel.

In view of such reports, Mr Perez issued the following statement to the board of directors:

we are neglecting the demands of some potential customers: Tourists who wish to bring some gifts back home. The effect of fixed (air tickets) and variable costs (accommodation) makes it an expensive day away from home. Visitors hate to spend half a day in a shopping mall because this takes them away from our beauties, resorts, golf courses, and restaurants, which are the primary purpose of their visit. I think that Peony has the resources and skills to target such market through the Internet commerce and, thereby, profit from our sunk costs in electronic data processing and avoid personnel layoffs. In this manner, Peony may also become a truly global firm and join the exclusive club of companies doing business on the market space.

To attain such goal, Peony launched an ICD that was chaired by Ed. The announcement of Ed's chairmanship stated that he had the 'vision, skills, energy and leadership to make Peony a successful competitor in the global market'. The set up of the ICD required from Peony additional expenditures in personnel, marketing, electronic bookkeeping, computerized dispatching, and office space.

Basically, the division comprised two departments: marketing and information systems, as other ICD activities were either provided by the corporate gift division of Peony (i.e. finance) or outsourced (i.e. logistics). Employees of Peony who succeeded in the traditional business of corporate gifts constituted the core of the marketing department. Their move to the ICD was motivated by expectations of increasing sales in an expanding market as well as by an incentive system that was perceived as 'accurate' to monitor performance and whose basic tenet consisted of enforcing collective indicators of performance over individual measures, as shown below.

The marketing department, with the assistance of a consultancy firm, launched an advertising campaign of the ICD business. It comprised extensive exposure at hotels' lobbies and rooms, public transportation (i.e. shuttle buses, cabs, and coaches), and intensive mailing distribution across the three elder locations. Negotiations were especially difficult with hotels. Hotel management argued that the ICD's products competed with those offered at hotels' shops and, thus, publicizing ICD products might jeopardize future hotels' rents. Finally, hotels accepted to become a venue for advertising the ICD products in return for receiving supplies of Peony's corporate gift division at marginal prices. Other advertising actions of the ICD division included search engines and banners. In general, the marketing policy of ICD encompassed free shipping; high-quality merchandise; 24 hour delivery at below-the-market prices; additional discounts to orders enabling delayed delivery; and a frequent buyers programme that targeted the elders segment as well as shoppers from outside the region.

The information systems department of ICD liaised with a consultancy firm to design and develop its technological infrastructure. The resulting system provided a satisfactory online market space: it was friendly and easy to use for people who lacked computer skills; it was available in five languages; it provided customers with automatic confirmation of orders; it contained a sophisticated firewall to protect data accessible from outside the firm; security patches of the system were regularly updated; the system of online shopping, lastly, was certified by a world-class firm of information systems assurance, whose logo was displayed in the home page. As a consequence of its built-in security, the system did not experience significantly successful attacks from hackers, but also the harsh firewalls instilled difficulties in the links to the internal inventory of the firm.

Products marketed by the ICD were not substantially different from the merchandise traditionally sold by Peony and, thus, the supply chain of the ICD largely built on that of Peony's corporate gift business. In common with the corporate gift division, the supply chain of the ICD was characterized by its reliance on Mr Perez's knowledgeability of suppliers for items such as T-shirts, handicrafts, garments, souvenirs, jewellery, and children's items. To speed up the process of building a supply chain, Mr Perez made a short-list of reliable, potential suppliers. Negotiations resulted in 'static' prices over the 1-year term of the contracts and two deliveries per week, in case of demand.

Systems of Management Control

Imbued with the technological culture of Internet commerce, the ICD requested from the finance department a management control system that departed from that existing in Peony. In short, Ed argued that the ICD and

Peony developed different technologies that could not be captured through a single system of management control. Though the argument appealed to the finance department, the final outcome still kept some of the traits of the system in use in the corporate gift division.

As noted above, a distinctive characteristic of the management control system at ICD consisted of its collective understanding of performance. By doing this, it departed from the individually based approach that was enforced in the corporate gift division. The latter was based on the notion of an 'account' manager. An account typically represented a customer that might be either a large company, or a group of small companies that produced significant sales turnover. Compensation packages comprised three elements: (i) a fixed salary; (ii) a pension fund that matched contributions made by employees up to a limit, and (iii) a variable salary that was contingent on performance. Performance, in turn, comprised individual and firm's measurements. The former included a yearly statement of responsibilities, indicators, and objectives. For example, for each account, it measured the annual attainment of targets as well as the reliability of the monthly forecast of sales. The latter consisted of a yearly bonus that depended on Peony's profitability (i.e. net income). Employees regarded this system as 'very stressing' in so far 'the good, old times of steady growth in sales were over and the yearly sales goals stated by the firm were more and more ambitious'. There were also complaints about the collective portion of the variable salary, as the bonus just implied a 2 per cent increase over the flat salary. In short, our interviewees complained about insurmountable problems to increase their personal income from such system.

In contrast, the ICD employees assessed positively the enforcement of an incentive system based on collective performance. On the one hand, they said that such system would enable teamwork within the division and coordination between different areas (i.e. marketing and information systems management). Further, along the deployment of quantitative measures of performance (i.e. sales volume), the ICD's system also enforced qualitative aspects such as 'generation and development of ideas' and 'responsiveness to market needs', which were regarded as 'constitutive parts of [their] jobs and crucial elements to succeed in the global market'. Finally, criteria of performance assessment at ICD also encompassed job-related issues to account for the inherent complexity of each individual job.

The systems of management control of the corporate gift division and ICD also kept some similarities. First, both systems relied on criteria of static prices with suppliers. As noted above, Mr Perez negotiated prices with vendors for both the corporate gift and ICD divisions, and this usually implied a 12-month contract that served the purposes of stabilizing prices. Therefore, eventual alternatives enabled by commerce on the Internet were ruled out at the ICD (i.e. exposed pricing, where every vendor may see everyone's bid). Second, information on cost data was classified at Peony. Mr Perez contended that such data were of strategic importance for the firm and that unrestricted access may ultimately bring about leaks of such sensible data to competitors. Therefore, salespersons were not aware of the merchandise costs and, thus, it was difficult for them to ascertain the best courses.

Getting Results

ICD entered operations by late spring 1999. Initial results showed the subsequent pattern of the firm's Internet commerce. First, sales were subject to considerable volatility, which made any planning difficult and posed serious troubles to estimate a critical mass of the ICD. Volatility in turnover aggravated existing difficulties in inventory planning caused by troublesome links to the internal database of the ICD. Second, the ICD sales amounted to 7 per cent of total Peony's turnover during its first 12 months of operations. Such figure was below the most conservative expectations enshrined in the ICD business plan. Further, the board of directors supported Mr Perez's idea to allocate marketing costs to the divisions as a function of their respective sales and calculate a single net income figure for the entire firm. Though these measures might help support a division with significant potential, like ICD, it worsened the organizational climate. Employees of the corporate gift division argued that their annual bonus diminished as a consequence of the losses of the ICD. Additionally, the corporate gift division was supporting the ICD by selling merchandise to a considerable number of hotels at marginal prices.

In summer 2000, the marketing department conducted a survey to ascertain the causes of the poor performance of the ICD. First, it was found that many potential customers distrusted the ICD return policy. In spite of the guarantee on 'satisfaction or the money back', customers showed reluctance to spend time in returning merchandise from their hometowns. Second, the ICD's loyalty programmes did not appeal to customers as much as expected. Potential customers spent short stays in the region and made piecemeal purchases from locations outside the county, which caused difficulties for the development of loyalty programmes.

Finally, whereas the marketing department observed that the 'resort' segment might produce positive performance, those of elders and visitors to the world-class attraction became niches, which were difficult to penetrate. On the one hand, the survey conclusively indicated that the elders lacked the necessary skills to do shopping on the Internet, which added to concerns about the security of online transactions. Interestingly, the survey suggested that the elders pondered visiting the shopping malls in search of gifts for their grandchildren over making purchases at the best possible prices on the Internet. On the other hand, the survey showed that visitors to the world-class attraction used to spend just one night in such places. Such short stays made it difficult to guarantee on time delivery for this segment of visitors. As a result of the survey of the marketing department, the ICD decided to concentrate its marketing efforts on visitors to the resorts, but keeping a low profile in the elders and world-class attraction segments. These decisions ultimately implied a need for downsizing the division.

Discussion

The extant literature on management control systems in the Internet commerce provides many perceptive insights into the technological side of the systems. By focusing on the technical aspects of management control systems in the e-business environment, investigation of the organizational implications of such systems has been widely neglected. Our study focuses on a family-owned firm that launched an Internet division to sell gifts and souvenirs to the millions of tourists that every year visited its region.

Our results reveal that the system of management control mediated the organizational conflict arising from Peony's decision to develop commerce on the Internet. This finding has some additional implications. First, even in highly centralized firms (i.e. family-owned firms), decision-makers are accountable for their actions in rational and analytical ways (Giddens 1984). To enhance that image of rationality, Peony enforced a decision-making process that heavily relied on reports issued by different departments (i.e. report of the finance department to assess implementation of an ERP system; report of the marketing department about the potentials of the Internet commerce). These reports were used to inform decision-making.

Our findings suggest that Mr Perez had intimate, albeit widely perceived, willingness of deploying an ERP system in Peony and entering the Internet commerce, and expected that technical reports provided support for such 'decisions' for otherwise it is difficult to explain the contents and structure of the reports. For example, the assessment report of the ERP implementation stated that the project failed to meet the 2-year payback requirement. In spite of this, the reports advised implementation of the ERP system on grounds of difficulty of obtaining reliable indicators as well as on the crucial importance to set up a system of electronic interface with critical customers. In a similar vein, the report that assessed the decision of setting up an ICD relied on soft data of revenues (i.e. the number of visitors was used as an indicator of potential sales), whereas the estimation of expenditures was considerably neglected (i.e. costs were simply deemed as non-significant). Interestingly, such soft reports contrasted considerably with the harsh system of management control that characterized Peony's regular business: 2-year payback criterion to assess long-term investment decisions, tough indicators of employees' performance assessment were determinant to set up compensation packages. Comprehensive market research was not undertaken until commerce on the Internet consistently reported poor results (i.e. surveys of the marketing department to examine causes of low sales in the elder and world-class attraction segments).

In other words, the vocabularies and calculation technologies deployed by management control systems provided a beneficial depiction of the Internet commerce that proved fully disentangled from any real object and, thus, exemplifying a Baudrillardian notion of hyperreality (Baudrillard 1994: 118; Macintosh *et al*. 2000: 14).

Our findings, thus, concurred with Meyer and Rowan's (1977: 349) contention that organizations use 'legitimated vocabularies' to the attainment of 'collectively defined, and often collectively mandated ends'. By deliberately adopting a 'soft' profile, the management control system became legitimating for managerial decisions that echoed pressures from either powerful constituents (i.e. Oliver 1991; on the implementation of an ERP system) or the wider institutional environment (i.e. Granlund and Lukka, 1998*a*—the need to become a global firm through the set up of an Internet commerce division). Compliance with such pressures would ultimately result in Peony becoming isomorphic with its environment (DiMaggio and Powell 1983).

Second, the rhetoric used by the management control systems attempted to garner support for the e-business decision from those that could question the financial feasibility of launching an Internet division (DiMaggio 1991). For example, the report of the finance department stressed the beneficial aspects of entering commerce on the Internet: by taking advantage of existing sunk costs, avoid layoffs, minimal additional investments. In a similar vein, attempts to reap organizational support for the ICD were exemplified in the official silence about the allocation of marketing expenses to divisions as a portion of total sales and the calculation of a single net income figure for the entire Peony. This exerted a negative impact on the compensation packages of employees of the corporate gift division.

Our results lend support for the notion that organizational survival requires compliance with institutional pressures as well as attainment of a performance threshold (Deephouse 1999; Dirsmith *et al*. 2000; Granlund *et al*. 1998). First, as a consequence of poor performance of the ICD division, two market segments were frozen (elders and world-class attraction), which, we contend, indicates that the process of institutionalization of Internet commerce may be classified into the pre-institutionalization category (Tolbert and Zucker 1996). In the case of full institutionalization, Peony had felt obliged to carry on its e-business commerce. This finding indicates that symbolic and instrumental work arguments are intertwined (Dirsmith *et al*. 2000; Giddens 1984), and that such interaction might occur at the stage in which the process of institutionalization is not yet completed (Tolbert and Zucker 1996). This is so, given that what is taken for granted and implemented by firms often disregards their economic impact (i.e. the audit function).

The poor financial performance of the ICD may be partially attributed to optimistic assessment of revenues arising from Internet commerce and the conservative estimation of costs. In our view, the ICD also missed some of the opportunities that commerce on the Internet offers to eliminate inefficiencies in a firm's supply chain (Chorafas 2001: ch. 4). For example, agreements on static prices simply transferred into the ICD the weaknesses of the corporate gift division. Instead, one might suggest that e-business firms might have looked at systems of smart pricing, where every vendor has access to everybody's bids (Carroll and Broadhead 2001; Zilliox 2001).

The contributions of the population ecology provide an alternative explanation for Peony's failure in the Internet commerce (Barnett and Carroll 1995). In contrast to the adaptive literature, theorists of the population ecology support a model of structural inertia. Such a model establishes that firms changing any of their core features (i.e. mission, technology, marketing strategy, and authority) are exposed to higher failure rates than counterparts that do not undertake such changes. In this respect, the deployment of the ICD by Peony involved changes in some of its core characteristics: technology, through substituting the brick and mortar kind of business by Internet commerce; marketing strategy, which involved targeting a population of tourists and temporary visitors to the region instead of firms; and authority, which implied the deployment of more 'democratic' incentive systems (i.e. those incorporating into the system some collective indicators of performance).

Family-owned firms encompass a number of idiosyncratic characteristics that enable an examination of the impact of institutional pressures on organizations. Such firms, for example, are characterized by centralization and concentration of ownership and management. The entrepreneur, in short, absorbs considerably the uncertainty stemming from technology or the market (Amat *et al.* 1994). Should the entrepreneur be positive to pressures from the external environment, such demands would be easily incorporated into the firm for the absence of significant organizational buffers. In this manner, entrepreneurial compliance to pressures stemming from powerful constituents indicating the convenience of the implementation of an ERP system or from the wider institutional environment to become an early entrant into the Internet commerce and a global firm face low, intra-organizational opposition. In such a context, the successful history of the firm (Giddens 1984), and the authority of the entrepreneur (owner of the firm and chief executive officer), makes troublesome a stiff opposition by subordinates.

Limitations and Extensions

Our investigation has some limitations that may encourage future work. First, empirical evidence supporting this study has been gathered from a family-owned firm. Though more research in such settings is needed, the idiosyncratic characteristics of family-owned firms suggest caution as to the generalizability of our conclusions. Therefore, there are possibilities for additional research on firms with a different ownership structure (i.e. public firms). Second, this study focused on the role of management control systems in the early stages of the implementation of Internet commerce in a firm. We think that future research on management control practices in firms with more experience in doing business online will shed light on the interplay between such systems of management control and the Internet environment.

The findings of our research also raise a series of theoretical questions that still remain unanswered from an institutional perspective and that we believe are worthwhile candidates for further exploration.

One of the main tenets of new institutional theories (e.g. DiMaggio and Powell 1983) is that firms gain legitimacy by complying with external institutional pressures. The case of Peony is quite paradigmatic in this respect, as noted above. We believe this presents a second potential contribution of this study. However, it also illustrates how the process of isomorphism is far from being linear and unidirectional. Whereas the case shows a need to succumb to external pressure for becoming a global and networked firm (i.e. the e-commerce and the ERP imperatives), it also illustrates how other institutionalized rationalities and practices (i.e. the need to attain a performance threshold) need to be accomplished too. In this respect Peony's management control system plays a dual role. On the one hand, it facilitates the introduction of the e-commerce initiative, providing a legitimate vocabulary for it. On the other, it is also the carrier of, and confers visibility to, another institutional pressure (i.e. the need to attain a certain level of performance), which cannot simply be discarded by the eruption of this new initiative (Dirsmith *et al.* 2000). To what extent then is the 'new' economy 'new' if the rationale that permits its diffusion is still anchored to quite 'old' and conventional economic performance measurement systems and the rationalities they embed?

This brings into focus the main critiques that institutional theories are facing. First, as argued in Hasselbladh and Kallinikos (2000) institutional theories have concentrated on the diffusion of existing institutions but very little is said on the processes of institutionalization. Our case points to the need for understanding and theorizing those conditions which make the 'new' emerge and how opportunities can be perceived as such and considered as a viable alternative to 'old' ideas and practices. Why some managerial ideas and practices manage to achieve visibility and take the place of others whereas many fail to do so is still a research issue to be addressed in a more analytical way. Our case illustrates that the study of management control systems can be an insightful line of research in this direction. They play a two-fold role (of facilitators and of inhibitors of innovation), which is still unexplored.

Second, the case illustrates how institutions are not as homogeneous and definite as some institutional theories seem to assume. It shows how the emergence of 'new' management ideas and practices is the result of a continuous process of struggle between competing, and sometimes contrasting, imperatives (i.e. the need to be global and performative).

Whether a new set of ideas manages to impose itself as new is not a simple matter of production and diffusion of a certain managerial belief (or practice), which can become a fad and/or a fashion once it is institutionalized (i.e. Mazza and Alvarez 2000). The problem is to see how these practices and ideas are constantly reworked and reinterpreted in their voyage to success and worldwide spread (Holm 1995). The diffusion process is not simply a change in space and time but it is constitutive of the very meaning of that specific idea, which cannot be decontextualized from the process itself. The institutional sequence of production to diffusion fails to recognize this complexity and, specifically, the multi-faceted role of management control systems. Studies on the emergence of activity-based costing (Jones and Dugdale 2002) are quite enlightening examples of how the process of translation (Latour 1987) of management ideas is actually constitutive of the idea itself. We believe that studies of management control praxis (Quattrone and Hopper 2001) have quite a lot to offer to address such issues. The evidence shown in this chapter is hopefully a step in this direction.

References

Ahrens T. and Chapman C. (2002), 'The Structuration of Legitimate Performance Measures and Management: Day-to-Day Contest of Accountability in a U.K. Restaurant Chain', *Management Accounting Research*, 13/2: 151–72.

Amat, J., Carmona, S., and Roberts, H. (1994), 'Context and Change in Management Accounting Systems: A Spanish Case Study', *Management Accounting Research*, 5/4: 107–22.

Barnett, W. P. and Carroll, G. R. (1995), 'Modelling Internal Organizational Change', *Annual Review of Sociology*, 21: 217–36.

Baudrillard, J. (1994), *Simulacra and Simulation* (Ann Arbor, MI: University of Michigan Press).

Berger, P. L. and Luckman, T. (1967), *The Social Construction of Reality: A Treatise in the Sociology of Knowledge* (Garden City: Doubleday).

Bjørnenak, T. (1997), 'Conventional Wisdom and Costing Practices', *Management Accounting Research*, 8/4: 367–82.

Burchell, S., Clubb, C., and Hopwood, A. (1985), 'Accounting in its Social Context: Towards a History of Value Added in the United Kingdom', *Accounting, Organizations and Society*, 10/4: 381–413.

————————Hughes, S., and Nahapiert, J. (1980), 'The Roles of Accounting in Organizations and Society', *Accounting, Organizations and Society*, 5/1: 5–27.

Burns, J. and Scapens, R. W. (2000), 'Conceptualising Management Accounting Change: an Institutional Framework', *Management Accounting Research*, 11/1: 3–25.

Carmona, S., Ezzamel, M., and Gutiérrez, F. (1998), 'Towards an Institutional Analysis of Accounting Change in the Royal Tobacco Factory of Seville', *Accounting Historians Journal*, 25/1: 115–47.

Carroll, J. and Broadhead, R. (2001), *Selling Online: How to Become a Successful E-Commerce Merchant* (Chicago: Dearborn).

Carruthers, B. (1995), 'Accounting, Ambiguity, and the New Institutionalism', *Accounting, Organizations and Society*, 20/4: 313–28.

Carruthers, B. G. and Espeland, W. N. (1991), 'Accounting for Rationality: Double-Entry Bookkeeping and the Rhetoric of Economic Rationality', *American Journal of Sociology*, 97/1: 31–69.

Chorafas, D. N. (2001), *The Internet Supply Chain: Impact on Accounting and Logistics* (New York: Palgrave).

Covaleski, M., Dirsmith, M. W., and Samuel, S. (1996), 'Management Accounting Research: The Contributions of Organisational and Sociological Theories', *Journal of Management Accounting Research*, 8: 1–36.

Deephouse, D. L. (1999), 'To Be Different, or To Be the Same? It's a Question (and Theory) of Strategic Balance', *Strategic Management Journal*, 20/2: 147–66.

DiMaggio, P. J. (1991), 'Constructing an Organizational Field as a Profesional Project: US Art Museums, 1920–1940', in W. W. Powell and P. J. DiMaggio (eds), *The New Institutionalism in Organization Theory* (Chicago: University of Chicago Press), 267–92.

——and Powell, W. W. (1983), 'The Iron Cage Revisited: Institutional Isomorphism and Collective Rationality in Organizational Fields', *American Sociological Review*, 48 (April): 147–60.

Dirsmith, M. W., Forgarty, T. J., and Gupta, P. (2000), 'Institutional Pressures and Symbolic Displays in a GAO Context', *Organization Studies*, 21/3: 515–37.

Giddens, A. (1984), *The Constitution of Society* (Cambridge: Polity Press).

Gimeno, J., Folta, T., Cooper, A., and Woo, C. (1997), 'Survival of the Fittest? Entrepreneurial Human Capital and the Persistence of Underperforming Firms', *Administrative Science Quarterly*, 42/4: 750–83.

Glover, S. M., Liddle, S. W., and Prawitt, D. F. (2001), *Ebusiness: Principles and Strategies for Accountants* (Upper Saddle River: Prentice Hall).

Granlund, M. (2001), 'Towards Explaining Stability in and Around Management Accounting Systems', *Management Accounting Research*, 11/1: 3–25.

——and Lukka, K. (1998*a*), 'It's a Small World of Management Accounting Practices', *Journal of Management Accounting Research*, 10: 153–73.

————(1998*b*), 'Towards Increasing Business Orientation: Finnish Management Accountants in a Changing Cultural Context', *Management Accounting Research*, 9/2: 185–211.

————and Mouritsen, J. (1998), 'Institutionalised Justification of Corporate Action: Internationalisation and the EU Corporate Reports', *The Scandinavian Journal of Management*, 14/4: 433–58.

Greenstein, M. and Feinman, T. M. (2000), *Electronic Commerce: Security, Risk, Management and Control* (Boston: Irwin-McGraw Hill).

Hasselbladh, H. and Kallinikos, J. (2000), 'The Project of Rationalization: A Critique and Reappraisal of Neo-Institutionalism in Organization Studies', *Organizations Studies*, 21/4: 697–720.

Holm, P. (1995), 'The Dynamics of Institutionalization: Transformation Process in Norwegian Fisheries', *Administrative Science Quarterly*, 40/3: 398–422.

Jones, C. and Dugdale, D. (2002), 'The ABC Bandwagon and the Juggernaut of Modernity', *Accounting, Organizations and Society*, 27/1–2: 121–64.

Latour, B. (1987), Science in action. How to follow scientists and engineers through society, Cambridge Mass: Harvard University Press.

Macintosh, N. B., Shearer, T., Thornton, D. B., and Welker, M. (2000), 'Accounting as Simulacrum and Hyperreality: Perspectives on Income and Capital', *Accounting, Organizations and Society*, 25/1: 13–50.

Malmi, T. (1997), 'Towards Explaining Activity-Based Costing Failure: Accounting and Control in a Decentralized Organization', *Management Accounting Research*, 8/4: 459–80.

—— (1999), 'Activity-Based Costing Diffusion across Organizations: An Exploratory Empirical Analysis of Finnish Firms', *Accounting, Organizations and Society*, 11/4–5: 649–72.

Mazza, C. and Alvarez, J. L. (2000), '*Haute couture* and *Prêt-à-Porter*: The Popular Press and the Diffusion of Management Practices', *Organization Studies*, 21/3: 567–88.

Meyer, J. W. (1986), 'Social Environments and Organizational Accounting', *Accounting, Organizations and Society*, 11/4–5: 345–56.

—— and Rowan, B. (1977), 'Institutionalized Organizations: Formal Structure as Myth and Ceremony', *American Journal of Sociology*, 83/2: 310–63.

Oliver, C. (1991), 'Strategic Responses to Institutional Processes', *Academy of Management Review*, 16/1: 145–79.

Quattrone, P. and Hopper, T. (2001), 'What Does Organisational Change Mean? Speculations on a Taken for Granted Category', *Management Accounting Research*, 12/4: 403–35.

Scapens, R. and Roberts, J. (1993), 'Accounting and Control: A Case Study of Resistance to Accounting Change', *Management Accounting Research*, 4/1: 1–32.

Scott, W. R. (1995), *Institutions and Organizations* (Beverly Hills: Sage Publications).

—— and Meyer, J. W. (1983), 'The Organization of Societal Sectors', in J. W. Meyer and W. R. Scott (eds), *Organizational Environments: Ritual and Rationality*, (Beverly Hills: Sage Publications), 129–53.

Strang, D. and Meyer, J. W. (1993), 'Institutional Conditions for Diffusion', *Theory and Society*, 22/4: 487–511.

Suchman, M. C. (1995), 'Managing Legitimacy: Strategic and Institutional Approaches', *Academy of Management Review*, 20/3: 571–610.

Tolbert, P. S. and Zucker, L. G. (1996), 'The Institutionalization of Institutional Theory, in S. Clegg, C. Hardy, and W. Nord (eds), *Handbook of Organization Theory*, (London: Sage), 176–90.

Vaivio, J. (1999), 'Exploring a "Non-financial" Management Accounting Change', *Management Accounting Research*, 10/4: 409–37.

Zilliox, D. (2001), *Get-Started: Guide to E-Commerce* (New York: Academy of Management Association).

9

Not for Profit—for Sale
Management Control in and of an Internet Start-Up Company

Jan Mouritsen and Kristian Kreiner

The Life of an Internet Company

> E-Firm really needs 'de-flexibilisation'. We are a bit too much on the chaotic side, and we need some standards and procedures to structure our processes.
> (founder of E-Firm)

It started as the classical story of an Internet start-up firm. Two entrepreneurs—still students at the time, founded it in 1994, and a small flat constituted the business premises. The founders were enthralled by information technology and especially by the most hip technology at the time: web technology. The firm—let us call it E-Firm—was founded on the business idea of providing e-solutions to other business firms. In the beginning, e-solutions were equivalent to home pages, but gradually the firm developed its services into e-commerce and e-based business strategy. And after a few, tumultuous years the firm was acquired by another player in the field and disappeared as an independent business entity.

The life of E-Firm was classical in terms of its operations, depending upon a very verbal and communicative management. The history of the company, its competencies, the explosive development of the technology, and the customers' need for the type of services that E-Firm could provide, were constantly narrated, explicated and adjusted by the founders. It seems as if managerial eloquence is a precondition for success in such start-ups. Without extensive experience or demonstrable successes, the trust of others was reliant on the images and visions that the managers were able to create by words and Power Point presentations.

In this chapter we reflect on E-Firm from the perspective of a critical moment in the history of the company. The year is 2000 when the ownership of the firm is highly negotiated. We use the managers' PowerPoint presentations as our data, and we focus on how the past as well as the future is presented. We investigate how E-Firm was made sellable and turn to management's main message at the time—'de-flexibilisation', as they had expressed it.

The account made by the management of the E-Firm is interpreted as a form of rationalization. We assume that the accounts are as real as reality comes in high tech companies. The market, the technology, and the structure of E-Firm become real, or at least more real by being presented in a consistent and communicable whole. The managerial controls were real, at least in their consequences, of making E-Firm a sellable entity. If other people are willing to pay money for it, we interpret that it exists in some sense. We discuss here how E-Firm became real—an entity which would be worth somebody else's money. We suggest that management controls played a central role in this.

The Management's Public Account of the Firm

In this section, we reconstruct the pitch developed by management during the lifespan of E-firm.

Embedding a Start-Up in a Technology-Driven Market

In 2000, one of the founders of E-Firm recounted the firm's past and future as depicted in Fig. 9.1. E-Firm started out making web sites with static information, often in the form of product information. Gradually, the sites became more dynamic, first in the form of marketing sites where brand identity and product qualities could actively be impressed on the public. This

Our arena

Mission critical aspect			
Low	Medium	High	Very High
Static Web presence Product information	Brand identity Greater graphics content E-mail and search capabilities	Faster response times E-commerce capabilities Business-to-consumer focus Internet seen as new distribution channel	Business-to-business focus Creation of new electronic markets Essential tool for maintaining and expanding customer base Focus on robust data warehousing systems Front office automation Integration of front and back office platforms
Information	Marketing	Interactive	Integrated

| 1994 | 1995 | 1996 | 1997 | 1998 | 1999 | 2000 | 2001 | 2002 | 2003 |

Fig. 9.1. The rationalized evolution of E-Firm (Year 2000)

moved gradually to interactive sites where business transactions could be performed online. Finally, the integrated sites that were envisioned to organize whole business networks and value chains emerged. Different types of technical solutions became critical in the different phases of the development, as indicated in Fig. 9.1.

Over the short span of years the products offered by E-Firm became more and more complex, as solutions to increasing numbers of business functions were integrated in the web sites. The product also became less and less technical, in the sense that issues of identity, strategy, and social organization in relation to the web technology deployed became a much larger part of the solutions being developed. Thus, on the one hand, web sites continued to be core to the E-Firm's products and services. On the other hand, that core counted for less and less of the value added that the products and services of E-Firm offered to its customers. More and more, E-Firm was selling business conceptions, visions, and strategies, for which, if implemented, E-Firm's web technologies would be available.

The Value Added for Customers

Web technology continued to be core, though its salience to the competitiveness of the company decreased as E-Firm went from helping customers to present their product on the Internet, to helping customers transform themselves and their business in a fundamental way (see Fig. 9.2). The focus moved away from the technology itself, and gradually over time, it shifted towards *organizing and managing technologies* rather than to technologies themselves.

Fig. 9.2. The development of corporate competencies, as defined by management

The core of the firm's activities became gradually displaced, and the firm altered its focus—in the eyes of its management—from a technology firm to a more general strategy consulting firm specializing in e-business applications. The 'Development' of the firm has been presented by management as a gradual and marginal adoption of new competencies that would contextualize the technological base of the firm. This 'Development' started off with attention being given to interaction between the firm and its customer with the two-way interaction between firm, customers, and suppliers and ultimately to the future. The 'Development' suggests that E-Firm was envisaged to gradually become more and more oriented towards the strategies to be pursued at top-management level in client firms. Therefore, the 'Development' is also an attempt to attach itself to higher and higher levels of management in these client firms. In a sense, the E-firm's history is one of continued marginalization of the core technology on which it was created.

Management as an Afterthought to Play

It may seem counter-intuitive to stress management and control for an Internet company if one takes on the suggestion that management and control are left-overs of the industrial, modernist age, while something other than this might be more apt in a networking, enterprising, and post-modern era (see Koogle, 2000; Shapiro and Varian 1999; Margretta 1998; Parolini 1999; and Tapscott *et al.* 2000). As Strannegård and Friberg (2001) suggest, the post-modern world is a fragmented one where firms and individuals exist in paradoxical relation with each other. People are, as Strannegård and Friberg say, always elsewhere, physically, intellectually, and in terms of identity. There is little in the way of systematic and continuous ways of life. In their study of an Internet company, they describe how the 'new new' was always coming in: always the latest telecommunication and information technologies, always the latest trend in furniture and colour, always new hiring, and always a circulation of people and services. The 'new new' as a way of life would contradict ideas of systematic management. They note how notions of play and identity may push notions of discipline and management out. It was more important to start projects than to manage projects. Management was a surprise; an afterthought to play.

Strannegård and Friberg's analysis of an Internet company stresses the undecidedness of management. It does not discuss the problems facing managers to keep things together. The flux and fluidity pressing themselves onto the firm are effects of strategies to be 'new new' but they are not merely resources in constructing the firm. They are also integral to uncertainties, paradoxes, and contradictions, which constantly press themselves onto managers. These uncertainties, paradoxes, and contradictions stand in contrast to the optimism of the fluid society where people, information technology, and financial flows intermingle in new and surprising—sometimes very surprising—ways

(Mandel 2000; Schiller 2000). The frailty of the Internet business models is perhaps more clear to managers that have to keep them together than to the nomads of people who travel from one firm to another. Therefore, for managers the problems of somehow organizing and keeping things together is a formidable task, that is perhaps more important in a 'post-modern' society than in a 'modern' one.

The story of E-Firm can be written as one suggestive always of what management could and should be, and the 'post-modern' world's mantras of flexibility and innovation, which have to be manoeuvred carefully. The flexible and innovative firm is one which has partly been managed from the stage of 'real affairs'. In their discussion of the 'New Commercial Agenda', Munro and Haterly (1993) suggest that the 'new' firm is one where middle-managers and workers coordinate directly with customers and suppliers in tightly coupled interaction on issues of products, services, exchanges, and commitments. Top-management, in contrast, are envisaged as bearers of the shareholder value imperative, where they coordinate primarily with the financial and capital markets. This is also the concern that has fuelled some of the discussion of the empowered, individualized firm (Bartlett and Ghoshal 1997; Johansen and Swigart 1994) and the concerns surrounding intellectual capital (Mouritsen *et al.* 2001*a, b*). The dilemmas facing managers in such situations have been expressed in terms of how it may be possible to invest in intangibles and at the same time retain power to capitalize on this investment. The dilemma is that much 'intellectual capital' is said to be in the heads of people and therefore beyond the reach of managers (Nonaka and Takeuchi 1995; Stewart 1997).

However, this is not satisfactory to managers. The prospect of not being able to hold on to resources is no solution, and therefore they embark on various strategies with a view to reducing this risk (Mouritsen *et al.* 2001*b*). This chapter follows the dilemmas of managing a growing firm in volatile markets—the Internet phenomenon—where little is known about appropriate business models (Clark and Neill 2001; Porter 2001; Treese and Stewart 1998; Weill and Vitale 2001) and the kinds of management controls that are possible in such firms?

In the literature, management control is often related to the application of certain techniques such as budgets and financial reporting systems. There, management control is identified as a set of mechanisms that exist 'outside' the situation being analysed, and therefore management control cannot be 'surprising'. It can only be a matter of degree compared with the intensity of the techniques used in particular situations. Our view differs. This is outlined below.

Management Control

While accepting that often budgets and financial reporting systems are part of a firm's control package, there may be other means through which control is achieved. To us, management control is not understood as the particular kind of management tool put in place, but rather it is a matter of how it is possible for a person (a manager) to get access to and somehow command resources. As such, management control is generally about the practices and technologies mobilized in order to establish oneself as an obligatory passage between resources and effects. It is about the efforts devised by managers to keep things together—the work involved in maintaining some form of continuity. This view draws to an extent on Latour's (1991) view that 'technology is society made durable'. A technology—a management technology—is a mechanism that allows somebody to establish it-, him-, or herself as able to somehow put resources together, influence their deployment and development, and monitor the effectiveness of their application (Hansen and Mouritsen 1999). It may be that budgets and financial reporting systems do this, but in some situations this may be more effective with only limited attention to such systems, as will be made clearer below.

With this perspective, the chapter tracks the development of the firm's management and control largely from its inception in very tiny localities through rapid growth, and mergers and demergers to the point where the original founders left the firm after being bought by a much larger international Internet company. In a sense, the chapter tracks the firm's history during the period when it still had a strong sense of identity and when the original founders of the firm were still in its management group. The empirical elements of the study are of three kinds. Power Point presentations used by managers throughout its history to present E-Firm and the images shown in this chapter are excerpted. Second, evidence from internal reports developed over time about the management of the firm are used. Last, conversations with managers and some employees contribute to the analyses. This last dimension of the method was impressionistic—in that it derives from unstructured interactions—last mobilized in the context of other objectives. These 'datapoints'—particularly the Power Point presentations—are carefully constructed pieces of communication, which help illuminate the managerial concerns held for the firm's image. The tensions of management and the ideas of the product and services are 'all over' these presentations as they try to make sense of the firm, and as they attempt to rationalize the steps made to change and develop the firm.

The Web Technology as Presentation—The Firm as a Meeting Place

In 'the beginning'—1994—in an apartment two students receptive to new technologies became receptive to the idea of entrepreneurship also. Once they realized that they had not yet got their degrees from university, the label entrepreneur seemed a welcome one. In the late 1990s, no one in Denmark was surprised by the background of entrepreneurs. The really great ones never completed their degree. Proper entrepreneurs rejected conventional frames of reference in terms of career path, particularly where education played a part.

In the start-up phase, E-Firm had no employees. It was a network enterprise without permanent employment, as programmers and other staff were students who used E-Firm not merely as a place for work—but for work, rest, and play. It was a place used as a mechanism to meet, to explore new technology, to fill out the spaces of time between lectures and assignment work. It was partly a mechanism to make money, but also—and perhaps even more decisively—a place to explore technologies, to 'hang out'. Very different kinds of life experience coalesced on this place—a whole spectrum of work and play was in evidence here.

It was a 'pizza' company. The pizza firm was on E-Firm's web site, and there was access to having pizzas ordered over the Intranet. As a pizza firm, it was 'nerdish'. Such a work identity very specifically mirrors the culture of program developers (see Fig. 9.3). Informality supported play and leisure time. 'Formal' management controls—such as budgets and systematic financial reporting—were not 'in place' because work time was not regarded as a scarce resource. The two individuals' presence was an 'in between' form of time bridging rest and play to university work which was then seen as a serious concern for most participants of the E-Firm experience. The very fact that formal controls were not in place may well have augmented the sense of

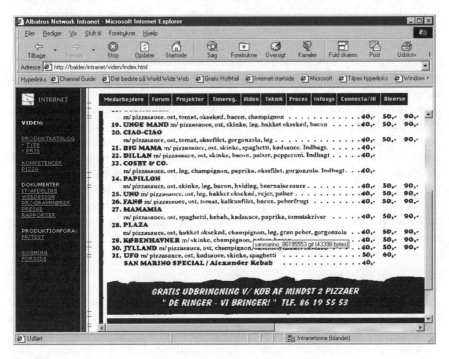

Fig. 9.3. The E-Firm's pizza identity—online pizzas for employees

resources not being scarce. As hours spent went uncounted, and as no system was in place to make them visible, there was an overt control gap.

People were participants rather than employees. Their time was not counted, and as payment was project based and related to specific agreed upon tasks, the financial structure was utterly flexible. The participants were 'hired by the project', and therefore payment was a truly variable cost. In a sense, management control here amounted to paying direct labour for the direct hours spent on projects, if such inducement/contribution ratio were to be inferred at all. Time was not a scarce resource in a financial sense. Sometimes, participants were paid to press the buttons of the PC—in times of work—and in other situations they just pushed the keyboards anyway because it was fun. Time recognition was meagre because participants saw the place not merely in terms of work, but also as the 'place to hang out', and the place to 'look into new technology'. The working place was not only working time, it was also to a certain extent, leisure time. Time was not a metre of accountability. Time was abundant and as such it could not be economized. There was no criterion for tracking it.

Life was a bit more serious for the entrepreneurs. They had the task of developing a business and had to create customers. They had management concerns, but these were not related to the management of internal people; they were related to the management of external people—the customers. Their space was larger than the place of E-Firm, it was the market place beyond—or related to—issues of technology. The division between the customer and the participants turned out later to be one of the delicate issues in the growth of the firm.

Time metering was meagre initially, as noted above, but time transformed itself gradually from a space of leisure and learning to one of scarcity. One aspect of this was the gradual development of participants' lives and the reach of their obligations. They tended to get additional obligations as they moved to the finish line of their university education or when they got involved with boy/girlfriends. The place gradually became displaced from being the *only* place for leisure time. Therefore, the probability that it would be easy to mobilize participants to engage in projects for customers at the right times worsened. Participants started to see their time as limited and scarce, internal management problems gradually emerged. The management of time became an issue when time was no longer abundant, and when it had to be paid for. It now became work rather than leisure.

Integration as a Solution—the Demanding Customer

From a management point of view, it is not difficult to develop a web site. It can be seen as largely a one-person job who can program in HTML. And in a sense, a web site is a simple service, which can be managed at a distance because the programming work is largely independent of interactions with customers. It is a technological thing. When E-Firm moved into e-solutions that required it to somehow integrate the web site with other customers' operations, new challenges arose. The first was that the customer wished to actually talk to E-Firm on a regular basis and be able to talk to the persons that were producing their solution. The phone had to be answered! But often people could be attending university classes or just out on a date with their boy/girl friend. It was difficult for a customer to find E-Firm, and therefore it had to establish itself as something 'tangible'. Telephones had to be answered, project managers had to be appointed, sales people had to be able to trust that E-Firm could deliver in time.

A gradual formalization of controls was related to seeing the firm as something that could present itself to customers as an entity—as a container of decision-making authority, which could arrange people and products in relation to each other. This involved an aspect of coordination between the internal and the external world. When customers wanted a solution, they needed to talk to the designer, programmers, and project managers. If these were part-time and if they had split loyalties towards the firm, their girl/boy friends and their education, the system was not adequately predictable for customers to be comfortable in their interaction on a continuous basis with the firm.

The idea of the firm as a mechanism to supply something required it to be a coordinated place that could act 'as one' towards an external audience. Under such circumstances, time ordering had to be observed. The firm had to bind its employees to business.

Integration as a Solution—the Complementary Firm

The gradual formalization of controls around time ordering implied a concern for predictability in operations and relations with customers. This theme had parallels in the area of strategy. When the firm gradually got 'its act together' in terms of self-presentation to its customers, it also faced the problem of what the possible supply was. When the service was a 'simple' home page, the impact on the customer's situation was 'faint'. When E-Firm gradually developed its aspiration into more specific strategic interests and wanting to supply not only the home page, but also e-business solutions and providing consulting on strategy matters relating to e-solutions, it found itself increasingly as having to organize the competencies needed to keep a hold on the firm's activities. This involved attention to stratifying the competencies of people and attention to project management systems that could help integrate people and technologies around complex customer projects involving strategy and technology at the same time. Thus, this required a project planning system that could help allocate time-resources and not only make sure they were available during a particular period of the day (see Fig. 9.4).

One aspect of this is the 'knowledge management web' and the project costing system. The illustration of layers of web pages on top of each other

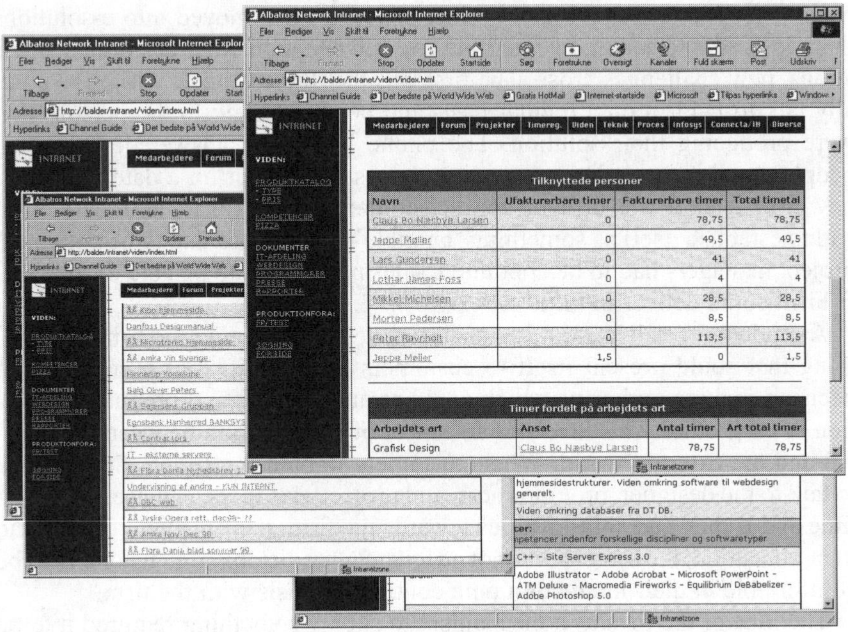

Fig. 9.4. Tools for managing E-Firm's resources

accord with a management perspective. The knowledge management part of it specifies what each employee—they are now employees rather than partners—are able to do, which technologies they master, which customers they know, and which projects they work on. It is a database of the competencies of each individual person, and it can be used to find knowledge in the firm, and thus also to allocate resources towards projects (see Fig. 9.5).

In addition to the pressure to make projects cohere, there were also pressures to economize resources and allocate them sensibly. This was problematized as follows in an internal report:

Previously, sales consultants spent lots of time writing and developing presentations of the firm, and frequently they started anew each time they had a new presentation. Now, they have a set of standard presentations, which they can draw on. They thus save time that they can use to find new customers.

Previously the project managers spent time writing a large number of proposals of which a large share never succeeded. Together, the project managers have created a flexible blueprint for their proposals that has been tested with a number of customers and they have reached significant improvements in productivity. Now it takes about half the time to make a proposal and they have built in a better assurance against proposals that promise too much or ask for too little.

There is obviously the possible danger that these standards will hamper the employee's creativity in presenting the firm or developing proposals. We are

What about the following rather than the simple question, how will you describe yourself?: 'I am sure that you will make a mark at all the attributes described below, but your modesty will not allow that. Please, put a mark at the competencies that others would point to in order to characterise you. Remember, we check references'.

Chose five of the following items

Knowledge about the industry	Technical knowledge	Knowledge of Business	Cross (functional knowledge)
Hard work and attention to results	Think expansively	Make plans	Demonstrate leadership
Act with integrity	Communicate effectively	Project management	Solve problems and make decisions
Influence others	Champion Improvements	Solve conflicts	Dedicated to customer success
Innovation & learning	Partnership	Team-worker	Do more with less

Fig. 9.5. Arenas of competence

knowledgeable about this limitation and work towards minimising it and the employees' sense of the process being too tight without room for variation and renewal.

Creativity can be abundant—it is a management issue to determine the kind of creativity that is relevant. If creativity does not 'coincide' with the rules, then the coherence of complex projects building on various disparate competencies from programming via design to strategy faces jeopardy. Moreover the potential financial effects are in jeopardy. Therefore, as can be seen from the illustration above (Fig. 9.4), the project accounting system—which counts hours and allocates them to projects—help sort out efficiency by which resources have been put on projects.

As projects are so complex, they need complementary resources. This is illuminated by the knowledge web page (Figs 9.4 and 9.5) and the efficiency of this allocation is measured against projected financial results. Because of these complexities, managerial controls could be appropriate. They could distribute complexity and make the project accessible. It can then be seen from a distance, on a piece of paper, as a representation which can help navigate E-Firm by connecting disparate spaces into one. One that is on paper. Management controls, in effect, are not in a contradictory relation to complexity and fluidity.

Circulation as a Solution—the Financial Space— the Circulation of the Firm

As the firm grew, it still presented itself as a (post) modern Internet company with flexible structures and systems, but gradually this presentation was modified. Flexibility was to be controlled, because the firm could not be allowed to become anarchic. This was interesting not least because management realized that the firm had to find alliances and partners to maintain a pace of growth. Here, the flexibility of the post-modern firm was a liability, because to be able to fit into another firm's strategy in terms of possible alliances or perhaps even direct mergers, the firm had to be able to explain itself. Not only was strategy a matter for its own development. It was a mechanism by which it could present itself as an appendix to other firms' strategies. For this to be possible it had to have two things in place—it first had to specify organizational competencies so that the complementarity with another firm could be made clear, and secondly it had to show control of its resources.

The 'History' illustrated above concerns the period after E-Firm's transformation into a limited company. Over a very short period of time, E-Firm attempted to engage in various collaborative relationships in order to develop the business (see Fig. 9.6). It was sold to ABC, it was partly repurchased and resold to DEF, which then within weeks merged with JKL.

This attracted new complementarities, but it also shows why E-Firm had to be a unit—not only a flexible network. For mergers to work, the merging entities have to be entities that can be incorporated into a whole. This requires the individual firm to be able to show itself and present itself in such a way that it fits another firm's strategy. To be able to do this, management and stacking controls are required, because they are the entities, which can speak for a whole set of resources that stand in structured relation to each other. This is how mergers can develop the reach of the firm, and one of management's slides illustrates this very well: there are offices all around Europe (see Fig. 9.7).

This presentation is one that holds on to all resources at one time. It shows very precisely that the space commanded by E-Firm is no longer the place in the apartment where copresence was possible. The map is a different metaphor where the firm can only be assembled and reached by means of a technology. This is a management technology, which connects the spaces of the firm together in one move. This is the map.

Milestones in our history:
Sale, purchase, sale

1998 - Primo: set up as limited company, NN in as an owner
1999 - 1st Quarter; sales of 51% to ABC Company
1999 - 4th Quarter; negotiation to repurchase the 51% of shares
2000 - 1st Quarter; repurchase of 26% of the shares from ABC Company
2000 - 1st Quarter; letter of Intent concerning a merger with DEF Ltd.
2000 - 1st Quarter; DEF begins talk with GHI Ltd. about merger
2000 - 1st Quarter; merger with DEF Ltd.
2000 - 1st Quarter; merger with JKL Ltd.

Fig. 9.6. The evolution of E-Firm

Geographical map

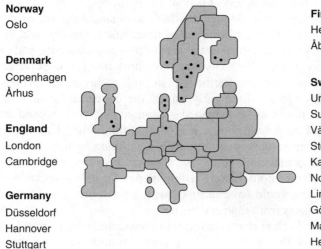

Norway
Oslo

Denmark
Copenhagen
Århus

England
London
Cambridge

Germany
Düsseldorf
Hannover
Stuttgart

Finland
Helsinki
Åbo

Sweden
Umeå
Sundsvall
Västerås
Stockholm
Karlstad
Norrköping
Linköping
Göteborg
Malmö
Helsingborg

Fig. 9.7. The space of E-Firm (Year 2001)

Discussion and Conclusion

This brief story shows how flexibility was gradually transformed—how deflexibilization was rationalized and communicated. In a time span of just a few years an anarchistic small start-up company developed a more structured form of management. This structuring was a way to develop a 'professional firm' that could be flexible towards both customer wishes and the wishes of possible alliance partners. In order to become flexible in those respects, flexibility towards employees and local practices had to be reduced. The E-Firm had to demonstrate management competence, and this demonstration consisted largely of the installation of management controls. These controls allowed time to be considered and measured as a scarce resource that required strategic and rational allocation. They also allowed time to be considered as a cost relative to the various projects, and as an investment in new organizational competencies. A systematic management of internal resources (mainly time) was considered a prerequisite for being flexible in relation to customers' demands and as such a prerequisite for being attractive to potential partners and buyers. To make a claim to being an entity, manageable as a whole, mobilizable as a whole, and sellable as a whole, management used the 'rigidity' or 'modernity' of the infrastructure of management controls. Flexibility was a highly complex phenomenon that did not reside outside management controls—rather the particular form of flexibility was defined by the attachments of management actions to competencies through the technologies of managing that made them available to organization and coordination.

It is a story of the transformation of time, space, identity, and the body. It is a transformation, which takes the idea of play and creativity, and disciplines it to suit growth and complexity. The transformation is one of recasting management, from being an afterthought to play, to becoming management of play. The playfulness of the early stages, the disregard for time as a scarce resource that needs to be managed systematically, was in itself mobilizing time and making it less scarce. E-Firm was the home of local people with interest and competence in web technology; 'hanging out' with like minds, disregarding normal work hours, and apparently so creative in their design of home pages that customers were willing to pay for it. It is impossible to know whether E-Firm would have survived with a more business-like approach to time and business from the very beginning.

However, it is clear that management considered a business-like approach necessary when the services sold got more complex and the expectations of the customers were raised. As an integral part to this development, the management itself became mandatory—it became the obligatory point of passage for all processes and decisions. The volunteers of the early days could not be required to be at work at regular and predictable hours, also because they grew older, got established in families, and depended on a regular income themselves. Play had—not only from a management point of view, but also from the employees' point of view—to be managed in order to produce predictability in certain directions. Predictability in presence and availability, so that phones would be answered and the clients' urgent problems attended to quickly. Predictability in pay and employment, so that a wardrobe of sorts and healthier food than pizza could be afforded. From being an afterthought to play, management moved up as forethought in preparation of play. 'Management of the play' was deemed necessary, and the management controls became ways in which play became manageable. Possibly, the amount of playfulness changed in this process. It did not disappear but was staged in new ways and in new areas because without playfulness, creativity and the integrated solutions on which E-Firm depended could not materialize.

The deflexibilization of E-Firm unrolled without clear protest from the employees. Possibly, this development suited them well in view of the fact that their circumstances had changed as well. The playful hanging-out with like-minds was fine for people in their early twenties, but 6 years later (1994–2000) the attractiveness of a life as a student would now have to be assessed by a person in the early thirties, with different material and social needs. It is possible that the institutionalization of E-Firm as a firm does not reflect the 'natural' evolution of start-ups, but rather reflects the personal and 'social' evolution of the participants involved in the firm. The requirement of the clients and the services may be convenient ways of ascribing the changing internal attitudes to an outside force, rendering 'adaptation' an undisputable necessity.

The other possibility is that the change had little to do with the requirements of clients and solutions, and instead had much to do with the ambition to sell the firm. The ambition was to put E-Firm on the map, literally and symbolically. Literally, it ended up with offices marked on a map of Europe (see Fig. 9.7). Literally, the business premises used to be a space to be filled with student interaction, etc. Now it had to become a space with a significant meaning—a place, as it were, that would communicate the presence and integration of a diversity of competencies and a management structure that can ensure rational exploitation of such diversity. The 'place' was the symbol of the entity that could not only provide integrated solutions to clients; it was also the symbol of a transferable network of intellectual resources and capabilities. It provided the notion of an entity that could be managed as an entity—and sold as an entity.

This is related to space—the place of activities and the distribution of encounters between people. This concerns the intersection between being present and being absent to each other and the mechanism that—after all—ties all people to the same sort of fate—namely the survival of the entity that outgrows any particular sense of presence and 'smell'. Space increasingly becomes representative to the degree that the firm has to be on a map over Europe. This goes far beyond copresence being the starting point of new technology.

In a sense, the firm in its new guises was not only oriented towards making itself a profitable place; it was just as much interested in capitalizing its competencies to be realized in a merger. It was indeed 'for sale' rather than only 'for profit'!

The original entrepreneurs are no longer with the firm, and the firm itself discontinued its existence as an independent entity. It was sold before the crash of the Internet stock in Spring 2000. We do not know what the entrepreneurs were paid. But they are still smiling. They may have profited from the 'for sale' strategy!

References

Bartlett, C. A. and Ghoshal, S. (1997), *The Individualized Firm* (New York: Harper Business).

Clark, P. J. and Neill, S. (2001), *Net Value. Valuing Dot-com Companies—Uncovering the Reality Behind the Hype* (New York: Amacom).

Hansen, A. and Mouritsen, J. (1999) 'Managerial Technology and Netted Networks', *Organization* (1999, vol 6, no. 3, pp 451–471).

Johansen, R. and Swigart, R. (1994), *Upsizing the Individual in the Downsized Organization* (London: Century).

Koogle, T. (2000), 'Building Yahoo', *Business Strategy Review*, 11/4: 15–20.

Latour, B. (1991) 'Technology is Society Made Durable', in Law, J. (ed.) *A Sociology of Monsters* (Sage publications)

Magretta, J. (1998), 'The Power of Virtual Integration: An Interview with Dell Computer's Michael Dell', *Harvard Business Review* (March–April): 73–84.

Mandel, M. J. (2000), *The Coming Internet Depression* (New York: Basic Books).

Mouritsen, J., Johansen, M. R., Larsen, H. T., and Bukh, P. N. (2001*a*), 'Reading Intellectual Capital Statements: Describing and Prescribing Knowledge Management Strategies', *Journal of Intellectual Capital*, 2/4. pp. 359–83.

Mouritsen, J., Larsen, H. T., and Bukh, P. N. (2001*b*), 'Valuing the Future: Intellectual Capital Supplements at Skandia', *Accounting, Auditing and Accountability Journal*, 14/4: 399–422.

Munro, R. and Hatherly, D. (1993), 'Accountability and the New Commercial Agenda', *Critical Perspectives on Accounting*, 369–95.

Nonaka, I. and Takeuchi, M. (1995), *The Knowledge Creating Company* (Oxford University Press, 1995)

Parolini, C. (1999), *The Value Net* (Chichester: Wiley).

Porter, M. (2001), 'Strategy and the Internet', *Harvard Business Review*, (March–April) 63–78.

Schiller, R. J. (2000), *Irrational Exuberance* (Princeton: Princeton University Press).

Shapiro, C. and Varian, H. R. (1999), *Information Rules: A Strategic Guide to the New Economy* (Boston: Harvard Business School Press).

Strannegård, L. and Friberg, M. (2001), *Already Elsewhere—om lek, identitet och hastighed i affärslivet Stoekholum: Raster Förlag*.

Stewart, T. (1997) Intellectual Capital–*The New Wealth of Organization* (Nicholas Brealy Publishing, 1997)

Tapscott, D., Ticoll, D., and Lowy, A. (2000), *Digital Capital. Harnessing the Power of Business Webs* (Boston: Harvard Busines School Press).

Treese, G. W. and Stewart, L. C. (1998), *Designing Systems for Internet Commerce* (Reading, MA: Addison-Wesley).

Weill, P. and Vitale, M. R. (2001), *Place to Space. Migrating to E-Business Models* (Boston: Harvard Business School Press).

10

Management Accounting in the New Economy:
The Rationale for Irrational Controls
Leif Sjöblom

Introduction

Hindsight is an exact science. With the Internet boom behind us, it is time to go back and ask ourselves 'what went wrong?' and draw lessons from the 'new economy' phenomenon. This chapter explores the mindset of Internet entrepreneurs and the internal management control systems during the rise—and fall—of the new economy. Understanding this mindset is important in that the new economy cannot be fully understood from a purely 'rational' perspective. The learning points of this autopsy are not new—many new economy entrepreneurs violated basic management principles that have been well accepted for years.

There is no generally accepted strict definition of the 'new economy'. One key feature of the new economy has been said to be the separation of the economics of information from the economics of things (Evans and Wurster 2000). New 'pure play' economy companies tried to exploit the value of information without getting involved in the intricacies of producing the goods. They routinely used the Internet as a low cost but rich channel of communication with the customer. In addition to the pure play new economy companies, many old economy companies—manufacturers of things—were also new economy players in the sense that they used the Internet to reach their customer base via new means. Since these ventures were often decentralized and independent of their parent organizations, they are also the subject of this chapter.

Over the years, I have had the opportunity to interact with many new economy entrepreneurs. A lot of them are mavericks who managed their companies with no control systems whatsoever—neither financial nor operational and

I am grateful to a number of people who agreed to be interviewed for this project. Although these people provided valuable information and ideas, they may not agree with the opinions and conclusions expressed in this article. Many thanks to Andy Baker, Rob Churchward, Alex Banz, Rens Schoenmakers, Teppo Paavola, Paul Pyzowski, T.J. Huizer, Frode Lervik, Nestor Gismondi and many more who prefer to stay anonymous. I am also grateful to Al Bhimani for all the constructive feedback on numerous iterations of the chapter.

without structured development or marketing processes in place. Their stories provide some insights into the mindset of the new economy entrepreneurs, but they are not the main target group.

For this study, I targeted a subset of the new economy firms based on two criteria. First, the companies should at least have attempted to implement some elements of traditional control systems, like a budgeting process, and second, they should at least have been partially successful in their stated objectives. Companies that have never generated any significant revenues were excluded. A total of seventeen entrepreneurs, venture capitalists, consultants, and chief financial officers/finance directors were interviewed. They represent ten companies directly and another 20–30 companies indirectly via venture capitalists. The business segments covered are diverse: Internet consulting services, interactive games, workflow tools for print jobs, neural network systems for capturing intellectual capital, portals for healthcare, retailing, comparative shopping, pet food, and so on. Three companies are described in more detail in the Appendix to the chapter. The sample is small, but the findings are surprisingly consistent across the sample.

The interviews were open ended and they centred around three major questions:

1. To what extent are today's problems in the new economy caused by external factors (such as pressure from investors) and to what extent by internal factors (such as planning and control systems)?
2. How did the control system evolve over time? What performance indicators were used? Were they useful or not?
3. With hindsight, what would the incumbent have done differently?

The common feature of all control systems was that the emphasis was on predicting future revenues. Cost control did receive a degree of attention, but revenues were always considered more important. There was only limited evidence that companies with traditional budgets and control systems outperformed their peers. They no doubt survived a little longer, but most suffered as much as the companies 'on the wild side'. This implies that although traditional control systems may be helpful in keeping costs under control in a stable environment, they were not sufficient for the new economy. More comprehensive systems may be needed to manage the major risks of a new venture—the market risk, the product risk, and the people—particularly in turbulent times.

The next part of the chapter summarizes the common factors that, according to the interviewees, drove the behaviour of the new economy companies. A short discussion of the implications for the design of control systems follows. The wide range of management control issues is illustrated through three mini case studies in the Appendix. The first company is an Internet technology/service provider that paid little regard to managing its rapid growth. Bertelsmann-On-Line (BOL), a well-known European Internet book retailer, provides an example of a new economy company with a detailed business plan and strict financial discipline. Workthing, a UK Internet job-listing agency, gives insights into a company with strong awareness of the business risks and a diagnostic control system to monitor these risks.

The New Economy Mindset

The interviews highlighted a number of external and internal factors that have had a major influence on how the companies were managed and on their ultimate fate. Three external factors—overly optimistic market size estimates supplied by credible sources, a perception of a race for the number one position, and valuations driven by inflated future revenue expectations—were all factors that worked against prudent financial management.

External Factors

The Internet received a lot of attention from the media, consultants, and investors during the late 1990s. It was perceived as having the potential to severely disrupt traditional business models. The gospel of the day was 'pursue e-business or die'. Even old economy companies like Intel accepted the mantra: 'Only the paranoid will survive'. These perceptions and the media attention they received created external pressures that had a considerable influence on the mindset of the new economy companies.

The market potential was enormous: There was an undisputed impression that the Internet was an enormously big thing that would fuel economic growth for several years. These impressions were reinforced by market research companies such as Forrester and Jupiter, which estimated the market size at orders of trillion dollars. The sheer size of the market, the implied growth rates, and the low entry barriers attracted many new entrants. Business plans could easily be sold to venture capitalists because it only took a very small market share to justify the return on investment figures. The external pressure caused by the inflated market size estimates, as well as the large number of ventures entering the market, accounted for much of the 'irrational' behaviour of the market. Almost all interviewees mentioned that their internal revenue targets had been adjusted upward by the board of directors to reflect these unrealistic market size estimates.

The business models assumed that the 'winner takes all': For many old economy companies, the trend has been for the top performers in an industry to make a disproportionately high share of the overall industry profits. Companies such as Nokia and Cisco, for example, were disproportionately more profitable than their followers in their respective markets (McKinsey 2001).

In the B2C segment of the new economy, there were compelling reasons as to why the first player to establish a critical mass would be the winner. Once a customer had chosen a particular website, there was to be no reason for him or her to switch. And since acquiring new customers was significantly more expensive than keeping existing customers, the first mover would have a significant cost advantage. Network effects—the 'nobody goes to an empty disco' phenomenon—would further consolidate the position of the market leader. 'Owning the customer' became the name of the game, and this created a perception of a race to become number one in the market.

The scale associated with being the market leader was also important. The new economy business models were highly scalable, which meant that once the critical mass was achieved, profitability would increase dramatically. And being the dominant player could give a company disproportionate market power to set standards which would force the suppliers into a commodity position.

In some segments, there was a degree of merit in the first mover argument. Early entrants such as Amazon and AOL established strong positions in their home markets. In the existing B2C world a handful—0.04 per cent—of all e-commerce sites generate 80 per cent of all consumer visits (Braddock 2001). But many business plans forgot that consumers are seldom as rational as consultants picture them. The mobile communications industry experiences churn rates—customers switching from one supplier to another—of 20–25 per cent despite the lack of compelling arguments that any one operator was superior to another.

Perhaps the most dysfunctional aspect of the winner takes all argument was the response of those companies that started late or fell behind in the race. The response to being behind target was simply to 'outspend the competition'. With few business drivers under direct control, this often meant spending money on anything perceived to add value. This meant, in particular, advertising and customer acquisition.

Stock market valuations were driven by revenues (or revenue potential): Although the argument that the winner takes all is not self-evident, it was widely accepted by both financial analysts and investors. Once market leadership had been established, it was assumed that the profitability issue would take care of itself. The new economy was driven by stock market valuations, and valuations were based on estimated future revenues. Hence, the search for revenues at any cost became crucial. This further fuelled the spending spree on advertising and customer acquisition.

Customers are a prerequisite for revenues and the number of customers was seen as a natural leading indicator of future revenue. Netscape initially achieved a phenomenal valuation because of its large customer base. The fact that this was achieved by giving away the product free did not dampen enthusiasm. Web traffic and related measures (see Fig. 10.1) became popular proxies of choice for the customer base and for future revenue potential.

The need to acquire additional customers as fast as possible also resulted in a large number of acquisitions. A study of eighty-six Internet acquisitions (Rajgopal *et al.* 2000) found that 77 per cent of the variability in acquisition price could be explained by web traffic. The average price was $167 per monthly visitor. But the number of visitors was not related to current revenues

Customer base

- number of web page hits,
- number of unique visitors,
- number of first time visitors.

Stickiness/loyalty

- number of registered users,
- duration—time spent on the site,
- churn rate—number of customers lost in a period,
- frequency—how often does a customer visit the site?,
- velocity—time from initial click to purchase,
- abandoned purchases,
- recency—when did a customer last visit the site?.

Conversion

- purchase rate/number of purchases per visit.

Fig. 10.1. Typical leading indicators of revenue potential used by new economy companies

or profits. Clearly, investors were confident that web traffic would eventually turn into revenues and profits.

Internal Factors

Although companies agreed almost unanimously on the three external factors affecting the behaviour of new economy companies, there was much more diversity in the opinion on the internal factors. The following picture emerged:

Lack of market and end user understanding: Many ventures failed to undertake basic customer and market segmentation analysis. Although many customers may be willing to buy books and CDs online, this does not automatically imply that anything can be sold online. The vast majority of the services offered by the companies were at best 'nice to have' but rarely truly essential. For example, the online market for pet food attracted several entrants—all of which failed. In highly fragmented markets such as books and music an aggregator has a potentially important function to fulfil. Some opportunities may exist to differentiate the service. For example, Amazon provides not only a large selection of books at attractive prices but also book reviews and targeted recommendations based on the customer's profile. But extending such a concept to the sale of pet food becomes less evident. Even when there was a real end user need, many markets did not have a structure that was open to a major shake-up. For example, the pet food industry was highly concentrated and the incumbent pet food suppliers were in the best position to offer online services.

Many ventures completely underestimated basic issues such as customer churn. One venture capitalist told me that he never saw a churn assumption in the hundreds of business plans he received. The customer base was assumed to grow at astronomical rates and all customers would remain perfectly loyal.

Another wishful assumption was the length of the sales cycle. Many entrepreneurs considered that: 'if we build it, they (the customers) will come—and soon'. The time and expense required to develop the market often turned out to be excessive.

Overspending on media and brand building: The major cost categories of a new economy company were marketing and brand building. The first problem was that because of external pressures many companies were actively encouraged to spend more money on marketing and advertising. The resources were, however, not spent wisely. Companies frequently overpaid for what they got, and significant sums were spent on general brand building that was unlikely to turn into revenue.

Wrong people: People who pursued e-business opportunities had often never worked in a particular industry but founded new economy companies in those very industries. Frequently, the external perspective the new people brought was useful if one sought to shake up an industry. But most of the time it is equally important to know the customers, their needs, and the market dynamics.

One key resource that most companies felt they did not need was a chief financial officer (CFO). Raising money was not a problem, and there was simply no obvious or immediate need for a CFO when the company had no revenues. Most professional CFOs that I interviewed were brought into the business by the parent company—in many cases an old economy company—to 'put the house in order' several months after the startup came into being.

In sum, the stereotypical new economy company was one in which the business opportunity was not well defined, the entrepreneurs had unreasonable expectations—fuelled by outside pressure from investors—and important human resources were lacking.

Implications for Management Control Systems

The purpose of a management control system is to help management focus on the core business opportunity, to support resource allocation, and to provide timely corrective action whenever necessary. In high-risk environment, such as that within which new economy firms operated, the importance of properly designed control systems would seem critical.

The interviews suggested that although a large number of 'no control' companies failed, many companies that implemented traditional financial controls—such as budgets and spending limits—did not fare much better. However, management control is a much more holistic concept than simply having a budget and financial controls. Simons (1995) provides a useful framework with four 'levers of control' that reinforce and complement each other to help managers steer their business. The framework is presented in Fig. 10.2.

The four levers represent an increasing recognition in the management accounting literature that many managers face multiple—and many times conflicting—objectives. Most organizations acknowledge the need for customer responsiveness, creativity, flexibility, and empowerment. But on the

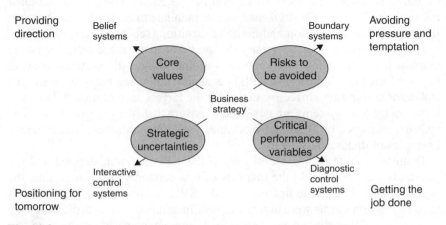

Fig. 10.2. Four levers of control (*Source*: Adapted from Simons (1995))

other hand, disasters such as Baring's Bank and Enron indicate that creativity and empowerment can extend too far, and that there simultaneously is a need for strict control. In addition, many companies struggle with the conflicts between short-term financial goals and longer term objectives.

Kaplan and Norton (1995) posited the Balanced Scorecard as a diagnostic tool that would give a more holistic and balanced view of the management control trade-offs. The lead–lag relationships between different performance indicators are useful in managing conflicting short-term and long-term objectives. Since financial performance indicators are often perceived to lack relevance, reliability, and timeliness (Sjöblom 1998), the balance between financial and non-financial performance indicators is a welcome attempt to compensate for the limitations of purely financial measures.

While the Balanced Scorecard is primarily a diagnostic control system, the four levers framework suggests that an even more holistic view of management control is needed. The four perspectives in many instances conflict with one another.

Belief systems or core values (providing direction): Managers need to articulate the business strategy and the direction they want their employees to pursue. The underlying business strategy needs to be translated into core values. Many new economy ventures had no clearly defined core values—or at least no core values based on a realistic assessment of the needs of a specific market segment. In some cases, the implicit core value was 'growth' (or perhaps, if one wants to be cynical, 'going public'). This often translated into 'growth at any price'. While high growth inevitably is part of any new venture, there were no breaks to translate this into 'manageable growth'. In other cases, the core values were more refined and more explicit, but nevertheless based on wishful thinking. The business opportunity was based on a product or service offering that was 'nice to have' rather than truly essential for the customer segment. The more successful new economy companies had clear core values. For example, BOL had a clear mandate to compete with Amazon in terms of market position and brand recognition (see Appendix, case II).

Diagnostic systems (getting the job done): For many managers, diagnostic systems are synonymous with control systems. Diagnostic systems measure key performance indicators (KPIs), evaluate them against predetermined standards and trigger corrective actions if the targets are not met. In layman's terms, diagnostic systems are designed to ensure that 'the job gets done'. The systems employed by BOL and Workthing (see Appendix, case II and III) are examples of diagnostic systems.

Diagnostic systems are useful only if the KPIs are well defined and the standards are objective. In the majority of new economy companies, this was never the case. The causal link between the KPIs and revenues and profits was tenuous, and standards were highly inflated. In addition, it was difficult to take corrective action if there was a variance. As mentioned earlier, one of the few variables within the control of management was media spend; many companies responded by spending more on advertising (the only variable they could control) when they were behind on customer acquisitions. Hence, it should not come as a surprise that diagnostic systems provided limited—or even counterproductive—value to these companies.

Another pitfall with diagnostic systems is seen to be that what gets measured gets done. If the system is not well balanced, even a well-designed system may create problems. The variables in Fig. 10.1, which are typical variables quoted by many interviewees, are purely geared towards revenue. It is hardly surprising that these companies frequently had cost control problems. As a counterexample, Workthing (see Appendix) uses a 'balanced scorecard' diagnostic system that is tailored both to the revenue potential and to the downside risk of the venture.

Boundary systems (avoiding pressure and temptation): In a highly uncertain environment with rapid growth, some breaks are necessary. But very few new economy companies had activities that were explicitly off limits. This was often justified by the flexibility needed to respond to rapid change and by the winner takes all argument. But the flip side of this was that the whole issue of risk management was neglected. New markets were frequently entered without really understanding the requirements of the markets or without having the necessary resources. The possibility of failure was simply unthinkable; the response to missed targets was overspending on advertising and media.

Ironically, although financial strength creates flexibility to respond to unforeseen circumstances, having too much money often results in lack of focus and, ultimately, failure (Laird and Sjöblom 2002). Tight financing forces management to be more focused and allocate scarce resources more carefully. The venture capital market, which provides some financial discipline, broke down during the emerging new economy era. Too much money was available to fund even weak business plans. And few companies used tight budgets as an internal boundary system.

Interactive systems (positioning for tomorrow): Planning for strategic uncertainties is a form of scenario planning in which constantly changing external threats (and opportunities) to the business are explored and contingency plans created. It is perhaps the least developed of the four levers in many old economy companies, which may explain why some companies were initially slow to react to the new economy opportunity. However, during the later stage of the new economy, old economy companies expended a lot of effort and resources on this kind of analysis—primarily as a defense mechanism against the external threat. Interestingly, the new economy companies largely ignored it—it was simply unthinkable that the new economy would fail. Business plans concentrated only on the upside potential; churn was an opportunity, not a threat. With the exception of Workthing, I came across very few companies with a clearly articulated exit plan in case they failed to achieve their milestones. Table 10.1 compares and contrasts the old and the new economy using Simons' framework.

Table 10.1. Levers of control in the old and new economies

Control lever	Typical old economy company	Typical new economy company
Business strategy	Developed over a long time. Well defined, with well-developed customer segments	Not well defined, often technology push, often based on wishful thinking. Customer needs and segments not clearly understood. Many product offerings were 'nice to haves' rather than essential
Core values	Often defined and communicated through mission statements. Established 'culture' makes core values implicit even if they are not formally communicated	Typically not well defined because strategy was not well defined. The 'winner takes all' mentality resulted in growth as an implicit core value. In some extreme cases, 'going public' and 'making money on the stock market' were the real value system
Diagnostic control systems	Formal, well established, often not developed to the point where they really support strategy	Typically revenue based and not well balanced. Because of expected high growth rates the standards were inflated. Few variables were really under management control and lead/lag relationships were not well understood
Boundary systems	Both explicitly and implicitly through budgets, capex reviews, and supervision	Very few activities were explicitly off limits. Money was abundant and not a real constraint
Interactive control systems	Typically the least developed control lever of established companies	Almost non-existent as a defensive tool

Note: The table represents generalizations based on a fairly large sample and does not necessarily apply to any single company.
Source: Simons (1995).

There is no doubt—even without the benefit of hindsight—that the new economy companies were highly risky. Simons (1999) has expanded his four levers framework to include a risk exposure metric that can be used to evaluate the pressure points in a company and to gauge the likelihood of breakdowns that could threaten a company's existence. Table 10.2 shows how the risk exposure metric would work for a typical new economy company.

Table 10.2 The risk exposure metrics for new economy companies

		Risk score (subjective)
Growth		
Pressure for performance	Significant peer pressure and pressure from financial investors because of the unrealistically high expectations	Very high
Rate of expansion	Significant growth in number of customers, number of web page hits and (for a few companies) revenues	Very high
Inexperience of key employees	By definition the new economy was new, so very few people were experienced. In addition, many new economy startups employed people who did not have enough experience in the relevant industry	High to very high
Culture		
Rewards for entrepreneurial risk taking	The financial rewards for success were often astronomical, while the consequences of failure for the individuals were limited. Many new economy entrepreneurs are millionaires despite the fact that their business failed	Very high
Executive resistance to bad news	The response of throwing good money after bad money when falling behind budget indicates resistance to bad news. In some companies it was simply inconceivable that the new economy could fail	High
Level of internal competition	I did not observe this as a major issue in the companies I interviewed	Low/ Medium
Information management		
Transaction complexity and velocity	Rapid expansion and technology teething problems	High
Gaps in diagnostic performance measures	There were some obvious gaps in many performance measures. This is discussed in more detail in the article	High
Degree of decentralized decision making	Very high even in companies with old economy parents	High

Source: Simons (1999).

Conclusion

At the outset of this investigation, one key question was whether the melt-down in the new economy was a result of a lack of controls or inadequate control systems. This would have been a very satisfying outcome for the management accountant, who might have claimed, 'I could have told you'. But the significant number of companies who adhered to conventional financial controls but still did not reap the rewards of their effort suggests that the answer is not straightforward.

Two possible views—both with some merits—are likely to prevail. Financial markets and public sentiment are frequently regarded as capable of overreacting to new events. In other words, the majority view is likely to be that new economy was just hype. As a psychological phenomenon, the new economy was neither new nor unique. If Charles Mackay (1841) were still alive, he might have further written about 'popular delusions and the madness of the crowds' along the same dimensions as the Dutch Tulip mania of the seventeenth century.

If we view the new economy as hype, we can draw one conclusion. Management control systems are tools designed by rational managers to help them implement the strategic objectives of their companies. As hindsight has shown, the rationality of the new economy phenomenon was many times dubious. Many important business decisions were made based on a superficial understanding of the business. Even in cases where the business model made some sense, the strong external pressure of the 'market' forced the decision-making process to become irrational. But control systems are systems designed for *Homo economicus*—the rational thinking manager depicted by economists—and we cannot expect them to work well in a non-rational environment. The control system is at best a management tool to achieve a set of objectives. But the logic of those objectives and the implementation process are ultimately the responsibility of management.

Since markets often overreact, writing off the new economy as hype may also be an overreaction. An alternative view might thus be that, even though it is likely to remain a minority opinion. The Internet is a rich, low cost information media that has the potential of transforming many industries. The potential of the new economy may have been overrated, but in many segments it is still significant. The real winners are likely to be the ones that can mobilize the business to take advantage of the new opportunity while simultaneously 'controlling' the destiny of their ventures.

As researchers and practitioners, we all recognize the limitations of the existing state-of-the-art management control systems. As academics, we do not understand exactly WHAT makes a certain control system work. As managers, we do not understand exactly HOW we should best implement the system. A need may be there for both theory and practice to evolve and adapt to new challenges. The emerging trend in management accounting research is that of a shift away from highly specialized diagnostic systems to a more holistic and more behavioural general management perspective. The 'failure' of many rational companies in the new economy suggests that this is the right direction for future research.

APPENDIX

Three Case Studies on New Economy Control Systems

The range of management control systems has gone from 'no control' in the early days to 'cash is king'. Many companies that have survived are now purely driven by their cash balances, with limited flexibility for any kind of strategic initiatives. Although these two extremes no doubt represent a large proportion of the new economy, this chapter targeted companies that fell between the two extreme points:

Case I: Technology Company

The practical limitations of control systems in a rapidly growing company can be highlighted by a 'pure play' North American company that provided full service—website design, domain and infrastructure hosting, and consulting—to Fortune 1000 companies. Financial investors, who were well aware that the market was looking for revenues and revenue potential, backed the company. Since the company had started later than some of its main competitors, the objective was to grow and catch up at any price. The investors assured them that lack of money would not be an excuse for not growing. Indeed, the company grew from 200 to 800 people between mid-1999 and the end of 2000. But when the new economy collapsed, the company downsized to 300 people in the space of 6 months before finally declaring bankruptcy.

Most service companies have a sales cycle of 3–6 months, which means that revenues are reasonably predictable for the next one or two quarters. In this environment, particularly if growth rates are reasonable, budgets are a reasonable way of controlling the business. This was not, however, the case in the turbulent Internet business. The company could receive a phone call in the morning, meet the client for lunch, and have a signed multi-million dollar contract by the end of the day. With revenues almost impossible to predict, and growth as the main target, the company had to sign up new employees based on highly uncertain growth forecasts.

Rapid growth is always a risky strategy, but it is not necessarily a bad one if the risks can be contained and if the potential upside is large enough. The real problem was that when the dot-com valuations plunged, this caused a complete reversal of the mindset of clients and investors:

1. The new economy companies were no longer an immediate threat to old economy companies. Many Fortune 1000 companies dramatically slowed down their investments in the Internet.
2. During the new economy boom, the dot-com companies had managed to create a 'mystique' whereby they were perceived to be the only ones who truly understood the new economy. Now the traditional players—like EDS, IBM, and Accenture—have once again become acceptable partners.

With the slowdown in revenues, the company went from experiencing substantial losses to horrendous losses. And with no growth opportunities to justify further investments, cash became the only relevant control variable. But with the depressed stock market, the financial investors did not see an opportunity to cash in their investment and they pulled out.

The outcome cannot be considered as just a failure of the control system. The only way to have avoided the outcome would have been to acknowledge the high risk and to have stayed out of the business. The company's strategy was reasonably clearly defined and not too different from that of established companies. But it was a risky strategy in a highly turbulent environment, and ultimately the strategy did not work out. One contributing reason was clearly the external factors discussed previously—the revenue-based stock market valuations and the perception that growth and size are critical to success. In a situation such as this, it would have been desirable to be explicit about the downside risk and plan for any contingencies. But this was not the mindset of the company—the company chose a risky growth strategy that did not pay off at the end of the day.

Case II: Bertelsmann-On-Line (BOL)

Bertelsmann-On-Line was the German media giant Bertelsmann's response to the on-line retailing phenomenon. Bertelsmann decided to enter the media e-commerce sector for two main reasons: First, given Bertelsmann's strength in the European markets in publishing and direct-to-customer businesses, Bertelsmann had a very good starting position to become one of the leading players in this field. Indeed, BOL managed to secure #1 or #2 market position in most countries shortly after launch. Second, given the threat that pure-play Internet companies such as Amazon posed on Bertelsmann's market position in the direct-to-consumer businesses, it was a mandate for BOL to compete with Amazon, both in terms of brand investments and time-to-market targets.

BOL was by intention designed as a 'start-up' inside Bertelsmann to enable BOL to move fast in the extremely time-competitive Internet markets of those days. In the early days, the top priority was to launch the business. Amazon had a significant first mover advantage, and there was extreme time-to-market pressure to launch the functionalities of the catalogue and the website and to build the company.

The evolution of financial controls inside BOL was normal for a start-up business. Initially, compared to old economy standards there was less discipline and real thought behind the spending. This was particularly the case for marketing and media spend, where the whole sector frequently overpaid for what it got. To establish more financial discipline, Bertelsmann brought in a CFO with considerable experience from a number of old economy companies such as Electrolux, Lafarge, and Dunlop.

The first action was to re-evaluate all media deals in terms of value for money and to reallocate the budgets accordingly. Media buyers were forced to start thinking in terms of benefits. In the past, there had not been enough accountability as to whether a certain media deal worked or not. Now, the spending could not be justified by the general brand awareness it created but had to be explicitly related to the number of new customers and, eventually, profits. And no suppliers would be paid without a purchase order. Initially the approach was not well received, but over time the mentality did change.

The reporting system was revamped. A traditional Budget–Forecast–Actual system was put in place and each line item evaluated. If the item could not be justified, it was stripped out. The information was reviewed quarterly—what had gone wrong that quarter, what had been done right, what were the corrective actions and what was the plan for the next quarter. Each department created a weekly operating action plan, which was shared with other departments. An unintended benefit of this was increased awareness across departments and better coordination of activities.

In addition to traditional financial controls, a number of non-financial leading indicators related to the website were used. Among the more obvious ones were the number of daily hits, number of orders (including fallouts and successes) and number of registrations. The whole order and delivery process was carefully monitored, as were repeat purchase rates and fulfilment rates. For example, BOL knew that once the service levels fell below a certain level, the number of customer service calls would increase dramatically.

BOL differs from many new economy start-ups in that it had a detailed business plan in place at all times. The plan was approved by Bertelsmann's board, and contained the key success parameters of the business (such as customer purchase rates, repeat buyer rates, overall marketing spending levels, etc.). These performance indicators were well understood from the direct-to-consumer businesses of Bertelsmann.

Like other start-ups, BOL's diagnostic control system evolved over time. The system was useful in steering the business, and the financial discipline no doubt saved BOL lots of money. But although BOL is still in business, it has not been successful in taking over the #1 position in global media e-commerce. The reasons for this are more related to the fundamental attractiveness of the market than to the internal control systems. Some of the lessons learned are:

1. First mover advantage was indeed important in the B2C market. Amazon managed to enter key European markets before BOL through the acquisition of the local market leaders (Telebuch in Germany and a local company in UK). Amazon's extremely high market capitalization enabled it to use its shares as cheap acquisition currency. With the enormous media coverage of Amazon in the United States and especially the development of its stock price, Amazon had a unique chance to build an Internet brand at comparably low costs. Amazon executed very well on its marketing and advertising strategy. In other markets— like the Netherlands, which Amazon never entered—BOL managed to position itself as the market leader, and built strong market share.

2. Retrospectively, one can say that although time-to-market is important, the pace of BOL's geographical expansion was probably too fast. Markets and competition have not developed equally fast in all regions. Managing complexity, especially multiplying the IT landscape into eleven geographies without having the chance to consolidate the system architecture in the meantime was the main challenge. This manifested itself in systems and databases that were not flexible enough to cope with the different market requirements, and this in turn led to additional expenses down the road.

There was too much reliance on external projections of market size and growth rates. This created unrealistic expectations and led to the entire sector heavily overspending on marketing. With hindsight, BOL could have awaited the collapse of the market and held back the marketing spend until the market had consolidated—but only with the danger of being marginalized in the meantime. With more realistic market size estimates, much of the overspending could have been avoided.

Case III: Workthing

Workthing is an example of a carefully planned and prudent extension into the new economy. Workthing is an online job listing service associated with the *Guardian* newspaper in the United Kingdom. The service is a complement to, and to some extent in competition with, the printed job listings of the newspaper. The online service is a strategic investment, where the parent is willing to absorb reasonable start-up costs in order to build the business. Similar to BOL, Workthing is neither the largest player nor the first entrant into this segment. The risks are significant. But the parent company is well aware of the risks and is only willing to support the start-up costs as long as the future revenue potential is there. Workthing's control systems are designed around the challenge of predicting future revenues, but with a strong emphasis on risk management and risk containment.

Initially, Workthing developed a 'Balanced Scorecard' approach with 26 KPIs:

- 10 financial indicators,
- 4 web traffic related indicators,
- 4 customer/jobs related indicators,
- 3 brand indicators,
- 3 service level indicators, and
- 2 headcount indicators.

Over time the system has evolved and many KPIs have been dropped. For example, obvious measures such as number of CVs listed and number of jobs listed turned out not to be useful. This may be counterintuitive, but anyone who has used an Internet search engine recognizes the problem. It is not really helpful to receive 3,000 listings when you do a search for a new job. What you want is a small number, say 5 to 10, of highly relevant job listings. The same applies to an employer who searches a database of CVs. Indeed, Workthing's selling proposition is the narrow, targeted search that results in a limited number of high quality matches.

For internal purposes, the number of KPIs is now down to 14: Five financial measures, five website usage related measures and four brand and service related measures. In addition, since promotion is the highest cost item, the company hires an outside agency to perform an audit of its media spend to ensure that it gets the best possible deal in the market.

Although the fourteen KPIs are available to the parent company, the number is too high for high-level monitoring of the business. Instead, five alert points—or minimum hurdles—are carefully monitored. If any one of these falls below expectations immediate action is taken. The five alert points are:

- net sales,
- per cent cost deviation from budget,
- per cent of cost base that is variable in three months' time. The target is 90 per cent or, in other words, 90 per cent of the cost base can be eliminated in 3 months' time,
- number of page views, and
- brand awareness (external measure).

The success of any online business ultimately depends on customer acceptance. The risks are clearly significant. Although the final verdict is still out, Workthing appears to have struck a good balance between the business opportunity and how to manage the downside risk.

References

Braddock, R. (2000), 'The Internet: The Novel', *Financial Analyst Journal* (September–October).

Evans, P. and Wurster, T. (2000), *Blown to Bits* (Boston: HBS Press).

Kaplan, R. and Norton, D. (1996), *The Balanced Scorecard* (Boston: HBS Press).

Laird, I. and Sjöblom, L. (2002), 'Commercialization of New Technology—Success Factors and Pitfalls'. IMD Working paper.

Mackay, C. (1841), *Extraordinary Popular Delusions and the Madness of Crowds* (reprinted in 1995 by Crown Publishers).

McKinsey & Co. (2001), 'The Winner Takes It All'. Presentation to the Swiss Society of Investment Professionals, Geneva October 3.

Rajgopal, S., Kotha, S., and Venkatachalam, M. (2000), 'The Relevance of Web Traffic for Stock Prices of Internet Firms'. Stanford GSB Working paper.

Simons, R. (1995), *Levers of Control* (Boston: HBS Press).

——(1999), 'How Risky Is Your Company?' *Harvard Business Review* 77(3): 85–94.

Sjöblom, L. (1998), 'Financial Information and Quality Management—Is There a Role for Accountants?', *Accounting Horizons*, December.

Part 3
Reshaping Accounting

11
Management Control and E-Logistics

Maurice Gosselin

Introduction

During the 1980s and the 1990s, globalization, deregulation, and advances in information technology have modified the economic environment in which manufacturing firms evolve. In operations management, the concept of supply chain management has enabled many firms to shorten their manufacturing cycles and to provide their customers with higher quality products. The development of e-business and, more specifically of e-logistics has emphasized this new perspective.

While these changes occurred in operation management, innovations in management accounting such as activity-based costing, capacity cost management, balanced scorecard, and target costing have emerged and, to a limited extent, they have affected the design of management accounting systems in many enterprises (Gosselin 1997; Guilding *et al.* 2000). In the control area, the focus has been on mechanisms outside the traditional accounting area such as strategic control (Langfield-Smith 1997) and other emerging forms of organizational control.

Over the past decade, the development of new communication channels has enabled firms to share information more rapidly at low costs and has reduced the relative importance of intermediaries such as brokers. Despite this change, in 2000, US companies spent more than $1 trillion—about 10 per cent of the gross national product—on activities related to logistics and distribution systems (Delaney 2001). Transportation costs accounted for 60 per cent of costs while inventory-carrying costs for around 40 per cent (Viswanadham and Gaonkar 2001). Some of these costs could be managed differently and even reduced with new information technologies, e-business approaches and e-logistics. These reductions could represent a competitive advantage for firms. Since business to business (B2B) exchanges enable more speed and greater flexibility, several traditional control mechanisms are adapted or abandoned. Thus, the design of management accounting systems may be deeply affected by the development of e-logistics, B2B, and other new communication technologies.

The main objectives of this chapter are to examine how firms adapt their management control systems in the context of e-business and e-logistics, identify research opportunities on management control systems in the context of e-logistics, and reflect on the changing role of management accounting in this environment. This chapter includes first a brief review of the evolution of management control over time. The context of e-business and e-logistics is subsequently examined. Following this is a discussion about the most important changes that may ensue in management control systems within organizations that have invested in new communication technologies such as e-commerce and e-logistics.

Changes in Management Controls

Management control practices have evolved over time. During the nineteenth century, management control systems focused primarily on cost control particularly in terms of direct labour and material costs (Kaplan 1984). The emergence of large and vertically-integrated firms called for the development of more sophisticated management accounting and control systems. The growth in the size of firms, the creation of functional organizations, and the need to decentralize decision-making required the use of control devices that focused not only on costs but on controlling the performance of responsibility centres and the implementation of business strategy.

Anthony's (1965) definition is still appropriate in capturing this modern vision of management control, 'The process by which managers assure that resources are obtained and used effectively and efficiently in the accomplishment of the organisation's objectives'. Similarly, in their book, Atkinson *et al.* (2001) defined control as, 'The set of procedures, tools, performance measures and systems that organizations use to guide and motivate all employees to achieve organizational objectives'. These definitions are not always reflected in management accounting books. The vision of control is usually separated from other dimensions of control such as strategic control and operational control. The emphasis is also mainly placed on accounting-based controls such as variance analysis or financial performance measures. A brief review of the evolution of management control can help to better understand why this is the case.

At the turn of the twentieth century, the most important dimension of management control was cost control. The emergence of scientific management had emphasized the need for managers to dictate to workers how to perform tasks. Standard costing systems and variance analysis developed in the 1920s were used to control workers' behaviour. Management control systems were essentially used to compare actual results with expectations. Thus, the basic model for control consisted of three phases. First, plans are developed for the period. Second, at the end of the period, performance is observed and third, actual results are compared with plans and excessive deviations are analysed. This traditional vision of management control has been used in most management accounting books. For instance, Dopuch *et al.* (1969) defined control as, 'A system of process in which expectations and actual performance are compared and comparisons serve as a basis for determining the proper responses to operating results'. This narrow definition of management control was advanced during the 1950s and more rapidly about 20 years ago. As organizations became more complex, management control systems were adapted to take into consideration the influence of employee behaviour and incentive schemes on processes. This led to the integration of agency theory and the principal–agent model by academics into the initial model described earlier (Baiman 1982, 1990; Demski and Feltham 1978). The application of agency theory in the area of control has focused mainly on two control mechanisms, budget participation (Birnberg *et al*. 1990; Kren 1997) and incentives and compensation (Young and Lewis 1995).

This focus on individual behaviour did not encourage researchers to take into consideration factors that influence control frameworks design at the organizational level. Thus, in the 1970s, the contingency framework for management accounting was postulated (Hayes 1977; Khandwalla 1972). Contingency theory suggests that there is no single universally appropriate control system that applies to all organizations in all circumstances (Otley 1980). Studies that have drawn upon this theory have focused on the effects of several categorizations of the effects of contingent variables on management control systems. The first models like Otley's (1980) considered three contingent variables: technology, organizational structure, and environment. This model was expanded during the 1980s. One of the latest studies in that area (Fisher 1995) considered five categories of contingent variables: external environment, strategy, technology, unit and industry variables, knowledge and observability factors. Contingency theory has been criticized for its lack of clarity (Schoonhoven 1981). Chapman (1997), in his article, discussed the need for improving the credibility of contingency studies.

Chenhall and Morris (1986) developed and tested a contingency model of the perceived usefulness of management accounting systems. In this landmark study, they examined the effects on management accounting system design of perceived environmental uncertainty, organizational structure, and organizational interdependence on four information characteristics: Scope; Timeliness; Aggregation; Integration. Scope represents the extent to which a firm uses external, non-financial, and future-oriented information. Timeliness is the frequency and speed of reporting while aggregation refers to the use of decision models. Integration concerns the impact of interacting effects of various functions.

Chenhall and Morris (1986) demonstrated that decentralization was associated with a preference for aggregated and integrated information, perceived environmental uncertainty with broad scope and timely information, and organizational interdependence with broad scope, aggregated, and integrated information. The effects of perceived environmental uncertainty and organizational interdependence were, in part, indirect through their association with decentralization.

This framework was developed with reference to traditional business operations. In the context of the digital economy, and more specifically of the redesign of supply chain through e-logistics and e-procurement, the framework needs to be adapted to take into consideration changes that occur in management accounting systems.

In the 1990s, the research on management focused on the investigation of control mechanisms outside the traditional accounting area such as strategic control (Langfield-Smith 1997) and certain forms of organizational control, and to better understand the relationship between these controls and traditional accounting controls. With the emergence of the digital economy, the focus has now moved to the design of management control systems that emphasize customer relationship management, supply chain management, and collaborative processes.

While these changes were taking place, accounting professional bodies proposed a new definition of control. The Committee of Sponsoring Organizations of the Treadway Commission published the report *Internal Control—Integrated Framework* (COSO 1992) and issued guidelines on how to design, assess, and report on the control systems of organizations. In this report, control is regarded as, 'Comprising those elements of an organization that, taken together, support people in the achievement of the organization's objectives'. Control elements are grouped into five interrelated components: control environment, objectives and risks, information and communication, control activities, and monitoring. Control environment is the foundation of all other components of internal control. Control environment factors are grouped into three categories: corporate governance, organizational structure, and organizational culture and values. In the context of e-business, these three categories will be significantly affected.

The second component of the control systems is the assessment of objectives and risks. This level of control includes objective setting, strategic planning, and risk management. The third component pertains to information and communication of control. The fourth part of the control system corresponds to a large extent to what we have considered so far as management control systems. It includes budgeting, performance measurement, and incentives systems. In the context of e-business and e-logistics, these systems will be modified substantially. The last element is the monitoring control group activities that provide senses of the organization's evolution. They include issues such as monitoring the environments (internal and external) and the performance, as well as assessing the effectiveness of control.

In this first decade of the twenty-first century, in the context of the digital economy, the perspective on control needs again to be developed. The emergence of e-logistics and the fact that many organizations have decided to focus on their core business require that management control be extended to the entire value chain. In the context of the digital economy, the following trends will affect management control systems:

- partnership in control;
- collaboration within the value chain;

- enterprise extension;
- information sharing;
- process specialization;
- integrated service providers;
- auditing for management control systems.

In the next section, we examine the characteristics of the environment where e-business and e-logistics impact management control systems. This will aid our understanding of the influence of the advent of the digital economy on management control.

The E-Business Environment

It took 38 years for radio to achieve a 50 million people audience. Television required a 13 year period, personal computer 10 years while the Internet took only 4 years. Time is an important factor in the digital economy. E-business is facilitating increased outsourcing of logistical functions and the growth of third party logistics. Organizations that can incorporate these major changes to their activities are going to have a competitive advantage during the next few years.

Several management consultants have studied organizations that have been able to make these changes. The Gartner Group has issued ten recommendations to help organizations adapt their processes to the new business environment. These are classified into six categories that highlight the major differences between the traditional and the digital economy. In his book, 'The E-volving organization', Moore (2000) also identifies six characteristics of firms that operate in the digital economy:

- operate at net speed;
- execute dynamic strategy;
- have a global reach;
- enable e-initiatives;
- engage in internal collaboration;
- integrate with partners.

Operating at Net Speed

Speed is one of the major characteristics of accounting and of the e-culture. In the 1950s, a 'good' accountant was someone who was able to calculate rapidly and without errors. During the 1970s, accountants spent a lot of time using computer cards to provide information to mainframe computers. Now accountants need to be able to deploy powerful integrated information systems. Technology is changing at a rapid pace and its costs are decreasing with time. Information, which used to be a scarce resource, is now often overwhelming.

The Internet enables information systems to exchange information and create a global network. This has enabled firms to deal directly with their suppliers (B2B) and their customers (B2C), and has thereby reduced or eliminated intermediaries and decreased the costs of ordering, shipping, and delivering. It is now possible for customers or firms to order on a real time basis, 24 hours a day and 7 days a week as and when goods are desired. To survive in more competitive web-enabled environments firms must respond to these changes, especially where customers have become more demanding.

The Acxiom 100-day project provides an example of the control related changes which companies will have to face. This company is involved in the software industry. The president of the company believes that it is not possible today to plan, develop, and produce software at 100 per cent unless it accepts to lag behind competition: 'Every company must answer the question for itself about which functions or products they can release as 80 percent finished and which require zero defects to meet customer expectations.' To internalize this philosophy, Acxiom decided to limit to 100 days the development of its projects after which delivery to the customers must occur. Since no employee wants to be responsible for the failure of the project, each works faster and longer hours (Staten 2001). Such changes will affect control priorities.

Execute Dynamic Strategy

Gartner suggests that organizations should not plan more than 24 months ahead. According to Moore (2000), businesses in the digital economy need to change their strategic management process. They have to revise their strategy more often if they want to keep their competitive advantage over their competitors. The development of dynamic strategies requires a more flexible structure and more participation from employees in the decision-making process. In many e-businesses, employees are participating in shareholders equity programs to enhance goal congruence.

Have Global Reach

The Internet enables firms to eliminate geographical frontiers. As such, the level of competition increases dramatically since all producers and vendors can make bids on several markets. The new cost accounting techniques that were developed during the last few years help firms to manage their costs and reduce transportation costs. In such a context, management control systems have to be changed to enable firms to ensure that resources are obtained and used effectively and efficiently.

Enable E-Initiatives

Many managers who are now in their forties or their fifties have self-learned how to use computers for accounting and management purposes.

Organizations now need managers who are aware of the new information technologies but also who are able to suggest improvements to the systems they are responsible for. Moore (2000) suggests that, 'Technology is not an absolute, but an awareness of what is currently possible and economically appropriate.' Firms involved in the digital economy need to find incentives that will motivate employees and managers to develop e-initiatives. Incentive and reward systems, as part of management control systems, can be used to promote the development of these initiatives.

Engage in Internal Collaboration

Teamwork is another factor that has to be considered in the context of an e-business. Management control systems have to be redesigned to enhance teamwork. Companies such as Acxiom favour the creation of a work group with specific objectives. This process enables the firm to obtain more flexibility and increase the speed of the decision process. This internal cohesion stimulates the competition between the teams within the company and increases worker productivity. Once the team has met the goals, it is dismantled and a new team is created for a new project. 'Cutting across traditional functional silos for the profit of multifunctional teams is the norm in e-culture. Speed is all-important, and wearing your functional hat too firmly will delay getting product to market (president, Acxion)'.

This internal collaboration helps to create a culture of employee empowerment. This is why several decisions are now decentralized. Furthermore, the level of vertical differentiation is reduced. Horizontal exchanges are performed outside traditional hierarchical schemes. This new context has a major impact on organizational structure, which has been shown to be a major determinant in the design of management control systems.

Integrate with Partners

Many firms consider cooperative strategies as their corporate strategy (Hitt *et al.* 2002). Internet and new information technology are in many respects tools that enable firms to execute this type of strategy (Suutari 2000). Some traditional firms have developed partnerships with dot-com enterprises to be able to rapidly access this new technology (Schweitzer 2000). This enables them to minimize risks associated with information technology and to reduce the costs of implementation. However, it affects the structure of the firm since it requires the integration of partners within the firms. It also implies that management control systems have to be redesigned according to the new strategy. This integration brings the problem of integrating different organizational cultures.

In the next section, we examine how in one specific area of e-business and e-logistics, changes in management control are taking place.

E-Logistics

E-logistics is a dynamic set of communication, computing, and collaborative technologies that transforms key logistical processes to be customer centric, by sharing data, knowledge, and information with the supply chain partners. These key logistical processes are ordering, delivery, transportation, and warehousing. Becoming customer-centric implies that firms will emphasize customer relationship management and end-to-end value delivery through collaborative exchanges.

E-logistics provides integration architecture and tools to support collaborative logistics through the enterprise, between enterprises and to individual users, allowing synchronization using data from different systems and resources. Ideally, it involves the creation of a real-time command and control system that monitor the fulfilment of activities throughout the entire trading partner network. The implementation of e-logistics involves important changes to management control systems.

It is estimated that logistic costs represent between 10 and 15 per cent of the cost of products (Delaney 2001). Controlling logistic costs can help a value chain and its related firms to gain a competitive advantage. For instance, the US Food and Beverage industry has lost $7 to $12 billion per year through incorrect data flows between suppliers and retailers (Bernstein 2001). Cisco wrote off $2.5 billion in excess inventory owing to poor management of its outsourced contractors. Micron Technology witnessed similar problems and it wrote off $260 million of memory products inventory which represented 32 per cent of 2001 sales (Valdero 2001).

Dibner *et al.* (2001) of Mercer conducted a survey in 2001 on logistic services. They reported key factors for dissatisfaction as being:

- low quality customer service;
- poor communications;
- documentation problems;
- paper intensity.

Respondents indicated that creating new supplier partnerships, shifting inventory to suppliers, and implementing supplier e-commerce relationships were effective ways to control logistic costs.

E-logistics has a major impact on logistic costs incurred by companies that have commenced trading electronically with their supplies. The firms are witnessing a reduction of 20 per cent in their costs (Phillips 2000). These cost reductions are the result of a major transformation of the supply chain within the value chain. On the other hand, the success of e-logistics relies on efficient management control systems. In 1999, the US Federal Trade Commission levied $1.5 million dollars in fines against internet retailers for missed customer shipments and poor service issues. Conversely, an Accenture survey conducted in 1999 showed that 25 per cent of online holiday purchases were unsuccessfully delivered. The same survey conducted in 2000 showed a decrease to 8 per cent.

Schwartz (2000) suggests that there are four main ways e-business will impact logistics (referred to as the four 'Ds').

1. *Dematerialization*: B2B and B2C enables firms to adopt real-time pro-duction because of processes such as just-in-time. In such context, firms reduce their levels of inventories and minimize the amount of assets.
2. *Disintermediation*: Electronic business eliminates or reduces the number of intermediaries since customers can buy goods directly from suppliers. The airline industry is witnessing a reduction in the amount of commis-sions that are paid to travel agencies and their replacement by purchases through the Internet of airline companies or specialized travel sites.
3. *Deverticalization*: Enterprises will find it less attractive to integrate vert-ically. They will prefer to build up partnerships with other businesses in the value-chain or focus their activities around their core business (Hitt *et al.* 2002).
4. *Development of Products/Services*: E-business enables firms to develop new products and services for new customers and markets at a more rapid pace.

Trends in E-Logistics

Viswanadham and Gaonkar (2001) identified three trends in e-logistics. First, supply chain management will move to end-to-end value delivery through collaborative exchanges. Such an approach implies a modification of the tra-ditional supply chain to synchronize scheduling between suppliers, logistic providers, and manufacturers. This approach will be developed through real-time integration between the various logistic providers, private exchanges, and independent trading exchanges.

The second trend is outsourcing. The development of Internet is making it easier to coordinate activities between partners. Outsourcing logistics is fairly new and its implementation in many firms is a result of the new e-business environment. This last trend is called 'customer-centricity'. Instead of trying to fit the customer needs into a standard transportation and warehousing model, firms work with the business customers to develop a customized logis-tics solution that is optimal. These trends have a major impact on manage-ment accounting systems in that the definition of control as noted above needs revision and a review of the conceptual frameworks of management control systems becomes essential.

Trends in logistics will force firms to:

- better manage their logistical processes;
- improve the management of transportation activities;

- standardize trade documents with suppliers and customers;
- improve ordering and delivery activities;
- set commodity quality standards;
- outsource logistic management;
- facilitate third party logistics information systems.

This emphasis on improving logistics will have the following impact on management control systems:

- increase in the use of integrated performance measurement systems;
- favour employee empowerment instead of supervision;
- broaden stakeholders focus;
- emphasize the relationships based on trust instead of contracts.

Management Control and E-Logistics

Several models have been developed to examine the effective design of management accounting systems and organizational contingencies. The Chenhall and Morris (1986) model was developed to test the relationship between external environment uncertainty, organizational structure, the organizational interdependence, and the perceived usefulness of Management Accounting System. Operating at net speed, executing a dynamic strategy and having a global reach are directly related to the level of perceived environmental uncertainty. Pressures from the environment will induce firms to deal directly with their suppliers (B2B) and their customers (B2C), reduce or eliminate some intermediaries, and decrease the costs of ordering, shipping, and delivering. As mentioned earlier, this trend will require major changes to management control systems. Decentralization and organizational interdependence are key elements of firms that need to enable e-initiatives and engage in internal collaboration.

In the digital economy, as depicted in Figure 11.1, the three contextual factors become more important. Therefore we may assume, as shown in Figure 11.2, that the levels of perceived environmental uncertainty, decentralization, and organizational interdependence will be higher in organizations operating in the digital economy.

According to the Chenhall and Morris (1986) study, perceived environmental uncertainty was associated with broad scope and timely information, decentralization with a preference for aggregated and integrated information, and organizational interdependence with broad scope, aggregated, and integrated information. Based on these findings and on the content of Figure 11.3, firms that are engaged in the digital economy will likely have a preference for more broad scope, timely, aggregated, and integrated information.

The validity of these propositions will need to be demonstrated in empirical studies.

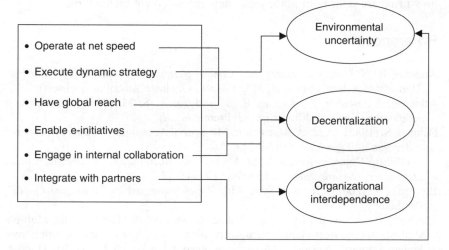

Fig. 11.1. Links between contextual settings and the characteristics of the digital economy

	Traditional economy	Digital economy
Perceived environmental uncertainty	+ +	+ + + + + +
Decentralization	+ +	+ + + + + +
Organizational interdependence	+ +	+ + + + + +

Fig. 11.2. Contextual factors and the digital economy

	Traditional economy	Digital economy
Scope	+ +	+ + + + + +
Timeliness	+ +	+ + + + + +
Integration	+ +	+ + + + + +
Aggregation	+ +	+ + + + + +

Fig. 11.3. Characteristics of management accounting systems in the digital economy

Conclusion

The purpose of this chapter has been to examine how the design of management control systems is affected by the digital economy and more specifically the implementation of e-logistics. Empirical research based on the Chenhall and

Morris (1986) study will be needed in the near future to better understand how firms are putting in place these new management techniques.

References

Anthony, R. N. (1965), *Planning and Control Systems: A Framework for Analysis* (Division of Research, Boston, MA: Harvard Graduate School of Business).

Atkinson, A., Banker, R., Kaplan, R. S., and Young, S. M. (2001), *Management Accounting* (Upper Saddle River, NJ: Prentice-Hall).

Baiman, S. (1982), 'Agency Research in Managerial Accounting: A Survey', *Journal of Accounting Literature*, 1: 154–213.

——(1990), 'Agency Research in Managerial Accounting: A Second Look', *Accounting, Organizations and Society*, 15: 341–71.

Bernstein, R. (2001), 'Kraft in Sync With Shaws Supermarkets Consumers Goods'. Technology.

Birnberg, J. G., Shields, M. D., and Young, S. M. (1990), 'The Case for Multiple Methods in Empirical Management Accounting Research (with an Illustration from Budget Setting)', *Journal of Management Accounting Research*, 2 (Fall): 33–66.

Chapman, C. S. (1997), 'Reflections on a Contingent View of Accounting', *Accounting, Organizations and Society*, 22: 189–206.

Chenhall, R. H. and Morris, D. (1986), 'The Impact of Structure, Environment and Interdependence on the Perceived Usefulness of Management Accounting Systems', *The Accounting Review* 51 (January): 16–35.

COSO (1992), *Internal Control—Integrated Framework* (New York: Committee of Sponsoring Organizations of the Treadway Commission).

Delaney, R. (2001), Reverse Logistics Executive Council (October).

Demski, J. S. and Feltham, G. A. (1978), 'Economic Incentive in Budgetary Control Systems', *The Accounting Review*, 67/3: 336–59.

Dibner, B., Meyers, D., and Tahir, M. (2001), *E-logistics and the 2000 Bulk Supply Chain Survey* (New York: Mercer Management Consulting).

Dopuch, N., Birnberg, J. C., and Demski, J. (1969), *Cost Accounting Data for Management*, 4th edn (Homewood, IL: R. D. Irwin).

Fisher, J. (1995), 'Contingency-Based Research on Management Control Systems: Categorization by Level of Complexity', *Journal of Accounting Literature*, 14: 24–53.

Gosselin, M. (1997), 'The Effect of Strategy and Organizational Structure on the Adoption and Implementation of Activity-based Costing', *Accounting, Organizations and Society*, 22/2: 105–22.

Guilding, C., Cravens, K. S., and Tayles, M. (2000), 'An International Comparison of Strategic Management Accounting Practices', *Management Accounting Review*, 11: 113–35.

Hayes, D. C. (1977), 'The Contingency Theory of Management Accounting', *The Accounting Review*, 52 (January): 22–39.

Hitt, M., Ireland, R., Hoskisson, R., Rowe, W. G., and Sheppard, J. P. (2002), *Strategic Management: Competitiveness and Globalization—Concepts*, 1st Canadian edn (Toronto: Nelson Thomson Learning).

Kaplan, R. S. (1984), 'The Evolution of Management Accounting', *The Accounting Review*, 33/3: 390–418.

Khandwalla, P. N. (1972), 'The Effect of Different Types of Competition on the Use of Management Control', *Journal of Accounting Research*, 10 (Autumn): 275–85.

Kren, L. (1997), 'The Role of Accounting Information in Organizational Control', in V. Arnold and S. G. Sutton (eds), *Behavioral Accounting Research: Foundations and Frontiers* (Sarasota, FL: American Accounting Association).

Langfield-Smith, K. (1997), 'Management Control Systems and Strategy: A Critical Review', *Accounting, Organizations and Society*, 22: 207–32.

Moore, G. A. (2000), *Inside the Tornado: Marketing Strategies from Silicon Valley's Cutting Edge* (New York: Harper-Collins) 1st. edn. New York: HarperBusiness 1995?.

Otley, D. (1980), 'The Contingency Theory of Management Accounting: Achievement and Prognosis', *Accounting, Organizations and Society*, 5: 413–28.

Phillips, Paul (2000), 'E-Business: What is it and Does it Matter to Accountant?', *Management Accounting* (February), 78(2): 40–2.

Schoonhoven, C. B. (1981), 'Problems with Contingency Theory: Testing Assumptions Hidden with the Language of Contingency Theory', *Administrative Science Quarterly*, 26: 349–77.

Schwartz, B. (2000), 'E-business: New Distribution Models Coming to a Site Near You', *Dot.com* (February): 4.

Schweitzer, C. (2000), 'Creating a Dot-Com-Compatible Culture', *Association Management* (December): 30.

Staten, M. (2001), 'Customer Relationship Management as a Privacy Enhancer', Working paper.

Voirannée: 2000 Titre de article: "chefs d'enterprise, attention" p. 10–11 Suutari, R. (2000), 'Vous souvenez-vous de . . .', *CMA Management* (September): 13.

Valdero, P. (2001), 'Improving the High Tech Supply Chain', Working paper.

Viswanadham, N. and Gaonkar, R. (2001), 'E-Logistics: Trends and Opportunities', working paper. The Logistic Institute–Asia Pacific

Young, M. S. and Lewis, B. (1995), 'Experimental Incentive-Contracting Research in Management Accounting', in R. H. Ashton and A. Hubbard Ashton (eds), *Judgment and Decision-Making Research in Accounting and Auditing* (Cambridge, UK: Cambridge University Press). 55–75.

12

Internet-Based Information Systems in the Not-for-Profit Sector

Hans-Ulrich Küpper

Introduction

Organizations in the not-for-profit sector have different needs in comparison to profit-oriented organizations. Often they pursue several objectives. Internet-based systems enable these needs and objectives to be met more effectively as they allow a closer connection to the stakeholders of the not-for-profit organization (NPO). This chapter discusses how Internet technologies help to achieve this.

In the following section the characteristics of organizations in the not-for-profit sector and the different types of NPOs are discussed. The Internet is important for all NPOs. It is an instrument for presenting their mission, goals, activities, and structure to a broader audience. A sports club, for example, is able to show its different activities, or a political party can describe its political programmes and use the Internet as a marketing instrument to recruit new members. The Internet also helps announce upcoming events, or inform as to the results of past events. The Internet will bring about further important changes to information systems within NPOs.

This chapter focuses on economic issues relating to NPOs, which may be in public or in private ownership. The determinants of information system requisites in terms of special non-economic objectives are discussed. This is followed by a section on the special structure necessary for a suitable information system for NPOs. The information and Internet technologies enable an effective information system for such organizations to be designed. This will be illustrated in the last section of the chapter taking universities as a special and important example of a public NPO.

Institutions in the Not-for-Profit Sector and Their Characteristics

Special Characteristics of Organizations in the Not-for-Profit Sector

The activities of most companies in a market-based economy are oriented towards profit. Shareholders invest money in order to get dividends. Therefore it might be surmised that all decisions by managers and the management information systems they use to select the best alternatives are driven by this objective.

Although there are different perspectives in the literature on how to define not-for-profit sector organizations, they have one common characteristic. The principal objective of an NPO is not to seek to realize profit. It has been noted that: 'A nonprofit corporation is not prohibited from making a profit, but there are limitations on what it can do with its "profits" ' (www.not-for-profit.org/page2.htm). If it realizes profits, the organization does not need to pay the profits to the shareholders or members of the organization. A basic feature of these organizations can thus be viewed in terms of a 'nondistribution constraint' (Streim 2002). People are not 'shareholders' in the same way as those of organizations seeking to obtain income. They are not primarily focused on the return of capital but rather on non-commercial objectives.

NPOs are founded to serve 'a purpose of public or mutual benefit other than to the pursuit or accumulation of profits' (www.not-for-profit.org/page2.htm). They seek to render services for their members, for other social groups or for society. Ordinarily there is a lack of such services as they are not satisfied by profit-oriented companies or by the government. Organizations in the not-for-profit sector pursue different not-for-profit-making objectives. These objectives may be oriented towards public interests such as education, public health, etc. or towards the group interest of a club. They may 'fulfil certain *material or service functions* . . . stipulated by their owners' (Oettle 1990: 1516). In general one can view NPOs as being organized, private, not-for-profit-distributing, self-governing and voluntary (Salamon and Anheier 1997: 33).

The objectives of the organizations in the not-for-profit sector determine their decisions on output and activities. Normally their output is not a tangible asset but a service. This means that in the production process, human activities usually play a role. Labour thus represents a crucial part of input and costs. The services of not-for-profit organizations are not traded on liberal markets. Therefore there must exist other types of regulations. These are important for their decision-making processes as well as their management information systems.

Important Types of Organizations in the Not-for-Profit Sector

In modern societies, the not-for-profit sector is an important part of the whole economy. Although most Western countries have a system of liberal or social market economy the not-for-profit sector covers a significant share of the gross national product. The organizations of the not-for-profit sector may be classified by different criteria. Figure 12.1 reveals the first criterion, which is ownership. There are public and partly public NPOs as well as private NPOs (Streim 2002). The former attempt to fulfil public tasks for the citizens of a country. Public governments and public companies for traffic, health, education, and culture belong to this class. Telecommunication companies, electricity companies,

Ownership		Object	Types
National NPO	Public NPOs	Fulfilment of public tasks	Public administration public enterprises
Parastatal NPO	Corporations subject to public law	Fulfilment of delegated tasks, in part with membership by obligation	Social insurances
Private NPO	Economic NPO Political NPO	Lobby for the members Activities to support political aims	Associations of enterprises Political parties
	Social NPO	Fulfilment of social tasks	Welfare services

Fig. 12.1. Types and examples of not-for-profit organizations

and social securities may be examples of partly public NPOs. The production of their services often requires high investments and can be very expensive. Therefore, the economic activities of these public or partly public organizations are important even if they pursue a not-for-profit objective. Much resource is required to run public hospitals, schools, and universities as well as public libraries, theatres, and museums. The economic impact is thus significant.

Private NPOs may be classified by the characteristics of their tasks and services as economic, socio-cultural, political, and social organizations. Economic NPOs such as cooperatives, trade, labour, professional, and similar associations promote the economic aims of their members. They do not pursue economic objectives themselves but perform special services for their members. These members, which act economically, are companies, labourers, customers, and so on. In contrast the members of other types of NPOs act in other ways in their pursuit of socio-cultural, political, or social objectives (e.g. see Fig. 12.1).

Determinants of Information Needs for Not-for-Profit Organizations

The Central Role of Accounting in the Profit Sector

Possibly the most important information system across companies in the profit sector is the accounting system. It measures past and estimates future business activities in monetary terms. The results form the basis for plans and control mechanisms underlying the decisions and processes of the whole company as well as those of their divisions and departments. Most decisions in all areas of a private firm like procurement, operations and marketing management, investment and finance are based on accounting information.

Accounting systems use and give information on monetary data like assets and liabilities, revenues, expenses and costs, gains and losses. Profit oriented organizations as well as NPOs need an accounting information system if they are to act economically. But the fundamental difference is that NPOs pursue not-for-profit objectives. This is important for the use and the structure of their accounting systems.

In the profit sector the first goal of a company is to realize profit and to increase shareholder value. These are central objectives in both the short and the long run. They primarily need an information system, which shows the influence of their businesses, decisions, and activities on these economic goals. Therefore traditional accounting systems calculate the shareholder's equity in the balance sheet, the net income and costs, the contribution margin, or the profit of an activity of a period in an income statement.

One central consequence of this is that the structure of the whole information system in financial accounting as well as in managerial accounting is determined by this purpose. All processes of a profit-oriented company influence the input and the output of the company measured in terms of costs and revenues. Their consequences on the profit goal determine the solution of all accounting problems: the valuation of assets and liabilities, the estimation of depreciation, the calculation of marginal or full costs, and so on.

Special Information and Accounting Issues in Not-for-Profit Organizations

As traditional accounting systems are oriented towards profit and as this goal is not the most important objective of NPOs, standard financial and managerial accounting systems are inappropriate. Cost or profit goals may be important for NPOs to the extent that they need to work efficiently and contain costs. Efficiency may be part of their system's objectives but this goal, which is tied to the profit purpose is usually dominated by other not-for-profit goals.

NPOs usually need information and accounting systems, which are oriented towards their primary objectives. Otherwise the use of traditional accounting systems could be inimical to their pursuits. If, for example, a state university used traditional financial and cost accounting systems geared for the commercial sector needs, its decisions on the selection of students and professors, the structure and the contents of the studies, research projects, etc. could be oriented towards costs instead of quality. With profit-oriented accounting systems, NPOs cannot be managed and controlled adequately.

Companies in the profit sector are integrated in a national and global economic system whereby they must pursue profit goals like shareholder value and periodic net income. These profit goals are standard for all commercial companies. Therefore, the accounting systems exhibit a common structure. In the not-for-profit sector there are a lot of different organizations with different missions, tasks, and goals. They often have cultural dynamics, which differ from those in profit-seeking organizations. Whereas the culture in the profit sector is tied to economic goals and markets, the culture of NPOs is influenced by special service tasks as well as their members and the goals of these members. Consequently, the information and accounting systems of NPOs differ more than those in the profit sector. Their information systems have to be more specialized in order to fulfil the special purposes of each organization. Thus the problem of structuring their information system must be analysed in more precise terms.

Determinants of Management Information Systems

Where NPOs are not obliged by law or other regulatory bodies to publish special reports like balance sheets or income statements, the primary purpose of their information system is to give data for the decision-making and the control processes of their managers and their members. They require a specific type of management information system (see Fig. 12.2).

The structure of management information systems in NPOs depends on two parameters: the users of the information and their decision problems; the management system of the organization.

The effectiveness of an information system depends on the use of its results. Therefore its construction must be oriented towards the decisions and activi-

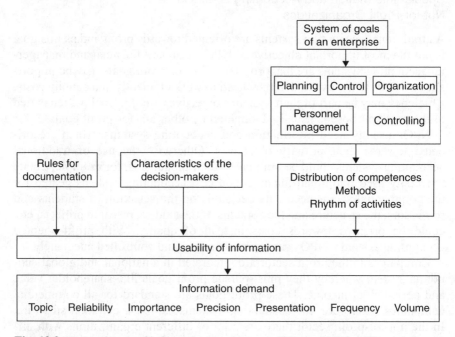

Fig. 12.2. Determinants of information requirements (Küpper 2001*b*: 142)

ties of its 'customers'. In the first place these are the managers of the organization. They need data to make decisions in order to fulfil their tasks. The more appropriate data they get and the better these data show the consequences of their decisions the more they will use the information system. Therefore the tasks of the different managers of an organization determine the necessary output and design of an information system. In order to analyse the information demand, one has to look at the managers of the organization and their tasks, decision problems, and activities. They should get all information that could be relevant to solve their problems. The evaluation of different alternatives and the selection of an optimal alternative depends on their goals. Therefore the objectives of the organization and their managers determine the relevance of information.

To construct an effective information system one should not only look at the individual managers of an organization and their decisions and control problems but also at the entire management system. Important components of the management system are planning and control, the organizational structure, the management incentives and management development system, and the controlling system. For example, the distribution of tasks or competences and the hierarchical structure with different divisions and departments determine which persons must get special information. The models and methods, which are used to plan and control the business processes determine the type of data which are needed. In many companies strategic and operative planning processes are regulated and have to follow a given timetable. Then the rhythm of planning and control as well as of decision-making will determine the time at which information must be available.

As NPOs have special cultural dynamics, it is important that the information system matches their individual culture. For example, the culture of a hospital or a university is quite different from the culture of a sports club, a parish, or a political party. As the Internet is increasingly used by people of differing socio-economic groups, this will make it easier to align the information system to the culture of NPOs. If most members use the Internet in their professional and their private activities, they will readily accept an Internet-based information system. Therefore the Internet becomes a 'medium' for installing information systems.

Structural Components of the Information Systems of Not-for-Profit Organizations

Characteristics of the Information Issues in Not-for-Profit Organizations

Whereas commercial accounting systems are the core of the information system in the profit sector and most of their information is monetary, NPOs need more diversified information systems. They have to work with and produce non-monetary as well as monetary data in order to produce measures of the not-for-profit objectives of the organization.

These data reflect the activities of the organization. For this purpose they relate to the input, the processes, and the output of its activities. Therefore the information system must include data which show

- the input of material, labour, machines, money, and other resources,
- the duration, the capacity utilization, and other characteristics of its processes, and
- characteristics of its output.

In an NPO the output cannot be characterized by monetary data like revenues. Its characteristics depend on the task of the organization. In a (not-for-profit) hospital this may be the number of patients, of surgeries, etc., in a public university the number of students, examinations or scientific papers for example. In order to measure the 'efficiency' of individual processes or the whole NPO, output and input data should be related to each other. Such efficiency ratios should relate to the objectives of the NPO. Otherwise they cannot be meaningful in assessing their processes.

Technical Characteristics of Information Systems in Not-for-Profit-Organizations

Modern information systems are computer based. In order to get a powerful Internet-based information system it should consist of two types of systems that are essential: several operative systems, and a data warehouse system.

The operative systems produce the current monetary and non-monetary data. Components of this part of the information system may be a bookkeeping system, computerized financial and/or cost accounting systems, non-monetary administration systems for staff, inventories, etc. Such systems help to plan and control the ongoing processes during the year. Their concern relates only to a limited area of the organization.

Conversely, there is a special requirement for a data warehouse system in not-for-profit organizations. This type of computerized information system provides the technical basis to develop a management decision system. Whereas the operative information systems only contain data of the current period, data warehouses store historized data of a lot of periods. Therefore they are useful for different analyses, for example, to see the development of relevant measures over time. Data warehouses can be characterized with four typical aspects (Inmon 1996):

- subject-oriented: their structure depends on the specific information needs of the decision-makers;
- integrated: in a data warehouse the data of different operative systems are brought together and consolidated;

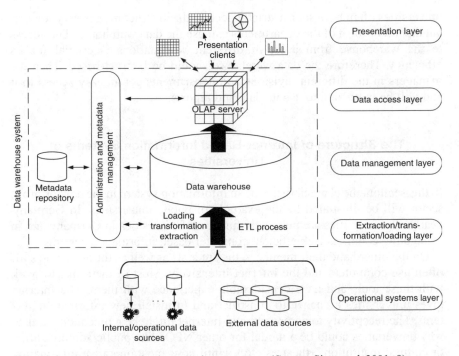

Fig. 12.3. Components of a data warehouse system (*Source*: Sinz *et al.* 2001: 9)

- time-varying: data warehouses contain historical data, and will be actualized periodically (e.g. daily, monthly);
- non-volatile: stored data will not be changed or deleted.

Figure 12.3 shows the architecture of a data warehouse system, which contains three different levels (Böhnlein/Ulbrich-vom Ende 2000). The lower lever is the interface to the operative systems. It manages the input of the data. This level contains instruments to extract the relevant data from the operative systems, to check and correct them, and to update the data warehouse. The middle level is used for data saving. Mostly it is constructed on the basis of a relational data bank system with special instruments to index and to save the data. That level can be organized in different ways as a virtual, central, or distributed data warehouse system as well as a data mart with or without a central data warehouse (Inmon 1996). At the highest level, there is an On-line Analytical Processing (OLAP)-server to provide the data to the users. This server contains the multidimensional structures for the applications and the presentation software. The OLAP concept supports the interactive use of the data. The administration of the whole data warehouse is controlled by special instruments like a metadata repository for administration and monitoring.

In an organization with a high degree of decentralization all decision-makers should have access to the data warehouse. As NPOs like hospitals or universities often have such a strictly decentralized structure it is very important that all or most of the departments can use the data warehouse. The access to the warehouse from a lot of different workstations is crucial for its efficiency. Therefore the data warehouse should be Internet-based. Then the managers in the different divisions and departments get an easy access to it and will be motivated to use its data and reports.

The Structure of Internet-Based Information Systems of Universities

In this section, the characteristics of an information system in the not-for-profit sector will be illustrated by the example of public universities. In Germany, nearly all universities are publically financed. Universities in Germany and in some other countries lack efficient computer based information systems.

On the other hand their members, the students as well as the academic staff often use computers and the Internet intensively. Most of them like to work with these tools and have considerable experience with them. The Internet gives universities a chance to construct and to install new information systems. The receptivity to computers and Internet might be a precondition as to why universities could be a model for other NPOs like public administration or cultural institutions (theatres etc.). Until now, most operative information systems are not Internet-based whereas data warehouses are developed as Internet-based systems. As universities have a comparatively decentralized structure, their operative systems will be designed on the basis of the Internet technology as well.

Operative Information Systems in Public Universities

Universities have a lot of different tasks and activities. To manage these processes they need various administrative and information systems. There are, on the one hand, different systems to control economic processes, which are similar to the systems used in the profit sector. On the other hand, universities need special academic information systems to administer the processes of education and research.

In order to design effective information systems for universities they must be oriented towards the demand of the potential users. Therefore to design an information system there must be a model of the university such as that in Fig. 12.4 (Küpper/Sinz 1998: 5; Küpper 2001a: 462).

This model reflects the determinants of the information systems. At the base, there are the business processes of education and research, which are supported by service processes in the libraries and administration. These processes are controlled by several academic and non-academic managers (president, chancellors, deans, professors, etc.). These managers are the

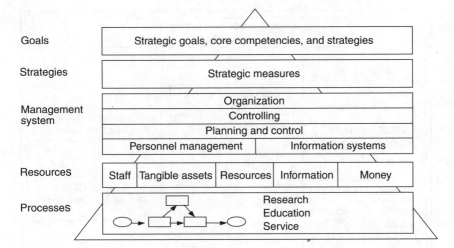

Fig. 12.4. Layer-based model of a university

decision-makers who decide on the input of the resources. The decisions are influenced and coordinated by the management system, the strategies and the strategic goals of the university on top.

Economic Information Systems of the University

Although public universities are not-for-profit oriented they have a lot of economic activities. They have to control a large monetary budget, which may be financed by government, fees, fund raising, and other sources. To manage their expenses, an accounting system based on a bookkeeping system may be required. As the central goals of universities are non-economic they should use special financial and cost accounting systems, which differ from those systems in the profit sector (Küpper 2000; Küpper 2001*a*).

Financial Accounting System

The basis of a financial accounting system is the cash flow statement which reveals the flow of money received from the government and others. In a public university a balance sheet can primarily show and classify assets. As the liabilities of such universities are often not high, they are not of great interest. As long as universities do not offer their activities in education and resarch on a free market and as they do not pursue a profit goal, an income statement is useless and could be misleading. Instead of this, it could be useful to show the changes of the net values of its assets in time. Then the financial accounting system of a university may consist of three types of economic information systems (Fig. 12.5), the cash flow statement, the balance sheet

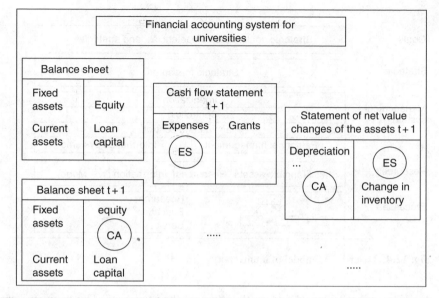

Fig. 12.5. Components of a financial accounting system for public universities (CA, changes of the assets; ES, expense surplus)

and a statement of net value changes of the assets. Such a system is used as a basic instrument to review the university by auditors and by government.

Cost Accounting System

In order to support decisions universities need a cost accounting system, too. The main problem in constructing this system is the lack of market-based sales revenues as long as most of the revenues are given by government. The problem of the allocation of the public grants to the different education, research, and service activities is not solvable without arbitrariness. Therefore a performance information system of a university should show the monetary expenses and costs of input on the one side and the non-monetary ouput in education, research, and service processes on the other side (Fig. 12.6). Performance indicators can be formed as ratios between output and monetary or non-monetary input measures. As the universities undertake different types of activities and pursue different goals in education, research, and services their performance cannot be measured by one indicator. These performance measures are calculated in a third part of this internal accounting system.

In Germany the chancellors of the universities make some efforts to get an accounting system suitable for universities. The basic principle for the university cost accounting system is to separate between a basic system and different purpose oriented systems for planning and control. The basic system

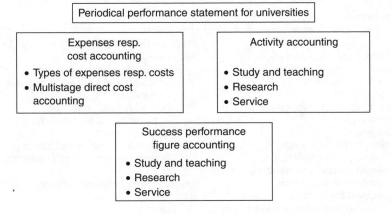

Fig. 12.6. Components of a performance statement for universities

contains raw data about cost and revenue issues. It includes the realized and the estimated data of the expenses and costs, the revenues and the non-monetary measures of university output. They must have a high degree of reliability. Cost allocation shall be reserved to the other type, the purpose oriented systems, as the used allocation principles and allocation mechanisms depend on the respective planning or control problems.

The statements of expenses, cost accounting, and activity accounting in Fig. 12.6 belong to basic accounting systems. As shown in Fig. 12.7 the expenses should be classified into operating and investment activities. The most important current expenses and costs are related to the input of material, external services, labour, information, fees, capital, etc. They have to be complemented by the expenses for the investments in buildings, machines, computers, and so on. Whereas the current expenses correspond to the cost, the expenses for investments lead to depreciations in cost accounting. Therefore the current expenses and costs may be completed by the depreciation on buildings, machines, computers, etc. In order to calculate these costs one has to allocate the purchase expenses of the property to its useful life. As the basic accounting system is not aligned to special planning or control problems one should take the straight-line depreciation method. On the other side the revenues of a public university may be classified by public grants, fees, research grants, revenues on capital stocks, interest, etc.

In a further step, all costs have to be attributed to cost centres. The hierarchical structure of a university leads to a multistage system of centres. The most important centres may be the chairs, the departments, the faculties, the administrative departments, and the board of a university. In order to avoid cost allocation, the basic system should only show the direct cost of each stage. Then one gets multistage direct cost accounting as a second component of university cost accounting.

Types of expenses	Types of revenues
Current expenses for	*Revenues from allocation of funds and for*
Material and purchased goods	*own activities*
(incl. literature, materials for	Allocation of funds
teaching and studying)	for teaching, study, and research (in
Purchased activities	general)
(incl. binding books, expert	for teaching and study
reports etc.)	for promotion of the scientific and
Personnel	artistic novices
Employees with tenure	for further education and training
Employees without tenure	for social promotion of the students
Social security contributions	etc.
and pension provision	*Revenues from international cooperations,*
Support for the scientific sector	*etc.*
Other expenses for personnel,	
for example, for recruitment etc.	*Revenues from research and technology*
Travel expenses, separation,	*transfer*
compensation	Allocation of funds for research from the
Further education and training	state, federal government, DFG ...
etc.	Revenues for research from the private
	sector of the economy
	Research assignments of private people,
	the industry or technology transfer
Usage of rights and services	Revenues from public relations, publishing
	activities
Communication,	Revenues from special assigned tasks
Contributions etc.	Revenues from licences, patents and
	commissions etc.
Taxes,	
Interests, etc.	*Revenues from cooperations*
Capital investments for	
Rights equivalent to real property	*Revenues from other securities and loans of*
and buildings	*the finance assets*
Technical installations and	
machines	
Other equipment, office furniture	*Other interests etc.*
and equipment (incl. computers)	

Fig. 12.7. Basic system of university expenses and revenues

As long as the different education and research activities of public universities are not sold on markets the output of an university cannot be measured monetarily without arbitrariness. In Germany students don't need to pay fees. Therefore the public universities in such a system need an activity accounting with non-monetary measures. A classification of important output measures in education and study, research and service gives Fig. 12.8.

The necessity of a specific activity accounting is one of the reasons why traditional accounting software cannot fulfil the objectives of cost accounting

Academic studies and teaching	Research	Service
Students	Promotion of scientific novices	Libraries
Places in higher	Post-graduate studies	Acquisitions
education	Courses	Users, etc.
First-year-students	Doctorates	
Undergraduate students	Habilitations, etc.	
Graduate students		
Drop out of students, etc.		
Teaching		Personnel administration
Number of courses	Utilization of scientific results	Attended persons
Course hours	Scientific publications	Recruitments, etc.
Tests	Patents, etc.	
Tests in undergraduate		
studies	Third-party funds from	
Tests in graduate studies	Industry	Student administration
graduates	Public institutions	Finance administration

Fig. 12.8. Classification of university output measures

in a university. In this situation it is possible to develop new software systems based on the Internet technology. The activities in education and research are done in different departments and faculties. The data on teaching, tests and examinations, post graduated courses, papers, publications, and so on are distributed on several decentralized centres. To get a non-redundant centralized data pool you need decentralized information based on the Internet technology. By this way one can get a high degree of efficiency.

The success of a public university cannot be measured by profit. As they pursue different objectives in education, research and service accounting has to determine different performance measures. In Germany there has been no agreement on those performance measures, which might represent the success of a public university. Therefore Fig. 12.9 shows some examples of performance indicators of universities (Arbeitskreis Hochschulrechnungswesen 1999).

The periodical statements of expenses and cost accounting, activity accounting, and success performance indicators are the basis for benchmarking, planning, and control. To compare several universities and to get benchmarks they have to publish similar data. In order to analyse the efficiency of university chairs, departments, faculties, or service centres one has to compare performance figures of these centres within the same university and with comparable centres of other universities (if one can get their data). Furthermore universities need cost and activity information for several decisions. For example, they have to decide on the centralization or decentralization of administration like examination centres or the initiation of a new study course. Then one has to collect and to estimate the relevant data to find

Academic studies and teaching	Research	Promotion of scientific novices	Service
Applicants per place at university	Publications per professor	Post-graduate students per professor	Library Acquisition of books per staff members in library
Resp. per student in first semester	Publications per academic staff	Post-graduate students per graduates	
Students per professor	Third-party funds per professor	Number of doctorates per professor	
Number of tests per professor	Third-party funds per academic staff	ØDuration of doctoral studies	
Graduation rate (based on number of first-year-students)	Scientific award per academic staff	Habilitations per professor	
Graduates per professor	Patents per academic staff	ØDuration of habilitation	
ØDuration of studies per degree programme			
ØAge of graduates			

Fig. 12.9. Classification and examples of universitary performance measures

the optimal alternative. In these calculations difficult problems of cost allocation have to be solved.

As monetary measures are not as important as in the profit sector, universities need additional non-monetary information systems. Very important are personnel administration systems and systems to plan and to control the allocation and the use of rooms and material.

The activities of a university take place in different schools and departments, which may be located in a broader area. In order to decide on the level of the departments, the faculties and the top of the university, and to get accounting and other reports of these levels, the data of all these decentralized locations have to be brought together. Internet-based systems enable this data integration. Therefore modern bookkeeping, accounting, and administration systems are Internet-based. That seems to be more important in universities and other NOPs than in the profit sector because of their high decentralization of the decision-making, administration, and accounting processes.

Academic Information Systems

The core of university activities consists of education and the research processes. Whereas the latter depend on the individual decisions of the scientists, the education of the students must be organized and coordinated by the faculties. The great number of students in several courses cannot be controlled without effective administration systems. Furthermore the enrolment in some courses, their master schedules and their examinations are often regulated by law. Then the standards in the processes of the selection of students and of examination are very high and can be reviewed by justice.

Universities must have effective systems to administrate the students, the courses, the local allocation of the different classes, and the examinations. Using these systems they have to inform the lecturers and the students about the timing and the local allocation of the courses, the results of examinations and other important aspects of the education. Internet-based information systems help to organize such information processes much more efficiently.

Although the individual scientists are free in their research, effective information systems are helpful to support their research processes by library administration systems etc. and to show their scientific results in publications, awards, citations, and so on. Web sites and Internet reports can transport the information on universities, faculties, departments and their members as well as their courses, and scientific activities worldwide. In this way information is available to a lot of people.

Internet-Based Data Warehouse Management Information System

The Structure of a University Data Warehouse System

German universities lack management information systems. Most decisions are made without sufficient information. Therefore in the last year a prototype of a data warehouse system for the Bavarian universities has been developed. It serves as a computer based decision support system to the managers of the universities and to the ministry; it is called CEUS. The motivation to develop such an Internet-based system came from the Bavarian ministry of science, research, and arts as it perceived the lack of readily available information.

The relevant decision-makers of the university system are the ministry and the parliament, the presidents, the chancellors, and the boards of the universities, as well as the faculties with their deans and boards. There are three levels of user groups: the state, the university, and the faculty. The managers of each level make different decisions, for example, on the allocation of grants and other resources to the universities (by the ministry), the centralization or decentralization of functions within a university (by the president), or the scheduling of courses and examinations (by the professors of a faculty). The information demands of the three levels differ. Furthermore the decision-makers of each level are partly autonomous.

As a consequence these decision-makers need different information. Especially this information has to differ in the grade of aggregation. For example, the managers of the university demand more aggregated information compared to the managers of the faculty; the ministry and parliament ask for information aggregated on the level of a university. Mainly because of these reasons the data warehouse system of the Bavarian universities contains data warehouses on three levels (see Fig. 12.10):

- a data warehouse for each faculty,
- a data warehouse for each university,
- a data warehouse for the Bavarian state.

The lower level includes data on the education, examination, research, and service processes of a faculty. These data must come from the operational administration systems of the faculty and the university, for example, the student administration system of the university, the examination's administration system of the faculty (or the university), and the bookkeeping system of the faculty. In Germany only some of the bigger and efficiently organized faculties use such operational systems. Only these faculties will get their own data warehouse.

The warehouses of the university will be installed in all universities if they have the required operative information systems and if they are necessary as a data source for the data warehouse of the state. Moreover the demand on quantitative data is higher on this level than on the faculty level.

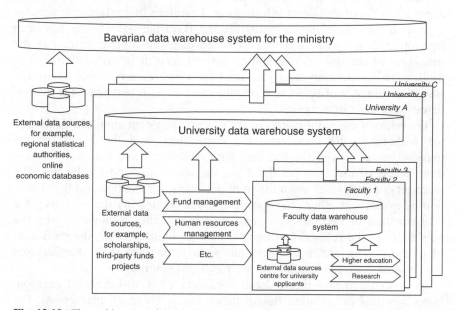

Fig. 12.10. The architecture of the data warehouse system of universities (Sinz *et al.* 2001: 10)

The data warehouse of the state gains its data not only from the universities. A further important source of data is the 'Bavarian State Office for Statistics and Data Processing'. This office periodically gathers and checks data on universities as it is demanded by law.

The access to each data warehouse is controlled by the respective level. The upload of data into a higher level data warehouse is regulated by the lower level. This is necessary in order to assure data protection. Besides this, trust and acceptance seem to be key factors for the success of this data warehouse system.

A data warehouse system usually has to be developed gradually. In the first step of installing the system each data warehouse will receive data concerning students, exams, staff, and finance. Every student is registered with different characteristics such as his age, sex, native country and region, address, course of study, and so on. The data on examinations show the results of the courses, credit points, the dates of examination, etc. The professors, assistants, and the administrative staff belong to the class of staff. Accounting data will be stored in the class of finance.

The Process of Installing a Management Information System

The task of developing and installing such a management information system requires two types of processes: computer related and management related processes. Important steps of the first type are the choice of a suitable data warehouse software, its adaptation to the special structure of the university system, the construction of the interfaces to the operative administration systems, the check of their data, and the test of the whole system. Important steps of the management related processes are the analysis of the information demand and the training of the user groups.

In order to supply the decision-makers with the appropriate information and to avoid an information overload an analysis of the information demand in the ministry and the universities with their faculties is necessary. There are deductive and inductive methods to analyse the information demand. The deductive methods include the analysis of the relevant laws, statutes, and other documents as well as the formal organization of the universities. One has to list up the important decision problems of the ministry, the university and the faculty and to investigate which information is most important for supporting decision-making. Inductive methods include interviews and questionnaires.

In order to get a well-founded view of the information demand, a combination of deductive and inductive methods seems to be necessary. First the tasks and the goals of the relevant managers in the ministry, the boards of the universities and the faculties have to be identified by an organizational analysis. Then one can make first interviews with a few representatives of these groups (see Fig. 12.11). In the next step the information demand of the decision-makers in the ministry and the university are analysed theoretically in a systematic way (deductive-logical analysis). These three steps constitute the basis to formulate

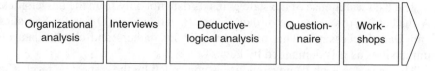

Fig. 12.11. Important steps within an analysis of information demand

specific questionnaires for the members of the ministry, the president and the vice-presidents, the chancellor and the members of the board of the university, as well as the deans and vice-deans for research and for study of several faculties. Last the results of the questionnaire should be tested and controlled in several workshops with selected representatives of each group.

Another critical issue for the successful use of this information system lies in the motivation of the managers to work with such a computer based instrument. This motivation can be increased by a qualifying training programme. It is important to have qualified personnel on each level. This personnel can also help to instruct the other managers of the respective level.

The Internet-Based Use of a Data Warehouse Management Information System

The management information system can be used in different ways. The customers on each level get standardized reports. This report system is designed during the development of the system and will only be changed in larger intervals. These reports are always designed specifically for a user group like the board of a university or a faculty.

The essential advantage of a data warehouse system lies in the opportunity to build individual reports in a fast and easy way. Within a very short time one is able to analyse and to combine different data, time-series and charts out of the huge multidimensional data-structures. This ability should only be provided to selected user groups. So different access authorizations have to be defined. Whereas students can only get standard reports, managers at each level are authorized to extract a lot of information from their data warehouse and to make their own reports. This expedites the relevant information for their decisions.

The reports are usually distributed by the Internet so that the report system gains in effectiveness and efficiency. Using the Internet the decision-makers of the different levels who are located at different places are able to use their own data warehouse in an effective way. The orientation of the stored data towards their information demand and the technical efficiency of such an Internet-based data warehouse increase the probability that the system will be used as a management information system. In this way the data warehouse system is an effective instrument to support the management.

Conclusion

The computer and especially the Internet technology enable a new class of information systems. That seems to be very important for the not-for-profit sector. Organizations with not-for-profit objectives cannot use traditional profit-oriented information systems without considerable adjustments. Often NPOs pursue several non-monetary objectives and have a structure with a high degree of decentralization. Their decisions may be allocated to a lot of different persons who are located at different places. In this case the Internet gives the opportunity to construct an efficient information system without installing a special intranet of the company.

The effectiveness of modern data warehouse systems is very high. They can be used in multiple ways. Every report can be generated to a special problem, situation, and purpose. That gives the chance to fulfil the information tasks in a NPO, which often have a higher degree of diversity as in a profit-oriented company. One important prerequisite is that the managers find the information, which is relevant and useful for their decisions and activities. Therefore the construction of the data warehouse must be based on an intensive analysis of their information demand. Furthermore the users must have learned how to use the data warehouse technology. The development of such an Internet-based system not only relates to the technical side but also has to be accompanied by a training programme. Then one can reach the aim that the Internet-based information system will be used as a management information system.

The decentralization offered by Internet technologies as well as their simplicity facilitate the management of NPOs. This technology has an increasing degree of dissemination in professional and private areas. NPOs will react to this development. The more their members become used to working with the Internet and email, it will become desirable for them to install information systems based on the Internet. One can expect that the Internet will push forward the development and the dissemination of effective information systems in the not-for-profit sector.

References

Arbeitskreis Hochschulrechnungswesen der deutschen Universitätskanzler: Schlußbericht 1999.

Böhnlein, M. and Ulbrich-vom Ende, A. (Februar 2000), Grundlagen des Data Warehousing: Modellierung und Architektur, Bamberger Beiträge zur Wirtschaftsinformatik Nr. 55, Bamberg.

Inmon, W. H. (1996), *Building the Data Warehouse*, 2nd edn (Wiley: New York).

Küpper, Hans-Ulrich (2000), 'Hochschulrechnung auf der Basis von doppelter Buchhaltung und HBG?', in *Zeitschrift für betriebswirtschaftliche Forschung*, 348–69.

—— (2001*a*), Rechnungslegung von Hochschulen, in *Betriebswirtschaftliche Forschung und Praxis*, 578–92.

—— (2001*b*), Controlling, 3rd edn (Stuttgart, Schäffer-Poeschel).

—— and Elmar Sinz (eds) (1998), 'Gestaltungskonzepte für Hochschulen. Effizienz, Effektivität', Evolution (Stuttgart, Schäffer-Poeschel).

Oettle, Karl (1990), 'Not-for-profit Organizations', in E. Grochla, E. Gaugler *et al.* (eds), *Handbook of German Business Management* (Stuttgart) 1513–20.

Salamon, Lester M. and Anheier, Helmut, K. (1997), Defining the nonprofit sector: A cross-national analysis (New York, Machester).

Sinz, E. J., Böhnlein, M., Ulbrich-vom Ende, A., and Plaha, M. (2001), Architekturkonzept eines verteilten Data Warehouse-Systems für das Hochschulwesen, in *Proceedings of Wirtschaftsinformatik* 2001 (Augsburg, WI) 19–21 September.

Streim, Hannes (2002), 'Not-for-profit Unternehmen', in H.-U. Küpper and A. Wagenhofer (eds). *Handwörterbuch Unternehmensrechnung und Controlling* (Stuttgart).

13
Paradoxes of Management and Control in a New Economy Firm

Kari Lukka and Markus Granlund

Introduction

He is afraid that the bean counters that have taken charge in the firm will destroy the good things. He stills thinks the German acquisition was excellent; only that the take-over phase did not succeed as expected. Other main owner parties think dreamers' era is now over. Kuokkanen disagrees. 'Surely one cannot build such a firm without dreams. We should encourage people to dream about big things.'

(Mr. Ilpo Kuokkanen, the initiator and prior President of the internet operator Jippii Group, when the German operations of the firm had turned out to be a disaster. Helsingin Sanomat, 9 September 2001)

The New Economy

Though it is debatable what the 'new economy' (NE) means, there appears to be a widely held common understanding that the core issues of the NE are its digital orientation, its thorough linkage with the Internet, and its tendency to be global. However, there are other dimensions of the NE as well. One of these is the fast emerging biotechnology cluster, which—when combined with the information technology (IT) cluster—has the potential of making the world and human life very different from what it is (e.g. Castells 2000).

One key characteristic of the NE is that it tends to reduce the significance of geographical location, whilst stressing the importance of speedy action. The role played by country borders is diminishing in the NE environment. The ability of governments, or even that of the cooperating organizations they form, to regulate things appears to decrease all the time (Castells 2000). Whereas action at a distance (cf. Latour 1987; Roberts and Scapens 1985; Robson 1992) in global firms, for instance, can take place very rapidly and cheaply today, this does not apply to the functioning of many regulatory bodies. Operations can be relocated globally increasingly quickly. Opportunities to control things by coercion appear to be decreasing. Cooperation between parties is increasingly prevalent.

The hepful comments of Mikka Alasaarela, Pekka Aula, Antti Oksanen, Vesa Partanen, Jani Taipaleenmäki, and Tero-Seppo Tuomela are gratefully acknowledged.

The NE has an important linkage to economics: the very notion of NE was indeed constructed on the basis of the huge and continuous growth of the US economy in the 1990s, without particular inflation or other economic disturbances. Based on this, it was even hypothesized that the globally oriented, IT-based economy would have changed the conventional regularities of economic behaviour: that a continuous unproblematic growth, without cyclic movements would have materialized. In the late 1990s, the capital market players started to pay increasing attention to the new economy firms (NEFs), and huge sums of loan and venture capital were invested in them. Many of the NEFs became listed in stock exchanges, and the global mergers and acquisitions movement affected them as well. High risks were taken with NEFs when they absorbed capital from new investors. In many cases, they had no completed commercial products, nor had they so far ever made any profit—profits were expected to be earned in the more or less distant future. Actually, capital market studies have shown that in the case of NEFs, there has in general been little association between their market value and their earnings (e.g. Engel *et al.* 2001), and when there is, the correlation is negative: bigger losses increase, not reduce, NEFs' market values (e.g. Hand 2000). The economic argument underlying this phenomenon is that current losses reflect strategic expenditures (e.g. for customer base creation), not poor performance as such.[1]

The peak of the belief in the economic value of the NE was during early 2000, when the stock prices of NEFs were extraordinarily high, based on their P/E-ratios (or growth rate adjusted P/E-ratio, PEG-ratio) in comparison to other firms. However, later in the same year, the bubble of the NE sector went bust. The extremely high expectations were suddenly regarded as far too optimistic, and stock prices of most of the NEFs crashed. NEFs started to sack personnel and a number of bankruptcies followed. The belief in new economic regularities vanished, and the conventional wisdom was realized to still hold true. However, this should not be taken to suggest that the NE would have collapsed: the rapidly developing, IT-based, and globally oriented NE is still in existence, though it is now viewed with more reasonable expectations as for their financial potential.

The New Economy Firms

The NE emerged relatively rapidly during the 1990s, in spite of the vast development of IT over several decades. The beginning of the 1990s witnessed the emergence of multimedia developers and the birth of the so-called new-media firms, focusing on the CD-ROM business. When the Internet

---

[1] This kind of relationship may be a temporary phenomenon only, reflective of the hectic boom of the NE during the study period.

made its breakthrough in the mid-1990s, the world-wide web (WWW) very rapidly caught most of their attention. Multimedia developers changed their focus from CD-ROMs to the Internet, and a number of new firms emerged, providing Internet-related technologies and services (e.g. various softwares, web-site and portal design aid, contents for the web-sites and portals, and consulting). E-commerce, dot-coms, accounting systems operating through the Internet, and outsourcing of accounting technologies through the Internet (e.g. Application Service Providers, ASPs) were significant issues of the last years of the 1990s (cf. Aula and Oksanen 2000). In 2001 the Internet expanding to include mobile solutions and third generation mobile-phone networks gained particular currency. E-business was believed to possibly move towards mobile business ('m-business') within a few years.

A distinction has been made between NEFs and firms representing the 'old economy'.[2] NEFs include many types of firms, from 'dot-coms', which operate primarily virtually (such as Amazon, eBay.com, or EQ Online) to several other types of firms, which are closely connected to the Internet (technology providers, www-site or-portal designers, content producers, and consultants). Currently this distinction of two categories of firms has yet become increasingly blurred, since many of the old economy firms have invested in digitalization in general, and e-commerce in particular (cf. the term 'clicks-and-mortar' firm; Williams 2001). These can be called 'hybrid firms', since they attempt to combine key features of the NE to their conventional business activities (Aula and Oksanen 2000). This chapter focuses on the 'true' NEFs, which are either dot-coms themselves, or support this kind of business orientation, by providing adequate technologies or services.

The pioneering NEFs of the 1990s were mostly small enterprises, which were either driven by artistic ambitions related to multimedia solutions or by an intention to create advanced new IT-technologies. The culture of these firms was very special, being fundamentally based on strong commitment to the technical or artistic potential of their personnel, especially that of the leading figures. They operated primarily on the basis of intrinsic motivation (e.g. Deci and Ryan 1985; Frey 1997): driven by direct emotional links of their personnel to what they were doing and developing. Their activities were linked together with the vision of the firm and the 'story' of its leading actor circulated. It was a 'we-culture', based on personal, continuous, and informal communication. The dedicated, mostly very young personnel were ready to work very long hours, and the working life was not clearly distinguished from private life (Aula and Oksanen 2000).

In the beginning of the 1990s, NEFs operated in quite modest financial and market frameworks, and focused on the development of their core abilities and products. During the course of the decade, the spectrum of NEF activities

---

[2] At the extreme, it is argued that there are only two types of firms: 'dot-coms' and 'wanna-dots' (Kanter 2001).

expanded, alongside the growth of the Internet technologies. Gradually NEFs started to regard growth as an important target for their operations. Growth was measured primarily by indicators like turnover, total head count, number of engineers, and the number of clients, and towards the end of the 1990s, increasingly by the market value of the firm. However, profitability was not regarded as a critical issue of the day; NEFs lived in the 'next-world' in that regard. In contrast, the market value of NEFs was viewed as increasingly crucial for several reasons. Often, linked to an agreement with a venture capital investor, was the intent to become listed in a stock exchange through a successful initial public offering (IPO). Also, many of the small NEFs merged, or were acquired by other firms. Opportunities emerged for the pioneering owner-managers to profit from selling their firms during the late 1990s, just before the stock price crash took place in spring 2000 (Aula and Oksanen 2000).

The role played by venture capital investors needs to be considered to understand NE-sector developments over the last few years. In the late 1990s boom period of the NE, venture capitalists typically invested in a relatively large portfolio of NEFs, with a view to being able to exit from them relatively rapidly after an IPO. As for the NEFs in their portfolios, their first priorities were seeking fast growth and the development of an image of successful companies in the market. Venture capital investors tended to apply a probabilistic approach, expecting only a small portion of their portfolio's NEFs to really succeed. They accepted high risks of failure in individual business cases. In this sense, the viewpoint of venture capitalists differed significantly from those of individual NEFs, for which—as for any firm—the survival of their own business was a high priority (cf. Aula and Oksanen 2000; Foster and Kaplan 2001).

NEFs have emerged over less than a decade, witnessing growth, but they have also been affected extensively by the economic downturn from spring 2000. Many NEFs have ceased to exist before being able to launch their first product in the market: their 'burn rate'[3] was too high compared to their ability to raise new funds or create revenue stream. In 2001 the NEF sector was in a state of severe crisis. One commonly reported explanatory candidate is that NEFs have simply been 'out-of-control' organizations. In particular, it has been argued that their financial control systems have been far from adequate.[4]

---

[3] Burn rate, a typical and central financial indicator of NEFs, measures the rate at which a new company is spending its capital while waiting for profitable operation. Typically, a new company, especially in new, fast-growing fields such as Internet commerce, expects in its early stages to spend money faster than it can generate revenues. The term is often seen in financial reviews and discussions about new Internet companies, where the question is whether revenue will begin to flow in sufficient amounts before the invested capital plus revenue is 'burnt up'. See http://whatis.techtarget.com/definition/0,,sid9_gci211716,00.html (retrieved 12 October 2001).

[4] In Finland, for instance, there has been much criticism of the way that the Helsinki Stock Exchange and the investment banks have undertaken NEF listings. Contention has been that they should have more carefully evaluated the management control systems of listing candidates. See for example, Säntti (2001) and Pietiläinen (2001).

Management and Control in the New Economy Firms

NEFs have been viewed as providing good examples of 'sensational leadership' as outlined by Holmberg and Ridderstråle (2000). The leaders of NEFs have been said to advance creative development of new products and services, rather than investing in the control of their organization's personnel and its functioning. One of the main vehicles for their leadership is story telling: the circulation of the mission of the firm, often by the example of the leading figures' own actions. This kind of leadership is characteristic of the 'dream-society', argued by Jensen (1999) soon to come and replace the prevailing 'information society'. Rather than emphasizing reason and rationality, in the dream society emotions, stories, and narratives play key roles. The personnel of NEFs are most typically talented youngsters who are not used to being supervised and controlled. In the boom years of the late 1990s and early 2000, if that would have been attempted, they could have quite quickly relocated themselves to a competing NEF. Just before the stock crash it was even argued that they typically could not be hired, but it was they who selected the firm for which they liked to work (Holmberg and Ridderstråle 2000).

NEFs are inherently like 'organized anarchies', which defy traditional notions of rationality (Cooper *et al.* 1981; March and Olsen 1976). In this light, organizational decision-making is depicted as a loose mixture of problems, solutions, participants, and choice opportunities. The coherence of organizational decision-making has a feature of randomness: problems, solutions, and actions are connected by their simultaneous occurrence rather than by their logical ordering (March 1987). Decision-making is not necessarily driven by goals, since they are often endogenous rather than exogenous elements of the process: goals are often discovered *ex post facto*, through action (Weick 1969). In the 'garbage-can' context, intelligent behaviour is referred to as a 'technology of foolishness' (March 1978), and intuition driven 'playfulness' is viewed as an integral part of organisational life (Cooper *et al.* 1981).

NEFs have features that are common to expertise-oriented organizations, such as universities or R&D departments in business firms. In these, the core issue of activities is the effective and innovative application of human knowledge, which in some cases is linked with applications or innovations of high technology. There exists literature on management control problems of these organizations, and the notion of 'loose coupling' is considered crucial in this context. Loose coupling presupposes that an organization can have both rational (i.e. coupled) and indeterminate (i.e. decoupled) elements simultaneously. Hence, it is important to acknowledge that a meaningful definition of loose coupling really consists of *both* looseness *and* coupling. Orton and Weick (1990) call this the dialectical definition of the notion.[5]

---

[5] The idea of loose coupling can be recognized, for instance, in the book by Foster and Kaplan (2001), when they discuss the cooperation between creative processes and operational excellence.

Loose coupling appears to be a highly relevant concept in analysing NEFs. On the one hand, it is looseness that contributes to their flexibility—to the critical factor regarding their very existence. On the other hand, one might ask, whether one of the key issues in their recent troubles is limited coupling. In fact, there is reason to believe that many of the (unsuccessful) NEFs have been factually decoupled organizations, since they have practically lacked developed coordination mechanisms. We will suggest below that achieving a genuine loose coupling position could be a theoretically valid response to the management control problems typical of NEFs. However, of course even functioning management control will not be enough if the firm's strategy is not apt to lead to achieving a sufficient competitive advantage (e.g. Porter 1996, 2001).

Granlund *et al.* (1998) have analysed the narratives of corporate annual reports of Finnish food manufacturing firms in order to demonstrate how companies live in a world of functional and institutional stories. These stories are essential in the pursuit of legitimacy from the different stakeholders of the company. In the context of the Finnish food industry of the mid-1990s, they drew on such notions as globalization, European Union, re-engineering, 'bigger is better', and strategy. These stories constructed a vision of a 'better future'. NEFs are replete with similar stories. However, regarding them, it still remains obscure what this 'better future' might actually mean. Detailed comprehensive analyses have been scarce, and their content has typically been abstract in the eyes of an average investor, not least since it is sometimes difficult to even describe what a NEF under investigation is actually doing and what its products are. In such a situation, what is truly needed is stakeholders' faith in the company's future. Indeed, it has been suggested that it is basically good faith and confidence that holds loosely coupled organizations together and allows them to function (Meyer and Rowan 1977; Orton and Weick 1990). This obviously engenders challenges for the management of NEFs. Whilst stories and narratives are an important part of the 'rhetorical management' needed for the creation and maintenance of good working spirit and faith in the future (cf. Granlund *et al.* 1998), at the same time, management control should be implemented in order to secure rationality of overall operation.

In the NEF context, particularly in the early years of the 1990s, management of any type was not welcomed. Trust, communication, and extreme flexibility were highly valued and viewed as central to operations instead of rules and formal procedures, which management typically comprises. However, when the pioneering NEFs started to really grow, merge, become listed, and sold at the end of the 1990s, the 'business as usual' attitude became more pervasive—despite the fact that this was quite often regarded as destructive for the original mission and operation culture of the firm (Aula and Oksanen 2000). The central paradox in the management and control of NEFs thus is how to combine rebellious creativity, unlimited individual freedom, and the pursuit of ultimate flexibility with the 'normal' demands of business organizations.

The Inherent Tension

Tensions are, as such, a quite normal feature of organizational life: eternal debates around centralization or decentralization, local or global focus, short term or long term, change or stability, focus on cost control or quality, and focus on manufacturing or customer service exemplify this. In fact, the economy appears to be in a continuous pendulum kind of a movement from one extreme to another. It can be argued that effective management means accepting the existence of these tensions and an ability to find a functioning balance between competing agendas (cf. Ahrens and Dent 1998; Evans 2000).

As outlined above, in the case of NEFs, one of the most significant tensions is that between creative flexibility and management control (cf. Foster and Kaplan 2001). Whilst this issue was no doubt acknowledged, it did not cause much attention before the stock price crash of the year 2000. Thereafter it suddenly seemed to be of crucial importance to be able to combine the two very different agendas. The paradox that had been regarded as only theoretical up to that point, if noticed at all, became very real. Consequently, the question concerning the potential significance of more rigorous management control technologies was very seriously raised. Accounting-based controls have been at the centre of this debate. However, putting accounting controls into place within NEFs is far from being an unproblematic task.

On the one hand, in the context of NEFs, accounting related controls might appear to have only limited intrinsic value. Accounting is developed for, and focuses on, tangible operations, and it has been acknowledged for a long time that intangible issues, such as the value of knowledge potential linked to the firm's personnel, are severe problems for accounting measurement. Since the operations of NEFs are to a large extent based on intangible resources, the accounting viewpoint to control may appear somewhat ill focused. It has even been argued that 'the accountant is measuring the company's capital at night—that is, when all employees have gone home' (Jensen 1999: 16).

On the other hand, accountability is a key feature of the market economy and NEFs are eventually part of that. Whilst there seems to have been a belief in the late 1990s and in 2000 that the accountability principle could somehow be relaxed in the NE context, that belief has already turned out to be radically wrong. Since accounting is the key measurement technology within the accountability networks of market economies (Ijiri 1975), the relevance of accounting (of at least some form) is guaranteed. Accounting can be viewed as a 'window back to reality' for NEFs. Through accounting, the somewhat omitted principles of running independent business units, with their pressures on profitability, liquidity, and solidity, become mediated to NEFs, similarly as to firms of other type. Accounting as the common denominator is still needed also in a sensational leadership environment, even though emotions and imagination would be their major focus issues (Holmberg and Ridderstråle 2000: 42). However, the particular features of NEFs can have radical implications on what kind of accounting is relevant, and particularly feasible, in their context.

But can the two quite radically different agendas be made compatible? On the one hand, some kind of management control methods seem to be desperately needed in order to bring adequate order into the managerial chaos often inherent in NEFs, and to keep them viable under market pressures. On the other hand, such methods tend to be felt as threatening the original ways of doing things in these firms. Whilst management control includes many approaches and techniques, such as formal organization, scheduling, formal meetings, rules and procedures, we concentrate here only on one of its subsets, namely management accounting techniques, such as cost accounting, budgeting, and performance measurement and evaluation. We ask whether such techniques can be applied in NEFs, and if they can, in what manner? We address the question of what kind of management control could fit into the complex operational agenda of NEFs.

The Challenge and Facilitation of Cultural Change

The 'Culture of Flexibility' and its Management

As was noted above, NEFs represent expert organizations. Literature on the management of expert (or knowledge-based) organizations emphasizes the special nature of this working environment. Offering a fertile ground for unlimited creativity is said to be the key to success for expert organizations (e.g. Von Krogh *et al.* 2000). On the other hand, many authors consider that performance measurement is needed to enable control in this type of organization as well (e.g. Sveiby 1997; Sveiby and Lloyd 1987). Whilst this appears plausible, it is somewhat peculiar that this argument is typically made as if putting controls in place into expert organizations would be unproblematic from a cultural perspective. The collision between control and creativity is not properly assessed, and the issue of financial control *vis-à-vis* creativity and flexibility seems to be ignored in earlier studies. While it is true that knowledge creation, flexibility, and adaptability should be supported (Hamel and Prahalad 1994; Peters 1987; Skyrme 1999), it also seems evident that this cannot be done at any cost.

Flexibility is a key term in the context of expert organizations, such as NEFs. In recent management accounting studies, flexibility is typically discussed in terms of technical flexibility.[6] In the present study flexibility is defined more broadly, as a fundamental part of a culture,[7] characterized by

---

[6] Flexibility regarding, for example, products, subcontractors, and production (see Mouritsen 1999; Mouritsen and Hansen 2000).

[7] Culture is defined as the commonly shared basic assumptions concerning meanings, norms and values, reflected in e.g. organizational symbols and rituals (see e.g. Schein 1997).

entrepreneurial enthusiasm, creativity, innovativeness, individual freedom, virtuality, young age, non-professional management, and a mix of business and pleasure. The common enemy is bureaucratic control, and financial control perhaps the peak of it. Though close connection between flexibility and competitiveness is typically acknowledged (Mouritsen and Hansen 2000; Stalk and Hout 1990), in NEFs this is normally not stressed: the 'flexibility culture' has emphasized creativity and related issues over financial realities and even competitiveness. In NEFs, flexibility is the primary issue, and competitiveness is not given too much attention: it is considered to follow from flexibility.

To link management and flexibility is far from being an easy task. From the management viewpoint, flexibility is problematic, *inter alia*, since it may lead to overall heterogeneity of operation, to coordination problems, and thus to difficulties especially with strategic management, because it is difficult to achieve synergies. While describing what it is like to lead an ice-hockey team, Juhani Tamminen, an experienced Finnish ice-hockey coach, concluded that a team is like a small bird. If you hold it in your hand too loosely, it will fly away. On the other hand, if you hold it too tightly, it will die. Similarly, in NEFs the management should be able to allow certain freedom, but to still engage in control.

NEFs represent organizations applying the predominantly so-called 'non-accounting' style control (Hopwood 1974). Choudhury (1988) suggests that there can be at least three types of reasons for the absence of accounting in an organization: reliance on trust (accountability is acknowledged but trust, rather than accounting, is used for that end), constructive ambivalence (the use of accounting is considered to conflict with other, more important targets, such as innovativeness), and symbolic absence (accounting is regarded to represent something that is preferred to be avoided). In this classification, the limited use, or even non-use, of accounting in NEFs falls probably most often to the second or third of these categories. The second points to the tension, which can be understood in quite rational terms, and of which there is evidence from many expert organizations. The third category poses a tension, which in the NEF context probably has a more value-laden character: accounting is not used since it is regarded as 'unnecessary evil' as such—as part of the normal bureaucratic business culture, for which NEFs, at least originally, were meant to offer a more exciting alternative. For this reason putting financial controls in place into NEFs is a challenge of cultural change.

Financial Control Diffuses into the Non-Financial Culture

NEFs are at the moment forced to develop their control systems and also provide more financial data on their operation (Granlund and Taipaleenmäki 2000; Zeller *et al.* 2001). NEFs have constantly been warning about poor (short-term) financial results. It seems obvious that financial control systems, if they existed, have failed in many of these companies. For example, in Finland (in 2001) IT consultants and communication security software providers seem to be encountering major financial problems (Hammarsten and Rainisto 2001). Most, if not all, NEFs have also increasingly warned about radically falling growth figures. Of course, convenient control systems alone would not have secured more profitable growth, but the investors normally expect, at the minimum, that company management is at least well aware of the financial position of the firm (cf. Granlund and Lukka 1998*a*). This has not been the case in many collapsed NEFs: evidence has been presented in economic magazines that financial control has collapsed in NEFs. This could probably have been avoided with different attitudes towards financial management and with well-designed management control systems.[8] However, as mentioned above, this alone could not have secured healthier overall development, if there were problems with the mission or strategy of the firm, preventing them from achieving competitive advantage (Porter 2001).

The external pressure to develop financial control systems in NEFs arises from the fact that today investors and analysts control this particular issue. Earlier this was not followed as such, but attention was directed merely to issues like managerial visions, products under development, market expectations, and especially the future growth potential of the company.[9] This pressure involves economic as well as institutional characteristics: it is an economic pressure since, for example, continuation of venture capital financing may depend on whether a NEF can demonstrate that it has implemented proper financial control systems. The institutional pressure originates, for example, in new financial accounting requirements due to public listing, or in corporate group pressure if a NEF is taken over in a corporate acquisition, typical to this business environment (cf. Granlund and Lukka 1998*b*). In general, the external pressure to implement and develop management control systems in NEFs is connected to gaining legitimacy from the stakeholders. Without formal management control systems organizations appear irrational and thereby lack legitimacy, which may again cause, for example, financing problems.

These strong pressures to bring financial controls into NEFs no doubt highlight the contrast between different professional frames of reference (Armstrong 1985; Giddens 1979; Spybey 1984). For people who value technological progress and behavioural flexibility over financial realities, the cultural bases of action—and the interpretative scheme through which these bases are communicated—are different to those who draw their actions primarily from

---

[8] It should be noted that despite current troubles within the NEF sector, there are many NEFs in rapid though sound development. Hence, although our analysis focuses on the inherent features of NEFs, and on managerial tensions that derive from them, there are no doubt examples of NEFs, which have already been able to tackle the issues we examine.

[9] One finds stories of potential investors who want to visit NEFs simply to see whether they truly exist, that is, that there are real people working somewhere in these companies.

financial control systems and the operating principles that underlie such a scheme (Macintosh and Scapens 1990). These schemes (or mediators), such as accounting systems, can facilitate shared learning in providing a commensurable conceptual system—a 'window back to reality' in the context of NEFs—through which a new culture can be produced and reproduced (Dent 1991; Giddens 1979, 1984). On the other hand, the findings of Chenhall and Morris (1995) indicate that a financial control system can be conveniently used beside other interpretative schemes that are applied in organizational communication and action in entrepreneurial companies—largely comparable to NEFs. In the context of NEFs, it can be tentatively concluded that it is possible to successfully embed the principles of financial control into the culture of flexibility—in a loosely coupled way.

Latour (1987, 1991) has outlined virtual operation, which means action and control at a distance, enabled by networking and new information technologies. Applying Latour's ideas of inscriptions (quantifications, 'materialisations') and their translations into this discussion suggests that management control systems take part in the translation processes occurring between general concerns (e.g. for profitability) and organizational action (cf. the ideas of Giddens 1979, and Dent 1991). While connecting Latour's ideas to the examination of flexibility, Mouritsen (1999) concludes that in his case company two competing translations between profitability and organizational action debated how production flexibility, productivity, and innovation would lead to commercial success. The formal 'paper version' of management control (traditional, formal financial management) suggested, among other things, that flexibility is expensive and needs to be controlled. In contrast, the 'hands-on version' of management control emphasized the role of people rather than information in running the complex production process.[10] This contrast between flexibility and formal control is likely to emerge also in NEFs, if management control systems are implemented in them in a way which constrains flexibility too much (cf. Chenhall and Morris 1995).

Indeed, Mouritsen and Hansen (2000) concluded, drawing again on Latour, that in the four case firms they studied, flexibility (defined largely as product/ production flexibility) was not in contrast to management control. The different forms of flexibility in each company were supported by certain management control inscriptions, which aligned flexibility with competitiveness. As Mouritsen and Hansen (2000: 27) explain:

Each of the four cases illustrates how management controls could support, translate, distribute and create continuity for a certain type of flexibility. Through and around these management controls were certain stories about the relationship between flexibility and competitiveness crafted... these managerial controls keep in place each

---

[10] The role of technology and its management (see e.g. Skyrme 1999) in this setting can be seen as being both a driver and an enabler for the organisational action in which the major tension seems to exist between 'financial management' and 'people management'.

firm's 'flexibility-identity'. This was why flexibility and management control were not at odds... the current form of flexibility was strong because it had the help of management controls. They, namely, point out its relationship to competitiveness.

As was noted above, flexibility should be supported by management controls. However, in the context of NEFs, this logic does not seem to apply as easily since the link to competitiveness has been missing from the operating principles. But the pressure to strive for competitiveness is there today, and so is the challenge of cultural change, too. The key issue in this regard is the ability of a financial control system to translate the problem, the concern for financially sound operation, so that the creative personnel can interpret the solution to the problem as being within their very own interests (Chua 1995; see also Dent 1991; Latour 1987). This has direct implications as regards, for example, the application of reward systems in NEFs. Mere relying on stock options in this regard, even if their terms can be adjusted, does not look as functional today as it did before the stock price crash. There is thus demand also for other bases for rewards, such as financial and non-financial performance indicators produced by a management control system.

Whenever a culture is challenged, problems and conflicts will emerge (e.g. see also Burns and Scapens 2000; Dent 1991; Hatch 1993; Schein 1997). Uncertainty about the new, unfamiliar operation practices characterizes all major changes in organizational operation. Such changes always call for learning of new and at least partial unlearning of the old. Argyris' (1977) theory of double-loop learning further explains this in dealing with situations where underlying values and assumptions are to be changed (Argyris 1993; see also Argyris and Schön 1978). The learning of financial fundamentals may necessitate double-loop learning in NEFs, especially among the creative R&D personnel. 'Simple' single-loop learning of new practices without changes in adopted norms and values is not as challenging as the learning of new business fundamentals, for instance.

Towards Flexible Management Control Systems

Based on the above discussion on the challenge and facilitation of cultural change, it seems that 'flexible management control' is feasible for NEFs. Such management control loosely couples the 'new economy spirit' (reflecting indeterminacy) and financial management (reflecting rationality). It supports innovativeness and flexibility, but at the same time attempts to ensure profitability in the long run (cf. Orton and Weick 1990). This is perhaps not so much a systems question, but a managerial question, that is, how systems are to be used. Of course, special attention has to be paid to the design of control systems for the needs of NEFs' managers.

Simons' (1995*a,b*) ideas on the use of control systems are applicable here, as we first try to outline the possible uses of management control systems in

NEFs. All the four proposed levers of control could be seen as important in the NEF context. Diagnostic control systems are increasingly important in that they direct attention to the financial outcomes and enable corrective actions. However, especially in NEFs they can be very problematic if used as a basis of straightforward, commanding management. As regards rewards, diagnostic control systems may have limited importance in NEFs, where the rewards are based on stock options. Boundary systems are needed to direct behaviour according to the selected strategy and to restrict opportunistic behaviour. However, boundary systems should be applied carefully in NEFs, so as not to set too tight limits. Interactive control systems are, for their part, important in the design of new strategies that should possibly replace old ones. They can play a crucial role in raising questions about the business fundamentals (strategic uncertainties): which products should be provided, which customers should be targeted, which technology will survive and how long, etc. (see also Chenhall and Morris 1995; Simons 1999). Belief systems are clearly important in this context as they connect to the discussion of the NEFs' general mission and performance overall, and to the possible need for double-loop learning. This is an important role especially now, as accounting systems are, in the end, marking off the successful NEFs from the unsuccessful ones. Belief, systems drawing on 'stories' often guided the operation in NEFs exclusively in the past. However, today there exist significant pressures to develop boundary systems and diagnostic control systems, in particular. Still, the motivating role of belief, systems should stay in place.

Our outlining of flexible management control systems for NEFs, informed by the idea of loose coupling, continues by following the argument 'simple is beautiful' (e.g. see Granlund and Lukka 1998*a*). Such simplicity in management control underlines that the grounds for technical simplicity still need to be solid. Support for this can be found, for instance, in Chenhall and Morris' (1995) comparative analysis of management accounting systems in entrepreneurial and conservative organizations. Their findings imply that in a company operating along entrepreneurial principles—similarly as NEFs do—simple but solid management control may be feasible, as it is used beside organic decision and communication practices. The 'simple but solid' management control implies that, technically, there is no need to invent new tools for management control in NEFs (cf. Maccarone 2001). However, business and strategic specifics should be incorporated in the design of management control systems in NEFs, as is the case in any business environment (e.g. Chenhall and Morris 1995; Chenhall and Langfield-Smith 1998; Langfield-Smith 1997).

An important determinant in design activities is supposedly the strategy and development phase of a NEF (Granlund and Taipaleenmäki 2000). It is questionable whether all NEFs have had (or have even today) a strategy. An explicit aim in many cases was, at least earlier, to get listed through an IPO and get 'easy rich', to put it bluntly. The strategy was an emerging, abstract idea concerning ways to reach this end. In the existing situation, most of the surviving NEFs tend to have employed a more specific strategy, or are trying to do so (cf. Porter 2001). However, based on informal discussions with NEF representatives, the idea of strategy still tends to be an implicit issue for NEFs. In general, there seems to exist very little publicly available information about what these strategies are and how they are developing.[11] Because strategy related goal ambiguity seems to be gradually vanishing, the purpose of management control systems may at the same time be seen to be becoming clearer in NEFs: the basic purpose of management controls to guide people towards a common target is, indeed, more meaningful in such a context.

For the smallest NEFs, basic costing and budgeting is probably enough, but with growth and geographical spread, more advanced information needs will emerge (cf. Granlund and Taipaleenmäki 2000).[12] It seems obvious that at least in the early stages of a NEF's development trajectory, heavy management accounting systems are neither appropriate regarding the challenge of cultural change nor even necessary in functional terms. However, 'lighter' versions of activity-based costing, balanced scorecard, non-financial measures in general, target costing, or whatever modern management accounting technique may later on prove to be useful in strategic and operative management of a NEF. As NEFs may operate as members of various company networks, the control of such networks becomes also important (Mouritsen and Hansen 2000). Various calculations regarding the costs and benefits of network relations is a demanding task, not only technically, but also in terms of trust (Tomkins 2001). Target costing, capital investment calculations, open books accounting, etc. are all techniques that may be taken advantage of, as durable business networks are built and maintained in the later evolution phases of NEFs. However, we have to bear in mind that even when NEFs grow, adding complexity to their management control systems may not be desired. The loose coupling between formal management control and the flexibility culture also means that the control system has to be light and flexible enough to be able to adapt to the many changes, for example, in the form of mergers and acquisitions, that constantly encounter NEFs.

Budgeting probably forms the backbone of management control in NEFs. Rolling forecasting/budgeting, in particular, can be a useful tool in the turbulent

---

[11] Based on Miles and Snow's (1978) typology we could suggest that probably most, if not all, NEFs have been 'prospectors' (more or less implicitly), that is, searching for new responses to emerging trends, creating new innovations, and even initiating changes in the market place. Some NEFs could be seen as 'reactors' as well, which have tried to follow leading NEFs and respond to changes in the market place, even if without coherent plans.

[12] Informal discussions with controllers working in NEFs, suggest that in many cases, especially in the smallest NEFs, it all starts from introducing cost concepts to the R&D experts and the like. After that it is possible to ask the experts to roughly register different types of costs to different projects etc. If this is accepted, it is much easier to proceed in the development of a financial management system. At the moment this seems to be more acceptable among the experts than it was some time ago, since, as has been mentioned, investors are now checking, not only the financial condition of NEFs more carefully, but also the functioning of their financial control systems.

environment surrounding NEFs, as it can be used more flexibly to set and monitor at least loose financial targets more so than under traditional annual budgeting. In NEFs, the calculation and control of cash flows could be emphasized, as they can conveniently be used to communicate the 'wretched' nature of operating in a business world, where capital markets play a crucial role (cf. the idea of financial control systems facilitating cultural change). The fact that venture capital investors are particularly interested in measures such as burn rate further emphasizes their importance in NEFs. Factually, it is possible to derive the base of the cash budget from the burn rate figure (cash sufficiency). Hence, cash flow based rolling budgeting and the calculation of cash flow based financial indicators seem to fit the operating and managerial environment of NEFs.

Cost management is in general important for effective and efficient resource allocation. There may be many relevant cost objects that warrant separate analyses in NEFs, varying from the traditional product/service/ customer to less traditional delivery channel (internet), a certain module of R&D, or even a whole technology generation. Naturally, also for NEFs, the design of cost management systems has to start from managerial information needs. The subjects of control and decision-making in NEFs may of course be different from the ones in traditional businesses, and thereby have an effect on the design of, for instance, an ABC system. For example, website optimization[13] can be a typical problem for a NEF (Zeller *et al.* 2001). The resource consumption—and consequently costs—of having a website as a trade channel is driven by, for example, the complexity of the website, number of site pages, and number of changes made on the site.

A survey on e-business performance measurement, conducted by Accenture (former Andersen Consulting), revealed that the responding NEFs were actively seeking improvements to their management accounting systems (Williams 2001). NEFs wanted most to improve user click-stream analysis, customer tracking/profiling, data warehouse measures, and the entire performance measurement system.[14] The most significant barriers preventing improvement were said to be lack of time, unavailability of required technology, difficulties in data collection, and the fact that the company has too many other priorities. While there are certain specific issues in the list of desired improvements that are different from the needs of companies operating in traditional businesses, the problems seem to be common—problems that have been well documented in a number of earlier studies (see Anderson and Young 1999). The obstacle regarding priorities is interesting here, as it may reflect an attitude towards management control that still exists in the culture of the responding NEFs: financial control is still fighting for its position among the

---

[13] Website optimization basically compares to managing the traditional retail floor.
[14] It seems obvious that the responded NEFs are not commencing ones, but NEFs that have already been able to somehow establish their position in the market place and implemented basic management control systems.

important issues. On the other hand, it may also be a sign of the fact that simple but solid accounting procedures have been put in place and they are in the current situation working well enough.

How the creative functions of a NEF should then be controlled? This is a general question regarding R&D control (Nixon 1997, 1998; Taipaleenmäki 1999, 2000): most of the expertise in NEFs is channelled to research and development. R&D is a challenging trade-off environment, where speed, quality, costs, and functionality should typically be balanced. In NEFs particularly, costs seem to have been downplayed in this trade-off. This is challenging because it is many times more difficult to even evaluate whether the R&D function should be treated as a cost or a profit centre. Different forms of target costing or life cycle costing in general could be applied in a light manner to control the direction of R&D in NEFs, but not so that they are felt to unduly constrain innovative behaviour (cf. Kaplan 1984; see also Taipaleenmäki 1999). Non-financial measures can also be seen as important in this context, as well as more generally in the management of NEFs. This can be said to flow most of all from R&D intensity, characteristic to NEFs. Especially time (duration of development work, time to milestones, time to product/service release, etc.) is a crucial issue to manage and thus measure in this operating environment. Time is also fairly directly connected to the cash flows of a NEF.

The most important issue in the discussion above perhaps still reverts to the fact that it is not so much about which techniques are adopted, but about how they are applied. The most important issue is not what the level of system sophistication is (Maccarone 2001)—although it is feasible in technical and cultural terms to follow the principle of 'simple but solid'—but how the specific measures are applied in strategic and operative management so that they will not constrain innovativeness and flexibility unnecessarily (cf. Kaplan 1984; Chenhall and Morris, 1995). Even a simple measurement can be used wrongly in this particular context. The key issue in this context is loose coupling. In terms of Simons' (1995*b*) framework, we can conclude that the challenging mobilization of management control systems for different purposes requires special attention as the management control wholeness is designed in a NEF. Whilst careful implementation of simple but solid control tools means visible development of diagnostic control systems and boundary systems, embedding or adding financial issues in NEFs' beliefs systems implies a challenging, cultural change. We have to bear in mind that it is not only the basic principles of financial control that people in NEFs are or have been learning, but also the very basic principles of business activity in general.

Conclusions

This chapter has examined the inherent tension of the NEFs: that between their tendency to stress creativity, flexibility, and ultimate freedom of operation and the need to also keep these firms in control, in order to keep them viable in market pressures. We have outlined the development and major character-istics of the so-called new economy as well as those of the typical firms of the new economy, the NEFs. We examined closely the contradictions between the original operation culture of NEFs, focusing on flexibility, and the emerging agenda, which also includes technologies of management control. The latter agenda, highlighting the significance of having adequate financial control sys-tems in place, is regarded as the 'window back to reality' for NEFs, in a situ-ation where the extremely high expectations of the late 1990s suddenly crashed in 2000. It is argued that the emergence of this competing agenda means a deeply rooted cultural change in many of the NEFs, encompassing features of double-loop learning.

The chapter has also highlighted the kind of management and financial controls that could be viewed as both relevant and feasible for NEFs. In Simons' (1995*a,b*) vocabulary, we argue that the on-going cultural change in NEFs means a tendency to put more pressure on boundary systems and, in particular, diagnostic control systems, however, still keeping the important motivating role of beliefs systems in place. Based on the notion of loosely coupled systems, it is suggested that management and financial control sys-tems arc nccdcd in order to keep NEFs alive under market pressures, but that they should be carefully designed and implemented and kept relatively light and simple in order to leave enough room for creativity and flexibility, which are, after all, the corner stones of NEFs' way of doing things. Relatively unso-phisticated financial control technologies, such as cash flow orientated budget-ing, are considered as the key solutions here to start with the cultural change. Hence, it is suggested that the control paradox of NEFs can be solved by being faithful to the key principles of loose coupling: by coordinating the elements and functioning of the organization in order to make them coupled enough, but doing this in a loose enough manner not to spoil the creative, indeterminate features of the organization.

References

Ahrens, T. and Dent, J. F. (1998), 'Accounting and Organizations: Realizing the Richness of Field Research', *Journal of Management Accounting Research*, 10: 1–39.

Anderson, S. W. and Young, S. M. (1999), 'The Impact of Contextual and Process Factors on the Evaluation of Activity-based Costing Systems', *Accounting, Organizations and Society*, 24: 525–59.

Argyris, C. (1977), 'Double Loop Learning in Organizations', *Harvard Business Review*, 55 (September–October): 115–25.

——(1993), *On Organizational Learning* (Cambridge, MA: Blackwell).

——and Schön, D. A. (1978), *Organizational Learning* (Reading, MA: Addison Wesley).

Armstrong, P. (1985), 'Changing Management Control Strategies: The Role of Competition Between Accountancy and Other Organizational Professions', *Accounting, Organizations and Society*, 10/2: 129–48.

Aula, P. and Oksanen, A. (2000), *Eepos. Suomalainen internet-unelma* [Eepos. The Finnish Internet dream] (WSOY: Juva).

Burns, J. and Scapens, R. (2000), 'Conceptualizing Management Accounting Change: An Institutional Framework', *Management Accounting Research*, 11: 3–25.

Castells, M. (2000), *The Information Age: Economy, Society and Culture. Volume I. The Rise of the Network Society* (Oxford: Blackwell).

Chenhall, R. H. and Langfield-Smith, K. (1998), 'The Relationship Between Strategic Priorities, Management Techniques and Management Accounting: An Empirical Investigation using a Systems Approach', *Accounting, Organizations and Society*, 23/3: 243–64.

—— and Morris, D. (1995), 'Organic Decision and Communication Processes and Management Accounting Systems in Entrepreneurial and Conservative Business Organizations', *Omega*, 23/5: 485–97.

Choudhury, N. (1988), 'The Seeking of Accounting where it is not: Towards a Theory of Non-accounting in Organizational Settings', *Accounting, Organizations and Society*, 13/6: 549–57.

Chua, W. F. (1995), 'Experts, Networks and Inscriptions in the Fabrication of Accounting Images: A Story of the Representation of Three Public Hospitals', *Accounting, Organizations and Society*, 20/2–3: 111–45.

Cooper, D. J. and Hayes, D., and Wolf, F. (1981), 'Accounting in Organized Anarchies: Understanding and Designing Accounting Systems in Ambiguous Situations', *Accounting, Organizations and Society*, 6: 175–91.

Deci, E. L. and Ryan, R. M. (1985), *Intrinsic Motivation and Self-determination in Human Behaviour* (New York: Plenum Press).

Dent, J. F. (1991), 'Accounting and Organizational Cultures: A Field Study of the Emergence of a New Organizational Reality', *Accounting, Organizations and Society*, 16: 693–703.

Engel, E., Gordon, E. A., and Hayes, R. M. (2001), 'Incentives and governance in entrepreneurial firms', *Managerial Accounting Abstracts (SSRN/ARN)*, Working Paper Series, 5:8.

Evans, P. A. L. (2000), 'The Dualistic Leader: Thriving on Paradox', in S. Chowdhury (ed.), *Management 21C* (Guildford and King's Lynn: Pearson Education).

Foster, R. and Kaplan, S. (2001), *Creative Destruction* (New York: Doubleday).

Frey, B. (1997), 'On the Relationship Between Intrinsic and Extrinsic Motivation', *International Journal of Industrial Organization*, 15/5: 427–40.

Giddens, A. (1979), *Central Problems in Social Theory* (London: Macmillan).

—— (1984), *The Constitution of Society* (Cambridge: Polity Press).

Granlund, M. and Lukka, K. (1998a), 'Towards Increasing Business Orientation: Finnish Management Accountants in a Changing Cultural Context', *Management Accounting Research*, 9/2: 185–211.

———— (1998b), 'It's a Small World of Management Accounting Practices', *Journal of Management Accounting Research*, 10: 153–79.

———— and Mouritsen, J. (1998), 'Institutionalised Justifications of Corporate Action: Internationalisation and EU in Corporate Reports', *Scandinavian Journal of Management*, 14/4: 433–58.

——and Taipaleenmäki, J. (2000), 'Management control and controllership in new economy firms', Working paper, Turku School of Economics and Business Administration, November.

Hamel, G. and Prahalad, C. K. (1994), *Competing for the Future* (Boston: Harvard Business School Press).

Hammarsten, H. and Rainisto, S. (2001), Hei, emmekös me äsken tehneet voittoa? [Hey, didn't we just make profit?], *Talouselämä* [Finnish Magazine '*Economic Life*'], 6: 52–4.

Hand, J. R. M. (2000), 'Profits, losses and the non-linear pricing of Internet stocks', Working paper, Kenan-Flager Business School, UNC Chapel Hill.

Hatch, M. (1993), 'The Dynamics of Organizational Culture', *Academy of Management Review*, 18/4: 657–93.

Helsingin Sanomat (9 October 2001), 'Speed blindness spoiled the dreams of Jippii', E1.

Holmberg, I. and Ridderstråle, J. (2000), 'Sensational leadership', in S. Chowdhury (ed.), *Management 21C* (Guildford and King's Lynn: Pearson Education).

Hopwood, A. G. (1974), *Accounting and Human Behaviour* (London: Haymarket).

Ijiri, Y. (1975), *Theory of Accounting Measurement* (Sarasota: AAA).

Jensen, R. (1999), *The Dream Society* (New York: McGraw-Hill).

Kanter, R. M. (2001), 'The Ten Deadly Mistakes of Wanna-dots', *Harvard Business Review*, 79/1: 91–100.

Kaplan, R. S. (1984), 'The Evolution of Management Accounting', *The Accounting Review*, 59/3: 390–418.

Von Krogh, G., Ichijo, K., and Nonaka, I. (2000), *Enabling Knowledge Creation: How to Unlock the Mystery of Tacit Knowledge and Release the Power of Innovation* (Oxford: Oxford University Press).

Langfield-Smith, K. (1997), 'Management Control Systems and Strategy: A Critical Review', *Accounting, Organizations and Society*, 22/2: 207–32.

Latour, B. (1987), *Science in Action* (Milton Keynes: Open University Press).

——(1991), 'Technology is society made durable', in J. Law (ed.), *A Sociology of Monters—Essays on Power, Technology and Domination* (Sage, London).

Maccarone, P. (2001), 'Defining performance measurement and control systems for e-commerce pure players', Paper presented at the 24th Annual Congress of the EAA, 18–20 April 2001, Athens, Greece.

Macintosh, N. B. and Scapens, R. (1990), 'Structuration Theory in Management Accounting', *Accounting, Organizations and Society*, 15/5: 455–77.

March, J. G. (1987), 'Ambiguity and Accounting: The Elusive Link Between Information and Decision Making', *Accounting, Organizations and Society*, 12: 153–68.

——and Olsen, J. P. (1976), *Ambiguity and Choice in Organizations* (Bergen: Universitetsförlaget).

Meyer, J. W. and Rowan, B. (1977), 'Institutionalized Organisations: Formal Structure as a Myth and Ceremony', *American Journal of Sociology*, 83: 340–63.

Miles, R. E. and Snow, C. C. (1978), *Organizational Strategy, Structure and Process* (McGraw-Hill).

Mouritsen, J. (1999), 'The Flexible Firm: Strategies for a Subcontractor's Management Control', *Accounting, Organizations and Society*, 24/1: 31–56.

——and Hansen, A. (2000), 'Management of technology and the technologies of managing', *Proceeding of the 2nd Conference on New Directions in Management Accounting*, 14–16 December 2000, Brussels, Belgium, pp. 517–45.

Nixon, B. (1997), 'The Accounting Treatment of Research and Development Expenditure: Views of UK Company Accountants', *European Accounting Review*, 6/2: 265–77.

——(1998), 'Research and Development Performance Measurement: A Case Study', *Management Accounting Research*, 9/4: 329–55.

Orton, J. D. and Weick, K. E. (1990), 'Loosely Coupled Systems: A Reconceptualization', *Academy of Management Review*, 15/2: 203–223.

Peters, T. (1987), *Thriving on Chaos: Handbook for the Management Revolution* (London: Macmillan).

Pietiläinen, T. (2001), Rahoitustarkastus arvostelee teknoyritysten pörssilistauksia [The Inspection Bureau of Financial Institutions criticises the listings of technology firms], *Helsingin Sanomat* [Finnish newspaper '*The Helsinki News*'], 11 April 2001, p. D1.

Porter, M. (1996), 'What is Strategy?', *Harvard Business Review* (November–December): p. 61–78.

——(2001), 'Strategy and the Internet', *Harvard Business Review* (March): 63–78.

Roberts, J. and Scapens, R. (1985), 'Accounting Systems and Systems of Accountability—Understanding Accounting Practices in their Organisational Contexts', *Accounting, Organizations and Society*, 10/4: 443–56.

Robson, K. (1992), 'Accounting Numbers as "inscription": Action at a Distance and the Development of Accounting', *Accounting, Organizations and Society*, 17/7: 685–708.

Schein, E. (1997), *Organizational Culture and Leadership* (San Fransisco: Jossey-Bass).

Simons (1995a), 'Control in an Age of Empowerment', *Harvard Business Review*, 73/2: 80–8.

——(1995b), *Levers of Control: How Managers Use Innovative Control Systems to Drive Strategic Renewal* (Boston, MA: Harvard Business School Press).

——(1999), 'How Risky is Your Company?' *Harvard Business Review*, 77/3: 85–94.

Skyrme, D. J. (1999), *Knowledge Networking: Creating the Collaborative Enterprise* (Guildford: Butterworth-Heinemann).

Spybey, T. (1984), 'Traditional and Professional Frames of Meaning in Management', *Sociology*, 18: 550–62.

Stalk, G. and Hout, T. M. (1990), *Competing Against Time: How Time-Based Competition is Reshaping Global Markets* (New York: Free Press).

Sveiby, K.-E. (1997), *The New Organizational Wealth: Managing & Measuring Knowledge-based Assets* (San Francisco, CA: Berrett-Koehler).

——and Lloyd, T. (1987), *Managing Knowhow: Add Value... by Valuing Creativity* (London: Bloomsbury).

Säntti, H. (2001), 'Hex listaa löperösti [Hex lists in a sloppy manner]', *Talouselämä* [Finnish Magazine '*Economic Life*'], 14: 58.

Taipaleenmäki, J. (1999), 'Luovuus ja kontrolli T&K:ssa [Creativity and control in R&D]', *Talouselämä* [Finnish Magazine '*Economic Life*'], 34.

——(2000), 'Management accounting in new product development: Case study evidence of management, accounting and knowledge creation in process-oriented product development environment', Paper presented at the 23rd Annual Congress of the EAA, 29–31 March 2000, Munich, Germany.

Tomkins, C. (2001), 'Interdependencies, Trust and Information in Relationships, Alliances and Networks', *Accounting, Organizations and Society*, 26: 161–91.

Weick, K. E. (1969), *The Social Psychology of Organizing* (Reading, MA: Addison-Wesley).

Williams, K. (2001), 'How do you Measure e-business Performance?', *Strategic Finance*, April: 16 and 21.

Zeller, T. L., Kublank, D. R., and Makris, P. G. (2001), 'How art.com™ Uses ABC to Succeed', *Strategic Finance*, 82/9: 24–31.

14

Management Accounting and the Knowledge Production Process

Hanno Roberts

Introduction

Knowledge is receiving widespread attention as being the source of competitive advantage and of economic growth. Terms such as the knowledge society and the knowledge-based firm have entered our vocabulary, and efforts are ongoing to dissect the knowledge concept and understand how it comes into being, what it is made of and how it works. Efforts range from the epistemological to the utilitarian, from delineating its distinctiveness and its position within the social sciences to developing specific tools and concepts for knowledge management.

The purpose of this chapter is to address knowledge in a utilitarian sense, and consider how to make use of it for management purposes. Knowledge here is understood in terms of applying accounting onto the knowledge production process. It implies the consideration of knowledge as an object that can be accounted for as well as opened up for manipulation by accounting technologies. Specifically, knowledge is assumed to be a resource, and defined as a financial resource in accounting: it can be registered, manipulated, utilized, exchanged, and transformed.

The approach adopted here is to develop an accounting-based concept of the knowledge production process. As with accounting, it is in the use of knowledge that its modalities are best illustrated, and that the knowledge resource displays its distinctive characteristics. In that sense, the knowledge production process should be conceived of as a manufacturing process, in which new knowledge is made, resources are used, and a positive return is generated. In instances where the accounting framework or terminology does not suffice to capture in full what knowledge is and does, we revert to terminology from the strategy field. For reasons of historical predisposition; strategy has considered knowledge resource as well as the resource concept since competitive advantage has been discussed. Increasing advances in strategy theory address explicitly the discretionary role of management in the so-called resource-based theory of the firm, with the knowledge-based theory of the firm and the concept of dynamic capabilities as the relevant subtopics for the purpose of this chapter.

The chapter is structured as follows. First, we discuss knowledge as a resource, and fuse it with accounting interpretations around its registration, accumulation, allocation, and utilization. The discussion is centred around interpreting knowledge as intellectual capital. Second, we discuss the knowledge production process as such, and argue that it is based on relations and relational capital, with connectivity as a key concept. We will argue that its accountable element is the human capital that enters into productive exchange. Finally, we conclude by summarizing the main points and provide suggestions as to the interfaces between accounting and knowledge, using a production process perspective.

Knowledge as a Resource

From a competitive strategy perspective, the resource concept is conceived as factor inputs acquired for less than their intrinsic value due to input market imperfections which arise themselves through information asymmetries (i.e. better managerial choices) and plain luck (Barney 1986, 1991). These resources provide the basis for sustainable competitive advantage; in other words, factor market impediments instead of product–market circumstances are the main providers of success while the main denominator is that of economic markets and efficiency.

Within the strategy field, the resource concept is subdivided into tangible and intangible assets, and further classified as either competences or relational resources, each of which have both individual and collective owners (see Figure 14.1).

In the situation that resources are collectively owned, one can speak of an overlap of the accounting and the strategy conceptions of a resource, that is, intangible assets as expressed in the financial statements. This leaves the individual ownership of both competences and relational resources falling outside

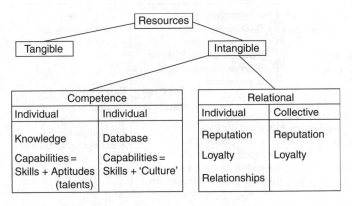

Fig. 14.1. Strategic resources (Løwendahl 1997: 87, Fig. 8)

the accounting framework, presumably because there is no underlying going concern nor separate legal entity principle.

Competence is defined as 'all aspects affecting the ability to perform a given task'. It encompasses knowledge that is based on existing information, skills that are acquired through apprenticeship and on-the-job training, and aptitudes or talents, which allow people to perform certain tasks in a way superior to that of their competitors (Løwendahl 1997: 81). Noteworthy here is that knowledge is defined as information based, while skills and aptitudes are defined in terms of abilities; this implies a separation between perceiving knowledge as an object, and perceiving it in terms of its effects—what you can do with it.

Relational resources include the reputation, client loyalty and customer base that are fundamental to organizational performance; these resources might be collective and shared or individual and idiosyncratic (Løwendahl 1997: 88). Relationships as such are conceived not as collectively but as individually owned.

When looking at the resource concept from an accounting perspective, the tangible versus intangible classification is largely followed. It is in the intangible category, however, that resource viewpoints are diverging. From an accounting perspective, client/customer loyalty and customer base are conventionally addressed under the heading of 'Goodwill' and expressed by either capitalizing or expensing the related monetary value. Typically, goodwill value tends to become visible only on moments of ownership transfer, where the acquiring firm tends to pay a negotiated amount over the book value of the acquired firm.

In fact, in the conventional accounting taxonomy of intangible assets, the method of acquisition (ownership transfer) of intangible assets is one of two key criteria used, see Figure 14.2. The other criterion being whether the asset is *both* identifiable *and* separable.

Method of acquisition	Assets specifically identifiable and separable	Assets **not** specifically identifiable and separable
Internally developed	For example: • R&D costs; • costs specifically attached to development of proprietary products or processes. **Expense**	For example: • customer relations; • (quality) reputation. **Expense**
Externally developed	**Capitalize** For example: • costs of obtaining a patent, copyright etc.; • organization costs; • beneficial contracts; • government concessions.	**Capitalize** For example: • Excess purchase price; paid on acquisitions (goodwill).

Fig. 14.2. Classification framework for intangible assets (Haskins *et al.* 1993: 455)

The conventional accounting distinction into stock (capitalize on the balance sheet) and flow (expense on the income statement) variables is present in this taxonomy. Typically, a stock is a property right—one owns the item and can exercise that ownership right on a market. Conversely, a flow is related to the utilization of a stock or property right. Utilization is a discretionary matter, and partial to degrees of usage, while an ownership right is an absolute and straightforward yes/no affair—it is yours or it is not. The latter befits a certainty versus uncertainty dichotomy and it is in the sphere of relative (un)certainty that flows and, thus, expensing play out.

However, within the field of strategic resource definitions, basically the internally developed and non-identifiable and non-separable items are the ones being addressed. That is, the focus is on the firm's unique competences and capabilities and not on their comparative similarity. Conversely, from an accounting perspective, these items tend to be under represented and only limitedly captured. Being firm, specifically built over time, they come in bundles instead of discrete packages that can be accounted for. Moreover, the bundled and time-dependent accumulation of these intangible assets is equally unique; there is no common denominator or standard against which to compare them or to aggregate them by. This places the criterion of identification as the most problematic criterion in establishing a resource definition that is acceptable to both accountants and strategists. If one cannot identify uniqueness because there is no standard for uniqueness, it does not make sense to engage in a subsequent effort of separation because it is unclear what needs to be separated from what. Similarly, the development of uniqueness needs an accumulation basis against which to assess increases or decreases in the development effort. Again, from an accounting perspective, uniqueness and the development of uniqueness by means of internally generated intangible assets, is unmanageable because of inadequate identification. However, developments in the area of performance measurement indicate that non-financial criteria categorized according to competitive dimensions might be an outcome here. This refers to the measurement parameters of the balanced scorecard.

In short, securing relevant identification criteria within the accounting field are a key need to develop resource definitions that are useful across a wider set of disciplines. If such a resource definition would exist, then the goals and purpose of an organization would be translatable into financial actions as much as they would be into managerial actions. As a result, the creation and the deployment of an organization's intangible assets in terms of its knowledge production and its knowledge production process, would visualize itself more readily.

Knowledge as Intellectual Capital

The knowledge production process is based on the intellectual capital of the organization, with the latter representing the combined knowledge resources

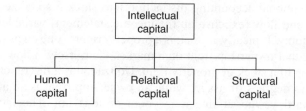

Fig. 14.3. Intellectual capital (adapted from Bontis 1998)

of the firm. Intellectual capital provides both the production factors for knowledge production and is also the recipient of the knowledge produced. Each time an organization produces a novel product/service, it also adds to its own knowledge base by accumulating experience and insights from the production process. Intellectual capital is, in a sense, a form of knowledge self-financing. Once the production process slows down or stops, the organization becomes 'poorer' because it accumulates experience more slowly.

In order to operationalize the concept, we adhere to the commonly accepted differentiation into human capital, relational capital, and structural capital, as indicated in Figure 14.3 (de Bontis 1998; MERITUM 2002; Nordic Industrial Fund 2001). Defined at the organizational level, human capital consists of the combined skills, experiences, insights, and education of the organizational participants. Following the above strategic resource definition, human capital is individually owned and coincides with the concept of human competencies. In popular terms, human capital is what leaves the organization after five in the afternoon. The organization can rent, hire, or lease human capital but cannot own it.

Relational capital—sometimes also called customer, external capital, or social capital—is the relational network between people and groups of people. It is defined by personalized interaction and provides the exchange arena for human capital and its constituting skills, experiences, education, and abilities. Relational capital coincides largely with the relation element of the above noted strategic resource definition. However, in contrast with human capital, some of the relational capital can be collectively owned. The aggregate exercising of individual skills and competences assembles into a collective whole for the group or organization. Similarly, the sustained and continued exchange of skills, experiences, and insights within the relational arena is only possible when there is a motivation to do so. The outcome effect of this motivation is the creation of loyalty to the collective, for example, the group or the organization. Relational capital, is thus owned by the collective but it has neither formal nor tradeable ownership rights attached to it. The role of the organization is limited to facilitating the arena for exchange, including devising the appropriate motivation systems and creating the opportunity for such exchange. The latter can be conceived in terms of information technology, such as intranets, or other communication platforms[1].

It is in the relational capital category that insights are exchanged, novel interpretations emerge, and sense is being made. Hence, it is relational capital that provides the basis for innovation and inventions as well as creates the market advantage of the firm (Nahapiet and Ghoshal 1998). Or, in accounting terminology, that new sources of value creation and new revenue streams are created.

Structural capital is the procedures, norms, systems, routines, and rules that make up the organizational skeleton. In contrast to human capital, structural capital is what remains in the organization after five o'clock, when the workday finishes. This set of routines is what institutionalizes an organization, and where organizing solidifies into organization. Typically, accounting as a rule-based management technology is a natural element of structural capital. Similarly, structural capital can for a large part be owned by an organization and expressed as an economic property in its financial statements. This is, for example, the case with software and related IT equipment.

Structural capital in that sense can be conceived as a formal and logical apparatus of organizational and managerial routines (Nelson and Winter 1982). Once the organization makes a selection out of this technical apparatus, it engages in a design activity and starts building intellectual capital systems. As with all systems design, the main choice here is whether to design top down or bottom up, that is, from the system to its usage and user, or from the user to the system. These two fundamental design choices are known in the strategy field as following either a knowledge codification strategy or a knowledge personalization strategy, respectively (Hansen *et al.* 1999). In terms of the intellectual capital subcategories, the interpretation of these two design strategies is to develop systems that emerge from personalized local knowledge or to develop systems that harvest existing praxis into aggregate homogeneous entities. This is not as simple as to state that a personalization strategy equals a dynamic humanistic perspective while a codification strategy equals a static artificial perspective. Rather, these two strategies are extremes on a continuum. Hybrids most likely exist in practice and will combine differential mixes of both approaches.

Intellectual capital as such refers to the knowledge resource of the organization. The use of the word 'capital', however, carries strong connotations of formal ownership and rigorous management as it implicates the accounting technology to be in use (Lev and Schwartz 1971). Consequently, the mere use of the word 'capital' hints at an attempt to legitimize the concept and have it gain credibility and respectability for the areas for which it is evoked. It therefore seems that the words both suggest intellectual capital as an object of management, opening it up for technological manipulation as well as a vehicle for

---

[1] In the work by Grant (1996) on the so-called Knowledge-Based Theory of the Firm he postulates that the only role of the organization is to coordinate knowledge. It implies that the only thing the organization truly owns is its coordination mechanisms.

change, managing organizational sense-making by means of the same intellectual capital terminology (Roberts 2000).

For the purpose of this chapter, we continue to view intellectual capital as an object for managerial decision-making. We postulate intellectual capital as a representative term for the varied and combined knowledge that an organization has as its disposal for competitive purposes. That is, intellectual capital has a passive property in its accumulated presence: it is there, waiting to be used. But in order to have it come into play, intellectual capital needs to be activated. To be mobilized, in strategy terminology. To activate intellectual capital, and to make an organization's knowledge potential work, its knowledge needs to be put into context and related to interpreting schemes. The main mechanism is for people to make sense of their observations and then start relating their interpretations to each other. Once that exchange process is established, knowledge is creating new knowledge, with alternative interpretations triggering new ones and accumulating throughout the process, thus producing novel world views. Or, concretely, novel ways to look at customers, processes, new products, or new service deliverables. Nonaka *et al.* (2000: 7) state this as:

Knowledge is dynamic, since it is created in social interactions amongst individuals and organisations. Knowledge is context-specific, as it depends on a particular time and space… Knowledge is also humanistic, as it is essentially related to human action. Knowledge has the active and subjective nature represented by such terms as 'commitment' and 'belief' that is deeply rooted in individuals' value systems. Information becomes knowledge when it is interpreted by individuals and given a context and anchored in the beliefs and commitments of individuals. Hence, knowledge is relational.

The knowledge production process is thus located in the relational capital element of intellectual capital. The personalized and individual knowledge of organizational participants becomes related—connected—to each other and creates the basis for innovation. The type of knowledge that an individual holds refers both to its explicit and its tacit dimension: the explicit version can be formally expressed and shared in a format that allows objective capture such as text, data, manuals, specifications, or algorithms. However, it is the tacit knowledge dimension of insights, actions, and emotions that provides the basis for analogies and metaphors that trigger subsequent understanding and interpretation. Tacit knowledge is by definition hard to formalize and, when attempting to do so, its value and meaning disappears. But it is exactly this ephemeral quality that acts as the fertilizer on the soil of explicit knowledge, requiring both types of knowledge to be present in order to produce a novel insight or an innovation.

Connectivity

The key principle of using knowledge, both the explicit and tacit versions, is that of connectivity. It refers to enabling the right people, or knowledge carriers, to find each other and connect their insights. Once connectivity is established, the transfer of knowledge and the exchange of insights can commence. For practical understanding, connectivity can be conceived in terms of identifying the 'right' people, locating them, and then bringing them together. Once connectivity is in place, more conventional forms of project or team management can be employed, for example, setting targets, providing facilities and other types of resources.

The key principle of connectivity is already well known in its operational versions. Within accounting, we term it allocation, for example, in distributing costs from a cost pool and allocating them to responsibility centres. For allocation purposes, we also need to identify the 'right' (activity) costs, locate their presence in the bookkeeping or cost registration system, accumulate or pool them, and then allocate them to cost centres according to a form of cost allocation, for example, activity based, hourly based, and time based. It is equally well known in accounting that rules for cost allocation can greatly affect computational outcomes and, consequently, influence managerial decision-making as well as organizational behaviour. For example, the erroneous effects of overhead costs allocation based on labour hours have been amply illustrated. Hence, the principle of connectivity has a strong resonance within the accounting technology and triggers various interpretation frameworks around what is good and proper management decision-making.

Similarly, in our other fellow resource management discipline, that of human resource management, connectivity is understood largely as staffing, notably project staffing. It allocates people to activities in the same way as costs are allocated to activities and activity areas; that is, for an optimal productive use of the scarce resource. Identifying the 'right' human competencies for a project or activity, then finding and locating these individuals (either inside, or outside by means of recruitment) and, finally, allocating them to a project team, are efforts highly identical to cost allocation. And as with accounting, the effects of erroneous allocation, that is, project staffing, are pervasive; insignificant output, high sick leave and absenteeism, and project overruns in terms of time and money. And, as with errors in cost allocation, more long lasting and strategic effects are likely to occur, for example, declines in labour market attractiveness, diminishing organizational flexibility, and an erosion of employee motivation and loyalty.

Connectivity effectively refers to how a resource such as knowledge comes into being. That is, via a sequential process of identification, location, and, finally, by making the link—connection. Before any connection can occur, one needs to identify what precisely it is one wants to connect. What kinds of competencies, skills, and relational aptitudes are required? As with the earlier discussed concern of providing criteria for uniqueness, the identification phase and its related identification criteria are a prime problem area.

However, identification of what one wants tends to be related to the larger purpose of the project and the overarching goals and objectives of the organization. What is the goal of the project one is identifying prospective members for? Typically, answers are of a strategic nature, and refer back to the specific detail of the human-resource based operationalization of the strategic objectives of the organization. This can be accomplished at a local or at a central level, with a preference for a locally grounded specification for reasons of information asymmetry and the local advantage in rich under-standings and expressions of needs (Westin and Roberts 1999). As a result, local definitions of needs and, therefore, of the specification of identifying cri-teria, tends to be a middle-management or project management affair; these are the persons who initiate and run the type of collective effort in which knowledge is produced and value is created. At the same time, it shows the relevance of adequate project descriptions, and the relevance of catchwords and phrases expressing the intention and purposes of a single project. When well expressed, the project description enables the identification of criteria of competences, aptitudes, and skills that are required. As an aside, it would mean that expressive aptitude would act as a key determinant of an ideal type project or middle manager in a knowledge-based organization.

An overall identification criteria, nevertheless, is that of requisite variety. This refers to maintaining the 'right' amount of diversity in the contributing parts *vis-à-vis* the whole of the parts, that is, the variety of the individual con-tributions relative to the homogeneity of overall purpose. The requisite variety criterion balances chaos with order in that it points at the need to have cross-functionality and multidisciplinarity build into the knowledge production. It balances the degree of openness of a knowledge endeavour: with too much openness and too much variety in disciplinary contributions, the knowledge outcome is insecure and chaos looms. With too little openness and variety, the knowledge outcome becomes rigidly introvert and crowds out alternative viewpoints and perspectives (Adler and Kwon 2002).

Locating is the next step and refers to actually finding the identified com-petences and skills (Roberts 1998). This element already has been developed to some extent in practice, under the heading of competence mapping or skills mapping. It provides an organizational map of the kind of individual abilities the organization has in house. Typically, competence maps are formulated on the basis of functional or keyword parameters under which a certain amount of individuals are grouped. These 'resource pools', however, have two draw-backs; first, the inventory is not the activity, and second, competences are mapped as far as they are within the organizational boundaries (i.e. appear on the company's pay list).

In order to have use of an inventory, its relationships with the underlying production process and, one step downstream, its customers need to be evid-ent. That implies grouping competences on the basis of their activity input (e.g. initiation, execution, design, pre-design, brainstorming, demonstration, etc.) and not on the basis of functional categories (e.g. IT skills, formal education, etc.) or key words (e.g. JAVA programming, cost analysis, distribution negotiations, etc.). An evident customer relationship with the requisite competence would refer directly back to the product/service offering and the terms and conditions of providing it (Norman 2001). In the latter case, a direct assessment between the competence maps and its pool of specific individuals would be possible. Or, stated in accounting terms, its value relevance becomes clear, with a valuation perspective based on present and evolving customer demands.

Furthermore, competences are only 'mappable' if they are played out within the managerial awareness set. And the key to that awareness set is the accounting technology; management will 'see' their organizational competences only when they are transmitted to them in terms of the costs and revenues that they generate. Or, stated differently, the 'governable person' worth mapping is the one on the pay list. Competences that are accumulated (partly) outside the organizational boundaries, with the boundaries defined by the accounting system, are invisible. Typically, this is the case with suppliers, customers, subcontractors, and freelancers. Within the field of intellectual capital, these forms of external knowledge are termed as customer capital or, simply, external capital, and a strong plea is made for including these external resource constituencies in managerial decision-making.

Resource pools that are not within the organizational boundaries are not kept in the books, and therefore, do not exist. As a result, it would imply a 'knowledge waste' (or knowledge cost) to maintain a registration on the single basis of an organizational denominator. Perhaps it would be more appropriate to register resource pools on the basis of knowledge transfer between collectives and other organizations; that is, to focus on alliances, partnerships, networks, and other organizational formats that centre around transfer and interaction, that is, the knowledge production process as such. From an accounting perspective, such a suggestion would hint at a much stronger consideration of the (minority) interests part of the asset section on the balance sheet, including refining criteria for stakes held in other entities and collectives.

Finally, the connection activity is based on factually bringing the 'right people' together. This connection might be in physical time and space or in virtual time and space. That is, bonding these individuals in terms of a formal project team or working party or in terms of a distributed community that is connected by IT means. What is the most appropriate and effective format depends on the specific objective and purpose of the effort, and is beyond the scope of this chapter.

However, the realization of connectivity is a collective effort, has exchange and learning as key focus, requires endurance, and allows for the appropriation of results. By definition, bringing people together to exchange insights and experiences constitutes a multiple person and collective address. It creates an opportunity for apt and identifiable individuals to concentrate on resolving an issue and, as a result of the exchange, to come to alternative insights. For practical purposes, this exchange process is defined as learning.[2]

However, bringing a requisite variety of people together and asking them to produce a new insight or product/service is not enough in itself. For people to start exchanging, they need to be motivated to do so. Apart from an initial motivation to start sharing, the effort needs to be made more lasting and permanent. In other words, membership of a knowledge-producing group is partly a reward but it needs to be supported over time by other means to achieve a sustainable dynamic. It is at this point that accounting technology might contribute as well. For example, as it is plausible that rewards need to be provided around a behavioural pattern of sharing, the reward basis would require some sort of 'sharing performance' assessment. It is in this debate that accounting technology might contribute, notably with respect to non-financial performance evaluation and management control frameworks based on interaction and dialogue.

The reward aspects of establishing the connection fulfil an equally important bridging role with the human resource function, which traditionally has claimed incentive and compensation systems as its functional turf. A soft merger between the two resource disciplines of accounting and HR on the two-sided coin of knowledge sharing rewards and their related performance assessment would establish a functional dialogue that could trigger other 'managerial technology' exchanges.

Connectivity, thus, refers to designing and establishing the (first) opportunity of tacit knowledge transfer. The explicit knowledge dimension comes later, that is, when new insights can be 'harvested' into improved procedures, processes, and products/services. That is, the translation from exchangeable idea to transactable object is delayed in time with the knowledge that production processes have a similar time line. The tacit knowledge dimension comes first. In terms of the intellectual capital model, this can be depicted by two main value creation moments—when human capital becomes relational capital, and when relational capital becomes structural capital (see Figure 14.4). Both moments are processes and best expressed in terms of dynamics and flows, while the three capital categories of intellectual capital are best understood in terms of stocks and inventories. These three can be registered and counted, inventoried and mapped, while the connections between the capital categories are the value creating processes that show *how* the capital is made productive. For example, issues of project staffing and their related criteria and mechanics are typically related to the first value creating moment, showing *how* the knowledge of individuals is put to work. Similarly, the improvements in project staffing procedures and methods are creating value as the structural capital stock of an organization is improving; the organization gets

---

[2] The cognitive aspect in relation to collective action and knowledge are discussed elsewhere, and is beyond the scope of this chapter (Spender 1998).

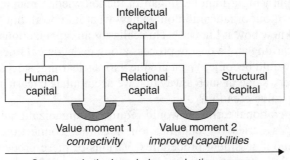

Sequence in the knowledge production process

Fig. 14.4. Intellectual capital, value creation, and the knowledge production process

better at what it does—its repertoire of capabilities and internal processes augments.[3]

As with the general design of connectivity, the two value creation moments point at the important role that sequencing plays (Grant 1998). Before actual connection can take place and the value creation bridge between human and relational capital can be made, the preceding phases of identifying and locating have to be completed. This suggests a sequential process, running from preparing the context to the final realization of the connection activity: that is, an outside-in design sequence, from preparing the embedding context to the final achievement of the tacit knowledge transfer and the exchange of insights, impressions, and experiences. Or, stated differently, by creating the necessary contextual conditions before value creation is actually likely to occur. These preparatory actions are partly a matter of deploying a series of functional tools from a diverse set of disciplinary fields, and partly a matter of establishing a time pattern of what needs to be deployed when, that is, timing matters. The latter is commonly understood as setting the learning pace and learning pathway of the organization, changing not only the organization's instrumentality but also its behavioural pattern. For example, even before the second value creation moment can be contemplated, the organization needs to have an awareness of itself in terms of its own procedures, processes, and routines because these are the capabilities that are going to change, once relational capital is becoming transformed into structural capital. But the term 'better' is only allowed when one knows what reference point there is, that is, the existing and functioning procedures and processes are

---

[3] This is the topic of a specific debate within Strategic Management and focuses on the dynamic capabilities of firms (Eisenhardt and Martin 2000; Helfat and Raubitschek 2000; Teece *et al.* 1997). It specifically draws out the simultaneous contribution of resources, and of routines and capabilities to the core competences of the firm. This triplet is stated as the simultaneous definition of the knowledge production function of the firm.

known. Paraphrasing a famous slogan in the knowledge management literature, it is not 'if our organization only knew what it knows!' but 'if our organization only knew how it knows!'. This calls for an organizational perspective
in terms of learning and a design process along pedagogical lines. As a result,
the question would become: What are the various learning stages, and how do
we design every stage in such a way that we accumulate ('learn') along a path
of increasing value creation?

In more operational terms, it would require an organizational intervention
consisting of a series of identification, location, connection, motivation,
expression, and assessment procedures. Various of these procedures already
exist within the accounting technology, albeit imperfectly; indicated above
were registration procedures, allocation principles, identification criteria,
(minority) interest valuations, non-financial performance measurement, and
management control frameworks. When considering the second value creation moment, from relational capital to structural capital, issues at stake have
to do with the institutional make-up of the organization at the microlevel.
Typically, this would involve the organization's method of expressing itself—
its reporting structure and format. Through the way the organization reports
externally, it expresses what it does and how it works. The financial accounting disclosures in terms of the annual statements are expressions of steward-
ship, showing how the organization has taken care of the monies entrusted to
it. Similarly, its *internal* reporting structure shows what kinds of information
management seeks to permeate within the organization and to focus its attention on. Again in a paraphrase of a well-known slogan, it is not that 'what gets
measured, gets done', but that 'what gets reported, gets attention'. If need be,
that attention can be further strengthened and directed by a series of performance measures, but without reporting, any sort or form of measurement
is futile. Intellectual capital research suggests that the reporting process
around the selected set of performance measures triggers the actual understanding of what is important (Johanson *et al.* 2001*a*,*b*).

Ordinarily, internal reporting is made up of a series of routines that are
interlinked throughout the organization and act as the communication, and
expression skeleton of what is important. For example, internal reporting
comprises a series of meetings, evaluation, and follow-up, and recognition
routines are built, each of which create further resonance on the information
item that was reported in the first place. The implication is that reporting
needs to be reconsidered in terms of its organizational capabilities and structural capital effects. The format, frequency, and functional orientation of
reporting should no longer be taken for granted when considered from a
knowledge production and intellectual capital perspective. Instead, the deliberate and conscious design of internal reporting structures and formats carries
a strong potential for value creation, and for bringing novel insights and new
product/service conceptions beyond the tacit knowledge boundary. And, as
with connectivity, when reporting is carefully designed in terms of the

routines within which it is embedded and that precede and follow it, reporting becomes a learning vehicle that can turn around organizational behaviour patterns.

In the illustration of the management model of a large Norwegian telecom firm (see Fig. 14.5), one can observe how the intellectual capital reporting (the 'house', see Fig. 14.6) is embedded in a continuous dynamic of the

Fig. 14.5. The integrated management model of Telenor (Brenna 2001)

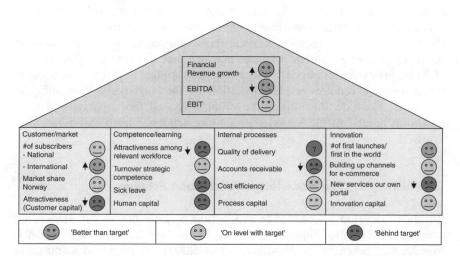

Fig. 14.6. 'The house'—the intellectual capital reporting model of Telenor (Brenna 2001)

strategy process. That dynamic is designed according to a conventional planning cycle of setting, executing, and evaluating the strategy. The reference point for evaluation is a simplified version of the Business Excellence model of the European Foundation of Quality Management (EFQM), which is a model frequently used as a blueprint for organizing the format of intellectual capital reporting (Ehrvervsudviklingsrådet 1997).

However, as can be observed, the strategy element is not only about strategy formation and operationalization, it also contains performance agreements as a reference point for the next phase of strategy implementation. The implementation is located at the business area level and strongly decentralized. Moreover, it is worth noting that the execution has a strong focus on activities, and project and team work, thus addressing the knowledge action at a first collective level, that is, where relational capital is to take effect.

The closing part of the cycle is the follow-up, in which measurement by means of value drivers (non-financial indicators that grow the business) as well as the business review is located. The business review is a good illustration of a routine that is linked to reporting and in which basically a richer meaning is extracted from the numbers. In the review between the management board and the business unit management, the results and actions of the unit are thoroughly discussed. Expectations, events and decisions along all the dimensions reported in 'the house' of intellectual capital are part of this multi-person dialogue, turning the business review into an interactive control mechanism (Simons 1994, 1995, 2000). However, the elements in the three stages of the cycle derive most of their functional benefit from the fact that they are all brought together into a pattern of action and dialogue. They are integrated as part of managerial and organizational behaviour and signal throughout the organization what is important. Various process elements such as the business reviews and the performance agreements are part of structural capital. When looking at the functional nature of each element, one can also observe that it is a cross-functional mix, originating from the fields of accounting, strategy, human resource management, project management, and IT. This carries the message that, when actually applied in practice, to account for knowledge requires a recomposition of the managerial technological apparatus. No individual discipline or field has all the answers, and their 'insertion points' in the knowledge activity sequence need to be carefully assessed.

The Knowledge Production Process

Efforts to develop a knowledge production process model can largely be attributed to Ikujiro Nonaka (Nonaka 1994; Nonaka and Konno 1998; Nonaka and Takeuchi 1995; Nonaka *et al.* 2000). He proposed a spiralling knowledge production process that creates knowledge out of the interaction between explicit and tacit knowledge, an interaction he labels 'conversion' as it refers to both an expansion in quality and in quantity (see Fig. 14.7). The knowledge conversion process is made up of four elements and defined by the acronym SECI, of Socialization, Externalization, Combination, and Internalization. In brief, socialization refers to the conversion of tacit knowledge by means of shared experience, for example as in an apprenticeship situation. Externalization is the articulation of tacit knowledge into explicit knowledge and an example provided is the quality control cycle where concrete improvements are made, based on on-the-job work experience. Combination is the conversion of explicit knowledge into larger sets and patterns of explicit knowledge, which are subsequently disseminated; a typical accounting report for a business unit is an example, where discrete parts of the puzzle are put together to create a wider overall formal understanding. Finally, internalization is the conversion back into tacit knowledge from existing explicit knowledge. Learning-by-doing following an instruction manual first is an example of this conversion. The SECI process, thus, is a continuous process of converting tacit into explicit into tacit knowledge; it spirals up in the sense that it is amplified when it is converted, where more leads to more, both in scale and scope, and higher levels of understanding are reached in the process.

Key element in the knowledge production process according to the SECI model is the interchange between tacit and explicit knowledge. Neither of the two dominates and both are mutually dependent.

The description of the knowledge production process based on intellectual capital focuses strongly on relational capital and on the two value moments—of creating connectivity, and of 'harvesting' insights into improved process, procedures, and routines. However, the intellectual capital-based model attempts to be more specific about the conversion as such; it locates conversion in establishing

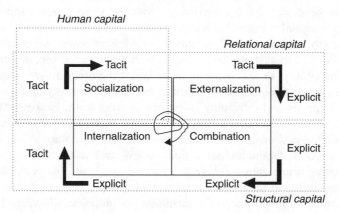

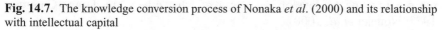

Fig. 14.7. The knowledge conversion process of Nonaka *et al.* (2000) and its relationship with intellectual capital

the collective bringing together of experiences and insights, as well as in articulating the acquired insights into improved organizational capabilities in terms of routines and processes, that is, in improving 'managerial technology capabilities'. In terms of the SECI model, the intellectual capital-based value moments are in the socialization and externalization categories, attempting to accomplish tacit-to-tacit and tacit-to-explicit conversion (see Fig. 14.7). It ignores the internalization element of converting from explicit-to-tacit because the intellectual capital model assumes a linear design sequence, starting with the individual but not ending with it or reverting back to the individual. That would result into a learning model for the individual in which the role of the organization is limited to a testing ground for his/her own cognitive exercises. Likewise, the combination element of the SECI model is where the factual accounting technology is already located; enabling individuals to see the wood from the trees as the prime knowledge function of the existing accounting apparatus. However, making sure that the wood fits the landscape, if not the territory, is what is intended in addressing (the role of accounting in) the knowledge production process.

In addition to describing the knowledge production process in terms of a conversion spiral based on the SECI stages, Nonaka also proposes a second main element, called *Ba*. In brief, the concept of *Ba* (the Japanese word for 'place') addresses the shared context in which knowledge is converted and exchanged. With *Ba*, Nonaka points out the importance of creating necessary enabling conditions before knowledge creation occurs. The characteristics of *Ba* are that it is based on interaction among individuals, that it is shared (i.e. collective property), and that it is continuously changing and fluid as it is defined by the participants and not by the task.

Referring back to the above discussion of intellectual capital as the basis for the knowledge production process, there exists a large overlap with the concept of *Ba*. This overlap is predominantly in the assertion that an adequate context is necessary for a knowledge production process to unfold. In the intellectual capital version, such context was addressed in terms of establishing (the connection as part of) connectivity. Motivation and incentives to start exchanging and to sustain the exchange over time, is the specific translation of *Ba*. The context in that sense is made up of the other project members or organizational participants that create a 'hot group' working climate of interesting colleagues and intriguing questions to work with. However, the intellectual capital version takes a stronger design stance in that not all motivation can be maintained on an intrinsic basis. It requires additional interventions that go beyond organizational attractiveness and job self-design. In that respect, using organization design as a motivational tool, for example, by delegating authority to semi-autonomous workgroups, is a commonly utilized mechanism as is the creation of information redundancy, allowing all parts of the organization to develop sense out of what others are doing (Galbraith 1977; Nonaka *et al.* 2000).

A 'soft' organizational design intervention that is more within the account-ing domain is internal reporting change. It goes to the heart of the informa-tion redundancy matter because reporting formats are possible that do not follow the organizational hierarchy ('open book management') or are based on an Intranet web page open for all. Equally, the frequency of reporting and the usual impossibility to aggregate the non-financial information content, create a 'semi-confusing information system' (Hedberg and Jonsson 1978) that triggers the search and dialogue behaviour of people in their attempts to reassert control over their work environment.

In other words, connectivity is as much about bringing people together as it is about bringing people and contexts together. The lessons learned in organ-izational design, dovetail the deliberate management of *Ba* and the creation of an enabling condition in order for knowledge production to take place.

Finally, the existing work on knowledge production processes also addresses the role of management and of managing the production process as such. Apart from suggesting organizational interventions in terms of creating redundancy of information and establishing semi-autonomous workgroups, managerial inter-ventions are of a more interactive nature. Particularly, a role for management is suggested in terms of a knowledge facilitator and of creator of specifically opportune language and vocabulary (Nonaka *et al.* 2000). Knowledge facilita-tion revolves around boundary spanning: seeing where the knowledge spiral is heading and what additional knowledge could be brought in. A boundary span-ner typically is someone who creates 'structural holes' (Burt 1992): that is, can cross over to other knowledge areas and bring these to bear on the issue at hand. It implies, however, that connectivity within groups is stronger than in between groups, thus necessitating a bridging function between the different groups to utilize their relational capital (Adler and Kwon 2002).

Overall, if the knowledge role of management is one of facilitation, bound-ary spanning and creating 'structural holes', it would also imply that the accounting function as such would need to become 'structurally' linked to other groups within the organization. This would further accentuate the need to become multidisciplinary in orientation and strengthen the discussion within the management accounting community on accountants being 'inter-nal consultants'. Particularly, such a multidisciplinary orientation would ben-efit from raising the awareness level of accountants on human resource and strategic management practices and concepts; project staffing, motivation and reward systems, competence mapping and apprenticeship type transfer mechan-isms would be obvious topical choices, while issues around dynamic capa-bilities, resource-based strategies and strategy implementation are first choices for strategy management.

The creation by management of an adequate language and vocabulary to facilitate knowledge production is receiving attention already within the intel-lectual capital field. Notably, the external reporting by means of intellectual capital statements tends to address this; part of such external reporting is the use of a so-called knowledge narrative that describes the organization's uniqueness and relates it to how the organization puts its own unique knowledge to work (Larsen *et al.* 1999; Mouritsen *et al.* 2001). Several new vocabularies are emerging together with intellectual capital reporting to capture this uniqueness. Indeed the term 'Intellectual Capital' itself being a case in point.

Moreover, in the business communication field, the use of narratives has been an accepted method to orchestrate corporate communication (van Riel 1995). Several other methods, notably related to measurement efforts of communication effectiveness, have emerged from the communications field, indicating an effort to deliberately manage the use of communication and its organizational antecedents (Roberts *et al.* 2002; Swedish Public Relations Association 1996; Tucker *et al.* 1996). Interestingly, all efforts imply an awareness that narratives are a means to combine (and not aggregate) disparate non-financial and qualitative information into a larger whole that suffers no loss of meaning, that is, stories are ways to see the wood from the trees and seem to be effective.

The ongoing research efforts within intellectual capital seem to suggest a strong importance of creating the adequate vocabulary, categories of meaning, and interpretative schemata to capture and address the way that knowledge plays out (Bjørkeng 2001; Roberts 1999). Notably, the problem is that knowledge is of an equivocal nature and hard to describe in direct terms; solution strategies emerge to describe knowledge indirectly, that is, by means of the narratives in which they are embedded, or to borrow terminology from related disciplines and imply a similar type of meaning in the new context of use.

Accounting Implications

The knowledge production process proposed in this chapter is rooted in the relational capital element of intellectual capital, and based on assumptions of connectivity, and of experience sharing and knowledge transfer. It assumes that there are two value moments—one preceding the creation of relational capital and one following it. Both value moments are based on organizational level conditions—one of enabling conditions, which one could term 'investments', and one of harvesting conditions, which one could term 'appropriation'. That is, the knowledge production process proposed considers a knowledge conversion that is subsequently appropriated. However, appropriation is not stated in terms of financial benefits and costs, but in terms of improved routines and increases in the effective functioning of the organization, typically expressed along parameters of flexibility and responsiveness. The appropriated 'return' of knowledge 'investment' thus occurs in the same dimension as its investment—that of organizational behaviour. Translating these returns into financial benefits would require a consideration of the identification (and the identification criteria) of the knowledge asset categories—what are the 'right' people, and what are adequate criteria for bundled assets? Moreover, it would require creating a financial expression for the improvement in organizational routines. A depiction of the knowledge production process as based on connectivity and relational capital is provided in Fig. 14.8. This model was developed for a medium-sized consultancy called MRB as part of an action research project on knowledge-based value creation in Norway (http://www.kunne.no/kunnskaping). As can be observed, the model stresses the connections between executing the core consulting assignment, which is knowledge-based, and the various resource inputs and outputs based on the related management routines to keep knowledge in a permanent state of flow and use. The assumption is that knowledge-in-use is what creates value and contributes to economic growth and wealth.

The accounting implications of the proposed knowledge production process are two-fold: first, the management accounting technology and its related toolbox would need a reconsideration on the basis of connectivity and, second, the management accounting orientation would need a shift towards issues of interactive control models.

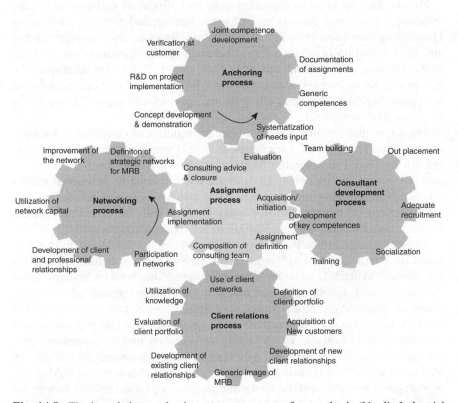

Fig. 14.8. The knowledge production process as a set of gear wheels (Nordic Industrial Fund 2000: 59)

The broad instrumental categories of registration, accumulation, and allocation are equally prevalent in the knowledge production process as they are in conventional manufacturing processes. But instead of costs, it is competences that are registered, skill and experiences that are accumulated in resource pools, and human capital that is allocated to activity areas, notably projects and teams. The principles for bookkeeping registration might equally evolve into principles that are relevant for knowledge registrations—for example, what are distinguishing criteria for 'bookkeeping' knowledge categories and what is the 'bookkeeping flow' between knowledge categories?

Similarly, are the criteria for cost accumulation and pooling of resources as applicable to the knowledge resource as they are to the financial resource? For example, given the fact that knowledge presents itself as a resource bundle, would it then make sense to establish grouping denominators for combinations instead of for itemized assets, developing 'networked assets'? And is accumulation a matter of conventional aggregation (counting and summing up) or is it a matter of combination and integration, as Nonaka seems also to suggest, to which a combinatory algorithm or a narrative needs to be applied?

Finally, the allocation of resources as in cost allocation to departments and responsibility centres already encompasses interdependence and reciprocity. Developing allocation criteria that specifically focus on this interdependence and the interaction (exchange flows) between groups (departments, centres) might be one step beyond the ones that already exist. For example, the accounting for shared services centres and for the use of call centres in service marketing cost allocation are showing signs of an ongoing evolution in this area (Dawson 2000).

The above instrumental endeavours might benefit from creating a disciplinary 'structural hole' in the human resource field where similar problems exist but are expressed in a foreign terminology and originate from a seemingly obscure conceptual universe. The criteria used in equally functional instruments around competence mapping, skills management, and project staffing would benefit from a comparative analysis along with the criteria for identification, classification, and application in the (cost) accounting field.

The knowledge production process has a strong human focus, in that it is based on interaction and exchange in the tacit dimension before the explicit dimension is evoked. The human 'knowledge carrier' has been under-represented in conventional accounting, and has generally been considered as a cost factor or, alternatively, as a resource on a similar footing to a capital asset that needs to be 'utilized', 'depreciated', and 'managed'. The fact that the human resource cannot be owned, can act on its own account, and has an internal production process called learning, has, at best, been acknowledged but did not lead to an accounting treatment that is relevant to its characteristics. Attempts to engage in human capital costing and accounting have been underway for the last 20 years, and receive much interest from practice, but have failed to contribute substantially to the accounting body of knowledge. Possible reasons are a disinterest from the academic community in researching the technical issues and problems, and the entanglement with issues around management control and implementation (Gröjer and Johanson 1998; Johanson 1998). But the latter could provide an exit from this conundrum.

Developments in management control frameworks such as the balanced scorecard, levers of control, and performance management blueprints such as the Business Excellence model, reveal an effort to integrate different functional perspectives, and to put human capital in a wider context of interpretation. Instead of considering it a cost factor, human capital is considered as a 'value driver' that generates revenue and enhances economic growth. With that consideration comes a re-evaluation of what human capital actually does and is. Its conceptualization as a resource is problematized again, but this time with a strong focus on the strategic implications of its interaction with other organizational elements and resources. For example, it is the human resource that engages in interactive control modes and which leverages the organization's attempt to cope with strategic uncertainty (Simons 2000) which is the human resource that coproduces value with the customer in the offering of goods and services (Norman 2001). Moreover, it is the human resource that implements organizational learning and drives performance, which makes itself a candidate of noteworthy category of non-financial performance measurement (Boudreau and Ramstad 1999; Olve *et al.* 1999).

Perhaps the human resource needs to be reconceptualized first from a management control and performance perspective before it can fruitfully (re-)enter the management accounting field, showing us where to look better and what to ask better the next time round. Calls for such a management control perspective as the starting point for management accounting research have been made earlier (Otley 1999). But it is particularly appropriate to involve these calls in developing accounting for the knowledge production process, where the interplay of the human resource, the knowledge resource, and the financial resource comes to light. As a result, a new role for the management accountant as a resource controller might emerge, combining the insights and perspectives that each resource definition can contribute to the wealth and well being of organizations.

References

Adler, P. S. and Kwon, S.-W. (2002), 'Social Capital: Prospects for a New Concept', *Academy of Management Review*, 27/1: 17–40.

Barney, J. B. (1986), 'Strategic Factor Markets: Expectations, Luck and Business Strategy', *Management Science*, 5: 1231–41.

——(1991), 'Firm Resources and Sustained Competitive Advantage', *Journal of Management*, 17/1: 99–120.

Bjørkeng, K. (2001), 'The Never-Ending Story: Emotional Aspects of Knowledge', paper presented at the Annual EGOS Conference, Lyon, France (SINTEF report STF38 S01904).

Bontis, N. (1998), 'Intellectual Capital: An Exploratory Study that Develops Measures and Models', *Management Decision*, 36: 2.

Boudreau, J. W. and Ramstad, P. M. (1999), 'Human Resource Metrics: Can Measures be Strategic?', in P. M. Wright, L. D. Dyer, J. W. Boudreau, and G. T. Milkovich (eds), *Strategic Human Resources Management in the Twenty-First Century*, Series Research in Personnel and Human Resources Management, Supplement 4 (Stamford: JAI Press), 75–98.

Brenna, B. (2001), *Intellectual Capital at Telenor*, presentation in the Symposium on Management Accounting and Control for the Knowledge-Driven Firm, 24th Annual Congress of the European Accounting Association, Athens, Greece.

Burt, R. S. (1992), *Structural Holes: The Social Structure of Competition* (Cambridge MA: Harvard University Press).

Dawson, R. (2000), *Developing Knowledge-based Client Relationships: The Future of Professional Services* (Boston: Butterworth-Heinemann).

Eisenhardt, K. M. and Martin, J. A. (2000), 'Dynamic Capabilities: What are they?', *Strategic Management Journal*, 21: 1105–22.

Ehrvervsudviklingsrådet (1997), *Videnregnskaber. Rapportering of styrning af videnkapital (Knowledge accounting. Reporting and Controlling Knowledge Capital)* (Copenhagen), http://www.efs.dk/icaccounts.

Gröjer, J. -E. and Johanson, U. (1998), 'Current Developments in Human Resource Costing and Accounting: Reality Present, Researchers Absent?', *Accounting, Auditing and Accountability Journal*, 11/4: 495–505.

Hansen, M. T., Nohria, N., and Tierney T. (1999), 'What is Your Strategy for Managing Knowledge?', *Harvard Business Review* (March–April): 106–16.

Hedberg, B. and Jonsson, S. (1978), 'Designing Semi-Confusing Information Systems for Organizations in Changing Environments', *Accounting, Organizations and Society*, 3/1: 47–67.

Helfat, C. E. and Raubitschek, R. S. (2000), 'Product Sequencing: Co-Evolution of Knowledge, Capabilities and Products', *Strategic Management Journal*, 21: 961–79.

Johanson, U. (1998), 'Why the Concept of Human Resource Costing and Accounting does not Work: A Lesson from Seven Swedish Cases', *Personnel Review*, 27/6.

——Mårtensson, M., and Skoog, M. (2001*a*), 'Mobilizing Change through the Management Control of Intangibles', *Accounting, Organizations and Society*, 26: 715–33.

————————(2001*b*), 'Measuring to Understand Intangible Performance Drivers', Working paper (Stockholm University: School of Business).

Larsen, H. T., Mouritsen, J., and Bukh, P. N. D. (1999), 'Intellectual Capital Statements and Knowledge Management: Measuring, Reporting and Acting', *Australian Accounting Review*, 9/3: 15–26.

Lev, B. and Schwartz, A. (1971), 'On the Use of the Economic Concept of Human Capital in Financial Statements', *The Accounting Review* (January): 103–12.

MERITUM (2002), *Guidelines for Managing and Reporting on Intangibles (Intellectual Capital Report)* (Madrid: Fundación Airtel Móvil).

Mouritsen, J., Larsen, H. T., and Bukh, P. N. D. (2001), 'Intellectual Capital and the "Capable Firm": Narrating, Visualising and Numbering for Managing Knowledge', *Accounting, Organizations and Society*, 26: 735–62.

Nahapiet, J. and Ghoshal, S. (1998), 'Social Capital, Intellectual Capital and the Organizational Advantage', *Academy of Management Review*, 23/2: 242–66.

Nelson, R. R. and Winter, S. G. (1982), *An Evolutionary Theory of Economic Change* (Boston: Harvard University Press).

Nonaka, I. (1991), 'The Knowledge-Creating Company', *Harvard Business Review* (November–December): 96–104.

——(1994), 'A Dynamic Theory of Organizational Knowledge Creation', *Organisation Science*, 5/1: 14–37.

——and Konno, N. (1998), 'The Concept of *'Ba'*: Building a Foundation for Knowledge Creation', *California Management Review*, 40/3: 1–15.

——and Takeuchi, H. (1995), *The Knowledge-Creating Company* (New York: Oxford University Press).

——Toyama, R., and Konno, N. (2000), 'SECI, *Ba* and Leadership: A Unified Model of Dynamic Knowledge Creation', *Long Range Planning*, 33: 5–34.

Nordic Industrial Fund (2001), *Intellectual Capital: Managing and Reporting* (Oslo).

Norman, R. (2001), *Reframing Business: When the Map Changes the Landscape* (Chicester: John Wiley & Sons).

Olve, N. -G., Roy, J., and Wetter, M. (1999), *Performance Drivers: A Practical Guide to Using the Balanced Scorecard* (Chicester: John Wiley & Sons).

Otley, D. (1999), 'Performance Management: A Framework for Management Control Systems Research', *Management Accounting Research*, 10/4: 325–453.

Roberts, H. (1998), 'Management Accounting and Control Systems in the Knowledge-Intensive Firm', paper presented at the 22nd Annual Congress of the European Accounting Association, Antwerp, Belgium.

——(1999), 'Ready for Intellectual Capital? A Multiple Case Study of 25 Firms in the Norwegian Graphical, Newspaper and Magazine Industries', paper presented at the 23rd Annual Congress of the European Accounting Association, Munich, Germany.

——(2000), 'Classification of Intellectual Capital', in H. Stolowy (ed.), *Classification of Intangibles*, CR 712/2000 (Paris: Groupe HEC), 197–205.

——Simcic, P., and Breunig, K. J. (2002), *Communicating the Knowledge Identity* (International Association of Business Communication Research Foundation) http://www.iabc.com.

Simons, R. (1994), 'How New Top Managers Use Control Systems as Levers of Strategic Renewal', *Strategic Management Journal*, 15: 169–89.

——(1995), *Levers of Control: How Managers Use Innovative Control Systems to Drive Strategic Renewal* (Boston: Harvard Business School Press).

——(2000), *Performance Measurement & Control Systems for Implementing Strategy: Text and Cases* (Upper Saddle River, NJ: Prentice-Hall).

Spender, J.-C. (1998), 'The Dynamics of Individual and Organizational Knowledge', in C. Eden and J.-C. Spender (eds), *Managerial and Organizational Cognition* (London: Sage).

Swedish Public Relations Association (1996), *Return on Communications* (Stockholm).

Teece, D., Pisano, G., and Shuen A. (1997), 'Dynamic Capabilities and Strategic Management', *Strategic Management Journal*, 18: 509–33.

Tucker, M. L., Meyer, G. D., and Westerman, J. W. (1996), 'Organizational Communication: Development of Internal Strategic Competitive Advantage', *The Journal of Business Communication*, 33/1: 51–69.

Westin, O. and Roberts, H. (1999), 'Rolling Down a River: Learning to Design a Local Information System', paper presented at the Fourth International Seminar on Manufacturing Accounting Research, Kolding, Denmark.

INDEX